Welcome

One of the things I most enjoy about working at the National Trust is imagining future generations visiting the places we look after. There's something wonderful about the idea that these places will keep being discovered and play an important role in people's lives for centuries to come.

So before you start exploring your new *Handbook*, I want to say 'thank you'. Your support makes it possible for us to look after all of the places in this book, so they can be enjoyed year after year.

I'd also like to draw your attention to the brilliant photograph on the cover of this year's *Handbook*. It was taken at Burton Bradstock, on the Jurassic Coast in Dorset, by National Trust member Paul Rook, winner of our very first cover photo competition in partnership with Panasonic.

Wherever you choose to explore, I hope you have a wonderful year – and why not take a moment to think about all the people who'll discover these places in the future, thanks to your support?

Jackie Jordan.

**Director of Brand, Marketing
and Supporter Development**

D1077576

Playing in the garden at Hatchlands Park, Surrey

Welcome to your 2017 *Handbook*

You'll find more than 500 places in this *Handbook*. Each one features a brief description of the stories and scenery that make it special. Plus some handy information to help you make the most of your visits. Here's what it all means…

This table shows you when places are open

Example place		M	T	W	T	F	S	S
House								
11 Feb–4 Nov	11–5	M	T	W	T	F	S	S
5 Nov–28 Nov	11–5	M	T	W	T	F	S	S
1 Dec–9 Dec	10:30–4:30	M	T	W	T	F	S	

Last entry to house and tea-room 20 minutes before closing.

These are seasonal opening times.

A letter means the place or facility is **open** on this day.

A grey dot means it's **closed**.

Any special notes about opening times are shown down here.

These symbols tell you a bit about the place. You'll find them above its description

1939	Acquisition date
🏠	Historic house
🏰	Castle/fort
✝	Church/chapel
⌂	Watermill
✖	Windmill
⌂	Other buildings
⌂	Public house
⌂	Archaeological site
⌂	Farm/farm animals
✿	Garden
🌳	Countryside/park
⛰	Coast
⌂	Nature reserve
⌂	Places to stay
⛺	Campsite
⌂	Licensed for weddings
⊤	Available for functions

These symbols tell you about accessibility. You'll find them towards the bottom of each listing

P♿	Designated parking
D♿	Drop-off point
♿	Transfer available
♿wc	Accessible toilet
♿	Catering accessible
♿	Shop accessible
⊃	Induction loop
▥	Photograph album
VT	Virtual tour
♿	Seats/seating available
⠿	Braille (guide or menu)
Ⓐ	Large print (guide or menu)
⌂	Steps/uneven terrain
⌂	Ramped access or slopes
⌂	Level access/terrain, paths
⇅	Lifts
⌂	Stairclimber
⌂	Stairlift
⌂	Narrow corridors
♿	Wheelchairs available
➡	Accessible route and/or map available
♿	Powered mobility vehicle

How to get there

At the start of each section, there's a simple map of the most popular places in that area. Each listing includes the place's address. You'll also see Sat Nav details for those out-of-the-way places where postcodes can be a bit misleading.

The postcodes listed under Sat Nav will take you near to a place, but not necessarily to it, so please look out for signs and be prepared to use road maps.

If you would like more comprehensive directions for all these places, along with detailed maps like those found in previous *Handbooks*, please order our free *Getting Here* guide. You can request your copy by calling 0344 800 1895 or visiting **nationaltrust.org.uk/gettinghere**

Alternatively, here are some useful resources to help you plan your journey:

By car: rac.co.uk/route-planner

By bike: sustrans.org.uk or 0117 926 8893

By train: nationalrail.co.uk or 03457 484950

By taxi (from a station): traintaxi.co.uk

By public transport (England, Wales and Scotland): traveline.info or 0871 200 2233

By public transport (Northern Ireland): translink.co.uk or 028 9066 6630

By public transport (London): tfl.gov.uk or 0343 222 1234

Please note

To give you time to enjoy your visit, last entry is **30 minutes before the closing times** shown in the opening arrangements tables, unless stated otherwise. Due to special events and adverse conditions, opening times sometimes change at short notice, so please **always check the online property page** before you leave, ideally on the day of your visit.

Everything you need to plan your visit

Website
Take a closer look by visiting **nationaltrust.org.uk**

app
500+ places in your pocket. Just search 'National Trust' in your app store

My National Trust
Now you can get the most from your membership by managing your details and preferences online. Register at **nationaltrust.org.uk/mynationaltrust**

Social media
Ask questions, share your experiences or just say 'hi'

Land Map
This interactive map shows when and how places came into our care. It also tells the story behind 300+ war memorials. Visit **ntlandmap.org.uk**

***Getting Here* guide**
Want printed directions and maps? Request your free copy on 0344 800 1895 or visit **nationaltrust.org.uk/gettinghere**

With a year's membership, here's a taste of things to come

From plotting scenic cycle routes, to finding the best blooms, or even snooping through a cache of lovers' letters, take time this year to rediscover the important things in life. (Even if that's just hanging upside down from an old oak tree.)

Find adventure at every turn

Look forward to tunnels, dens, rope swings and even mini castles when you come to visit our adventure playgrounds. What's more, we know that curious minds love to learn by getting hands on, so we've made a list of 50 things to do before you're 11¾.

Discover an adventure playground near you on page 429 of the themed index.

Get used to the unexpected ...

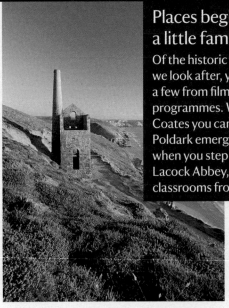

Places begin to look a little familiar

Of the historic places and wild spaces we look after, you might recognise a few from films and television programmes. When you visit Wheal Coates you can almost imagine Ross Poldark emerging from the mine. And when you step into the cloisters at Lacock Abbey, do you conjure up the classrooms from *Harry Potter*?

See page 437 of the themed index to plan your visit to popular film and television locations.

You could be more green-fingered than you know

Explore a few of the many gardens that we care for and you'll soon be recommending places to find the best blooms. There's no shortage of kitchen gardens to inspire you to start your own vegetable plot plans.

Turn to page 429 of the themed index to start ticking off your garden visit wish list.

Realise you're a bit of an expert ...

Unleash your talent for storytelling

Don't be surprised if you find yourself telling friends about the ring that inspired J. R. R. Tolkien to write *Lord of The Rings*, or the cabinet that was made for Pope Sixtus V in 1585. Many of the collections we look after have unusual stories behind them, which are yours to discover.

Find the best properties for unique collections on page 433 of the themed index.

Take the outdoors in your stride

Love walking but fancy something a little different? Saddle up and test your mettle on a mountain bike trail in the Lake District, or try your hand at canoeing round the islands at Derwent Water.

Turn to page 429 to start planning the activities you love (or can't wait to try).

Learn something new about yourself …

Indulge your inner gourmet

Fresh, sustainable food is something we're very passionate about in our cafés and shops. Even if you can resist the range of delicious pickles, biscuits and sweet treats, we defy you to turn down one of our famous scones.

Browse the *Handbook* to bookmark foodie destinations.

Skip the services and stretch your legs instead

Did you know that there are National Trust places just a short hop from many main roads? Next time you're in need of a quick stop, discover which destinations could be right around the corner.

See page 432 for easily accessible places to break up your journey.

Always find a reason to visit …

And if you're still left wanting more …

You can find out about the hundreds of special places and spaces we look after in this *Handbook*. Turn to the themed index on page 429 to start planning your visits today.

Along with your membership, you can support the National Trust in many ways, from visiting or volunteering, to making a donation or leaving a gift in your Will.

Find out how you can make a difference at nationaltrust.org.uk

Cornwall

Boscastle, Cornwall
Competition entry from Chris Bell

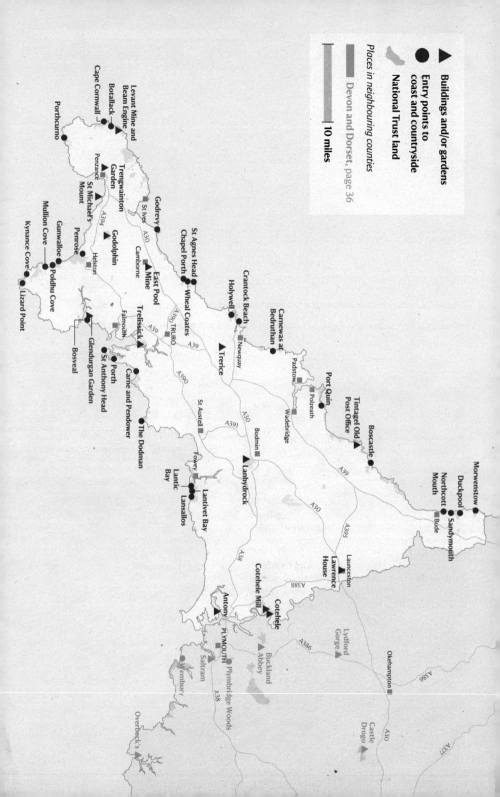

Buildings and/or gardens
Entry points to coast and countryside
National Trust land
Places in neighbouring counties
Devon and Dorset, page 36
10 miles

Cape Cornwall
Porthcurno
Levant Mine and Beam Engine
Botallack
Penzance
Trengwainton Garden
St Michael's Mount
Godrevy
St Ives
Trevose
A394
Godolphin
Penrose
Gunwalloe
Mullion Cove
Kynance Cove
Poldhu Cove
Lizard Point
Helston
Camborne
A30
St Agnes Head
Chapel Porth
East Pool Mine
Wheal Coates
Holywell
Crantock Beach
Carnewas at Bedruthan
Newquay
Padstow
Polzeath
Wadebridge
Port Quin
Tintagel Old Post Office
Boscastle
Morwenstow
Duckpool
Northcott Mouth
Sandymouth
Bude
A39
Falmouth
Trelissick
Bosveal
Glendurgan Garden
St Anthony Head
Porth
Carne and Pendower
The Dodman
TRURO
A39
A390
St Austell
A391
Fowey
Lantic Bay
Lansallos
Lantivet Bay
Lanhydrock
Bodmin
A30
A38
A30
A395
Launceston
Lawrence House
A388
Cotehele Mill
Cotehele
Antony
PLYMOUTH
Saltram
Trematon
Plymbridge Woods
A38
Buckland Abbey
A386
Lydford Gorge
Okehampton
A386
Castle Drogo
A30
A377
Overbeck's
Trerice

Surrounded by clipped yew hedges, magical Antony sits swathed in morning mist, creating an air of mystery

Antony

Torpoint, Cornwall PL11 2QA

🏠🌸♿ 1961

Still the family home of the Carew Poles after hundreds of years, this beautiful early 18th-century house has fine collections of paintings, furniture and textiles. The landscape garden offers sweeping views to the River Lynher and includes a formal garden with topiary, a knot garden and sculptures. **Note**: members admitted free to Woodland Garden (not National Trust) only when house is open.

Eat, shop, stay: self-service tea-room offering light lunches and afternoon tea. Picnics welcome in the grounds. Gift shop with souvenirs, plants and local produce. Small second-hand bookshop.

Things to see and do: **Indoors** Quizzes and trails. **Outdoors** Garden and family events. Modern sculpture throughout garden and Woodland Garden. Games and croquet on lawn. Quizzes and trails. **Dogs**: assistance dogs only.

Access: 🅿️♿🏛️🚻🎧📷🎡📶
House 🏠🚶♿ Grounds 🏠➡️♿
Parking: 250 yards.

Find out more: 01752 812191 or antony@nationaltrust.org.uk

Antony		M	T	W	T	F	S	S
House, garden, shop and tea-room								
4 Apr–31 May	12–5	·	**T**	**W**	**T**	·	·	·
1 Jun–31 Aug	12–5	·	**T**	**W**	**T**	·	·	**S**
5 Sep–26 Oct	12–5	·	**T**	**W**	**T**	·	·	·
Woodland Garden								
1 Mar–31 Oct	11–5:30	·	**T**	**W**	**T**	·	**S**	**S**

House: open 12:30 to 4:30. Timed ticket entry to house allocated on arrival. Also open Good Friday and Easter Sunday, Sundays 30 April and 28 May and Bank Holiday Mondays.

Boscastle

near Tintagel, Cornwall

♿🏰🚌 1955

There has been a fishing and trading port here for centuries and you can still watch boats come and go between the high cliffs that guard the snaking harbour entrance. Much of Boscastle can be discovered on foot, with footpaths leading in all directions. You can walk in the footsteps of the young Thomas Hardy through the wildlife-rich ancient woodland in the Valency Valley, or explore the rare medieval field system known as 'the Forrabury Stitches'

Boscastle: looking down on the village and natural inlet

Bosveal

near Mawnan Smith, Falmouth, Cornwall

🏠 ♿ 🚻 💤 1980

Many walks take in woodland valleys, secluded coves and the soft, sheltered shores of the Helford River and Falmouth Bay. **Note**: toilets and refreshments at nearby Glendurgan Garden and Durgan village (February to October). Holiday cottages at Bosloe and Durgan. For Sat Nav use TR11 5JR.

Find out more: 01326 252020 or bosveal@nationaltrust.org.uk

high above the village. Nearby is the striking lookout building on Willapark headland, and the historic churches of Minster and Forrabury. **Note**: toilet by main car park (not National Trust).

Eat, shop, stay: harbourside café with courtyard seating. Large shop and visitor centre offering a wide range of gifts, seasonal plant sales plus a wealth of guides and information about the local area. Second-hand bookshop. Five holiday cottages. Free wi-fi throughout.

Things to see and do: children's quiz/trail. Coasteering available nearby. Visitor centre shows short film about the 2004 flood. Why not combine with a visit to Tintagel Old Post Office, four miles down the coast? **Dogs**: welcome on walks and in café courtyard.

Access: 🏃 🚶 🚶 Grounds 🏃
Sat Nav: use PL35 0HD. **Parking**: 100 yards, pay and display, not National Trust (charge including members).

Find out more: 01840 250010 or boscastle@nationaltrust.org.uk

Boscastle	M	T	W	T	F	S	S
Shop, café and visitor centre							
Open all year	*	M	T	W	T	F	S	S

*Opening times vary throughout year, ranging from 10:30 to 4 in winter, to 10 to 5:30 in high summer. Closed 25 and 26 December.

Botallack

on the Tin Coast, near St Just, Cornwall

🅿 🍽 🏠 ♿ 🚻 💤 🔦 🍷 1995

Engine houses cling to the cliffs at Botallack, near St Just

On the wild Tin Coast, the famed Crowns engine houses cling to the foot of the cliffs in a landscape transformed by its industrial past. Part of the Cornish Mining World Heritage Site, and the filming location for Wheal Leisure in BBC's *Poldark*, from here Cornish miners changed the world. **Note**: industrial landscape with numerous mine shafts and mining remains – please keep to paths and tracks.

Eat, shop, stay: refreshments with views to the Isles of Scilly (opening days/times vary, telephone to check), local pasties, sandwiches, cakes, ice-cream, hot and cold drinks. Picnic blankets to borrow. Two can stay at romantic Botallack Count House Cottage, with dramatic coastal views.

Things to see and do: new exhibition in the Workshop celebrating the Tin Coast and *Poldark*. You can explore mining history on the outdoors trail and enjoy an easy clifftop walk to Levant Mine. **Dogs**: welcome everywhere on short leads. Please take care near mine shafts.

Access: ⓟ Ⓓ ⌖ ⌖ ⌖
Sat Nav: use TR19 7QQ. Beware, some Sat Navs misdirect. Keep to the B3306 until you reach Botallack village.
Parking: just beyond Botallack Count House.

Find out more: 01736 761853 or botallack@nationaltrust.org.uk

Wild and rugged Cape Cornwall juts out into the ocean on the historic Tin Coast

Cape Cornwall

on the Tin Coast, near St Just, Cornwall

🏛 ♿ ⌖ ⌖ 1987

The distinctive headland of Cape Cornwall juts out into the ocean where two great bodies of water meet. Once a heavily industrialised landscape, it is now part of the Cornish Mining World Heritage Site, and a wild and rugged home to many seabirds which nest on the Brisons rocks. **Note**: narrow lanes, unsuitable for caravans. Car park toilets open Easter to end of October.

Eat, shop, stay: light refreshments (not National Trust) available from Easter to end of October, including drinks, pasties, sandwiches, homemade cakes and, when available, crab and lobster landed at Cape Cornwall. Many facilities in St Just. Holiday cottage in nearby Cot Valley.

Things to see and do: perfect beach for rock-pooling and wild swimming. Working cove for crab and lobster fishermen. Views to the Isles of Scilly from the top of the Cape. Coastwatch hut to visit. **Dogs**: welcome, except on the beach and slipway.

Access: 🚻
Sat Nav: use TR19 7NN for Cape Cornwall car park. **Parking**: at Cape Cornwall, Porth Nanven (Cot Valley) and Ballowall.

Find out more: 01736 761853 or capecornwall@nationaltrust.org.uk

Carne and Pendower

near Veryan, Cornwall

 1961

Two of the best beaches on the Roseland peninsula: fine stretches of sand and rock pools, popular with families. Walks along the coast and inland reveal the area's wildlife – great for butterflies in summer and birds in winter. Lots of history to discover nearby, from Bronze Age to Cold War. **Note**: seasonal toilets in both car parks.

Eat, shop, stay: Tea by the Sea van at Carne (concession) serves tea, cake and tempting treats. The tenant-run Hidden Hut is at Porthcurnick Beach. You can stay close to Carne Beach at the five holiday cottages at Gwendra, or nearby at Caragloose.

Things to see and do: the beaches are ideal for swimming and rock-pooling. A path leads inland to Carne Beacon, one of Britain's largest Bronze Age barrows. Downloadable walking trails cover the wider area. **Dogs**: seasonal dog restrictions on beaches (please keep under control near livestock).

Access: 🚶
Sat Nav: for Carne use TR2 5PF; Pendower TR2 5PF (turn right at sign for Pendower Beach). **Parking**: car parks at both Carne and Pendower.

Find out more: 01872 580553 or carne@nationaltrust.org.uk

Carnewas at Bedruthan

near Padstow, Cornwall

🚻🅿 1930

Since Victorian times this has been one of the most popular destinations on the Cornish coast, known for its spectacular clifftop views of giant rock stacks striding across Bedruthan Beach (not National Trust). Those with a head for heights can climb down the cliff staircase to the beach (closed during the winter) but beware of being cut off by the tide. For a longer walk, follow the coast path to Park Head and the sheltered cove of Porth Mear beyond. Carpets of spring and autumn squill bedeck these clifftops and birds nesting from March include linnets, stonechats and skylarks. **Note**: unsafe to enter the sea here at any time.

Eat, shop, stay: shop offering a range of gifts, many locally sourced and produced, and popular tea-room (concession) with adjoining clifftop tea-garden. Picnic area. Bunkhouse and holiday cottages offering expansive sea views at Park Head.

Things to see and do: children's quiz and walks leaflet. Simple play area. Carnewas awarded 'dark sky status', so ideal for star-gazing. Why not combine with a visit to Trerice (9 miles away)? **Dogs**: welcome under control.

Access: 🅿️♿🌐🚻🅰️ Car park and cliff top 🧗➡️
Sat Nav: use PL27 7UW. **Parking**: on site.

Find out more: 01637 860563 or carnewas@nationaltrust.org.uk

Carnewas at Bedruthan		M	T	W	T	F	S	S
Tea-room*								
11 Feb–31 Mar	11–4	M	T	W	T	F	S	S
1 Apr–29 Oct	10:30–5	M	T	W	T	F	S	S
27 Dec–31 Dec	11–4	·	·	W	T	F	S	S
Shop								
11 Feb–26 Feb	11–4	M	T	W	T	F	S	S
4 Mar–5 Mar	11–4	·	·	·	·	·	S	S
11 Mar–31 Mar	11–4	M	T	W	T	F	S	S
1 Apr–29 Oct	10:30–5	M	T	W	T	F	S	S

Cliff staircase closed from 30 October to mid-February.
*Telephone 01637 860701 to check opening times in winter.

One of the most popular Cornish destinations since Victorian times, Carnewas at Bedruthan, below, still exerts a strong pull today, with its giant rock stacks and views. Chapel Porth, right, becomes a sweep of sand at low tide

Chapel Porth

near St Agnes, Cornwall

🏖️📶 1957

Nestled at the foot of a steep valley between high heathery cliffs, which turn a dazzling purple and yellow in late summer, Chapel Porth Beach is just a shingle strip at high tide but transforms into a huge expanse of sand at low tide. Now a popular family and surfing beach, Chapel Porth is steeped in mining history, with the remains of tin-processing buildings to be seen in the car park. Just up the valley you can discover what's left of Charlotte United Mine. Children love to splash in the stream and all ages love the famous hedgehog ice-cream. **Note**: seasonal toilets. Take care not to get cut off by incoming tide. Seasonal lifeguards.

Eat, shop, stay: Chapel Porth Beach café open daily in summer and most winter weekends (01872 552487). Picnics welcome. Pubs, cafés and shops nearby in St Agnes (none National Trust).

Things to see and do: this is great walking country – footpaths link you with Porthtowan and St Agnes Head and the World Heritage Site mine buildings at Charlotte United, Wheal Coates and Trevellas. **Dogs**: seasonal dog ban on the beach (Easter Sunday to 30 September inclusive).

Access: 🅿️♿🌐🚻🅰️
Sat Nav: use TR5 0NS. **Parking**: car park (very busy in summer).

Find out more: 01872 552412 or chapelporth@nationaltrust.org.uk

Time seems to stand still at rambling Cotehele, near Saltash, which sits high above the River Tamar

Cotehele ·

St Dominick, near Saltash, Cornwall PL12 6TA

🏠✝🏠❀♨✿⛵☂ 1947

The Edgcumbes built their rambling granite and slate-stone home high above the River Tamar, and it remained in their family for nearly 600 years. Time has stood still here. The Hall, with its ancient timber roof and displays of weaponry, and the warren of tapestry-clad rooms beyond have changed little since Tudor times. The 5-hectare (12-acre) garden features historic daffodils, terraces, ponds and orchards with 150 local apple varieties. The Valley Garden, with medieval stewpond and dovecote, leads to Cotehele Quay – thriving in Victorian times – where you'll find 1899 Tamar sailing barge *Shamrock*, lime kilns and the Discovery Centre. **Note**: the house has no electricity, so feel free to bring a torch.

Eat, shop, stay: restaurant near house serving hot lunches and cakes. Tea-room on quay offering light lunches, cakes and cream teas. Gift shop and plant centre. Art and craft gallery featuring West Country artists. Second-hand bookshop. Picnic area. Ten holiday cottages on estate.

Things to see and do: **Indoors** 'Just Hanging?' Discover the secret life of tapestries on a self-guided tour, continuing for 2017. First World War exhibition featuring local memories. **Outdoors** Play area. Year-round events and walks. **Dogs**: welcome throughout estate. Assistance dogs only in formal garden.

Access: 🅿♿🚻♿♿🅿♿🅿 ▣
Building 🅿♿♿ Grounds 🅿♿➡
Sat Nav: ignore from Tavistock, follow brown signs. **Parking**: at house and on quay.

Find out more: 01579 351346. 01579 352711 (Barn Restaurant). 01579 352713 (shop) or cotehele@nationaltrust.org.uk

Cotehele		M	T	W	T	F	S	S
House								
11 Mar–29 Oct	11–4	M	T	W	T	F	S	S
30 Oct–31 Dec*	11–4	M	T	W	T	F	S	S
Garden and estate								
Open all year	Dawn–dusk	M	T	W	T	F	S	S
Restaurant, tea-room, shop, plant sales, gallery								
11 Feb–10 Mar**	11–4	M	T	W	T	F	S	S
11 Mar–29 Oct	11–5	M	T	W	T	F	S	S
30 Oct–31 Dec	11–4	M	T	W	T	F	S	S

*Hall of house and Christmas garland only. Everything closed 25 and 26 December, except garden and estate.
**Tea-room on quay opens daily from 7 January. Restaurant opens 10:30 during main season.

Cotehele Mill

St Dominick, near Saltash, Cornwall PL12 6TA

🏠♨🛏 1947

A peaceful walk alongside the Morden stream from Cotehele Quay takes you to the restored 19th-century Cotehele Mill. On Thursdays and Sundays you can watch corn being ground into flour. Traditional woodworker and potter on site, as well as re-created wheelwright's, saddler's and blacksmith's workshops. Look out for baking days. **Note**: nearest toilets and parking at Cotehele Quay.

Eat, shop, stay: Cotehele flour, gifts and ice-cream for sale. The Edgcumbe tea-room at nearby Cotehele Quay serves light lunches and cream teas. Pasties available from the kiosk on the quay. Picnics welcome in meadow. Two holiday cottages.

Things to see and do: **Indoors** Events, including milling and bakery demonstrations, as well as dress-up days. Opportunity to mill grain at the hand quern. Interpretation boards. **Outdoors** Family trails. **Dogs**: welcome, but assistance dogs only in bakery and mill.

Access: 🅿♿🎦📷📓 Building 🔎 Grounds ♿
Parking: by arrangement only. Shuttlebus from Cotehele house.

Find out more: 01579 350606 (mill). 01579 351346 (Cotehele) or cotehele@nationaltrust.org.uk

Cotehele Mill		M	T	W	T	F	S	S
11 Mar–30 Sep	11–5	M	T	W	T	F	S	S
1 Oct–29 Oct	11–4:30	M	T	W	T	F	S	S

Corn is still ground into flour at the restored 19th-century Cotehele Mill

Crantock Beach

near Newquay, Cornwall

🏖 1956

Close to Newquay, this feels like a different Cornwall: Crantock Beach is an expanse of golden sand, great for sandcastles and surfing. Wonderful walking country – through the dunes on Rushy Green, alongside the gentle waters of the Gannel Estuary, or around the headland of West Pentire, carpeted with wild flowers.

Dunes at Crantock Beach, near Newquay. This expanse of golden sand is perfect for surfing and sandcastles

Eat, shop, stay: refreshments available at Crantock village and West Pentire. Fern Pit café (not National Trust), across the Gannel Estuary from Crantock Beach, is accessible by ferryboat at high tide during the main season or by footbridge at low tide.

Things to see and do: surf school and board hire. Spot seals from the coast path. There are vibrant displays of summer wild flowers to discover in the fields above nearby Polly Joke Beach. **Dogs**: welcome under control everywhere, including the beach.

Access: 🅿🔎
Sat Nav: use TR8 5RN for Crantock Beach and TR8 5QS for Treago Mill. **Parking**: on site (height restriction barrier when unmanned) and at Treago Mill for Polly Joke Beach (also known as Porth Joke).

Find out more: 01208 863046 or crantockbeach@nationaltrust.org.uk

The Dodman

Penare, near Gorran Haven, Cornwall

 1919

The highest headland on Cornwall's south coast, with massive Iron Age ramparts. Great walking, wildlife and beaches on either side. **Note**: car park at Penare. For Sat Nav use PL26 6NY and carry on down hill. Sorry no toilet.

Find out more: 01872 580553 or thedodman@nationaltrust.org.uk

Duckpool

near Bude, Cornwall

 1960

Remote beach with rock pools at the mouth of the wooded Coombe Valley, overlooked by cliffs carpeted with wild flowers. **Note**: toilets open seasonally. For Sat Nav use EX23 9JN.

Find out more: 01208 863046 or duckpool@nationaltrust.org.uk

East Pool Mine

Pool, near Redruth, Cornwall TR15 3NP

 1967

East Pool celebrates the extraordinary lives of the people who worked at the very heart of the Cornish Mining World Heritage Site. With two giant beam engines, preserved in their towering engine houses, this is a great place for all the family to discover the dramatic story of Cornish mining.

Eat, shop, stay: small shop selling lovely gifts, food and souvenirs, also a good selection of minerals and Cornish history books.

Visitors discover the dramatic story of Cornish mining at East Pool Mine, near Redruth

You can enjoy a hot drink (or even an ice-cream) indoors or at our picnic bench in the sun.

Things to see and do: view the working beam engine and hands-on exhibits. Family activities, trails and free guided tours. Trevithick Cottage, home of the celebrated Cornish engineer Richard Trevithick, is nearby at Penponds. **Dogs**: welcome in outdoor areas.

Access:  Grounds ➡ Taylor's Engine House Michell's Engine House
Sat Nav: use TR15 3ED; for Trevithick Cottage use TR14 0QG. **Parking**: parking in Morrisons superstore (far end). Also at Michell's Engine House, off A3047.

Find out more: 01209 315027 or eastpool@nationaltrust.org.uk
Trevithick Road, Pool, Cornwall TR15 3NP

East Pool Mine		M	T	W	T	F	S	S
Mine and Taylor's Engine House*								
21 Mar–28 Oct	10:30–5	·	T	W	T	F	S	·
Michell's Engine House*								
21 Mar–28 Oct	12–4	·	T	W	T	F	S	·
Trevithick Cottage								
5 Apr–25 Oct	2–5	·	·	W	·	·	·	·

*Open Easter Monday and Bank Holiday weekends in May and August (times as above). Visits can be booked in advance, November to March.

Glendurgan Garden

Mawnan Smith, near Falmouth,
Cornwall TR11 5JZ

🏠🌸♿🖼️🅿️ 1962

Glendurgan Garden was described by its
creators, the Quakers Alfred and Sarah Fox,
as a 'small peace [sic] of heaven on earth'.
Visitors can find out why it proved to be just
this for the Foxes and their 12 children by
exploring Glendurgan's three valleys, running
down to the sheltered beach at Durgan on the
Helford River. There's a puzzling maze, created
by Alfred and Sarah to entertain the family. You
can enjoy camellias, magnolias and primroses
in early spring, then rhododendrons and
bluebells in May, followed by the exotic greens
of summer and dramatic autumn colour in the
trees. **Note**: steep paths, steps, uneven terrain.

**Glendurgan Garden, near Falmouth: subtropical paradise
set in three valleys running down to a sheltered beach**

Eat, shop, stay: tea-house (concession)
serving homemade cakes, soups, sandwiches,
light lunches and daily changing specials.
Ice-cream and hot drinks at the beach.
Small shop and plant centre. Holiday lets –
from waterside cottages for two, to large
country houses for eight or more.

**A blaze of pink rhododendrons and exotic planting at
Glendurgan Garden, with the River Helford beyond**

Things to see and do: Durgan Beach on
Helford River. Durgan Fish Cellar provides local
history and wildlife information. Beach chairs
to borrow and children's activities. Ten-minute
introductory talks (call to check availability).
Dogs: assistance dogs only in garden.
Walks in surrounding countryside
(details available at Glendurgan).

Access: 🅿️♿♿♿ Garden entrance 🔼 Garden 🔼
Parking: on site.

Find out more: 01326 252020 or
glendurgan@nationaltrust.org.uk

Glendurgan Garden		M	T	W	T	F	S	S
11 Feb–30 Jul	10:30–5:30	·	T	W	T	F	S	S
1 Aug–31 Aug	10:30–5:30	M	T	W	T	F	S	S
1 Sep–29 Oct	10:30–5:30	·	T	W	T	F	S	S

Closes dusk if earlier. Open Bank Holiday Mondays.

Godolphin

Godolphin Cross, Helston, Cornwall TR13 9RE

🏠 🏛 ♿ ✿ 👥 🛏 2000

Hidden in shaded woodland, Godolphin escaped modernisation and contemporary fashions. The granite-faced terraces and sunken lawns of the Side Garden have seen little change since the 16th century, and Victorian farm buildings tell the story of Godolphin as a tenant farm. The estate, once busy with prosperous tin mines, is now part of the Cornish Mining World Heritage Site and is wonderful walking country, rich in archaeology, rare plants and wildlife. There are panoramic views from the top of Godolphin Hill. The historic house is a holiday home, where you can stay and experience the splendour that mining riches bought. **Note**: house is open on limited dates between holiday lets (please check before visiting).

Eat, shop, stay: small tea-room in the Piggery serving drinks, sandwiches, cakes, ice-cream. Local gifts and souvenirs. Picnic benches in the grassed farmyard or borrow a blanket to picnic in the orchard or garden. Soak up the atmosphere by staying in Godolphin House.

Things to see and do: gardener's potting shed has information on flora and fauna. View wildlife from conserved cider house.

Free guided tours, walks booklet and events. Barefoot trail Easter to October. Trengwainton Garden nearby. **Dogs**: welcome outdoors on short leads. Water bowl and dog biscuits available from reception.

Access: 🅿 ♿ 📷 ♿ 🍴 ♿ 🚶 House ♿ ♿ 🚻
Cider House ♿ ↕ Garden ♿ ♿
Parking: 300 yards.

Bypassed by modernisation and untouched by contemporary fashion, Godolphin, above and below, has seen little change since the 16th century

Find out more: 01736 763194 or
godolphin@nationaltrust.org.uk

Godolphin		M	T	W	T	F	S	S
Garden and outbuildings								
1 Jan–29 Oct	10–5	M	T	W	T	F	S	S
30 Oct–31 Dec*	10–4	M	T	W	T	F	S	S
Estate								
Open all year	Dawn–dusk	M	T	W	T	F	S	S
House								
Limited opening**								

*Closed 24 and 25 December. **House open first Saturday
to Thursday of every month, February to October
(except August), plus weekends 25 November to
10 December (please check house opening before visiting).

Godrevy

near Hayle, Cornwall

 1939

Long sandy beaches on St Ives Bay with
wildlife-rich cliffs and walks. Godrevy café
in dunes (concession) open most days.
Note: unstable cliffs and incoming tides.
Toilets open in top field. Parking limited in
wet weather and at busy times. For Sat Nav
use TR27 5ED. Café open daily most of the
year; weekends and fine days in winter.

Find out more: 01872 552412 or
godrevy@nationaltrust.org.uk

Gunwalloe

near Helston, Cornwall

⊞ 🔲 📱 🕿 📶 📱 1974

Two family-friendly sandy beaches and
reedbeds rich in wildlife. Between the two coves,
a medieval church shelters behind Castle Mound.
Note: lifeguards patrol Church Cove in summer
holidays. Seasonal toilets. Dogs welcome all
year at Dollar Cove, council-enforced ban at
Church Cove (Easter to 1 October).

Find out more: 01326 222170 (Rangers) or
gunwalloe@nationaltrust.org.uk

Holywell

near Newquay, Cornwall

 1951

A classic north Cornish beach with a sweep
of golden sand and a towering dune system.
There's lots of history to explore, including the
remains of an Iron Age castle on Kelsey Head,
a Bronze Age barrow on Cubert Common
and the holy well in a cave on the beach.

Eat, shop, stay: seasonal refreshments,
traditional seaside shopping and pubs at
Holywell and a convenience store and café year
round at Cubert, 2 miles (none National Trust).

Things to see and do: surf schools and board
hire. Beach great for rock-pooling and building
sandcastles. Seals can be seen from Kelsey
Head. Wildlife-rich grasslands and coastline.
Dogs: welcome everywhere, including the
beach, but under close control, especially
around livestock.

Access: 📱🖨 Coast 🦽
Sat Nav: use TR8 5PF. **Parking**: on site.

Find out more: 01208 863046 or
holywell@nationaltrust.org.uk

**Towering dunes, golden sands and a blue
sea at Holywell on the north coast**

Sunrise over Kynance Cove on the Lizard peninsula. The spectacular beach lies hidden among towering cliffs

Kynance Cove

on the Lizard peninsula, Cornwall

 1935

One of the world's most spectacular beaches, for centuries Kynance has been a magnet for adventurous tourists. The unusual geology in this part of the Lizard creates a rolling landscape of rare heathland, while on the beach – hidden among towering cliffs – are stacks, arches and islands of serpentine rock rising from white sand and turquoise water. The caves, accessible at low tide, offer a chance to get close to the colourful serpentine. The walk down to the cove takes you through a small section of Lizard heathland that's home to some of the rarest plants and creatures in this country. **Note**: level terrain/access route applies to viewpoint only.

Toilets in car park closed during winter.

Eat, shop, stay: café in cove (concession), with outdoor seating, open from Easter to November, serving crab sandwiches, pasties and cream teas.

Things to see and do: try to visit at low tide when there's plenty of beach to enjoy, for building sandcastles or taking a dip in the clean turquoise water. This beach is not lifeguarded. **Dogs**: council-enforced beach ban (7 to 7, Easter to 1 October), welcome on coast path.

Access: 🅿️🚾 Cove 👓 Viewpoint 👓➡️
Sat Nav: use TR12 7PJ. **Parking**: car park on cliffs above Kynance Cove.

Find out more: 01326 222170 (Property Office). 01326 291174 (Rangers) or kynancecove@nationaltrust.org.uk

Lanhydrock

Bodmin, Cornwall PL30 5AD

🏠✝🕸🦆🎫🍽 1953

A tragic fire in 1881 meant that the Agar-Robartes family had to rebuild most of their 17th-century home. Out of the ashes came the country house you see today, presented as if time has stood still with the family having just popped out to tea. There are more than 50 rooms to discover – from the extensive kitchens, which reveal the servants' daily lives, to the elegant Victorian luxury of the family rooms. Outside is a garden, full of colour all year round and famed for its magnolias, and ancient woodlands with miles of footpaths to explore. The off-road cycle trails have different routes to suit all levels of experience, and you can even hire a bike when you get here.

Two views of Lanhydrock. Rebuilt in 1881 after a fire, there are more than 50 rooms and extensive grounds to explore

Lanhydrock		M	T	W	T	F	S	S
House and garden								
1 Mar–31 Oct*	11–5:30*	M	T	W	T	F	S	S
1 Dec–31 Dec**	11–4	M	T	W	T	F	S	S
Estate and cycle trails								
Open all year	Dawn–dusk	M	T	W	T	F	S	S
Refreshments								
Open all year	10–5*	M	T	W	T	F	S	S

*House closes at 5 in March and October; refreshments close at 4 November to February. **Selected rooms only. Everything closed 25 December.

You can hire bikes to suit all ages and abilities to enjoy the off-road trails at Lanhydrock

Eat, shop, stay: Park Café, by the cycle hire and plant centre, offers homemade dishes year-round. At the house there's the Stables tea-room, plus waitress service in the Victorian restaurants. Shop sells local food and gifts. Second-hand bookshop. Holiday cottage (sleeps six).

Things to see and do: **Indoors** There's a remarkable early 17th-century ceiling in the Long Gallery which survived the fire and is the oldest room in the house. Family museum where you can find out about all the children in the Agar-Robartes family and, for young explorers, we have a free children's trail. Victorian festive fun at Christmas. **Outdoors** Guided tours (telephone for availability) help you discover one of the great Cornish gardens, as well as the more remote corners of the parkland and riverside woods. There are waymarked routes for exploring alone, as well as family-friendly cycle trails and a popular adventure playground. **Dogs**: dog-friendly walks throughout estate (assistance dogs only in house and garden).

Access: 🅿♿🏠🦽📷♿🚻📷🔊
House 🔊♿⬆🚶♿ Grounds ♿➡♿♿
Sat Nav: use PL30 4AB (1 Double Lodges).
Parking: 600 yards.

Find out more: 01208 265950 or lanhydrock@nationaltrust.org.uk

Lansallos

between Polperro and Polruan, Cornwall

 🏠♿🏛🛏🅰 1936

East of the Fowey Estuary is a long stretch of unspoilt coast loved by walkers, with abundant wild flowers and birds. From Lansallos church, a path ambles down the valley to a west-facing sandy beach. A picnic and a nose for adventure are all you need for the perfect day.
Note: nearest toilets at Lantivet Bay car park.

Lansallos: a path cuts through rock leading down to the west-facing beach

Eat, shop, stay: Highertown Farm campsite in Lansallos churchtown offers relaxed and unspoilt camping, or you could stay at Old and West House holiday cottages, with their far-reaching views over open countryside and the bay below.

Things to see and do: downloadable walking trails. Play trails alongside the valley path at Lansallos. Great coast for kite-flying, paddling and bathing. Walking west along the coast path leads to Lantivet and Lantic Bays. **Dogs**: welcome (close control near livestock).

Access: 🔲
Sat Nav: use PL13 2PX for Lansallos.
Parking: at Lansallos.

Find out more: 01726 870146 or lansallos@nationaltrust.org.uk

Lantic Bay

near Polruan, Cornwall

🔲🔲🔲 1959

Large shingly beach on a beautiful bay, great spot for paddling and picnicking, well worth the climb back up. **Note**: sorry no toilet. Beach is down a very steep path with steps. Beware of rip tides. Nearest postcode for Sat Nav is PL23 1NP.

Find out more: 01726 870146 or lanticbay@nationaltrust.org.uk

Lantivet Bay

between Polruan and Lansallos, Cornwall

🔲🔲🔲🔲 1976

Great starting point for walks along this unspoilt sweep of coast, with its small rocky coves. Access to coast path. **Note**: toilets in car park. For Sat Nav use PL23 1NP. National Trust holiday cottages at nearby Triggabrowne Farm.

Find out more: 01726 870146 or lantivetbay@nationaltrust.org.uk

Lawrence House

9 Castle Street, Launceston, Cornwall PL15 8BA

🔲🔲 1964

This Georgian town house, now a museum, hosts special exhibitions. Large display of costumes and a children's toy room.
Note: leased to Launceston Town Council. Open Monday to Friday, 3 April to 27 October, 10:30 to 4:30 (also open the second Saturday of each month).

Find out more: 01566 773277 or lawrencehouse@nationaltrust.org.uk

Levant Mine and Beam Engine

on the Tin Coast, near Pendeen, St Just, Cornwall TR19 7SX

🔲🔲🔲🔲🔲 1967

High up on the exposed cliffs of the Tin Coast is Levant, part of the Cornish Mining World Heritage Site, and at its heart, the restored 1840s beam engine running on steam. Here you can discover how Cornish miners,

Levant Mine and Beam Engine sits high up on the cliffs

A volunteer runs the restored engine at Levant

engineers and inventors risked everything to help shape the modern world. **Note**: exposed clifftop location, uneven ground and mine ruins. Please take care underfoot.

Eat, shop, stay: light refreshments, including hot and cold drinks, pasties and ice-cream with outdoor picnic benches. Small shop selling books, minerals, souvenirs and postcards. You can stay in the heart of the Tin Coast at nearby Botallack Count House Cottage (sleeps two).

Things to see and do: **Indoors** Restored beam engine steams daily. Free guided tours of mining landscape and archaeology. Tunnel to the man-engine shaft. Rock-breaking and mineral-washing activity. **Outdoors** Waymarked walks to Botallack and Geevor. **Dogs**: welcome on short leads.

Access: 🅿️ 🅳 🚽 ♿ 📷 🎧 🔦 📷
Reception ♿ 🔆 **Engine house** ♿ 🍴 🔆
Grounds ♿ ➡️ 🔆
Parking: 328 yards.

Find out more: 01736 786156 or levant@nationaltrust.org.uk

Levant Beam Engine		M	T	W	T	F	S	S
17 Feb–17 Mar	10:30–4:30	·	·	·	·	**F**	·	·
20 Mar–29 Oct	10:30–5	**M**	**T**	**W**	**T**	**F**	**S**	**S**
3 Nov–8 Dec	10:30–4:30	·	·	·	·	**F**	·	·

Engine steaming from 11. Hourly tours 11 to 3. Winter opening hours vary (please contact property for details).

Lizard Point

on the Lizard peninsula, near Helston, Cornwall

🐾 🏊 🎢 🐾 🛏️ 1935

This is mainland Britain's most southerly point, infamous as a site of shipwrecks in the past and overlooking what is still one of the busiest shipping lanes in the world. The cliffs and farmland are incredibly rich in wildlife. From the Wildlife Watchpoint you can see seals and occasionally dolphins, as well as the iconic Cornish choughs, which breed close by. At Bass Point, a short walk along the coast path, you'll find the tiny Lizard Wireless Station. This is dedicated to Marconi's world-changing experiments, which took place in this simple hut on the cliffs.

Eat, shop, stay: the highly rated Polpeor Café at Lizard Point (concession) open all year – weather-dependent – with outside seating and great views. Gifts on sale at the information point (Easter to end October). Quirky holiday cottage adjoining the Lizard Wireless Station on Bass Point.

Things to see and do: take a walk along the coast path for superb coastal views, or try one of the inland routes to search for rare

and unique plants. **Dogs**: welcome all around Lizard Point. Please note that livestock graze in some areas.

Access: 🅿️♿️🚾♿️🚼 Lizard Wireless Station ♿️
Sat Nav: use TR12 7NT.
Parking: at Lizard Point.

Find out more: 01326 222170 (Property Office). 01326 291174 (Rangers/Wireless Station) or lizard@nationaltrust.org.uk

Lizard Point		M	T	W	T	F	S	S
Wildlife Watchpoint								
1 Apr–16 Sep*	10–4	M	T	W	T	F	S	S

*Weather permitting. Telephone for opening times of the Lizard Wireless Station at Bass Point.

Mainland Britain's most southerly point, Lizard Point near Helston, below and bottom, has seen numerous ships founder on its treacherous jagged rocks

Morwenstow

near Bude, Cornwall

🏛️ | 1956

The realm of a great Victorian character – Parson Hawker. Hawker's Hut, driftwood-built, is on the cliff edge near his church. **Note**: sorry no toilets. For Sat Nav use EX23 9SR. Rectory Tea-rooms (tenant-run) open seasonally.

Find out more: 01208 863046 or morwenstow@nationaltrust.org.uk

Mullion Cove

on the Lizard peninsula, near Helston, Cornwall

🏠🏖️🏛️⛺ | 1945

Originally built in the 1890s, the picturesque harbour at Mullion Cove shelters a small fishing fleet from westerly storms. **Note**: toilets are seasonal. Dogs welcome. Kayaking and boat trips available. Campsite at Teneriffe Farm. For Sat Nav use TR12 7ES. Parking not National Trust (charge including members).

Find out more: 01326 291174 (Lizard Rangers). 01326 240293 (Teneriffe Farm Campsite) or mullioncove@nationaltrust.org.uk

Northcott Mouth

near Bude, Cornwall

🏛️ | 1981

Quiet and ruggedly beautiful, this small rocky beach opens up to expansive sand and rock pools as the tide drops. **Note**: sorry no toilets. Dogs welcome, under control. Lifeguards in high season. For Sat Nav use EX23 9ED.

Find out more: 01208 863046 or northcottmouth@nationaltrust.org.uk

Penrose

near Helston, Cornwall

🏠♿🚶🐕🛏️ 1974

Breakers crash onto Loe Bar at Penrose, top, and a visitor enjoys one of the inland paths around the estate

Home to Loe Pool, Cornwall's largest natural lake, Penrose is a mix of woods, farmland, parkland, cliffs and beaches: a great place to explore. There are 16 miles of bridleways and footpaths, including a trail around the pool and many coast path links. **Note**: to maintain the sense of peace at Penrose we don't allow watercraft on the pool.

Eat, shop, stay: Stables Café with parkland views (open daily, Easter to November, and at weekends all year). Picnics welcome in the neighbouring walled garden. There are several holiday cottages around Penrose, some hidden away and others with sea or lake views.

Things to see and do: you can hire a bike at Helston, try the easy-access route from Helston to the café, or pick a downloadable

trail to follow. Free outdoors guide/map available. **Dogs**: welcome under control, please note livestock graze in the fields.

Access: Helston Drive ♿ ➡️
Sat Nav: use TR13 0RD for Penrose Hill; TR13 0RA for Helston Drive. **Parking**: around Loe Pool (use Penrose Hill for Stables Café), and the Fairground car park (not National Trust) in Helston for Helston Drive.

Find out more: 01326 222170 (Rangers) or penroseestate@nationaltrust.org.uk

Penrose		M	T	W	T	F	S	S
Stables Café								
1 Jan–15 Apr	10–4	·	·	·	·	·	S	S
16 Apr–27 Oct	10–4	M	T	W	T	F	S	S
28 Oct–31 Dec	10–4	·	·	·	·	·	S	S

Also open through school holidays outside main summer season (telephone 01326 562353 to check).

Poldhu Cove

on the Lizard peninsula, near Helston, Cornwall

🏠♿🚶🐕⛺ 1984

Poldhu is an unspoilt beach popular with locals and visitors. The beach, dunes and reedbeds are designated as a Site of Special Scientific Interest for their rich wildlife. South of the cove the Marconi Monument and visitor centre celebrate Poldhu's role as the site of the first transatlantic wireless signal. **Note**: car park and toilets not National Trust. Members pay for parking.

Eat, shop, stay: the café at Poldhu Beach is open all year (not National Trust). A Trust

Sandy and unspoilt Poldhu Cove is popular with families

campsite is close by at Teneriffe Farm, near Mullion, and there are holiday cottages further away at Bass Point, Penrose and Cadgwith.

Things to see and do: popular surf school offers lessons for all the family. **Dogs**: council-enforced beach ban (7 to 7, Easter to 1 October). Welcome on coast path.

Access: 🅿️ Marconi Centre 🏖️ 🏖️ ➡️
Sat Nav: use TR12 7BU. **Parking**: on site (not National Trust).

Find out more: 01326 291174 (Lizard Rangers). 01326 240293 (Teneriffe Farm Campsite) or poldhucove@nationaltrust.org.uk

Port Quin

near Wadebridge, Cornwall

 1936

Once busy, Port Quin is now a peaceful sheltered inlet

Once a busy fishing port, Port Quin is now a peaceful sheltered inlet on an outstanding stretch of unspoilt coast. Nearby are the headlands of Pentire and the Rumps, with spectacular views and wild flowers; Lundy Bay at the foot of a wildlife-filled valley; and Pentireglaze Haven with great rock-pooling. **Note**: nearest toilets in Polzeath, 3 miles (not National Trust).

Eat, shop, stay: pubs, cafés and shops in Polzeath (not National Trust). Holiday cottages, including the quirky Doyden Castle and a number of coastal apartments and characterful cottages.

Things to see and do: seals, rare bats, corn buntings and puffins to spot. Well-preserved Iron Age ramparts on the Rumps. Sea kayaking and coasteering available nearby. **Dogs**: welcome under control. Seasonal dog ban on Polzeath Beach (including Pentireglaze Haven).

Access: Coast and beach 👣
Sat Nav: use PL29 3SU for Port Quin; PL27 6QY Pentireglaze and Pentire Farm; PL27 6QZ Lundy Bay. **Parking**: at Port Quin, Pentire Farm, Lead Mines (Pentireglaze) and Lundy Bay. Also at Polzeath (not National Trust).

Find out more: 01208 863046 or portquin@nationaltrust.org.uk

Porth

on the Roseland peninsula, near Portscatho, Cornwall

 1958

Creekside and coastal footpaths make for great walking and wildlife spotting. Towan Beach, next to Porth, is perfect for children. **Note**: for Sat Nav use TR2 5EX. The Thirstea Company seasonal van (concession) serves drinks, cakes, sandwiches and ice-cream. Toilets. Four holiday cottages.

Find out more: 01872 580553 or porth@nationaltrust.org.uk

Porthcurno

near Penzance, Cornwall

🚽 🏛️ 🏖️ 🏊 1994

Soft, white shell beach with popular freshwater stream, surrounded by turquoise seas. Great for watching birds, basking sharks and dolphins. **Note**: for Sat Nav use TR19 6JU. Parking and toilets not National Trust (charge including members).

Find out more: 01736 761853 or porthcurno@nationaltrust.org.uk

St Agnes Head

near St Agnes, Cornwall

🏠🚽🏛 1967

A brilliant patchwork of yellow gorse and purple heather carpets this dramatic coastal landscape. Just inland is St Agnes Beacon. **Note**: nearest café and toilets at Chapel Porth. For Sat Nav use TR5 0NU.

Find out more: 01872 552412 or stagneshead@nationaltrust.org.uk

St Anthony Head

on the Roseland peninsula, near Portscatho, Cornwall

🏠🚽🏛🛏 1959

Strategically important for centuries, St Anthony Head sits at the eastern entrance to Falmouth harbour

This headland at the eastern entrance to Falmouth harbour has been strategically important for centuries. It commands magnificent views up the Fal Estuary and across Falmouth Bay towards the Lizard, and there are still plenty of historic fortifications of various eras to be explored.

Eat, shop, stay: you can stay here in the old officers' quarters on the headland itself (two adapted for disabled visitors), or nearby at Bohortha and Porth. There are many wonderful spots for picnicking. At Porth there's a seasonal tea-van (concession).

Things to see and do: many historic military remains to discover. There's a bird hide for spotting peregrine falcons and you can walk the coast path or scramble down to lovely Molunan Beach. **Dogs**: welcome.

Access: 🚾♿
Sat Nav: use TR2 5HA. **Parking**: on site.

Find out more: 01872 580553 or stanthonyhead@nationaltrust.org.uk

St Michael's Mount

Marazion, Cornwall TR17 0HS

🏰✝❀🏛 1954

This iconic rocky island, crowned by a medieval church and castle, is home to the St Aubyn family and a 30-strong community of islanders. Visiting the Mount, you are immersed in history, islanders' tales and legends like the famous 'Jack the Giant Killer'. There's a subtropical terraced garden to explore, and spectacular views of Mount's Bay and the Lizard from the castle battlements. If the tide is high, you can take an evocative boat trip to the island harbour; at low tide you walk across the ancient cobbled causeway from Marazion on the mainland, as pilgrims have done for centuries.

The subtropical terraced garden on St Michael's Mount

Topped by a medieval castle and church, magical St Michael's Mount is reached by an ancient causeway which runs from Marazion, near Penzance

Note: steep climb to the castle over uneven, cobbled, historic pathway. St Aubyn Estates/National Trust partnership. Members have to pay for car parking and boat trips to the Mount at high tide.

Eat, shop, stay: Island Café for pasties, sandwiches and cream teas. Sail Loft for Newlyn fish, daily specials, cream teas, homemade breads and cakes. Both serve local ales and cider. Island Shop and Courtyard Shop sell local produce, jewellery, bags, arts and crafts.

Things to see and do: **Indoors** Children's quiz. Events, exhibitions. Find out more about the castle's history by asking our knowledgeable room guides. Sunday church services (Whitsun to September). **Outdoors** Garden trail for children. **Dogs**: assistance dogs only in castle and garden.

Access: 🅿♿🏛🎫🏷🚻 Castle ♿ Village ♿♿
Parking: numerous spaces in Marazion, opposite St Michael's Mount, not National Trust (charge including members).

Find out more: 01736 710265 (information, tides and boats) or stmichaelsmount@nationaltrust.org.uk stmichaelsmount.co.uk Estate Office, King's Road, Marazion TR17 0EL

St Michael's Mount		M	T	W	T	F	S	S
Castle								
19 Mar–2 Jul	10:30–5	M	T	W	T	F	·	S
3 Jul–1 Sep	10:30–5:30	M	T	W	T	F	·	S
3 Sep–27 Oct	10:30–5	M	T	W	T	F	·	S
Garden								
17 Apr–30 Jun	10:30–5	M	T	W	T	F	·	·
6 Jul–1 Sep	10:30–5:30	·	·	·	T	F	·	·
7 Sep–29 Sep	10:30–5	·	·	·	T	F	·	·

Last admission 45 minutes before castle closes (remember to allow enough time for travel from mainland). Telephone for details of opening arrangements in February, early March, November and December.

Sandymouth

near Bude, Cornwall

A pebbly cove at low tide, Sandymouth becomes a wide sweep of beach once the sea goes out

A popular destination, yet Sandymouth remains unspoilt and breathtakingly beautiful. You'll find an extreme difference between the beach at low tide – when it is a huge sweep of sand and rocky outcrops – and at high tide, when it shrinks back to a pebbly cove, backed by twisted cliffs.

Eat, shop, stay: Sandymouth Café (concession, open seasonally) has outdoor and indoor seating and also sells beach goods. Pubs, shops and cafés in Kilkhampton and Bude (none National Trust).

Things to see and do: surf school. Fantastic rock-pooling and coastal walks. Look out for the waterfall and amazing geological formations backing the beach. You may also catch sight of skylarks, song thrushes and stonechats. **Dogs**: welcome everywhere, including the beach, but under close control (especially around livestock).

Access: 🅿️🚻🔆 Coast and beach ♿
Sat Nav: use EX23 9HW. **Parking**: on site.

Find out more: 01208 863046 or sandymouth@nationaltrust.org.uk

Sandymouth
Café at Sandymouth open seasonally, telephone 01288 354286.

Tintagel Old Post Office

Fore Street, Tintagel, Cornwall PL34 0DB

More than a post office, this medieval hall-house has had many uses during its 600 years, and has numerous stories to tell. Today, it is furnished as the Victorian letter-receiving office that once served the village. The cottage garden at the rear offers a retreat from Tintagel's bustling high street. **Note**: nearest toilet 54 yards in Trevena Square (not National Trust).

Eat, shop, stay: small souvenir shop in the Post Room selling craft items, gifts and books inspired by the Old Post Office's history and events. Picnics are welcome in the relaxing cottage garden at the back of the house.

Things to see and do: **Indoors** Events held over the year, including traditional craft workshops, baking demonstrations and activities to provide entertainment during school holidays. **Outdoors** Family trail, games and dressing-up. **Dogs**: assistance dogs only.

The Hall at Tintagel Old Post Office. This humble 600-year-old building has many stories to tell

Access: 🅿️📷🔆⬤📷 Building ♿🔆🚻
Grounds ♿🔆
Parking: pay and display village car parks, not National Trust (charges including members). Nearest Trust parking at Glebe Cliff in Tintagel, ½ mile.

Find out more: 01840 770024 or
tintageloldpo@nationaltrust.org.uk

Tintagel Old Post Office		M	T	W	T	F	S	S
11 Feb–19 Feb	11–4	M	T	W	T	F	S	S
6 Mar–2 Apr	11–4	M	T	W	T	F	S	S
3 Apr–24 Sep	10:30–5:30	M	T	W	T	F	S	S
25 Sep–29 Oct	11–4	M	T	W	T	F	S	S

Seen from the air, the wonderful position of Trelissick on its own peninsula in the Fal Estuary becomes apparent

Trelissick

Feock, near Truro, Cornwall TR3 6QL

🏠🏛️✳️🎣🖼️🛏️🍴 1955

Trelissick is set on its own peninsula, with panoramic views over the Fal Estuary. The house provides the perfect setting to enjoy the ever-changing seascape and countryside steeped in Cornish history. Visitors can explore meandering paths through the woodland garden, leading to exotic plants and formal lawns with herbaceous borders bursting with colour. There are also longer walks to discover through the historic parkland, which sweep down towards the estuary, and along Lamouth Creek to the Iron Age promontory fort and 18th-century quay at Roundwood.

Eat, shop, stay: café open daily, with outdoor seating in the courtyard. The Barn Restaurant is available for functions and event hire. Gift and plant shop. Second-hand bookshop. Cornish art and craft gallery. Six holiday cottages on the estate.

Things to see and do: **Indoors** Don't miss the amazing views from Trelissick House. At Christmas the house and garden are illuminated during evening openings. **Outdoors** Trelissick beach is perfect for skimming stones and paddling. **Dogs**: welcome on woodland walks. Assistance dogs only in garden.

Access: 🅿️♿️🎧🔔📷✏️📶📷 Reception ♿️♿️ House ♿️♿️♿️ Garden ♿️♿️♿️➡️♿️♿️ **Parking**: 30 yards.

Find out more: 01872 862090 or trelissick@nationaltrust.org.uk

The graceful colonnade at the front of Trelissick, which commands a breathtaking view down the Fal Estuary

Trelissick		M	T	W	T	F	S	S
Garden, café, shop, gallery and bookshop*								
Open all year	10:30–4:30	M	T	W	T	F	S	S
House								
11 Feb–29 Oct	11–5	M	T	W	T	F	S	S
1 Dec–31 Dec	11–4					F	S	S
Parkland and walks								
Open all year		M	T	W	T	F	S	S

*Garden, café, shop, gallery and bookshop: 11 February to 29 October, close at 5:30. Garden closes at dusk if earlier. Late-night openings and garden illuminations for Christmas. Everything closed 25 and 26 December. Some areas, including the house, close occasionally for private events.

A satisfyingly well-ordered bed in Trengwainton's productive walled garden, built to the dimensions of Noah's Ark

Trengwainton Garden

Madron, near Penzance, Cornwall TR20 8RZ

❄ ⚲ 1961

Here in this warm and luxuriant garden, you can follow in the footsteps of the 1920s plant hunters to see plants that flowered in Britain for the first time. Award-winning magnolias and rhododendrons are still nurtured by those with a passion for plants, and subtropical species from around the world thrive in the shelter of the walled gardens, including a kitchen garden built to the dimensions of Noah's Ark. Winding wooded paths follow a half-mile incline to sea views across Mount's Bay, and the descent via the drive is bordered by a colourful stream garden and open meadows.

Eat, shop, stay: award-winning tea-room (not National Trust) with indoor and outdoor seating. Shop sells local gifts, food, souvenirs and Trengwainton-inspired plants. On a chilly day you can warm yourself by the woodburner. You can stay in an 18th-century former laundry-house (sleeping nine).

Things to see and do: seasonal spotter sheets and sensory trail. Events throughout the year. You can visit the Dig for Victory plot. Why not visit Godolphin on the same day? **Dogs**: welcome on leads.

Access: ♿ 🅿 🔊 🤟 ⬆ 🔲 🔊 ❗ Ⓐ Reception 🔲
Tea-room 🔲 Garden 🔲 ➡ ♿
Sat Nav: TR20 8RZ. **Parking**: 150 yards.

Find out more: 01736 363148 or trengwainton@nationaltrust.org.uk

Trengwainton Garden		M	T	W	T	F	S	S
12 Feb–29 Oct	10:30–5	M	T	W	T			S

Open Good Friday. Tea-room opens at 10.

Trerice

Kestle Mill, near Newquay, Cornwall TR8 4PG

🏛 ❄ ⚲ ▲ 🍵 1953

It's easy to lose yourself in this small yet enchanting place as you soak up the tranquillity of Trerice. Just a stone's throw from Newquay, it's nestled in a peaceful corner of rural Cornwall. This romantic Elizabethan manor house tells a story of prosperous origins, decline, partial ruin and 20th-century restoration. Today, the peace and quiet of Trerice is occasionally pierced by shouts of excitement from the kayling lawn (surely you will want to try a game of kayling or slapcock?), bringing back some of the bustle and noise that must have typified its time as a busy manor house.

Eat, shop, stay: self-service restaurant offering coffee, locally produced lunches, cakes and desserts, as well as our famous lemon meringue pie. Shop selling local products, souvenirs and plants. You can stay in the West Wing of the house, which is a holiday flat.

Things to see and do: **Indoors** Costume days, introductory talks and conservation events. Replica armour to try on. **Outdoors** Family activities and trails, Cornish 'kayles' and other traditional games. **Dogs**: welcome in car park only.

Dressing up for the fray at Trerice: a visitor is helped into a suit of armour

The enchanting Elizabethan manor of Trerice, now peaceful and quiet, was once a bustling hive of activity

Access: [icons] House [icons] Barn [icons] Garden [icons]
Parking: 300 yards.

Find out more: 01637 875404 or trerice@nationaltrust.org.uk

Trerice		M	T	W	T	F	S	S
25 Feb–29 Oct	10:30–5*	M	T	W	T	F	S	S
4 Nov–17 Dec**	11–4	.	.	.	.	.	S	S

*House opens 11. **Great Hall only, garden, shop and Barn restaurant open.

Wheal Coates

near St Agnes, Cornwall

[icons] 1956

Dramatic ruins on cliffs carpeted with heather and gorse, the old mine buildings of Wheal Coates are a Cornish icon. **Note**: nearest café and toilets at Chapel Porth. For Sat Nav use TR5 0NT.

Find out more: 01872 552412 or whealcoates@nationaltrust.org.uk

Additional coastal and countryside car parks in Cornwall

Strangles Beach	EX23 0LQ	St Agnes Beacon	TR5 0NU	Chyvarloe	TR12 7PY
Glebe Cliff, Tintagel	PL34 0DL	Reskajeage Downs	TR14 0JG	Predannack	TR12 7EZ
Lundy Bay	PL27 6QZ	Derrick Cove	TR14 0JG	Poltesco	TR12 7LR
Pentireglaze	PL27 6QY	Fishing Cove	TR27 5EE	Nare Head	TR2 5PQ
Trevose Head	PL28 8SL	Trencrom	TR27 6NP	Lamledra (Vault Beach)	PL26 6JS
Park Head	PL27 7UU	Carn Galver	TR20 8YX	Coombe Farm	PL23 1HW
Treago Mill (Polly Joke)	TR8 5QS	Cot Valley	TR19 7NS	Hendersick	PL13 2HZ

Devon
and Dorset

Corfe Castle, Dorset

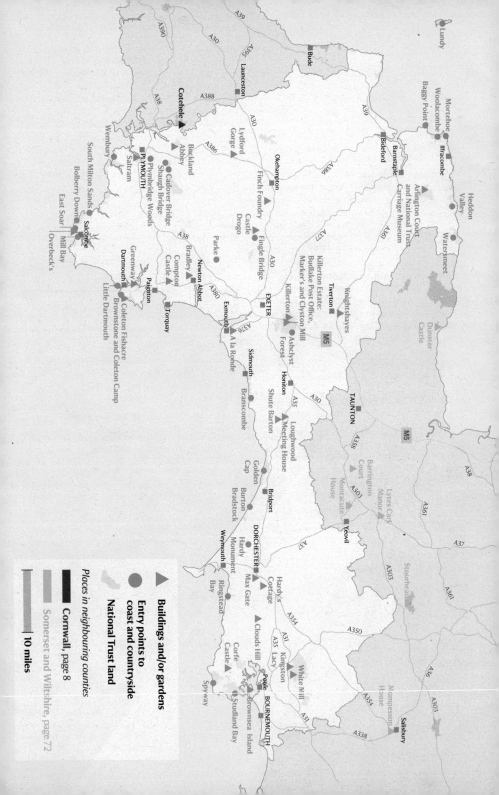

Lundy

Bude

Mortehoe
Woolacombe
Baggy Point
Ilfracombe
Heddon
Valley
Watersmeet

Arlington Court
and National Trust
Carriage Museum

Barnstaple
Bideford

Dunster
Castle

A39

A388

Launceston

Cotehele ▲

Lydford
Gorge

Okehampton

Finch Foundry

Knightshayes

Tiverton

M5

Wembury

Buckland
Abbey

Saltram

Cadover Bridge
Shaugh Bridge
PLYMOUTH
Plymbridge Woods

Castle
Drogo

Fingle Bridge

Killerton Estate:
Budlake Post Office,
Marker's and Clyston Mill

Killerton

EXETER

Ashclyst
Forest

South Milton Sands
Bolberry Down

East Soar
Mill Bay
Overbeck's
Salcombe

Bradley
Compton
Castle

Parke

Newton Abbot

A la Ronde

Exmouth

Sidmouth

Honiton

Shute Barton

TAUNTON

M5

Greenway
Dartmouth

Paignton

Torquay

Coleton Fishacre
Brownstone and Coleton Camp
Little Dartmouth

Branscombe

Loughwood
Meeting House

Barrington
Court

Montacute
House

Lytes Cary
Manor

Golden
Cap

Bridport

Yeovil

Stourhead

Burton
Bradstock

DORCHESTER

Hardy
Monument

Weymouth

Ringstead
Bay

Max Gate

Hardy's
Cottage

Clouds Hill

Corfe
Castle

Kingston
Lacy

White Mill

Mompesson
House

Salisbury

Spyway

Studland Bay

Brownsea Island

Poole

BOURNEMOUTH

A la Ronde

Summer Lane, Exmouth, Devon EX8 5BD

 1991

Full of creativity and treasures from around the world, this amazing 16-sided house was the work of cousins Jane and Mary Parminter in the 1790s. Step inside and you enter another world, one where their imaginations ran wild in design and ornamentation. They decorated walls with feathers, shells and pictures made of seaweed and sand, and every space contains mementoes from their travels. With the 360° touchscreen virtual tour, you can view the fragile shell gallery made from nearly 25,000 shells. Outside, there's a sense of harmony around the orchard, hay meadow and colourful borders, and views over the Exe Estuary.
Note: small and delicate rooms. Photography welcome without flash.

Eat, shop, stay: tea-room has indoor and outdoor seating with views of the Exe Estuary.

Hot and cold light lunches, homemade cakes and Devon cream teas. Picnic area in orchard. The shop features gifts, local food and keepsakes. Second-hand book sales.

Things to see and do: **Indoors** Self-guided tours. Monthly 'Hidden house' feature.
Outdoors Orchard, hay meadow and colourful borders. Views of Exe Estuary. Garden games and croquet. Events, including family trails and crafts. **Dogs**: dogs on leads welcome everywhere except inside house. Assistance dogs can access all areas.

Access: ⬚⬚⬚⬚⬚⬚⬚⬚
House ⬚⬚⬚ **Grounds** ⬚➡
Parking: on site.

Find out more: 01395 265514 or alaronde@nationaltrust.org.uk

A la Ronde		M	T	W	T	F	S	S
4 Feb–10 Feb	Tour	M	T	W	T	F	S	S
11 Feb–19 Feb	11–5	M	T	W	T	F	S	S
20 Feb–10 Mar	Tour	M	T	W	T	F	S	S
11 Mar–29 Oct	11–5	M	T	W	T	F	S	S

Grounds, shop and tea-room open 10:30 to 5:30.
Last orders in tea-room at 5. Last entry to house at 4.

In the garden at A la Ronde in Devon there are colourful borders and views over the Exe Estuary

Arlington Court and the National Trust Carriage Museum, Devon: a surprise and a delight

Arlington Court and the National Trust Carriage Museum

Arlington, near Barnstaple, Devon EX31 4LP

🏠 ✝ ⚙ ❁ ♿ ⛺ | 1949 |

Hidden in the lichen-draped landscape of North Devon, Arlington is a surprise and a delight. The starkly classical exterior of the house gives no clue to what lies inside – the passions of 11 generations of the Chichester family, including shells, ships and pewter. The stable block houses a nationally important display of carriages, from grand state coaches to humble governess carts. The garden is restored to its colourful Victorian glory, and the conservatory's exotic plantings reveal the Chichesters' world travels.

New 2017 exhibition: discover the ship collection of the Chichester family, plus Sir Francis Chichester's round-the-world voyage.

Eat, shop, stay: seasonal produce grown in the walled garden is used in the tea-room. Reduced menu in winter. Produce also made into Arlington chutney, made by a local producer. Two holiday cottages on edges of estate, sleeping two or three (dogs welcome).

Things to see and do: **Indoors** Spy on the bats in the attic. Children's activities. **Outdoors** Bring your walking boots to explore the extensive estate, including two woodland play areas. Daily children's activities (school holidays). **Dogs**: welcome on leads in garden, Carriage Museum and wider estate.

Access: 🅿 ♿ 🚍 ♿ ♿ 🐕 🖥 📺 ♿ ◦◦ ⊘
House ♿ ♿ ♿ **Museum** ♿ ♣ ♿
Grounds ➡ ♿ ♿
Sat Nav: from South Molton, don't turn left into unmarked lane (deliveries only).
Parking: 150 yards.

Find out more: 01271 850296 or arlingtoncourt@nationaltrust.org.uk

Arlington Court		M	T	W	T	F	S	S
11 Feb–29 Oct	11–5*	M	T	W	T	F	S	S
4 Nov–17 Dec	11–4	·	·	·	·	·	S	S

*Garden, shop and tea-room open 10:30. Grounds open all year, dawn to dusk.

Ashclyst Forest

near Broadclyst, Exeter, Devon

 1944

One of the largest woods in East Devon, with waymarked trails for exploring. A haven for butterflies, bluebells and birds. **Note**: for Sat Nav use EX5 3DT, follow signs to Ashclyst. Part of the Killerton Estate – toilets, café and shop nearby at main Killerton car park.

Find out more: 01392 881345 or ashclystforest@nationaltrust.org.uk

Baggy Point

near Croyde, Devon

1939

Baggy Point is the impressive headland at Croyde, once owned by the Hyde family and overlooking one of the best surfing beaches in the South West. Huge coastal views, great walks and opportunities to climb, surf and coasteer make it a must-do destination for anyone visiting North Devon. **Note**: toilets (not National Trust) on main beach slipway, 500 yards from Trust car park.

Eat, shop, stay: Sandleigh tea-room, garden and shop (tenant-run) serving drinks and food grown in the walled garden. Open-air covered seating area overlooking garden. Tea-room is next to car park, close to beach slipway. Car-park kiosk serving cold drinks and snacks.

Things to see and do: free children's activity pack (to borrow). Walks leaflets available from car-park kiosk. Arlington Court and the National Carriage Museum is nearby. **Dogs**: welcome on leads (except for seasonal ban on Croyde Beach from May to September).

Access: 🅿️🏟️➡️
Sat Nav: use EX33 1PA. **Parking**: car park in Moor Lane, Croyde.

Find out more: 01271 870555 or baggypoint@nationaltrust.org.uk

Young adventurers at Baggy Point in Devon, with the impressive headland beyond

Bolberry Down

between Salcombe and Hope Cove,
near Malborough, Devon

 1938

The starting point for discovering a spectacular
stretch of coast between Salcombe and Hope
Cove, including the headlands of Bolt Head
and Bolt Tail and the sandy beach at Soar Mill
Cove. The majestic ragged cliffs have claimed
countless ships over the centuries. There's an
easy-access route over the clifftops.
Note: sorry no toilet.

Eat, shop, stay: refreshments and meals
available at Port Light Hotel and Restaurant
(not National Trust). Walkers' Hut café
(tenant-run) at East Soar Outdoor Experience
serves hot drinks and homemade cakes and
there are also catered camping options and
a pretty holiday cottage.

Things to see and do: level circular trail,
accessible for most wheelchair users and
pushchairs. **Dogs**: welcome (on leads
where animals grazing).

Access:
Sat Nav: use TQ7 3DY. **Parking**: at Bolberry
Down and Hope Cove (not National Trust).

Find out more: 01752 346585. 01548 561904
(East Soar Outdoor Experience) or
bolberrydown@nationaltrust.org.uk

Bradley

Totnes Road, Newton Abbot, Devon TQ12 6BN

 1938

Unspoilt and fascinating medieval manor
house, still a relaxed family home, in a green
haven among riverside meadows and
woodland. Many charming original features,
such as the medieval cat hole and drip stones.
The quiet and peaceful chapel was licensed
for services in 1428. **Note**: sorry no toilet.

Medieval Bradley, Devon, is still a relaxed family home

Parking from 10:30 on open days.

Eat, shop, stay: table-top shop selling honey,
souvenirs, gifts and postcards. Picnics welcome in
the meadows surrounding the house and garden.

Things to see and do: events, including
open-air theatre. Walks in surrounding
countryside. For a truly medieval experience,
why not visit nearby Compton Castle?
Dogs: welcome in meadows and woodland.
Assistance dogs only in garden and house.

Access: Building 🔊🔊🔊
Grounds 🔊🔊➡
Sat Nav: TQ12 1LX directs to gate lodge (follow
driveway for parking). **Parking**: in meadow
(for designated parking call 01626 354513).

Find out more: 01803 661907 or
bradley@nationaltrust.org.uk

Bradley		M	T	W	T	F	S	S
4 Apr–28 Sep	11–5	.	T	W	T	.	.	.

Branscombe

on the Jurassic Coast, near Seaton, Devon

🏠📷🏞🚗 1965

Nestling in a valley that reaches down to the
sea on East Devon's dramatic Jurassic Coast,
the village of Branscombe is surrounded by
picturesque countryside with miles of tranquil
walking through woodland, farmland and
beach. Charming thatched houses, forge and
restored watermill add to the timeless magic of
the place. **Note**: nearest toilets at information
point, village hall and beach car park.

Branscombe		M	T	W	T	F	S	S
Manor Mill								
2 Apr–29 Oct	2–5	·	·	·	·	·	·	**S**
Old Forge								
Open all year	10–5*	**M**	**T**	**W**	**T**	**F**	**S**	**S**

Manor Mill also open Wednesdays 19 July to 30 August.
*Telephone 01297 680481 to check forge opening times.
For details of the Old Bakery tea-room opening,
telephone 01297 680764.

Eat, shop, stay: Old Bakery tea-room
(tenant-run) serving sandwiches, homemade
cakes and cream teas. Quality ironwork on
sale from the Old Forge. Forge Cottage, just
across the road, is a holiday cottage in an ideal
location for exploring the village and coast.

Things to see and do: trail (graded as easy)
winding up from the beach to the village,
passing Manor Mill, Old Bakery and Old Forge.
The beach is great for swimming and picnics.
Dogs: welcome on leads in the Old Bakery
garden, orchard, beach and wider countryside.

Access: 🅿 Building 🚻 ♿ Mill 🚻 ⛪ Grounds ♿
Sat Nav: use EX12 3DB. **Parking**: next to
Old Forge, limited spaces. Also village hall and
beach car parks (neither National Trust).

Find out more: 01752 346585 or
branscombe@nationaltrust.org.uk

**Branscombe in Devon, top, and Brownsea Island
in Dorset, below: two picturesque south coast gems**

Brownsea Island

Poole Harbour, Poole, Dorset

⬧🏠♿🎨🐦🛏 1962

The perfect day's adventure, this island wildlife
sanctuary is easy to get to but feels like another
world from the moment you step ashore.
The island sits in the middle of Poole Harbour,
with dramatic views to the Purbeck Hills.
Thriving natural habitats, including woodland,
heathland and a lagoon, have created havens
for wildlife, such as the red squirrel and a huge
variety of birds. The island is rich in history too.
It is the birthplace of the Scouting and Guiding
movements, and there are the remains of
daffodil farming, pottery works and Maryland
village to explore. **Note**: half-hourly boat
service from 10 (not National Trust).

Rare red squirrels live on Brownsea Island

Wheelchair boat service. No access to castle. Small entry fee to Dorset Wildlife Trust area (including members).

Eat, shop, stay: Villano Café, coffee bar and self-service drinks at the Outdoor Centre. Mobile ice-cream unit (peak periods). Engine Gift Shop selling Brownsea Island outdoors range, local produce, souvenirs and ice-cream. Scout and Guide Trading Post sells memorabilia. Two holiday cottages.

Things to see and do: family activities, tree-climbing trail, Tracker Packs and natural play area. Events. Walks and talks. Open-air theatre. Outdoor and visitor centres. Introductory walks and buggy tours for less-mobile visitors (booking advised). **Dogs**: assistance dogs only.

Access: 🧎🦽🅿🔄🛗📶🅰 Building 🦽 Grounds 🦽➡

Sat Nav: for Sandbanks Jetty use BH13 7QJ; for Poole Quay BH15 1HP. **Parking**: near Sandbanks and Poole Quay, not National Trust (charge including members).

Find out more: 01202 707744 or brownseaisland@nationaltrust.org.uk

Brownsea Island	M	T	W	T	F	S	S
Hourly boat service from Poole Quay and Sandbanks*							
4 Feb–12 Mar	10–4						S	S
Full boat service from Poole Quay and Sandbanks							
18 Mar–29 Oct	10–5	M	T	W	T	F	S	S

Shop and Villano Café open until last boat. *Special weekend openings: boats leave every hour from Poole and Sandbanks (shop, café and visitor centre will all be open). New for winter: Poole Harbour Bird Boats from Poole Quay (booking essential).

Brownstone and Coleton Camp

between Dart Estuary and Brixham, Devon

🏠📷♿🚶 1981

Rugged and captivating stretch of coast east of the Dart Estuary, with cliffs, beaches and traditional farmland. From Trust car parks you can easily reach the coast path for great walking and superb views. Close to Brownstone car park is one of the few remaining Second World War gun batteries. **Note**: public toilets at nearby Kingswear, or at the Trust's Coleton Fishacre (when open).

Eat, shop, stay: café at nearby Coleton Fishacre offering tea and homemade cakes or a hearty lunch. Five holiday cottages in the area, which enjoy after-hours access to Coleton Fishacre garden.

Things to see and do: spectacular coastal views. Peregrines, seals and dolphins can be spotted from the coast path. The Froward Point area is known for its rare flora. Bird hide at Man Sands. **Dogs**: on leads near livestock and on cliff paths.

Rugged coast near Brownstone and Coleton Camp, Devon

Access: 🚶🦽

Sat Nav: use TQ6 0EH for Brownstone; TQ6 0EQ Coleton Camp; TQ6 0EF Mansands and Scabbacombe. **Parking**: at Brownstone (for Froward Point and Brownstone Battery), Coleton Camp, Mansands (for Woodhuish and Mansands Beach), and Scabbacombe.

Find out more: 01803 753010 or coletoncamp@nationaltrust.org.uk

Buckland Abbey

Yelverton, Devon PL20 6EY

🏯 ✝ ❄ 🛏 🍴 | 1948 |

Hundreds of years ago, Cistercian monks chose this tranquil valley as the perfect spot in which to worship, farm their estate and trade. The Abbey, later converted into a house, today combines furnished rooms with museum galleries bringing to life the story of how seafaring adventurers Sir Richard Grenville and Sir Francis Drake changed the shape of Buckland Abbey and the fate of England. Outdoors you'll find the garden, including a walled kitchen garden, Cider House garden and wild garden; the impressive medieval Great Barn; community growing areas; orchards and woodland walks with far-reaching views and late spring bluebells. **Note**: Abbey interior presented in association with Plymouth City Museum.

Eat, shop, stay: Ox Yard Restaurant serves freshly cooked local produce, often using ingredients grown in the kitchen garden. Picnics welcome in garden and grounds. Shop selling gifts and plants. Gallery and second-hand bookshop. Holiday cottage.

Things to see and do: **Indoors** Don't miss the famous Drake's Drum. **Outdoors** Higher Paddock natural play area and zip wire for younger visitors. Year-round events, estate walks and trails. **Dogs**: welcome on leads in farmland and on woodland walks. Assistance dogs only in garden.

Access: 🄿 ♿ 🄶 🄻 🄹 🄿 🄳 🄹 🄿 🅀
Abbey ♿ ♿ 🄶 **Visitor Welcome** ♿ 🄶
Grounds ♿ ♿ ▶ ♿ 🄶
Sat Nav: do not use. **Parking**: 150 yards.

Find out more: 01822 853607 or bucklandabbey@nationaltrust.org.uk

Buckland Abbey		M	T	W	T	F	S	S
1 Jan–5 Feb*	10–4	.	.	.	.	.	**S**	**S**
11 Feb–29 Oct	10–5**	**M**	**T**	**W**	**T**	**F**	**S**	**S**
30 Oct–31 Dec†	10–4**	**M**	**T**	**W**	**T**	**F**	**S**	**S**

*Everything, apart from Abbey, open weekends (also open 2 January). **Abbey: opens one hour later and closes 30 minutes earlier. †November: access to Abbey Monday to Friday by tour only (places limited); Saturday and Sunday free-flow. December: free-flow access to ground floor only; 27 to 31 December access by tour only (places limited). Everything closed 24 to 26 December.

There is so much to discover, both indoors and out, at tranquil Buckland Abbey in Devon, above and below

Burton Bradstock

on the Jurassic Coast, near Bridport, Dorset

 1973

One of the main gateways to Dorset's Jurassic Coast, with easy access to spectacular sandstone cliffs and miles of unspoilt beaches. Hive Beach is a hugely popular family destination, part of Chesil Bank – the largest shingle ridge in the world. Nearby, Burton Cliff glows bright gold in the sunlight.

Eat, shop, stay: tenant-run Hive Beach Café on Chesil Bank serving local seafood.

Things to see and do: events through the year, some especially for families. Paddling, swimming and outdoor activities. Circular and clifftop walks. Hive Beach popular for scuba diving and angling. **Dogs**: welcome. Dog-free zone on Hive Beach, 1 June to 30 September.

Access: 🅿️ 🔽
Sat Nav: use DT6 4RF. **Parking**: on site.

Find out more: 01297 489481 or burtonbradstock@nationaltrust.org.uk

Cadover Bridge

on Dartmoor, near Shaugh Prior, Devon

 1960

Tranquil moorland by the River Plym with pools. Starting point for walks across open moors and tors or ancient woodland. **Note**: for Sat Nav use PL7 5EH.

Find out more: 01752 341377 or cadoverbridge@nationaltrust.org.uk

Castle Drogo

Drewsteignton, near Exeter, Devon EX6 6PB

 1974

High above the ancient woodlands of the Teign Gorge stands Castle Drogo. Inspired by the rugged Dartmoor tors that surround it, the castle was designed and built by renowned 20th-century architect Sir Edwin Lutyens. Nothing is normal at Drogo, as the castle is currently undergoing a major conservation project to save it, by making it watertight. The inside has been redisplayed taking inspiration from the stories of Drogo, bringing to life darkened spaces and displaying the collection in creative new ways. A scaffolding viewing tower enables you to see the craftsmanship of the modern-day stonemasons. **Note**: access may be restricted or changed due to building works. Restrictions apply to viewing tower.

Eat, shop, stay: popular licensed café in the visitor centre, with outside seating, serving light meals, homemade cakes and scones. Picnics welcome in garden and grounds. Shop stocking gifts, local beers, jams and a good-sized plant centre. Holiday cottage nearby at Chagford.

Things to see and do: **Indoors** Specialised guided tours, family trails and events.
Outdoors Lutyens-designed terraced garden, games on the lawn. Walks into the Teign Gorge with views across Dartmoor and riverside paths. **Dogs**: welcome on leads in grounds and wider estate. Assistance dogs only in formal garden.

Inspired by stories, the interior of Castle Drogo, Devon, has been redisplayed, while work to the exterior continues

High heathland and ancient woods around Castle Drogo offer excellent walking and views across Dartmoor

Access: 🅿️ 🚐 ♿ 👶 🦽 🍴 🐕 🏛️ ⬆️ 🅿️ ⚲
Building 🦽 👶 👁️ **Grounds** 🦽 👶 👶 ➡️ 🚐 👁️
Parking: 400 yards from visitor centre.

Find out more: 01647 433306 or castledrogo@nationaltrust.org.uk

Castle Drogo		M	T	W	T	F	S	S
Castle								
6 Mar–29 Oct	11–5	M	T	W	T	F	S	S
4 Nov–17 Dec	Tour**	·	·	·	·	·	S	S
Garden, visitor centre, café and shop								
1 Jan–5 Mar	11–4	M	T	W	T	F	S	S
6 Mar–29 Oct	10–5:30	M	T	W	T	F	S	S
30 Oct–31 Dec	11–4*	M	T	W	T	F	S	S
Estate								
Open all year	Dawn–dusk	M	T	W	T	F	S	S

*Closed 24 to 26 December. **Last tour at 3.
During restoration project the visitor route may change.

Clouds Hill

Bovington, Dorset BH20 7NQ

🏠 1937

In this tiny woodsman's cottage you can discover the essentials and the luxuries chosen by T. E. Lawrence after he had abandoned the 'Lawrence of Arabia' persona and remodelled himself as a private in the army at Bovington Camp. Much of the furniture and fittings was designed by Lawrence himself. **Note**: Mondays and Tuesdays admission by timed ticket with guided tour only, advance booking essential.

Eat, shop, stay: self-service tea, coffee and cake available. Small shop selling gifts, books and Lawrence memorabilia.

Things to see and do: you can visit the nearby homes of Thomas Hardy – Max Gate and Hardy's Cottage – along the very roads on which Lawrence himself rode. **Dogs**: welcome on leads in grounds only.

Access: ♿ Building 👶🚻 Grounds 🦽
Parking: on site.

Find out more: 01929 405616 or cloudshill@nationaltrust.org.uk

Clouds Hill		M	T	W	T	F	S	S
1 Mar–31 Oct	11–5	M	T	W	T	F	S	S

Timed tickets may apply on busy days. No electric light, so last admission at dusk.

Clouds Hill in Dorset: this tiny woodsman's cottage was once home to T. E Lawrence

Coleton Fishacre

Brownstone Road, Kingswear, Devon TQ6 0EQ

🏠❄️♿🏛️🛏️🍽️ 1982

This evocative 1920s Arts and Crafts-style house, with its elegant Art Deco interiors, perfectly encapsulates the spirit of the Jazz Age. The former country home of the D'Oyly Carte family, it has a light, joyful atmosphere and inspiring sea views. You can glimpse life 'upstairs and downstairs' and try on 1920s clothing in the popular handling room. In the RHS-accredited garden, paths weave through glades and past tranquil ponds and rare tender plants from New Zealand and South Africa; many exotic plants thrive beneath the tree canopy. You can walk down to a coastal viewpoint through the valley garden.

Eat, shop, stay: 1920s-inspired award-winning Café Coleton serving homemade cakes and hearty lunches. Art Deco-inspired shop selling souvenir guides, china, gifts, food, music and plants. If you stay in the Chauffeur's Flat or Coleton Barton Cottages, you have after-hours access to the garden.

Things to see and do: daily guided garden walks from Easter to October, led by a member of the garden team. Events, including theatre in the garden. Family trails and new wild play area. **Dogs**: welcome on leads on designated paths (map available from reception) and outside Café Coleton.

Access: 🅿️♿🚻♿📷 Building ♿♿♿ Grounds ♿➡️♿
Parking: 20 yards from reception; overflow parking 150 yards.

Find out more: 01803 842382 or coletonfishacre@nationaltrust.org.uk

Coleton Fishacre		M	T	W	T	F	S	S
11 Feb–29 Oct	10:30–5	M	T	W	T	F	S	S
4 Nov–24 Dec	11–4						S	S
27 Dec–31 Dec	11–4			W	T	F	S	S

With its joyful atmosphere, Coleton Fishacre in Devon, right top and bottom, encapsulates the spirit of the Jazz Age

Compton Castle

Marldon, Paignton, Devon TQ3 1TA

🏰✚❄️♿🏠 1951

A rare survivor, this medieval fortress with high curtain walls, towers and two portcullis gates, set in a landscape of rolling hills and orchards, is a bewitching mixture of romance and history. Home for nearly 600 years to the Gilbert family, including Sir Humphrey Gilbert, half-brother to Sir Walter Ralegh. **Note**: hall, sub-solar, solar, medieval kitchen, scullery, guard room and chapel open. Credit cards not accepted.

Eat, shop, stay: Castle Barton restaurant (not National Trust) opposite. Table-top shop selling souvenirs, gifts, postcards and ice-cream. Picnics welcome in the orchard. You can stay in the bewitching Watchtower, which is a holiday cottage.

Things to see and do: history and squirrel trails for children. 1½-mile circular footpath, accessible from opposite the castle – a great walk with wellies. Events, such as Easter Egg hunts. **Dogs**: welcome in the orchard. Assistance dogs only in castle and garden.

Compton Castle, Devon: ancient home of the Gilbert family

Access: 🅿️♿🚻📷 Building 🔼♿ Grounds 🔼♿
Parking: in Castle Barton's car park for cars and campervans, opposite entrance, 100 yards. Overflow parking on grass verges at castle entrance.

Find out more: 01803 661906 or comptoncastle@nationaltrust.org.uk

Compton Castle		M	T	W	T	F	S	S
4 Apr–26 Oct	10:30–4:30	·	**T**	**W**	**T**	·	·	·
Open Bank Holiday Mondays.								

Corfe Castle

Corfe, Wareham, Dorset BH20 5EZ

🏰♿🏠 1982

Corfe Castle, Dorset, stands silhouetted against the sky

This fairytale fortress is an evocative survivor of the English Civil War, partially demolished by the Parliamentarians in 1646. It's a favourite haunt for adults and children alike – all ages are captivated by these romantic ruins with their breathtaking views. There are 1,000 years of the castle's history as a royal palace and fortress to be discovered here. Fallen walls and secret places tell tales of treachery and treason around every corner. Corfe Castle's brooding presence is a backdrop to some of Britain's most beautiful coast and countryside. Corfe Common and Hartland Moor are close by – you can explore them by walking or cycling, discovering rare wild flowers and masses of wildlife along the way. **Note**: steep, uneven slopes; steps; sudden drops throughout castle. All/parts of castle close in high winds.

Eat, shop, stay: 18th-century tea-room serving cream teas. Summer garden with unrivalled castle views and an open log fire in winter. Shop in village square, offering products ranging from pocket-money treats to luxury locally made gifts. Visitor centre at the car park. Holiday cottage.

Things to see and do: our action-packed programme of fun family history events runs from April until September, with something every weekend and school holidays. Highlights include Saxon, Viking, Civil War and medieval archery re-enactments, falconry, open-air theatre and cinema and festive lights. Throughout the year, discover the castle

Why not share your pictures with us? #nationaltrust

The stunning setting of romantic ruined Corfe Castle becomes fully apparent when viewed from the air, left. The surrounding area, above, offers so many opportunities for fun, from cycling to hiking and nature watching

trebuchet, our timber-framed mason's lodge and children's quest. There's some fascinating wildlife and industrial archaeology in the area to be found by foot or bike. Landscapes range from rich chalk grassland around Corfe Castle, to the tranquil oasis of Middlebere and Hartland on the shores of Poole Harbour. Bird hides overlook the heathland and Middlebere Lake. **Dogs**: welcome on short leads.

Access: 🅿️🅳♿🎫🚾📷 Grounds 👣
Sat Nav: use BH20 5EZ. **Parking**: 800 yards uphill walk. Norden park and ride (½ mile) and West Street in village, neither National Trust (charge including members).

Find out more: 01929 481294 (ticket office). 01929 480921 (shop). 01929 481332 (tea-room) or corfecastle@nationaltrust.org.uk

Corfe Castle		M	T	W	T	F	S	S
1 Jan–28 Feb	10–4	M	T	W	T	F	S	S
1 Mar–31 Mar	10–5	M	T	W	T	F	S	S
1 Apr–30 Sep	10–6*	M	T	W	T	F	S	S
1 Oct–31 Oct	10–5	M	T	W	T	F	S	S
1 Nov–31 Dec	10–4	M	T	W	T	F	S	S

Tea-room closed for refurbishment 3 to 6 January.
Shop closed 3 January. Castle, shop and tea-room: closed
2 March and 25 to 26 December. *Shop and tea-room
closes at 5:30.

East Soar

between Salcombe and Hope Cove, near Malborough, Devon

🏖️🚶 1950

This is a great starting point for exploring the isolated and rugged coast between Bolt Head and Bolt Tail. There's lots of history to discover, including the remains of Bronze Age settlements, shipwrecks and a top-secret Second World War installation. There is a waymarked 1-mile route to Overbeck's, overlooking Salcombe. **Note**: sorry no toilet.

Eat, shop, stay: the quirky Walkers' Hut café (tenant-run) at East Soar Outdoor Experience serves hot drinks and homemade cakes. There are also catered camping options and a pretty holiday cottage. Nearby Overbeck's offers crab sandwiches and cream teas with sea views.

Things to see and do: this is a good stretch of coast for wildlife-spotting – look out for cirl buntings, silver-studded blue butterflies and large flocks of swallows and house martins gathering for their autumn migration.

Access: ♿
Sat Nav: use TQ7 3DR.
Parking: at East Soar car park.

Find out more: 01752 346585. 01548 561904 (Walkers' Hut) or eastsoar@nationaltrust.org.uk

Finch Foundry

Sticklepath, Okehampton, Devon EX20 2NW

🏠🌼🏖️ 1994

The foundry was a family-run business producing a range of tools for south-west industries, including farming and mining, in the 19th century. The huge waterwheels and tilt hammer spring into action during regular demonstrations. Outside is a delightful cottage garden with Tom Pearse's summerhouse

The tilt hammer in action at Finch Foundry in Devon

('Widecombe Fair' fame). **Note**: narrow entrance to car park, plus height restrictions.

Eat, shop, stay: small tea-room serving snacks, cakes, ice-cream, tea and coffee. Small gift shop, plant sales.

Things to see and do: **Indoors** Family activities, stories, demonstrations and tours of machinery. Live blacksmithing event on St Clement's Day in November. **Outdoors** Great starting point for moorland walks, delightful small cottage garden. **Dogs**: welcome in all areas except tea-room.

Access: 🏠🔧🔊📷⠿ Foundry 🔧🏚 Grounds 🔧
Sat Nav: EX20 2NW. **Parking**: on site (height/width restrictions).

Find out more: 01837 840046 or finchfoundry@nationaltrust.org.uk

Finch Foundry		M	T	W	T	F	S	S
4 Mar–29 Oct	11–5	M	T	W	T	F	S	S

Demonstrations of the working machinery throughout day. Open for St Clement's Day, 18 November (patron saint of blacksmiths).

Fingle Bridge

Teign Gorge, near Drewsteignton, Exeter, Devon

 1990

This is a popular spot at the bottom of the Teign Gorge on Dartmoor, where a 17th-century bridge crosses the river. There's much to explore

– downstream lie 27 miles of newly reopened footpaths through Fingle Woods; upstream you can climb towards Castle Drogo on a ridge high above the river. **Note**: uneven terrain. Fingle Woods are being restored and managed in partnership with the Woodland Trust.

Eat, shop, stay: you're welcome to picnic in the meadow by the river. Refreshments available at the Fingle Bridge Inn (not National Trust) and at Castle Drogo café, where there is also a National Trust shop, at the top of the gorge.

Things to see and do: abundant birdlife in Fingle Woods and the Teign Gorge, plus bats and butterflies. Iron Age hill forts, riverside walks and wonderful views. 'Wild Tribe' events in the meadow (booking essential). **Dogs**: welcome under close control.

Access: 🚾♿
Sat Nav: for Fingle Bridge car park use EX6 6PW; Castle Drogo car park EX6 6PB; Steps Bridge car park EX6 7EQ.
Parking: Fingle Bridge (access over narrow packhorse bridge) for Fingle Woods. Additional parking Castle Drogo main car park or Steps Bridge in Teign Valley.

Find out more: 01647 433356 or finglebridge@nationaltrust.org.uk

Golden Cap

on the Jurassic Coast, near Bridport, Dorset

 1961

Spectacular countryside estate on the Jurassic Coast – England's only natural World Heritage Site. The great rocky shoulder of Golden Cap is the south coast's highest point, with breathtaking views in all directions. Stonebarrow Hill is a good starting point for discovering the 25 miles of footpaths around the estate.

Eat, shop, stay: small volunteer-run shop and information centre (open Easter to October), with toilets and bunkhouse, in the old radar station at Stonebarrow car park, Charmouth. Six holiday cottages, mostly thatched, make ideal bases for getting to know the wider estate.

The sun rises over Golden Cap in Dorset, above.
A holiday home on a grand scale, Greenway in Devon,
below, sits within a relaxed woodland garden

Things to see and do: play trail on Langdon
Hill. Smugglers' trail on Stonebarrow Hill.
Family activities and events all year. Charmouth
Beach for fossils and traces of 185 million years
of Earth's history. **Dogs**: welcome.

Access: [access icon]
Sat Nav: for Stonebarrow use DT6 6RA;
Langdon Hill DT6 6EP. **Parking**: at Stonebarrow
Hill and Langdon Hill.

Find out more: 01297 489481 or
goldencap@nationaltrust.org.uk

Golden Cap

Stonebarrow shop and information centre open seasonally,
Easter to October.

Greenway

Greenway Road, Galmpton, near Brixham,
Devon TQ5 0ES

[icons] 2000

Here you are given a glimpse into the lives of
the famous and much-loved author Agatha
Christie and her family. Their atmospheric
holiday home is set in the 1950s, when
Greenway overflowed with friends and family
for holidays and Christmases. The family were
great collectors and the house is filled with
archaeology, Tunbridgeware, silver, porcelain
and books. The relaxed woodland garden
drifts down the hillside towards the sparkling
Dart Estuary and the Boathouse, scene of
the crime in *Dead Man's Folly*. Please consider
'green ways' to get here: ferry (shuttle service
available from quay), steam train, cycling or
walking. **Note**: booking essential for car
parking. Train halt approximately ½ mile
(woodland walk or shuttle bus).

Eat, shop, stay: licensed Barn Café serving
lunches, cakes and cream teas. Tack-room
open at peak times. Greenway-inspired shop
selling souvenir guides, Agatha Christie books,
plants and ice-cream. Second-hand bookshop
in café. Four holiday cottages enjoy access
to the garden.

Dart Estuary below Greenway, looking towards Dartmouth

Things to see and do: daily guided garden tours from March to October. Start your visit with an introductory film in the Stables. Events include open-air theatre. Family activities include croquet, tennis and trails. **Dogs**: welcome on garden paths on short leads (tethering rings available in courtyard).

Access: [icons] Buildings [icons] Garden [icons]
Parking: spaces must be booked – same-day booking possible by telephone. No parking on Greenway Road or Galmpton.

Find out more: 01803 842382 (Infoline and car-park booking). 01803 882811 (Greenway Ferry Company). 01803 555872 (Dartmouth Steam Railway and River Boat Company) or greenway@nationaltrust.org.uk

Greenway		M	T	W	T	F	S	S
11 Feb–29 Oct	10:30–5	M	T	W	T	F	S	S
4 Nov–24 Dec	11–4						S	S
27 Dec–31 Dec	11–4			W	T	F	S	S

Hardy Monument

Black Down, near Portesham, Dorset

[icons] 1938

Memorial to Vice-Admiral Hardy, Flag-Captain of HMS *Victory* at Trafalgar, designed to look like a spyglass. Views over the Channel. **Note**: nearest postcode for Sat Nav is DT2 9HY. Open Wednesday to Sunday, 5 April to 1 October, 11 to 4.

Find out more: 01297 489481 or hardymonument@nationaltrust.org.uk

Hardy's Cottage

Higher Bockhampton, near Dorchester, Dorset DT2 8QJ

[icons] 1948

You can find yourself 'far from the madding crowd', as you explore Hardy's rural childhood home and the birthplace of his literary land of 'Wessex'. Visitors are invited to make themselves at home, sitting next to the fire or wandering through the quintessential cottage garden. **Note**: nearest toilet at visitor centre.

Eat, shop, stay: postcards, gifts and Thomas Hardy's books are sold at Hardy's Cottage and Hardy's Birthplace Visitor Centre (near the car park). Café (not National Trust) at the visitor centre.

Things to see and do: nearby are Max Gate, Hardy's later home in Dorchester, and Clouds Hill, the retreat of Hardy's friend T. E. Lawrence. **Dogs**: welcome on leads in the garden and woods only.

Access: [icons] Building [icons] Grounds [icons]
Parking: 700 yards (not National Trust). Telephone for accessible parking arrangements.

Find out more: 01305 262366 or hardyscottage@nationaltrust.org.uk

Hardy's Cottage		M	T	W	T	F	S	S
1 Mar–31 Oct*	11–5	M	T	W	T	F	S	S
2 Nov–31 Dec**	10–4				T	F	S	S

Last admission 45 minutes before closing (dusk if earlier). Admission through visitor centre (open daily 10 to 4, café last orders 3:45), which is 15-minutes walk from cottage. *Mondays: entry by online advanced-booking tickets only (up to seven days in advance, booking closes 5 on Sundays). Timed tickets may apply on other days. **Closed 24 December.

Quintessential cottage garden at Hardy's Cottage, Dorset

Heddon Valley

on Exmoor, near Combe Martin, Devon

 1963

The dramatic west Exmoor coast, favourite landscape of the Romantic poets, offers not only the beautiful Heddon Valley, but also Woody Bay and the Hangman Hills to explore. There are spectacular coastal and woodland walks, as well as a car park, shop and information centre in the Heddon Valley.

Eat, shop, stay: shop selling walking equipment and clothing, maps, postcards, local history books, Exmoor products, gifts and ice-cream.

Things to see and do: all-terrain children's buggies and all-terrain mobility scooter available to borrow (call 01598 763556 to book mobility scooter). There are barbecues by the river that you're welcome to borrow. **Dogs**: welcome.

Access: [P] [D] [W] [M] [M] Countryside ➡ [K]
Sat Nav: use EX31 4PY.
Parking: opposite Trust shop.

Find out more: 01598 763402 or heddonvalley@nationaltrust.org.uk

Heddon Valley		M	T	W	T	F	S	S
Shop								
4 Mar–29 Oct	10:30–5*	**M**	**T**	**W**	**T**	**F**	**S**	**S**

*Opens 11 to 4 in March and from 4 September.

Killerton

Broadclyst, Exeter, Devon EX5 3LE

 1944

Would you give away your family home for your political beliefs? Sir Richard Acland did just that with his Killerton Estate in the heart of Devon, when he gave it to the Trust in 1944. The welcoming Georgian house is set in a huge estate of working farmland, woods, parkland, cottages and orchards. This year, the house is undergoing crucial conservation to make the roof watertight. Everything is open as normal, except the annual fashion exhibition, normally displayed on the first floor. There's calm and beauty year-round in the garden, with rhododendrons, magnolias, champion trees and formal lawns. You can explore winding paths, climb an extinct volcano, discover an Iron Age hill fort and take in distant views towards Dartmoor. **Note**: due to roof repairs, the first floor is closed (the fashion exhibition returns in 2018).

Eat, shop, stay: table service in the highly rated Killerton Kitchen restaurant. Lighter bites in the Stables Café or Dairy Café on busier days. Picnics welcome. Plant centre, bookshop and flagship shop selling gifts and award-winning estate produce. Five holiday cottages on the estate.

Enjoying the peace and quiet of the garden at Killerton in Devon, above, with the attractive parkland beyond

 Places may occasionally close for events or bad weather

Things to see and do: **Indoors** Interactive, family-friendly house. You're welcome to play the piano, read library books and sit on chairs. Family trail to find hidden mice. **Outdoors** Walk, run and cycle in the 2,600-hectare (6,400-acre) estate, made up of parkland, woods, orchards and rolling Devon countryside. Winding garden paths to the bear's hut, ice house and chapel. There are giant redwoods, rhododendrons and far-reaching views to discover. Many seasonal events and trails, including Easter Egg trails, cider and apple festival and Christmas at Killerton. **Dogs**: welcome in the parkland and estate. Assistance dogs only in garden and chapel grounds.

Access: 🅿️🎫♿🗺️♿♿🔄💻🎧📷📷
House ♿♿♿♿ **Grounds** ♿➡️♿
Sat Nav: postcode leads to house, so follow brown signs to main car park. **Parking**: main car park 280 yards. Additional smaller car parks, including Ashclyst Forest Gate, Ellerhayes Bridge, Danes Wood.

Find out more: 01392 881345 or killerton@nationaltrust.org.uk

Killerton		M	T	W	T	F	S	S
House and Killerton Kitchen restaurant								
11 Feb–24 Mar	11–4	M	T	W	T	F	S	S
25 Mar–29 Oct	11–5	M	T	W	T	F	S	S
25 Nov–31 Dec**	11–4	M	T	W	T	F	S	S
Chapel, garden, Stables café, shop and plant centre								
1 Jan–10 Feb	11–4*	M	T	W	T	F	S	S
11 Feb–31 Dec**	10–5:30*	M	T	W	T	F	S	S
Park								
Open all year	8–7	M	T	W	T	F	S	S

*Opens 9 on Saturday. **Special Christmas opening until 5 January 2018. Closes at 3 on 24 December, everything except park closed 25 December, house closed 26 December. Timed tickets at peak times. Garden and park open daily until 7 or dusk if earlier. Dairy café open at peak times.

Killerton Estate: Budlake Post Office, Marker's and Clyston Mill

Killerton Estate, Broadclyst, Devon

🏠♿ 1944

You can get a feel for life on the wider estate by searching out Marker's, a modified medieval hall-house with unusual painted screen; the picturesque working watermill at nearby Clyston; and Budlake, a thatched cottage that once served as the village post office, with a pretty cottage garden. **Note**: nearest toilets at Broadclyst car park and Killerton visitor car park.

Eat, shop, stay: Clyston flour available at the mill or at the Killerton gift shop. Wide range of food and drink on offer at Killerton. Five holiday cottages on the Killerton Estate – four of which are thatched.

Things to see and do: unusual and quirky things to spot, including the red telephone box and two-seater privy at Budlake. Flour ground at Clyston. Map available at Killerton. **Dogs**: on leads at Budlake and Clyston Mill. Assistance dogs only at Marker's.

Access: 🅿️♿♿ **Marker's** ♿ **Clyston** ♿♿➡️
Sat Nav: for Marker's and Clyston use EX5 3DX; for Budlake follow Killerton brown signs. **Parking**: for Marker's and Clyston use Broadclyst village car park. For Budlake use main Killerton car park.

Find out more: 01392 881345 or killerton@nationaltrust.org.uk

Budlake, Marker's and Clyston Mill		M	T	W	T	F	S	S
1 Apr–29 Oct	1–5	M	T	W	.	.	S	S

Picnicking on the rolling hills at Killerton, opposite, and picture-postcard perfect Budlake Post Office in Devon, left, sits surrounded by its pretty cottage garden

Kingston Lacy

Wimborne Minster, Dorset BH21 4EA

🏠🏛️♿🐾🛏️🏕️🚆 1982

Home to the Bankes family for over 300 years, Kingston Lacy is a monument to the family's exceptional taste and desire to surround themselves with beauty. After the family lost their Corfe Castle stronghold to the Parliamentarians in the Civil War, they moved here and gradually created an astonishing Italian palace in the heart of rural Dorset. Today you can discover an internationally acclaimed art collection, including paintings by Rubens, Velázquez and Titian, exquisite carvings and lavish interiors. There's even more to explore outside, with sweeping lawns, a Japanese Garden, kitchen garden, woodland and parkland walks – look out for the award-winning herd of Red Ruby Devon cattle – and a huge 3,500-hectare (8,500-acre) countryside estate to enjoy. **Note**: timed tickets only. Some rooms may close at short notice, please check before visiting.

Eat, shop, stay: hot meals at lunchtime, light bites, cream teas and cakes in the Stables Café. Drinks, cakes and ice-cream available in kitchen garden (March to October). The old kitchen shop stocks local food, plants, gifts and souvenirs. Second-hand bookshop. Holiday cottage.

Things to see and do: **Indoors** Lavish interiors, world-class art collection, sculptures and wood carvings. **Outdoors** The garden changes with the seasons from snowdrops, blossom and bluebells to summer flowers and autumn

colour. There are deckchairs for relaxing on the lawn, or why not explore the kitchen garden or join a garden tour? Activities all year include guided walks, family trails and evening events. Longer walks across the estate include a riverside route past Eye Bridge or the Iron Age hill fort of Badbury Rings, home to 14 varieties of orchid. **Dogs**: welcome on leads in café courtyard, park, woodlands and wider estate.

Access: 🅿️♿🚻🧷🐕‍🦺🔆📷📱📺🎧👓📹
Building 🪑 Grounds ♿➡️♿
Sat Nav: unreliable, follow B3082 to main entrance. Use BH21 4EL for Eye Bridge; BH21 4EE for Pamphill Green; DT11 9JL for Badbury Rings. **Parking**: on site or at Eye Bridge, Pamphill Green and Badbury Rings, where there is a charge on point-to-point race days (including members).

The lavish dining-room at Kingston Lacy in Dorset

Cricket on the lawn at Kingston Lacy

Knightshayes

Bolham, Tiverton, Devon EX16 7RQ

🏛 🏠 ❀ ♨ 🛏 ☂ 1972

One of the finest in the South West and the only existing 'garden in a wood', Knightshayes' garden is a masterpiece of architectural planting. As well as showcasing every continent's most beautiful, unusual discoveries, there are hidden glades and views across the Exe Valley. The Gothic Revival house is a rare example of the genius of William Burges, whose opulent designs are guaranteed to inspire extremes of opinion. Alongside this, the restored walled garden merges full productivity with aesthetic appeal. Practising traditional growing techniques, it's one of the best examples of a Victorian kitchen garden in the country.

Eat, shop, stay: Stables Café serving hot meals, made using ingredients from the kitchen garden, also soups, sandwiches, cakes and drinks. Conservatory tea-room serving snacks, cakes, ice-cream and drinks. Picnics welcome. Well-stocked shop and plant centre, with plants from the Knightshayes collection.

A masterpiece of architectural planting, the garden at Knightshayes, Devon, surrounds the Gothic Revival house

Find out more: 01202 883402 or kingstonlacy@nationaltrust.org.uk

Kingston Lacy		M	T	W	T	F	S	S
House								
1 Mar–29 Oct	11–5	M	T	W	T	F	S	S
Part of house: for exhibition or seasonal experience only								
1 Jan–28 Feb	11–3	M	T	W	T	F	S	S
1 Nov–26 Nov	11–4	M	T	W	T	F	S	S
1 Dec–31 Dec*	11–4	M	T	W	T	F	S	S
Garden, park, shop and café								
Open all year	10–4**	M	T	W	T	F	S	S

Last admission to house one hour before closing. House: open by timed tickets only (available entrance hall, limited availability on day), or online in advance. Some rooms and areas may close at short notice (please check before visiting). *Christmas experience: Friday, Saturday and Sunday in December, house open to 6 and garden (with light displays) to 7. Everything closed 25 December. **Closes at 6 in main season (1 March to 29 October).

The sun shines down on children visiting Knightshayes, with the William Burges-designed stables behind

Things to see and do: **Indoors** Family trails around the house. Traditional Victorian Christmas. **Outdoors** Play areas. Animal topiary. Kitchen garden restoration project. Events, including outdoor music in the summer, Christmas fairs and illuminations. **Dogs**: welcome on leads in parkland and woods; in formal garden, November to February only.

Access: ⓟ🅳♿🚿🖐🎧🐕🖼📷🎹👶📷
House ♿🅰♿ **Stables** 🅰♿♿ **Gardens** ♿➡♿
Sat Nav: do not use, follow brown signs on nearing Tiverton/Bolham. **Parking**: on site.

Find out more: 01884 254665 or knightshayes@nationaltrust.org.uk

Knightshayes		M	T	W	T	F	S	S
1 Jan–26 Feb	10–4	M	T	W	T	F	S	S
27 Feb–29 Oct	10–5	M	T	W	T	F	S	S
30 Oct–30 Nov	10–4	M	T	W	T	F	S	S
1 Dec–31 Dec	10–5	M	T	W	T	F	S	S

House opens 11. Selected rooms January to February; downstairs only November to December. Garden, café and shop open until 5:30 in July and August. Parkland and woodland open all year, dusk to dawn. Property closed 24 and 25 December. Saturday 22 July: mid-Devon show (expect delays).

Little Dartmouth

near Dartmouth, Devon

🏛♿🚴 1970

A gentle coastal landscape west of Dartmouth, with wonderful views, wild flowers and the remains of a Civil War encampment. **Note**: toilets at Dartmouth Castle (not National Trust). For Sat Nav use TQ6 0JP.

Find out more: 01752 346585 or littledartmouth@nationaltrust.org.uk

Loughwood Meeting House

Dalwood, Axminster, Devon EX13 7DU

✝ 1969

Atmospheric 17th-century thatched Baptist meeting house dug into the hillside. **Note**: sorry no toilet. Open daily, 11 to 5. Services held twice yearly (details at Meeting House).

Find out more: 01752 346585 or loughwood@nationaltrust.org.uk

Lundy

Bristol Channel, Devon

🏠✝🍴🏛🔭♿🚴🐕 1969

Undisturbed by cars, this wildlife-rich island, designated the first Marine Conservation Area, encompasses a small village with an inn, Victorian church and the 13th-century Marisco Castle. **Note**: financed, administered and maintained by the Landmark Trust. Ferry from Bideford or Ilfracombe. MS *Oldenburg* fares (including members), discounts available.

The first Marine Conservation Area, the island of Lundy in the Bristol Channel is rich in wildlife

Eat, shop, stay: tavern serving hot and cold food and drinks. Convenience shop selling souvenirs, Lundy stamps, snacks and ice-cream. Holiday cottages (not National Trust).

Things to see and do: scuba diving, walking, letterboxing, bird and wildlife-watching.
Dogs: assistance dogs only.

Access: [icons] Building [icon] Grounds [icon]
Sat Nav: use EX34 9EQ for Ilfracombe; EX39 2EY for Bideford. **Parking:** at Bideford and Ilfracombe, not National Trust (charge including members).

Find out more: 01271 863636 or lundy@nationaltrust.org.uk. The Lundy Shore Office, The Quay, Bideford, Devon EX39 2LY

Lundy

MS *Oldenburg* sails from Bideford or Ilfracombe up to four times a week from the end of March until the end of October carrying both day and staying passengers. A helicopter service operates from Hartland Point from November to mid-March, Mondays and Fridays only, for staying visitors.

Lydford Gorge

Lydford, near Tavistock, Devon EX20 4BH

 1947

This magical legend-rich river gorge (the deepest in the South West) offers a variety of adventurous walks. The gorge provides a truly breathtaking experience: around every corner the River Lyd plunges, tumbles, swirls and gently meanders as it travels through the steep-sided, oak-wooded valley. There are amazing features carved out by the water over thousands of years, from the 30-metre Whitelady Waterfall to the turbulent pothole called the Devil's Cauldron. Throughout the seasons there is an abundance of wildlife and plants to see, from woodland birds to wild garlic in the spring and fungi in the autumn.
Note: rugged terrain, vertical drops.

Eat, shop, stay: shop selling gifts, books, local food and drink, outdoor wear. Two tea-rooms serving light lunches, soup, sandwiches, cream teas, cakes and ice-cream. Takeaway drinks and food available.

Things to see and do: family events, wildlife-themed and bushcraft activities, children's play area, bird walk and bird hide along the old railway line.
Dogs: welcome on leads.

Whitelady Waterfall crashes down the steep, oak-wooded sides of magical Lydford Gorge, Devon

Access:
Buildings 🏛 Gorge 🚶
Sat Nav: EX20 4BH (Devil's Cauldron entrance); EX20 4BL (waterfall entrance). **Parking**: on site.

Find out more: 01822 820320 or lydfordgorge@nationaltrust.org.uk

Lydford Gorge		M	T	W	T	F	S	S
4 Mar–29 Oct	10–5*	**M**	**T**	**W**	**T**	**F**	**S**	**S**
30 Oct–23 Dec**	11–3:30	**M**	**T**	**W**	**T**	**F**	**S**	**S**

*Waterfall tea-room opens 11; closing dependent on weather. Last admission to gorge at 3:30 in October. **Only short walk to waterfall open: other gorge paths closed due to weather and maintenance. Shop and tea-room open at weekends. Short walk to waterfall also open during daylight hours in January and February.

Max Gate

Alington Avenue, Dorchester, Dorset DT1 2AB

🏠 ✤ 1940

Max Gate, home to Dorset's most famous author and poet, Thomas Hardy, was designed by the writer himself in 1885. This atmospheric Victorian house is where Hardy wrote some of his most famous novels, including *Tess of the d'Urbervilles* and *Jude the Obscure*, as well as most of his poetry.

Eat, shop, stay: Thomas Hardy's books, souvenirs and small gifts on sale. Tea, coffee, cakes and ice-cream available.

Things to see and do: visit nearby Hardy's Cottage, the thatched cottage in which the writer was born and grew up, and Clouds Hill,

Max Gate in Dorset: Thomas Hardy's home

the retreat of Hardy's friend T. E. Lawrence ('Lawrence of Arabia'). **Dogs**: welcome on leads in garden only.

Access: Building 🚶 🍴 Garden 🚶
Sat Nav: use DT1 2AJ. **Parking**: on the roadside in front of the house (50 yards, limited spaces, not National Trust).

Find out more: 01305 262538 or maxgate@nationaltrust.org.uk

Max Gate		M	T	W	T	F	S	S
1 Mar–31 Oct	11–5	**M**	**T**	**W**	**T**	**F**	**S**	**S**
2 Nov–31 Dec*	10–4	·	·	·	**T**	**F**	**S**	**S**

Closes dusk if earlier. *Closed 24 December.

Mill Bay

East Portlemouth, near Salcombe, Devon

🚶 🚗 1991

There are sandy beaches at Mill Bay, Sunny Cove and Seacombe Sands, with rugged walking past coastguard lookouts towards Prawle. **Note**: for Sat Nav use TQ8 8PU. Toilets and Mill Bay Beach not National Trust.

Find out more: 01752 346585 or millbay@nationaltrust.org.uk

Mortehoe

near Ilfracombe, Devon

🚶 🚗 🛏 🚶 1909

Gateway to a wild, remote coast with a rich history of wrecking and smuggling. Amazing walking, wildlife and sunbathing seals. **Note**: use EX34 7DT for village car park and toilets, not National Trust (charge including members). Town Farmhouse (tenant-run) offers cream teas in summer.

Find out more: 01271 870555 or mortehoe@nationaltrust.org.uk

Overbeck's

Sharpitor, Salcombe, Devon TQ8 8LW

🏠✿♣⚘ 1937

Tucked away on the cliffs above Salcombe is this hidden paradise: a subtropical garden, bursting with colour, filled with exotic and rare plants and surprises round every corner, which surrounds the seaside home of scientist and inventor Otto Overbeck. The views from the garden over the estuary and coast are truly breathtaking. Inside, among Otto's eclectic collections – glimpses of a bygone age – are his 'Rejuvenator', once believed to cure all ills, and the melodious giant music box called a polyphon (you can choose a disc to play). Generations of children return to discover Fred the friendly ghost. **Note**: entrance path and grounds are very steep in places.

Eat, shop, stay: licensed tea-room serving cream teas and light lunches (crab sandwiches a speciality), terrace with sea views.

Shop selling unique gifts such as 'First Flight', a statuette inspired by the bronze girl in the garden, books and plants.

Things to see and do: **Indoors** Activities, tours, trails and quizzes for children and adults. **Outdoors** Garden trails, tours. Statue garden, secret paths, woodland areas. The surrounding coast and beaches are great for exploring. **Dogs**: assistance dogs only.

Access: 🅿♿♿♿♿♿♿♿
Building 🏠 Grounds 🌿
Sat Nav: follow brown signs through Malborough. **Parking**: small car park at top of drive and on approach lane. Additional parking at East Soar (1½ miles along coast path).

Find out more: 01548 842893 or overbecks@nationaltrust.org.uk

Overbeck's		M	T	W	T	F	S	S
11 Feb–29 Oct	11–5	**M**	**T**	**W**	**T**	**F**	**S**	**S**

Tea-room closes at 4:45.

With breathtaking views, the subtropical garden at Overbeck's in Devon is bursting with exotic surprises

Parke

near Bovey Tracey, Devon TQ13 9JQ

 1974

Plymbridge Woods, Devon, link Plymouth and Dartmoor

Set on the south-eastern edge of Dartmoor, this tranquil parkland contains numerous delights. Riverside paths follow the course of the Bovey, as it meanders through woodlands and meadows rich in plant and wildlife. There is also a medieval weir, walled garden and historic orchard to explore.

Eat, shop, stay: Home Farm Café (not National Trust). Delicious, freshly cooked food from the seasonal menu board. Coffee, teas and homemade cakes. Parke Lodge holiday cottage at the entrance to Parke.

Things to see and do: orienteering trails to follow. Events, including our Apple Day in October. Self-guided woodland trails leaflet available in courtyard. Productive walled garden to explore. **Dogs**: welcome throughout (on leads where stock grazing).

Access: P♿ D♿ ☕ ♿ Countryside ♿ ➡ ♿
Sat Nav: use TQ13 9JQ. **Parking**: on site.

Find out more: 01626 834748 or parke@nationaltrust.org.uk

Parke	
Open every day all year	Dawn–dusk

Home Farm Café open 10 to 5; closes 4 in winter.
Open Friday and Saturday evenings.

Plymbridge Woods

near Plymouth, Devon

🏭♿ 1968

The wooded valley of the River Plym creates a tranquil 'green bridge' from the edge of Plymouth to the heights of Dartmoor. At its lower end, Plymbridge is the starting point for footpaths that lead through the woods, alive with birdsong, and alongside the river past fascinating industrial ruins that speak of the valley's busy past. There is also the family-friendly cycle path (NCN27), which runs along an old railway line, and wooded mountain-bike trail along with a variety of running routes. The Upper Plym Valley climbs past rocky crags to open onto the high moors.

Eat, shop, stay: mobile refreshment van in Plymbridge car park. Riverside picnic spots. A short cycle ride away is Saltram, with its popular Park Café and Chapel Tea-room in the garden.

Things to see and do: plenty of options for walkers, runners, cyclists and birdwatchers. Peregrine falcons can be watched from the viewpoint on Cann Viaduct in spring. Downloadable walking, cycling and orienteering trails available. **Dogs**: welcome under close control.

Access: P♿ ♿
Sat Nav: use PL7 4SR for Plymbridge. **Parking**: at Plymbridge.

Find out more: 01752 341377 or plymbridgewoods@nationaltrust.org.uk

Ringstead Bay

on the Jurassic Coast, near Weymouth, Dorset

♿📷 1949

This quiet, unspoilt stretch of the Jurassic Coast in West Dorset is like the seaside of childhood memories: a perfect sweep of shingle beach with rock pools inviting you to explore, backed by farmland and cliffs covered with flowers and butterflies. The seawater is incredibly clear and safe for bathing.

Eat, shop, stay: picnics welcome at the Trust car park at the top of the hill, with its views of the Jurassic Coast World Heritage Site. Shop and café at the beach car park (not National Trust).

Things to see and do: spectacular views of the bay and across to the Isle of Portland to enjoy. Why not walk out to the chalk headland of White Nothe? **Dogs**: welcome everywhere, especially on the South West Coast Path.

Access: 🦽
Sat Nav: use DT2 8NQ for Southdown.
Parking: on the clifftop farmland at Southdown Farm and at beach car park (not National Trust).

Find out more: 01297 489481 or ringsteadbay@nationaltrust.org.uk

Natural unspoilt beauty at Ringstead Bay on Dorset's Jurassic Coast, left, and Georgian perfection at Saltram in Devon, above

Saltram

Plympton, Plymouth, Devon PL7 1UH

🏠 ❄ ♿ 🏛 🍽 1957

Standing high above the River Plym, with magnificent views across the estuary, the rolling landscape parkland now provides wooded walks and open space for rest and play on Plymouth's outskirts. Saltram was home to the Parker family from 1743 and reflects the family's increasingly prominent lifestyle during the Georgian period. The magnificent decoration and original contents of the house include Robert Adam's Neo-classical Saloon, original Chinese wallpapers, 18th-century Oriental, European and English ceramics and a superb country-house library. Outside, the garden's planting offers something of interest all year, and there is also an 18th-century orangery and follies to explore. After wandering along scented pathways and the magnificent lime avenue, why not treat yourself to afternoon tea in the Chapel Tea-room?

Eat, shop, stay: Park Café serving meals, drinks, snacks and ice-cream. The Chapel

Why not share your pictures with us? #nationaltrust

Looking very small amid the splendour of Saltram in Devon, left, a little girl explores the magnificent house. While above, children play a game of croquet in the garden

Tea-room offering light lunches and afternoon tea with waitress service. Shop selling seasonal gifts, local food, books and plants.

Things to see and do: **Indoors** Open 363 days a year. Dressing-up, guided tours, baking in the kitchen, themed family trails, conservation in action, changing exhibitions and the house dressed for Christmas. **Outdoors** Seasonal spectacles of winter snowdrops, spring daffodils, summer blooms and autumn colour in the garden. The park is ideal for anyone wanting a stroll with the dog, a run, cycle or simply to feed the ducks whatever the weather. Activities, 50 things to do, guided walks and tours throughout the year. Why not book our outdoor classroom for a Forest School session or a child's birthday? **Dogs**: very welcome in the park (identified on- and off-lead areas).

Access: 🅿️🅿️🖼️🔔🎬📷🎨
House 🏛️♿ Grounds 🏛️➡️🛴♿
Sat Nav: enter Merafield Road, not postcode.
Parking: 50 yards.

Find out more: 01752 333500 or saltram@nationaltrust.org.uk

Saltram		M	T	W	T	F	S	S
House and Chapel Tea-room								
1 Jan–28 Feb†	11–3:30	M	T	W	T	F	S	S
1 Mar–31 Oct*	11–4:30	M	T	W	T	F	S	S
1 Nov–31 Dec†	11–3:30	M	T	W	T	F	S	S
Garden, Park Café and shop								
Open all year	10–5**	M	T	W	T	F	S	S
Park								
Open all year	Dawn–dusk	M	T	W	T	F	S	S

*West Wing route only 11 to 12, by guided tour. Whole house open from 12 (timed tickets). Last house admission 45 minutes before closing. Last orders at tea-room 30 minutes before closing. †Winter route in operation. Everything except park closed 25 and 26 December. **Closes 4, November to February.

Shaugh Bridge

on Dartmoor, near Shaugh Prior, Devon

🏛️⛱️🐾 1960

Ancient oakwoods and mossy boulders cloak the Plym Valley; riverside walks pass the atmospheric Dewerstone Rocks and industrial ruins. **Note**: for Sat Nav use PL7 5HD. Watch out for climbers on the Dewerstone Rocks.

Find out more: 01752 341377 or shaughbridge@nationaltrust.org.uk

Shute Barton

Shute, near Axminster, Devon EX13 7PT

🏛️❄️🔑 1959

Medieval manor house, with later Tudor gatehouse and battlemented turrets – now a holiday cottage. **Note**: open weekends 20 and 21 May, 17 and 18 June, 14 and 15 October, 18 and 19 November (guided tour only – no need to book).

Find out more: 01752 346585 or shute@nationaltrust.org.uk

South Milton Sands

Thurlestone, near Kingsbridge, Devon

⛱️🚽 1980

This popular beach – a long sweep of golden sand and rock pools – edges a sheltered bay of crystal-clear water and looks out to the iconic Thurlestone Rock offshore. The nearby wetland is home to many bird species and is an ideal place to spot rare migratory visitors.

Eat, shop, stay: Beachhouse café (tenant-run) serving breakfast, lunch and dinner (locally caught fish).

Kayaking around Thurlstone Rock at South Milton Sands in Devon

Things to see and do: great for swimming and watersports (RNLI lifeguard in summer). Wetsuits, as well as windsurf and paddle boards, for hire (seasonal). The South West Coast Path offers great walks. **Dogs**: welcome on coast path and beach.

Access: [P] [A] Café and toilets [&] Beach [&]
Sat Nav: use TQ7 3JY. **Parking**: behind beach.

Find out more: 01752 346585 or southmiltonsands@nationaltrust.org.uk

South Milton Sands
Beachhouse café seasonal opening, telephone 01548 561144.

Spyway

on the Purbeck coast, Langton Matravers, near Swanage, Dorset

[icons] 1982

Gateway to a distinctive landscape of grassy clifftops teeming with wildlife and dramatic coast, including Dancing Ledge. Fabulous walking country. **Note**: sorry no toilet. For Sat Nav use BH19 3HG.

Find out more: 01929 450002 or spyway@nationaltrust.org.uk

Studland Bay

Studland, near Swanage, Dorset

[icons] 1982

This glorious slice of Purbeck coastline is famed for its 4-mile stretch of golden sand, gently shelving bathing waters and views of Old Harry Rocks and the Isle of Wight. With four beaches to choose from, Studland is loved by young families and watersports fans of all ages, and it includes the most popular naturist beach in Britain. The vast swathe of heathland behind the beach is a haven for native wildlife and features all six British reptiles. Footpaths and bridleways through sand dunes, woods and wild open landscape encourage you to explore. Wildlife to spot includes deer, insects and birds, as well as numerous wild flowers. Studland was the inspiration for Toytown in Enid Blyton's *Noddy*. **Note**: toilets at Shell Bay, Knoll Beach and Middle Beach; also South Beach (not National Trust).

Volleyball on the sandy beach at Studland Bay in Dorset, above, and Old Harry Rocks, right

Eat, shop, stay: seaside café at Knoll Beach, with spectacular views of Old Harry Rocks, serves fresh, locally sourced food (inside and outside seating). Log burner in winter. Knoll Beach shop sells seaside-themed goods and local gifts. Thirteen holiday cottages in Purbeck.

Things to see and do: year-round events programme, including food events, family trails and a multitude of watersports and beach sports to try – geocaching, slacklining, orienteering, beach volleyball (at Shell Bay), snorkelling, swimming, beach table tennis, paddle-boarding, pedaloes, canoeing and sea kayaking, windsurfing and sailing.

And don't forget sandcastles and rock-pooling. You can hire bikes or go horse-riding to explore inland. Signposted trails for walking. Look out for the Second World War remains that tell of Studland's role in the build-up to D-Day. Five bird hides overlooking Poole Harbour and Little Sea. Discovery Centre for private hire. **Dogs**: on short leads (2 metres maximum), 1 May to 30 September. No winter restrictions.

Access: [P&] [&] [&] [&] Grounds [&] [&]
Sat Nav: use BH19 3AQ for Knoll Beach.
Parking: at Shell Bay (7 to 9); South Beach (9 to 11); Knoll Beach and Middle Beach (9 to 8, or dusk if earlier).

Find out more: 01929 450500 or studlandbay@nationaltrust.org.uk

Studland Bay	
Shop and café	
Open every day all year	9:30–5*

*26 March to 28 October, open to 6 at weekends. Reduced hours in winter (usually 10 to 4). Shop and café closed 1 and 2 March and 25 December.

Eat, shop, stay: tea-garden serving hot and cold food and drinks in a magnificent wooded setting. Shop selling Exmoor produce and gifts, walking gear and maps. Nearby holiday cottages offer the chance of a longer stay to explore the area.

Things to see and do: Exmoor Spotter chart for families and *Exmoor Coast of Devon* walks leaflet available. **Dogs**: allowed on leads in tea-garden.

Access: [D&] [&] Building [&] Grounds [&]
Sat Nav: use EX35 6NT. **Parking**: pay and display (not National Trust) on Watersmeet Road; steep walk down to house. Trust car parks nearby at Combe Park and Countisbury.

Find out more: 01598 752648 or watersmeet@nationaltrust.org.uk

Watersmeet		M	T	W	T	F	S	S
Tea-room and tea-garden								
4 Mar–29 Oct	10:30–5*	M	T	W	T	F	S	S
26 Dec–31 Dec	11–3		T	W	T	F	S	S

*March and after 3 September open 11 to 4. Shop opens 30 minutes after tea-room and tea-garden in main season.

Watersmeet

on Exmoor, near Lynmouth, Devon

[icons] 1955

This area, where the lush valleys of the East Lyn and Hoar Oak Water tumble together, is a haven for wildlife and offers excellent walking. At the heart sits Watersmeet House, a 19th-century fishing lodge, which is now a tea-garden, shop and information point. **Note**: deep gorge with steep walk down to house.

Wembury

near Wembury village, Plymouth, Devon

[icons] 1939

A great beach, and more: some of the best rock pools in the country, good surfing, masses of wildlife and views of a distinctive island – the Great Mewstone. Starting point for lovely coastal walks to Wembury Point and the Yealm Estuary. **Note**: toilet (not National Trust).

By shopping with us, you support special places – see inside back cover

The Great Mewstone seen from the beach at Wembury in Devon

Eat, shop, stay: Old Mill Café serves coffees, homemade cakes, soups, pasties and ice-cream, as well as beach shop (tenant-run). Part of the old mill house adjoining the café, Mill Cottage is an idyllic holiday let right on the shore.

Things to see and do: Marine Centre full of information. Rock-pooling, surfing and snorkelling. **Dogs**: welcome on coast path all year, and on beach 1 October to 30 April.

Access: [P] [symbols] Café [symbol]
Marine Centre [symbol] Beach [symbol]
Sat Nav: use PL9 0HP. **Parking**: just above beach.

Find out more: 01752 346585. 01752 862538 (Marine Centre) or wembury@nationaltrust.org.uk

Wembury
For details of the Old Mill Café seasonal opening, telephone 01752 863280.

White Mill

Sturminster Marshall, near Wimborne Minster, Dorset BH21 4BX

[symbol] 1982

An 18th-century corn mill with original wooden machinery, built on a Domesday Book site in a peaceful riverside setting. **Note**: open weekends, 25 March to 29 October, 12 to 5 (admission by guided tour, last tour 4).

Find out more: 01258 858051 or whitemill@nationaltrust.org.uk

Woolacombe

near Ilfracombe, Devon

[symbols] 1935

A golden beach and huge dunes, amazing surfing, perfect coves for rock-pooling and numerous headland walks with views of Lundy. **Note**: for Sat Nav use EX34 7BG (car park). Nearest toilets are by the beach (neither toilets nor car park are National Trust). Members have to pay for parking.

Find out more: 01271 870555 or woolacombe@nationaltrust.org.uk

Fishing at Watersmeet in Devon, opposite

Additional coastal and countryside car parks in Devon and Dorset

Devon				Danes Wood	EX5 3LH
Countisbury	EX35 6NE	Snapes Point	TQ8 8NQ	Ellerhayes	EX5 4PY
Combe Park	EX35 6LF	Prawle Point	TQ7 2BX		
Woody Bay	EX31 4QU	Scabbacombe	TQ6 0EF	**Dorset**	
Trentishoe Down	EX34 0PF	Man Sands	TQ6 0EF	Cogden	DT6 4RJ
Torrs Walk, Ilfracombe	EX34 8BA	Salcombe Hill	EX10 0NY	Lambert's Castle	DT6 5QJ
Hartland: Brownsham	EX39 6AN	Dunsland	EX22 7AA	Acton	BH19 3JN
Exmansworthy	EX39 6AR	Steps Bridge	EX6 7EQ	Dean Hill Viewpoint	BH19 3AA
East Titchberry	EX39 6AU	Hembury Woods	TQ11 0HW		
Stoke	PL8 1JG	Holne Woods	TQ13 7ST		

Row with Ringmore TQ7 4HR:

Somerset
and Wiltshire

Avebury, Wiltshire

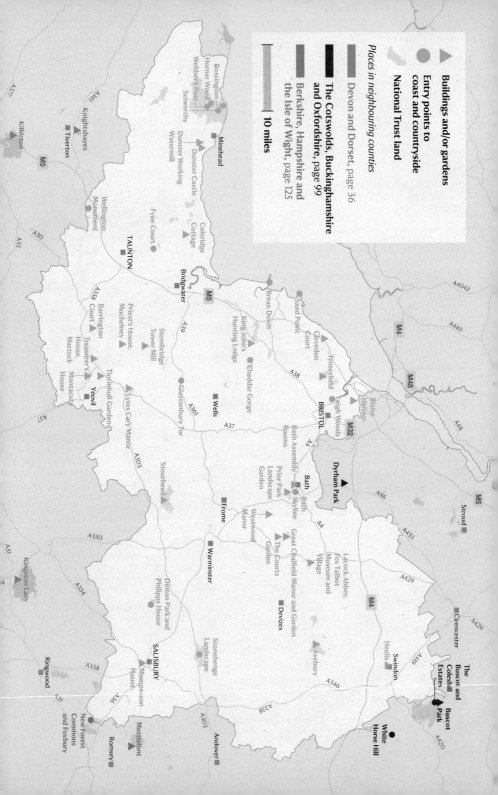

Places in neighbouring counties

Devon and Dorset, page 36

The Cotswolds, Buckinghamshire and Oxfordshire, page 99

Berkshire, Hampshire and the Isle of Wight, page 125

National Trust land

Entry points to coast and countryside

Buildings and/or gardens

10 miles

Killerton

Knightshayes

Tiverton

Wellington Monument

Bossington
Horner Wood
Webber's Post
Selworthy

Minehead

Dunster Castle
Dunster Working Watermill

Fyne Court

Coleridge Cottage

TAUNTON

Bridgwater

Barrington Court

Treasurer's House, Muchelney

Priest's House, Muchelney

Stembridge Tower Mill

King John's Hunting Lodge

Brean Down

Sand Point

Clevedon Court

Tyntesfield

Leigh Woods

Blaise Hamlet

BRISTOL

Montacute House

Yeovil

Tintinhull Garden

Lytes Cary Manor

Glastonbury Tor

Cheddar Gorge

Wells

Dyrham Park

Bath Assembly Rooms

Bath

Prior Park Landscape Garden

Skyline

Lacock Abbey, Fox Talbot Museum and Village

Westwood Manor

Great Chalfield Manor and Garden

The Courts Garden

Stourhead

Frome

Warminster

Devizes

Avebury

Stonehenge Landscape

Kingston Lacy

Dinton Park and Philipps House

SALISBURY

Ringwood

Mompesson House

New Forest Commons and Foxbury

Romsey

Mottisfont

Andover

White Horse Hill

The Buscot and Coleshill Estates

Buscot Park

Cirencester

Stroud

Swindon

Heelis

The Manor, Avebury, Wiltshire: sits on the edge of a pretty village surrounded by the world's largest prehistoric stone circle

Avebury

near Marlborough, Wiltshire

🏛️✝️🍷🏚️❄️🛏️🛌 1943

At Avebury, the world's largest prehistoric stone circle partially encompasses a pretty village. Millionaire archaeologist Alexander Keiller excavated here in the 1930s, and there is a museum bearing his name. Arranged in two parts, the Alexander Keiller Museum is divided into the Stables, displaying archaeological treasures from across the local area, and the Barn, a 17th-century threshing barn housing interactive displays and children's activities that reveal the story of this ancient landscape. Avebury forms part of the Stonehenge and Avebury World Heritage Site. Avebury Manor, on the edge of the village, was transformed in a partnership between the National Trust and the BBC, creating a hands-on experience that celebrates and reflects the lives of the people who once lived here. **Note**: English Heritage holds guardianship of Avebury Stone Circle (owned and managed by the National Trust).

Eat, shop, stay: Circles Café and the Manor tea-room (seasonal). Shop selling local gifts, including Avebury honey and books on the archaeology and mythology of the area. Holiday cottage (sleeping two) within the stone circle available all year.

Avebury		M	T	W	T	F	S	S
Manor and garden*								
11 Feb–25 Mar	11–4	M	T	W	T	F	S	S
26 Mar–28 Oct	11–5	M	T	W	T	F	S	S
29 Oct–31 Dec	11–4				T	F	S	S
Museum								
1 Jan–25 Mar	10–4	M	T	W	T	F	S	S
26 Mar–28 Oct	10–6	M	T	W	T	F	S	S
29 Oct–31 Dec	10–4	M	T	W	T	F	S	S
Stone circle								
Open all year	Dawn–dusk	M	T	W	T	F	S	S

Shop and café open daily. *Manor open 1 and 2 January, and closed 20 to 22 June. Last entry one hour before closing; timed tickets during peak times. In winter, part of garden and museum may be closed, and everything closes at dusk if earlier than 4. Everything, except stone circle, closed 24 to 26 December.

Avebury Manor kitchen, top, and a section of the celebrated ancient stone circle, above

Things to see and do: **Indoors** Specialist talks and guided tours of the manor. Family activities in the museum and events during holidays. **Outdoors** Guided tours of the stone circle all year. Talks and guided tours of the landscape. Hunt for the golden hare at Easter or for witches' cats at Hallowe'en. **Dogs**: assistance dogs only in Avebury Manor and garden and Circles Café. Elsewhere dogs on leads welcome.

Access: 🅿️🐕♿🚻🚼📷🏠🎒♿ Museum ♿♿ Manor ♿♿🚻♿ Grounds ♿♿▶️♿ **Sat Nav**: use SN8 1RD. **Parking**: 300 yards. Please do not park on village streets.

Find out more: 01672 539250 or avebury@nationaltrust.org.uk National Trust Estate Office, High Street, Avebury, Wiltshire SN8 1RF

Barrington Court

Barrington, near Ilminster, Somerset TA19 0NQ

🏠❄️🛏️🔔🍴 1907

Colonel Lyle, whose family firm became part of Tate & Lyle, rescued the partially derelict 16th-century Court House in the 1920s, surrounding it with a productive estate. A keen collector of architectural salvage, Colonel Lyle filled the house with his collection of panelling, fireplaces and staircases. Now without furniture, the light, empty spaces provide atmospheric opportunities to explore freely. The walled White Garden, Rose and Iris Garden and Lily Garden were influenced by Gertrude Jekyll, with playing fountains, vibrant colours and intoxicating scents. The original kitchen garden supplies the restaurant and continues the Lyle family's vision of self-sufficiency. **Note**: independently run artisan workshops (opening times vary).

Eat, shop, stay: Strode dining and tea-rooms offering tea, homemade cakes and main meals with ingredients often grown in the kitchen garden. Children's menu available. Gift shop selling gifts, plants and award-winning cider and apple juice. Second-hand bookshop. Holiday cottage in Strode House.

Things to see and do: **Indoors** House tours and children's trail, seasonal events. Activities in artisans' workshops. **Outdoors** Trails and tours. Seasonal events, including Easter Egg hunts.

Barrington Court, Somerset: now emptied of furniture, the light, open spaces inside the atmospheric 16th-century house offer a unique visiting experience

Dogs: assistance dogs only in formal garden.

Access: 🅿️🔊♿🚻🖼️📷📱🎧 **Building** ♿
Grounds ♿➡️♿♿
Sat Nav: misdirects visitors to rear entrance – follow brown signs from Barrington village.
Parking: 200 yards.

Find out more: 01460 241938 or barringtoncourt@nationaltrust.org.uk

Barrington Court		M	T	W	T	F	S	S
1 Jan–12 Feb	10:30–3						S	S
13 Feb–29 Oct ·	10:30–5	M	T	W	T	F	S	S
3 Nov–31 Dec*	10:30–3					F	S	S

*Closed 24 December. Telephone for details of artisan workshop opening times.

Bath Assembly Rooms

Bennett Street, Bath, Somerset BA1 2QH

🏠🔔🍴 1931

The Assembly Rooms were at the heart of fashionable Georgian society. The Fashion Museum is on the lower ground floor.
Note: limited access during functions.
Run by Bath and North East Somerset Council. Entry charge for the Fashion Museum (including members). Open daily, 10:30 to 5 (closes at 4 in January, February, November and December). Closed on 25 and 26 December. Access to all rooms guaranteed in August until 4:30.

Find out more: 01225 477789 or bathassemblyrooms@nationaltrust.org.uk

Bath Skyline

Bath, Somerset

 1959

One of Bath's unique features, leading to its World Heritage Site designation, is its 'green setting' – encircling meadows and wooded hillsides where you can walk and relax with grandstand views over the historic cityscape. There's a 6-mile Bath Skyline waymarked walk, plus shorter routes to follow from the city centre. **Note**: sorry no toilet or parking.

Eat, shop, stay: there are many great places to picnic around the Skyline. Food and snacks are available from local shops, the nearby city centre and the American Museum (charge including members) – none National Trust.

Things to see and do: at Claverton Down – Family Discovery Trail, woodland play area (open all year), Wild Wednesdays (school holidays from 10:30). Bath Parkrun every Saturday and regular city-to-countryside guided walks. Geocaching trail. **Dogs**: welcome under control (on leads in woodland play area). Cattle grazing April to November.

Access: 🚹 ➡
Sat Nav: use BA2 7AD for Claverton Down; BA2 7PD for Bushey Norwood; BA2 6EP

Grandstand views of the city from Bath Skyline, Somerset

for Bathwick. **Parking**: none on site, nearest city centre.

Find out more: 01225 833977 or bathskyline@nationaltrust.org.uk

Blaise Hamlet

Henbury, Bristol BS10 7QY

 1943

Delightful hamlet of nine picturesque cottages, designed by John Nash in 1809 for Blaise Estate pensioners. **Note**: access to green only; cottages not open. Sorry no toilet.

Find out more: 01275 461900 or blaisehamlet@nationaltrust.org.uk

Bossington

on Exmoor, near Minehead, Somerset

🏠🚹⚙🛏 1944

Part of the Holnicote Estate, Bossington is a peaceful coastal hamlet on the edge of the Bristol Channel with distinctive thatched cottages. From here you can wander down to the pebble beach, where there's plenty of coastal wildlife to spot and far-reaching views

The peaceful beach at Bossington, Somerset

to Wales and along the Exmoor coastline. **Note**: nearest toilets in car park.

Eat, shop, stay: barbecues provided in the picnic field next to the car park. Kitnors tea-room is open seasonally for cream teas and light lunches (not National Trust). Why not stay here longer? The picturesque part-thatched Lower House holiday cottage sleeps ten.

Things to see and do: look out for tall round chimneys above the stone bread ovens, old limekilns and Second World War sea defences. You can walk to the ruined coastguard lookout on Hurleston Point. **Dogs**: welcome on leads.

Access: 🚻
Sat Nav: use TA24 8HF. **Parking**: on site.

Find out more: 01643 862452 or bossington@nationaltrust.org.uk

Brean Down

near Weston-super-Mare, North Somerset

🏰 🏛 ♿ ✈ 🚶 1954

One of Somerset's most striking coastal landmarks: a dramatic limestone peninsula jutting out into the Bristol Channel. You can relax on the beach at the foot of the down or take a walk along this spectacular 'natural pier' to the fort, which provides a unique insight into Brean's military past. **Note**: steep climbs and cliffs; please stay on main paths. Tide comes in quickly.

Eat, shop, stay: Cove Café – with winter woodburner or summer courtyard and picnic

benches – serving cooked breakfasts, lunches or tea and cakes. Newly refurbished shop with popular ice-cream bar, buckets, spades, beach games and souvenirs.

Things to see and do: you can walk to the end of the down and discover the historic fort, spotting birds, feral goats and flowers on the way. Downloadable circular walk available. Events throughout year. **Dogs**: welcome on leads, please note stock may be grazing.

Brean Down in Somerset above the Bristol Channel

Access: 🚻 **Building** ♿ 🚽
Sat Nav: use TA8 2RS.
Parking: at Cove Café and shop.

Find out more: 01278 751874 or breandown@nationaltrust.org.uk

Brean Down	
Café and shop	
Open every day all year	10–4*

*Shop closes 5, March to October. Car park closes at 6. Café and shop closed 25 December.

Cheddar Gorge

in the Mendips, near Wells, Somerset

♿ 🚶 1910

At almost 400 feet deep and three miles long, Cheddar is England's largest gorge. It was formed during successive Ice Ages, when glacial meltwater carved into the limestone, creating steep cliffs. The gorge is a haven for wildlife and contains many rare plants, including the Cheddar pink. **Note**: terrain is steep away from the road. Caves and car parks privately owned (charge including members).

Eat, shop, stay: seasonal shop and information centre providing leaflets, information on National Trust membership, local information and walks, gifts and souvenirs. Free wi-fi and computer tablets available for use to help plan days out in the area.

Things to see and do: 4-mile circular gorge walk (details from shop and information centre) and Strawberry Line (NCN26) cycle route to Cheddar. **Dogs**: welcome on leads in shop and gorge.

Access: 🦽
Sat Nav: use BS27 3QE. **Parking**: car parks on both sides of gorge, not National Trust (charge including members).

Find out more: 01934 744689 or cheddargorge@nationaltrust.org.uk

Cheddar Gorge		M	T	W	T	F	S	S
Shop and information centre								
1 Mar–31 Oct	10–5	M	T	W	T	F	S	S

Also open weekends in November and December (until Christmas). Telephone to check additional opening times.

Clevedon Court

Tickenham Road, Clevedon, North Somerset BS21 6QU

🏠 ✺ 1961

Featuring rare domestic architecture from the medieval period, the house is in remarkable condition and has played home to Clevedon's lords of the manor for centuries. The house was bought by Abraham Elton in 1709 and it is still the much-loved family home of his descendants today. **Note**: the Elton family opens Clevedon Court for the National Trust.

Eat, shop, stay: kiosk serving cream teas and soft drinks.

Things to see and do: extensive collection of Elton Ware pottery, Nailsea glass and prints of industrial archaeology. Family guide and children's quiz/trail. **Dogs**: assistance dogs only.

Access: 🅿️ 🐕 ⌨️ 🖥️ 📷 •• 🖼️
Building 🦽 🏛️ Grounds 🦽
Parking: 50 yards (unsuitable for trailer or motor caravans). Alternative parking 100 yards east of entrance in cul-de-sac.

Find out more: 01275 872257 or clevedoncourt@nationaltrust.org.uk

Clevedon Court		M	T	W	T	F	S	S
2 Apr–28 Sep	2–5			W	T			S

Car park opens 1:15. House entry by timed ticket, not bookable. Open Bank Holiday Mondays.

Coleridge Cottage

35 Lime Street, Nether Stowey, Bridgwater, Somerset TA5 1NQ

🏠 ✺ 1909

Simple Coleridge Cottage in Somerset

A visit to the award-winning former home of Samuel Taylor Coleridge offers the chance to immerse yourself in the sights, sounds and smells of an 18th-century cottage. Coleridge's poetry is brought to life in this simple house – the birthplace of the literary Romantic Movement – and its cottage garden.

Eat, shop, stay: tea-room serving light refreshments. Shop selling gifts reflecting Coleridge's life and work.

Things to see and do: **Indoors** Writing with a quill, dressing up in Georgian

costume or following a family trail.
Outdoors You can listen to poetry in the garden, or look down the 17th-century well.

Access: 🖼️ 🏚️ 🅿️ Building 🔉 🕌 Garden 🔉 ➡️
Parking: in pub car park (not National Trust).

Find out more: 01278 732662 (Infoline). 01643 821314 or coleridgecottage@nationaltrust.org.uk

Coleridge Cottage		M	T	W	T	F	S	S
4 Mar–29 Oct*	11–5	**M**	·	·	**T**	**F**	**S**	**S**
2 Dec–17 Dec	11–3	·	·	·	·	·	**S**	**S**

*Private tours available on Tuesdays and Wednesdays by prior arrangement (please telephone for details).

The Courts Garden

Holt, near Bradford on Avon, Wiltshire BA14 6RR

❄️ 1943

This curious English country garden is a hidden gem. Garden rooms of different styles, shaped by the vision of past owners and gardeners, reveal themselves at every turn. You'll find herbaceous borders, quirky topiary, a peaceful water garden, arboretum, kitchen garden, naturally planted spring bulbs and a redesigned sunken garden.

Eat, shop, stay: seasonal kitchen garden produce and a selection of gifts and guidebooks for sale. Second-hand book sales support conservation work. Rose Garden

The Courts Garden, Wiltshire: one of many garden rooms

tea-room serving lunch and afternoon tea. Picnics welcome in the arboretum.

Things to see and do: discover garden history and seasonal highlights in the Orchard Room. Trails and a hidden wildlife garden for young explorers. Keen gardeners can pick up tips from the friendly team. **Dogs**: assistance dogs only.

Access: 🏞️ 🍴 🖼️ 🏚️ 🚻 🅿️ Garden 🔉 🔊 ➡️ ♿
Parking: 80 yards in village hall car park (not National Trust). Follow signs for overflow parking. Please avoid parking on village streets.

Find out more: 01225 782875 or courtsgarden@nationaltrust.org.uk

The Courts Garden		M	T	W	T	F	S	S
4 Feb–26 Feb	11–5:30	·	·	·	·	·	**S**	**S**
27 Feb–29 Oct	11–5:30	**M**	**T**	·	**T**	**F**	**S**	**S**

Special evening openings of the garden in June, telephone for details (tea-room not open). Tea-room last orders 45 minutes before closing.

Dinton Park and Philipps House

Dinton, Salisbury, Wiltshire SP3 5HH

🏛️ 🏚️ 🪑 1943

Neo-Grecian house in a tranquil park, designed by Jeffry Wyatville for William Wyndham in 1820. **Note**: the house is closed in 2017. The park is open daily all year. Sorry no toilet.

Find out more: 01672 538014 or sw.customerenquiries@nationaltrust.org.uk

Dunster Castle

Dunster, near Minehead, Somerset TA24 6SL

[icons] 1976

Dramatically sited on top of a wooded hill, a castle has existed here since at least Norman times. Its impressive medieval gatehouse and ruined tower are a reminder of its turbulent history. The castle that you see today, owned by the Luttrell family for over 600 years, became an elegant country home during the 19th century. The terraced garden displays varieties of Mediterranean and subtropical plants, while the tranquil riverside wooded garden below, with its natural play area, leads to the historic working watermill. There are panoramic views over the Bristol Channel and surrounding countryside from the castle and grounds.

Eat, shop, stay: 17th-century stables shop selling local and regional gifts and guidebooks. Light refreshments available at the Camellia House. Riverside tea-room and shop selling stoneground flour at Dunster Working Watermill. Places to eat and drink in Dunster village (not National Trust).

Things to see and do: Indoors Interactive exhibitions and 'Chapters' bring stories to life. Tours of kitchens and behind the scenes. Explore the vaulted Victorian reservoir beneath the Keep Garden. **Outdoors** Events, including living history. **Dogs**: welcome in parkland and garden on short leads.

Access: [icons]
Castle [icons] Stables [icon] Grounds [icons]
Parking: 300 yards (enter from A39).

Find out more: 01643 823004 (Infoline).
01643 821314 or
dunstercastle@nationaltrust.org.uk

Dunster Castle		M	T	W	T	F	S	S
Castle								
1 Jan–3 Mar	Tour	M	T	W	T	F	S	S
4 Mar–29 Oct	11–5	M	T	W	T	F	S	S
16 Dec–23 Dec	2–7	M	T	W	T	F	S	S
26 Dec–31 Dec	11–3		T	W	T	F	S	S
Garden, park, shop and tea-room								
Open all year	10–5*	M	T	W	T	F	S	S

Behind-the-scenes tours available all year (telephone for details). 'Dunster by Candlelight': castle open 4 to 9, Friday 1 and Saturday 2 December. Everything closed 24 and 25 December. *Close dusk if earlier.

Strategically sited on the crest of a wooded hill, Dunster Castle in Somerset, above, looks out over the surrounding countryside. Everyone can enjoy its sunny terraced garden, below. Nearby Dunster Working Watermill, right, is still operating hundreds of years after it was built. Opposite, top right, Fyne Court in Somerset

Dunster Working Watermill

Mill Lane, Dunster, near Minehead, Somerset TA24 6SL

 1976

Close to Dunster Castle on the River Avill, this fully operating 18th-century watermill is built on the site of a mill mentioned in the 1086 Domesday survey. With the recent installation of a new second waterwheel, this is now a very rare surviving example of a double-overshot mill. **Note**: admission to watermill inclusive with a Dunster Castle garden ticket.

Eat, shop, stay: the mill produces stoneground wholemeal flour from organic wheat, and the milling team packs porridge oats, jumbo oats and their own muesli mix – all for sale in the shop. The riverside tea-room and garden serves light lunches and afternoon teas.

Things to see and do: milling often takes place on the first Wednesday of every month from April until September. A circular walk suitable for families takes in the mill and castle. **Dogs**: welcome in the tea-room garden.

Access: ⬚ **Building** ⬚⬚⬚
Parking: at Dunster Castle car park, 800 yards (enter from A39).

Find out more: 01643 821759 (mill). 01643 821314 (Dunster Castle) or dunstercastle@nationaltrust.org.uk

Dunster Working Watermill	
Watermill and tea-room	
Open every day all year*	10–5

Closes at dusk if earlier. *1 and 2 December, open to 9 for 'Dunster by Candlelight'. Closed 24 and 25 December.

Fyne Court

near Bridgwater, Somerset

⬚⬚⬚⬚ 1967

This is a hidden gem in the Quantock Hills. While the house (former home of amateur scientist Andrew Crosse) no longer stands, the site remains simply beautiful within its woods and meadows. A great place for gentle walks, splashing in streams, building dens and discovering ruins. Information room in courtyard.

Eat, shop, stay: Courtyard tea-room serving light lunches, cream teas and cakes. Fyne Court Cottage (once a shooting lodge, then the family's retreat when the main house burnt down in a fire in 1894) is now a holiday cottage where you can stay.

Things to see and do: three walking trails, including an accessible trail. Natural play and den-building areas for families. You can observe the skies at the Skyglade and enjoy a picnic in the walled garden. **Dogs**: welcome on leads.

Access: ⬚⬚⬚ **Grounds** ⬚⬚
Sat Nav: use TA5 2EQ. **Parking**: on site.

Find out more: 01823 451587 or fynecourt@nationaltrust.org.uk

Fyne Court		M	T	W	T	F	S	S
Estate								
Open all year	*	M	T	W	T	F	S	S
Tea-room								
11 Feb–19 Feb	10:30–3:30	M	T	W	T	F	S	S
25 Feb–12 Mar	10:30–3:30	·	·	·	·	·	S	S
13 Mar–29 Oct	10:30–4**	M	T	W	T	F	S	S

*Opening times vary according to weather conditions.
**Extended opening hours in school holidays.

Glastonbury Tor

near Glastonbury, Somerset

 1933

Iconic tor, topped by a 15th-century tower offering spectacular views of the Somerset Levels, Dorset and Wiltshire. **Note**: sorry no toilet. For Sat Nav use BA6 8YA for nearest car park, not National Trust (charge including members).

Find out more: 01278 751874 or glastonburytor@nationaltrust.org.uk

Great Chalfield Manor and Garden

near Melksham, Wiltshire SN12 8NH

 1943

A monkey, soldiers and griffins adorn the rooftops of this moated medieval manor, looking over the terraces of the romantic

Moated medieval Great Chalfield Manor and Garden, Wiltshire, boasts topiary, roses and a spring-fed fish pond

garden with topiary houses, rose garden and spring-fed fish-pond. All is lovingly looked after by the Floyd family. The manor featured in the BBC drama *Wolf Hall*. **Note**: home to the donor family tenants, who manage it for the National Trust. Members attending annual plant fair before normal opening times pay for admission.

Eat, shop, stay: guidebooks, postcards and plants for sale. Enjoy tea and coffee in the Motor House, along with homemade cakes and soup.

Things to see and do: visits to the house are by guided tour (limited). The garden and parish church can be enjoyed at any time. Maps for cross-country walk to The Courts Garden are available. **Dogs**: assistance dogs only.

Access: [icons]
Manor [icons] **Garden** [icons]
Parking: 100 yards, on grass verge outside manor gates.

Find out more: 01225 782239 or greatchalfieldmanor@nationaltrust.org.uk

Great Chalfield		M	T	W	T	F	S	S
Manor								
2 Apr–29 Oct	Tour*		T	W	T			S
Garden								
2 Apr–29 Oct	2–5							S
4 Apr–26 Oct	11–5		T	W	T			

*Manor admission by 45-minute guided tour (places limited, not bookable) Tuesday, Wednesday and Thursday at 11, 12, 2, 3 and 4; Sunday at 2, 3 and 4. Group visits welcome Friday and Monday (not Bank Holidays); please contact the tenant, Mrs Robert Floyd on 01225 782239 (charge including members).

Heelis

Kemble Drive, Swindon, Wiltshire SN2 2NA

 2005

The Trust's award-winning central office is a remarkable example of an innovative and sustainable building. **Note**: shop and café open all year, except 1 January, 16 April, 24 to 26 December. Admission to offices by booked guided tour only.

Find out more: 01793 817575 or heelis@nationaltrust.org.uk

Shallow babbling brooks run between ancient oak trees in beautiful Horner Wood in Somerset

Horner Wood

on Exmoor, near Minehead, Somerset

 1944

One of the largest and most beautiful ancient oak woods in Britain, Horner Wood is part of the Holnicote Estate. Home to an unusually rich variety of wildlife, the 324 hectares (800 acres) of woodland clothe the lower slopes of the surrounding moorland and follow river and stream valleys. **Note**: toilets in car park.

Eat, shop, stay: you can picnic by the river or enjoy a light lunch or cream tea at Horner Tea Garden or Horner Vale tea-room (neither National Trust). There are four holiday cottages on the Holnicote Estate for staying a bit longer.

Things to see and do: there's a 17th-century packhorse bridge and a Tudor iron-smelting site in the woods, plus some of Britain's rarest lichens, mosses and bats, and the General,

a 500-year-old oak tree. **Dogs**: welcome under close control so as not to disturb wildlife and grazing animals. **Sat Nav**: use TA24 8HY. **Parking**: on site.

Find out more: 01643 862452 or hornerwood@nationaltrust.org.uk

King John's Hunting Lodge

The Square, Axbridge, Somerset BS26 2AP

 1968

This early Tudor timber-framed wool merchant's house (*circa* 1500) provides a fascinating insight into local history. **Note**: run as a local history museum by Axbridge and District Museum Trust. Open daily 1 April to 30 September, 1 to 4.

Find out more: 01934 732012 or kingjohns@nationaltrust.org.uk

Lacock Abbey, Fox Talbot Museum and Village

Lacock, near Chippenham, Wiltshire SN15 2LG

🏛️ ✝️ 🍴 ♿ 🛏️ 1944

You can see why Ela of Salisbury chose this spot for her abbey in 1232: nestled alongside the River Avon in a rolling Wiltshire landscape, Lacock invites you to stay. The Abbey bears testament to a legacy of almost 800 years of past owners with sophisticated taste, who sensitively turned it from a nunnery into a quirky family home, furnished with well-loved mementoes and furniture. Seasonal colour can be discovered in the wooded grounds, botanic garden, greenhouse and orchard. The museum celebrates William Henry Fox Talbot, who created the first photographic negative and established this as a birthplace of photography. Lacock has a homely feel, and the village, with its timber-framed cottages, is to this day a bustling community. **Note**: during winter please check the opening times for the first-floor furnished Abbey rooms.

Eat, shop, stay: many places to eat and drink in Lacock. Two National Trust shops, independent village businesses, the Stables tea-room and a beautiful holiday cottage make Lacock a great place to visit all year.

Things to see and do: **Indoors** The Abbey offers two distinct experiences: a peaceful ground-floor monastic cloister and first-floor furnished rooms. The museum provides an insight into the history of photography, which appeals to all ages and includes changing

Why not share your pictures with us? #nationaltrust

exhibitions. The birthplace of photography story is also brought to life through exciting displays in the Abbey. **Outdoors** The level grounds are great for picnics and walks. There are year-round family-friendly trails in the Abbey grounds, open-air theatre events and a play area in the village. Lacock is a famous filming location, and its appearances include *Harry Potter*, *Wolf Hall* and *Pride and Prejudice*. **Dogs**: 1 November to 31 March welcome on short leads in Abbey grounds.

Access: 🅿️♿🐕♿🎧🖥️🔊VT♿👓🔍
Abbey ♿♿ **Museum** ♿♿♿
Grounds ♿♿➡️♿♿
Sat Nav: may direct down closed road. Set to Hither Way, Lacock, for car park.
Parking: 220 yards. No visitor parking on village streets.

Find out more: 01249 730459 or lacockabbey@nationaltrust.org.uk

Lacock Abbey		M	T	W	T	F	S	S
Abbey cloister, grounds, museum, Stables tea-room, shops								
2 Jan–10 Feb	11–4	M	T	W	T	F	S	S
11 Feb–29 Oct	10:30–5:30	M	T	W	T	F	S	S
30 Oct–31 Dec	11–4	M	T	W	T	F	S	S
Abbey rooms (first floor)								
7 Jan–5 Feb*	11:30–3:30						S	S
11 Feb–29 Oct	11–5	M	T	W	T	F	S	S
4 Nov–26 Nov*	11:30–3:30						S	S
30 Nov–31 Dec*	11:30–3:30					T	F	S

Last admission to Abbey rooms 45 minutes before closing. Site closed 25 and 26 December and 1 January 2018.
*Great Hall only. Village businesses operate independently.

Lacock Abbey, Fox Talbot Museum and Village in Wiltshire: from far left to right, exploring the cloisters, the east front of the Abbey and a model of Fox Talbot's camera in the South Gallery

Leigh Woods

Bristol

🏛️ 🔟 ♿ 🐦 1909

Sitting on the very edge of Bristol, Leigh Woods offer a welcome taste of wilderness

A tranquil wilderness on Bristol's doorstep, with woodland, wildlife, Iron Age fort and wonderful views of the Avon Gorge and suspension bridge. Excellent network of paths, including 1¾-mile easy-access trail, links to the National Cycle Network and popular 'Yer Tiz' off-road cycle trail. Unique whitebeam trees grow in these woods. **Note**: toilet open during office hours.

Eat, shop, stay: picnics welcome.

Things to see and do: new natural play offer. Permanent orienteering course (map available to download). Iron Age hill fort – Stokeleigh Camp. Great views. Events programme. New welcome hub. Listen out for calls of peregrines. **Dogs**: welcome (but be aware of cattle in summer).

Access: 🖥️ ➡️
Sat Nav: use BS8 3QB for Leigh Woods car park (not National Trust). **Parking**: limited, on site (not National Trust).

Find out more: 0117 973 1645 or leighwoods@nationaltrust.org.uk

Lytes Cary Manor

near Somerton, Somerset TA11 7HU

🏛️ ✝️ 🔟 ♣️ ♿ 🛏️ 1949

This intimate medieval manor house, with its beautiful Arts and Crafts-inspired garden, was originally the family home of the Elizabethan herbalist Henry Lyte. After years of neglect Lytes Cary was lovingly restored in the 20th century by Sir Walter Jenner and is arranged as it was in his time. A stroll around the garden rooms, divided by high yew hedges, reveals collections of topiary (including the 12 Apostles), sensuous herbaceous borders and manicured lawns. A visit to this harmonious manor is wonderfully relaxing and uplifting.

Eat, shop, stay: small tea-room offering cakes and drinks. Picnic tables in the courtyard. Shop selling gifts, garden accessories and plants. Second-hand books. West wing is available as a holiday let.

Things to see and do: tranquil walks on the wider estate and children's outdoor natural play area. Allotments are bursting with creative and colourful designs. **Dogs**: welcome on leads on estate walks only.

Access: [icons]
Building [icons] **Tea-room** [icons] **Grounds** [icons]
Parking: 40 yards.

Find out more: 01458 224471 or
lytescarymanor@nationaltrust.org.uk

Lytes Cary Manor		M	T	W	T	F	S	S
House								
4 Mar–29 Oct	11–4:30	M	T	W	T	F	S	S
Garden, tea-room and shop								
4 Mar–29 Oct	10:30–5	M	T	W	T	F	S	S
Estate walks								
Open all year	Dawn–dusk	M	T	W	T	F	S	S

Parts of the garden may be closed off due to maintenance or
bad weather. Tea-room closes at 4:45.

**Wonderful yew shapes adorn the Arts and Crafts-inspired
garden, bottom, at Lytes Cary Manor in Somerset.
Inside the Great Hall, below, visitors learn
more about this romantic medieval manor house**

Mompesson House

The Close, Salisbury, Wiltshire SP1 2EL

[icons] [1952]

Mompesson House in Salisbury Cathedral Close, Wiltshire

Visiting Salisbury Cathedral Close, you
step back into a past world. As you enter
Mompesson House, featured in the film
Sense and Sensibility, the feeling of leaving the
modern world behind deepens. The tranquil
atmosphere is enhanced by the magnificent
plasterwork, fine period furniture and graceful
oak staircase, which are the main features
of this perfectly proportioned Queen Anne
house. The Turnbull collection of 18th-century
drinking glasses is of national importance.
The delightful walled garden has a pergola
and traditional herbaceous borders. A new
exhibition celebrates the 40th anniversary
of the National Trust redecorating, furnishing
and opening Mompesson to visitors.

Eat, shop, stay: tea-room with indoor
and outdoor seating, serving delicious
scones and cakes, light lunches and teas.
Small gift shop, plant sales and occasional
second-hand book stall. Turnbull Glass
Collection catalogue for sale.

Things to see and do: regular croquet
sessions on the lawn and occasional live
music, including Northumbrian Pipers.
Dogs: assistance dogs only.

Access: [icons]
Building [icons] **Grounds** [icons]
Parking: 260 yards in city centre, not
National Trust (charge including members).

Find out more: 01722 335659 or mompessonhouse@nationaltrust.org.uk

Mompesson House		M	T	W	T	F	S	S
11 Mar–5 Nov	11–5	**M**	**T**	**W**	**T**	**F**	**S**	**S**
25 Nov–17 Dec*	11–3:30	·	·	·	**T**	**F**	**S**	**S**

*'The Christmas House' – downstairs rooms open and decorated.

Montacute House

Montacute, Somerset TA15 6XP

1931

Built out of golden Ham stone, Montacute House commands a central position in the picturesque village sharing its name. A beacon of Elizabethan pomp and style, it contains oak-panelled rooms, tapestries, samplers and Britain's longest remaining Long Gallery, hosting portraits from the National Portrait Gallery. The surrounding clipped lawns, wibbly-wobbly hedges, hidden paths and parkland all entice exploration. Edward Phelips – a wealthy, ambitious lawyer and MP – built this grand mansion to advertise his lofty positon and success. Now, over 400 years later, he may well have enjoyed the fact that it featured in BBC2's acclaimed drama *Wolf Hall*.

Elizabethan Montacute House in Somerset

Eat, shop, stay: café serving a variety of homemade seasonal lunches and tempting cakes to be enjoyed inside or out – dogs restricted to courtyard please. Gift shop and plant sales. Monthly farmers' markets held March to December (excluding August). Two holiday cottages.

Things to see and do: **Indoors** National Portrait Gallery exhibition 'After Holbein'. **Outdoors** Regular 'Elizabethan Welcome' outdoor tours and seasonal events. Family trails and swings. Tintinhull Garden and Barrington Court nearby. **Dogs**: welcome in garden on gravel paths (short leads please). Assistance dogs only in café.

Access: ⊞ 🐕 🔔 🏛 ♿ :• ⊘
Building 🔲 🏛 ♿ **Grounds** 🏛 ➡ ♿
Parking: on site.

Find out more: 01935 823289 or montacute@nationaltrust.org.uk

Montacute House		M	T	W	T	F	S	S
House*								
1 Jan–26 Feb	12–3	·	·	·	·	·	**S**	**S**
4 Mar–29 Oct	11–4:30	**M**	**T**	**W**	**T**	**F**	**S**	**S**
4 Nov–31 Dec	12–3	·	·	·	·	·	**S**	**S**
Garden, parkland, café and shop								
1 Jan–3 Mar	11–4	·	·	**W**	**T**	**F**	**S**	**S**
4 Mar–29 Oct	10–5	**M**	**T**	**W**	**T**	**F**	**S**	**S**
1 Nov–31 Dec	11–4	·	·	**W**	**T**	**F**	**S**	**S**

*Some rooms may not be open. Everything closed 24 and 25 December.

Priest's House, Muchelney

Muchelney, Langport, Somerset TA10 0DQ

 1911

Medieval hall-house, built in 1308.
Note: private home. Sorry no toilet.
Open April to September, please call for
details of opening arrangements.

Find out more: 01935 823289 or
priestshouse@nationaltrust.org.uk

Prior Park Landscape Garden

Ralph Allen Drive, Bath, Somerset BA2 5AH

❖ 1993

Perched on a hillside overlooking Bath, this
elevated spot was chosen by Ralph Allen to show
off his estate to the city. The magical landscape
garden he created captures a moment in time:
1764, the year of Allen's death. There is a lot to
discover, from winding paths leading to hidden
retreats, to views over Bath. There are seasonal
family trails and a natural play area, and you
can even walk over the Palladian Bridge, one
of only four in the world. A tea-garden provides
a picturesque refreshment stop at the bottom
of the garden by the lakes. **Note**: house not
accessible. Steep slopes, steps and uneven paths.

Eat, shop, stay: Tea Shed by the lakes
serving light snacks, cakes and refreshments
(please note outdoor seating only, in
tea-garden). Small shop next to visitor
reception selling outdoor-related products
and pocket-money gifts.

Things to see and do: events and activities all
year. Free guided tours and seasonal trails. Tree
swings and natural play area. The Bath Skyline
6-mile circular walk is just minutes from the
garden. **Dogs**: welcome on short leads.

Prior Park Landscape Garden in Bath, Somerset:
the natural play area, top, and Palladian Bridge, above

Access: 🅿️ 🅿️ 🎫 📷 📶 👓 🎧 **Grounds** ♿ 🏔️
Parking: for disabled visitors only. Car parks in
city centre, 1 mile (steep, uphill walk). Frequent
bus services from bus station, Abbey and
Manvers Street (by bus station).

Find out more: 01225 833977 or
priorpark@nationaltrust.org.uk

Prior Park Landscape Garden		M	T	W	T	F	S	S
1 Jan–29 Jan*	10–4	.	.	*	.	.	**S**	**S**
1 Feb–29 Oct	10–5:30	**M**	**T**	**W**	**T**	**F**	**S**	**S**
4 Nov–31 Dec*	10–4	.	.	.	.	.	**S**	**S**

Last admission one hour before closing. Closes dusk if
earlier than 5:30. *Open 2 January and 26 December.
Tea Shed opening times vary.

Sand Point

near Kewstoke, Weston-super-Mare,
North Somerset

 1964

A natural pier into the Bristol Channel, north of
Weston-super-Mare and Brean Down. Perfect
for picnics; views across Sand Bay. **Note**: steep
climbs and cliffs – please stay on main paths.
Tide comes in quickly. Sorry, no toilets.
For Sat Nav use BS22 9UD.

Find out more: 01278 751874 or
sandpoint@nationaltrust.org.uk

Selworthy

on Exmoor, near Minehead, Somerset

 1944

Selworthy is a good place to start discovering
the wonderfully varied Exmoor landscapes
within the 4,856-hectare (12,000-acre)
Holnicote Estate. This is a timeless rural
landscape of thatched cottages, a fine medieval
church, walks through wooded combes and
sweeping views across the vale to Dunkery
Beacon, Exmoor's highest point. **Note**: nearest
toilets by Selworthy Green (not National Trust).

You can discover Exmoor from Selworthy, Somerset

Eat, shop, stay: Periwinkle tea-rooms
(not National Trust) is a favourite spot
for cream teas. Why not enjoy a picnic on
Selworthy Green? Or stay for a while in the
romantic thatched Ivy's Cottage (sleeps two).

Things to see and do: a walk through the
woods leads to Bury Castle, an Iron Age hill fort.
The whitewashed church of All Saints looks
out over the vale. **Dogs**: welcome on leads.

Access: 🚶
Sat Nav: use TA24 8TP. **Parking**: on site.

Find out more: 01643 862452 or
selworthy@nationaltrust.org.uk

Stembridge Tower Mill

High Ham, Somerset TA10 9DJ

⚙️ 1969

Built in 1822, this is the last remaining thatched
windmill in England – the only survivor of five
in the area. **Note**: private tenanted home.
No toilet, limited parking, assistance dogs only.
Open April to September, please telephone
01935 823289 for details opening arrangements.

Find out more: 01935 823289 or
stembridgemill@nationaltrust.org.uk

Stonehenge Landscape

near Amesbury, Wiltshire

🏛️ 1927

You can wander freely through thousands of
acres of downland within the Stonehenge and
Avebury World Heritage Site. The landscape
around the famous stones is studded with
ancient monuments, such as the Avenue and
Cursus, and abounds with wildlife. The shuttle
from the visitor centre also stops at Fargo

Stonehenge Landscape, Wiltshire: space to wander

woodland. **Note**: English Heritage manages stone circle, visitor centre/car park. Bookings via english-heritage.org.uk. Pay and display car park free to Trust members (booking essential). Trust members enter free (excluding International National Trust or affiliate membership organisation members).

Eat, shop, stay: café and shop at visitor centre (not National Trust).

Things to see and do: guided walks and family activities throughout the year. **Dogs**: welcome on leads and under close control. Assistance dogs only at stone circle.

Access: [icons]
Sat Nav: use SP3 4DX. **Parking**: at visitor centre (English Heritage), free to Trust members displaying Trust sticker. Booking essential to guarantee space. Limited parking at Woodhenge.

Find out more: 0870 333 1181 (English Heritage). 01980 664780 (National Trust) or stonehenge@nationaltrust.org.uk

Stourhead

near Mere, Wiltshire BA12 6QF

[icons] 1946

'A living work of art' is how Stourhead was described when it first opened over 250 years ago. The world-famous landscape garden surrounds a glistening lake. There are towering trees, exotic rhododendrons, classical temples and a magical grotto to explore. Stourhead House was one of the first in the country to showcase Palladian architecture. With a unique Regency library, Chippendale furniture and inspirational paintings, this was a grand family home, shaped by generations of the Hoare family. Outside, views stretch across the Wiltshire countryside, and the lawns are perfect for picnics. Great for walking and wildlife spotting, with 1,072 hectares (2,650 acres) of chalk downs, ancient woods, Iron Age hill forts and farmland to explore.

Eat, shop, stay: award-winning restaurant. Large shop with local food, crafts, gifts, garden and plant selection. 18th-century Spread Eagle Inn, ice-cream parlour serving takeaway snacks and refreshments, Red Lion country pub, farm shop and art gallery (not National Trust). Picnics welcome. Holiday cottage.

The Regency Library at Stourhead in Wiltshire

Entry is still possible at most places up to 30 minutes before closing

The garden at Stourhead, opposite and above

Things to see and do: **Indoors** The house is a great place to start your 'Harry's Story' journey. You can find out about the tragedies and joys of family life for Henry, Alda and their son Harry, the last owners of Stourhead. Alda wrote her letters in the Gothic Cottage, and you can share your memories there today. **Outdoors** The landscape garden changes in harmony with the seasons. From spring blooms and fresh greens of summer, to spectacular autumn colours and exposed winter views. There is also much to see in the productive walled garden. 'Harry's Story' trail reveals his family's garden paradise. **Dogs**: in garden on leads after 4 (March to October) and 3 (November), all day (December to February).

Access: ⬚⬚⬚⬚⬚⬚⬚⬚⬚
House ⬚⬚⬚ Landscape garden ➡ ⬚⬚
Parking: 400 yards. King Alfred's Tower, 100 yards.

Find out more: 01747 841152 or stourhead@nationaltrust.org.uk

Stourhead		M	T	W	T	F	S	S
Garden, shop and restaurant								
Open all year	9–5*	M	T	W	T	F	S	S
House								
25 Feb–12 Nov	11–4:30**	M	T	W	T	F	S	S
25 Nov–22 Dec†	11–3:30	M	T	W	T	F	S	S
Entrance Hall								
7 Jan–5 Feb	11–3	·	·	·	·	·	S	S
11 Feb–19 Feb	11–3	M	T	W	T	F	S	S
Behind Closed Doors Tours								
9 Jan–10 Feb	Tour	M	T	W	T	F	·	·
King Alfred's Tower								
4 Mar–29 Oct	12–4	·	·	·	·	·	S	S

For Behind Closed Doors Tours contact us for times and availability to avoid disappointment. *Close 6 in main season (3 April to 29 October). Shop: opens at 10. **Closes 3:30 after 29 October. †'The Christmas House': selected rooms open and decorated. Everything closed 25 December. King Alfred's Tower also open Bank Holidays and school holidays.

Tintinhull Garden

Farm Street, Tintinhull, Yeovil,
Somerset BA22 8PZ

⬚⬚⬚ 1953

The vision of Phyllis Reiss, amateur gardener, lives on in this small yet perfectly formed garden. You can stroll among clipped lawns, glinting pools and welcome shaded areas that punctuate 'living rooms' of colour and scent. It's just the place to sit, relax and get away from it all.

Eat, shop, stay: quaint tea-room serving cakes and cream teas. Small shop and plant sales. You can soak up the atmosphere for longer by staying in the holiday cottage which forms part of Tintinhull House.

Things to see and do: village history exhibition (Tintinhull Archaeological Society). Why not combine with a visit to Montacute House or Lytes Cary Manor? Gardens licensed for weddings. **Dogs**: welcome in courtyard only (reception has details of local walks).

Access: ⬚⬚⬚⬚⬚⬚⬚⬚
Building ⬚⬚ Gardens ⬚➡⬚
Parking: 150 yards.

Tintinhull Garden, Somerset: small yet perfectly formed

Find out more: 01935 823289 or tintinhull@nationaltrust.org.uk

Tintinhull Garden		M	T	W	T	F	S	S
18 Mar–4 Jun	11–5	·	·	W	T	F	S	S
6 Jun–25 Jul	11–5	·	T	W	T	F	S	S
26 Jul–29 Oct	11–5	·	·	W	T	F	S	S

Open Bank Holiday Mondays.

Treasurer's House, Martock

Martock, Somerset TA12 6JL

 1971

Completed in 1293, this medieval house includes a Great Hall, 15th-century kitchen and an unusual wall-painting. **Note**: private home. Sorry no toilets or parking. Open April to September, please call for details of opening arrangements.

Find out more: 01935 823289 or treasurersmartock@nationaltrust.org.uk

The impressive Victorian Gothic exterior of Tyntesfield, Somerset, below. Visitors admire the ornate chapel, while children play in the grounds, right top and bottom

Tyntesfield

Wraxall, Bristol, North Somerset BS48 1NX

🏠➕🔆🦽🖼🍽 2002

At its heart Tyntesfield is a Victorian country house and estate, which serves as a backdrop to the remarkable story of four generations of the Gibbs family. Their tale charts the accumulation of wealth from the guano trade, transformation of a Georgian house to a Victorian Gothic masterpiece and the collection of over 50,000 objects. Their achievements are celebrated through ornate Gothic carvings, flower-filled terraces and an expansive estate amid the Somerset countryside. With each visit you'll experience a new side of Tyntesfield, as we close one door and open another. **Note**: we may have some essential work taking place across the estate – sorry for any inconvenience.

greenhouse tours all year (check times on arrival). Extensive signed walks across the estate. For young explorers we have three play areas, including a woodland adventure and sculpture trail. Packed activities programme, including open-air theatre, music, family activities and living history. **Dogs**: welcome on two signposted woodland walks all year; in formal garden November to February.

Access: ♿🅿♿♿♿♿♿♿♿♿
House ♿♿♿♿♿ **Grounds** ♿♿♿♿
Parking: 550 yards.

Find out more: 0344 800 4966 (Infoline). 01275 461900 or tyntesfield@nationaltrust.org.uk

Tyntesfield		M	T	W	T	F	S	S
1 Jan–26 Feb	10–5*	M	T	W	T	F	S	S
27 Feb–29 Oct	10–6*	M	T	W	T	F	S	S
30 Oct–31 Dec	10–5*	M	T	W	T	F	S	S

Last entry to house one hour before closing. Timed tickets to house (limited numbers): booking via website advised. 24 and 31 December house closes at 2; garden, estate, restaurant and shop at 3. *House open 11 to 3, 1 January to 26 February and 30 October to 31 December; open 11 to 5, 27 February to 29 October. Shop and restaurant close 30 minutes before estate. Everything closed 25 December.

Eat, shop, stay: Home Farm visitor centre offers year-round homemade dishes using estate-grown ingredients. Shop with plant sales, second-hand bookshop and small play area. For light bites while exploring, try the Pavilion Café. Holiday cottages on the estate provide opportunities for longer stays.

Things to see and do: **Indoors** The house is open every day (except 25 December). House tickets sell out very quickly so booking via website advised. Guided tours take you 'behind the scenes' in the house (seasonal, please check times on arrival). Step back in time with 'A very Victorian Christmas at Tyntesfield', featuring fabulous Victorian festive fun. **Outdoors** Free garden and

Webber's Post

on Exmoor, near Minehead, Somerset

🏛♿♿♿ 1944

This fine lookout on the Holnicote Estate commands views over Horner Wood and the wild expanse of moorland stretching up to Dunkery Beacon, the highest point on Exmoor. With many trails, this is a beautiful setting for many different pastimes – walking, cycling, horse-riding, picnicking or simply enjoying the view. **Note**: sorry, no toilets.

Eat, shop, stay: it's a great spot for enjoying a picnic with classic Exmoor views across Horner Wood and moorland. There are four holiday cottages nearby on the Holnicote Estate, offering the perfect base for getting to know this beautiful area.

Things to see and do: there's an easy-access trail to Jubilee Hut, which celebrates Queen

Victoria's Diamond Jubilee in 1897. 4,000-year-old burial cairns to be discovered, and keep an eye out for Exmoor ponies. **Dogs**: welcome under close control so as not to disturb wildlife and grazing animals.

Access:
Sat Nav: use TA24 8TB and follow signs to Webber's Post. **Parking**: on site.

Find out more: 01643 862452 or webberspost@nationaltrust.org.uk

Wellington Monument

near Wellington, Somerset

🏛 1934

A striking memorial to the Duke of Wellington in an informal rural setting on the edge of the Blackdown Hills. **Note**: for Sat Nav use TA21 9PB. Sorry no toilet.

Find out more: 01823 451587 or wellingtonmonument@nationaltrust.org.uk

Westwood Manor

Westwood, near Bradford on Avon, Wiltshire BA15 2AF

🏛 ✝ ✿ 1960

Over the centuries, the residents of this small late-medieval, Tudor and Jacobean house have modified the building to their own tastes, each leaving a permanent mark. The interiors are rich with decorative plasterwork, fine furniture and beautiful tapestries. Particular highlights are two rare keyboard instruments: a spinet and a virginal. **Note**: Westwood Manor is a family home, administered by the tenants. Sorry, no toilet.

Eat, shop, stay: guidebook telling the fascinating history of Westwood, postcards and CD of Elizabethan music recorded on the virginal and spinet.

Things to see and do: children's quizzes (house suitable for over fives). Close to Lacock Abbey, The Courts Garden at Holt and Great Chalfield Manor and Garden.

Access: 🔲 ⠤ ⬜ Manor 🔲🔲 Garden 🔲
Parking: 90 yards.

Find out more: 01225 863374 or westwoodmanor@nationaltrust.org.uk

Westwood Manor		M	T	W	T	F	S	S
2 Apr–27 Sep	2–5		T	W				S

Groups (eight people plus): please contact the tenant on 01225 863374 to arrange a private tour outside normal opening hours.

Westwood Manor, Wiltshire: fine interiors and furniture

Additional coastal and countryside car parks in Somerset and Wiltshire

Somerset		King's Wood,		Wiltshire	
Sand Point	BS22 9UD	Mendip Hills	BS25 1DH	Whitesheet Hill	BA12 6RP
Staple Plain,		Ivy Thorn,		Win Green Hill	SP5 5AW
Quantock Hills	TA4 4DQ	Polden Hills	BA16 0TZ	Overton Hill	SN8 1QG
Holford	TA5 1SE	Walton Hill,		Pepperbox Hill	SP5 3QL
Quarts Moor	EX15 3UZ	Polden Hills	BA16 9RD	Cley Hill	BA12 7QU

The Cotswolds, Buckinghamshire and Oxfordshire

Haresfield Beacon, Gloucestershire

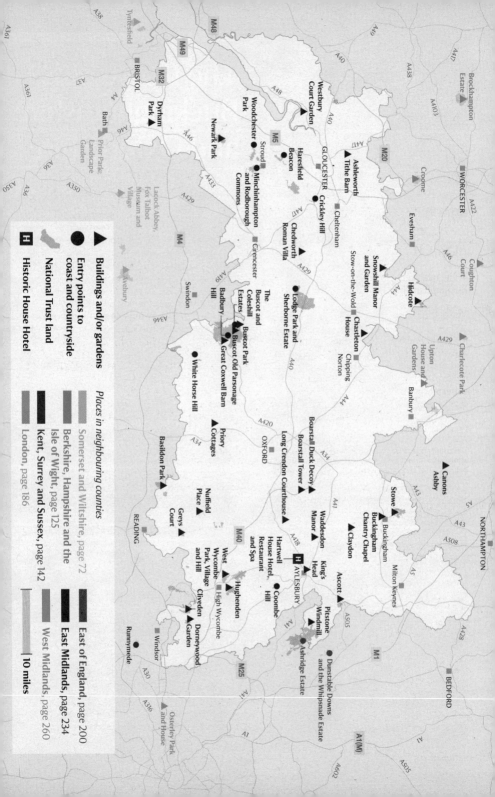

Places in neighbouring counties

Somerset and Wiltshire, page 72

Berkshire, Hampshire and the
Isle of Wight, page 125

Kent, Surrey and Sussex, page 142

West Midlands, page 260

East of England, page 200

East Midlands, page 234

London, page 186

Buildings and/or gardens

▲ Entry points to
coast and countryside

● National Trust land

H Historic House Hotel

|———| 10 miles

Map labels

A38, A361, A46, A48, M49, M48, Tyntesfield, BRISTOL, M32, A37, Bath, A4, Prior Park Landscape Garden, A36, A350, Lacock Abbey, Fox Talbot Museum and Village, A429, M4, Avebury, A346, SWINDON, A419, A420, A34, READING, M40, M4, A329, Windsor, A30, A316, A1, A308, Osterley Park and House, A1(M), BEDFORD, M1, A508, NORTHAMPTON, A43, A5, A428, A602, A505, A509, Milton Keynes, Buckingham, Dunstable Downs and the Whipsnade Estate, Ashridge Estate, M25, Runnymede, A4, Dorneywood Garden, Cliveden, High Wycombe, Hughenden, West Wycombe Park, Village and Hill, Hartwell House Hotel, Restaurant and Spa, AYLESBURY, King's Head, Coombe Hill, Pitstone Windmill, Ascott, Claydon, Waddesdon Manor, Chantry Chapel, Buckingham, Stowe, Canons Ashby, A41, A418, A34, Boarstall Tower, Boarstall Duck Decoy, Long Crendon Courthouse, OXFORD, A40, Nuffield Place, Greys Court, Basildon Park, White Horse Hill, Priory Cottages, Buscot Old Parsonage, Buscot Park, Great Coxwell Barn, Badbury Hill, The Buscot and Coleshill Estates, Lodge Park and Sherborne Estate, Chipping Norton, Chastleton House, Banbury, Upton House and Gardens, Charlecote Park, Hidcote, Snowshill Manor and Garden, Stow-on-the-Wold, A44, A429, Evesham, WORCESTER, Croome, Coughton Court, Brockhampton Estate, A417, A438, A40, A22, A46, A103, A22, Chedworth Roman Villa, Crickley Hill, Cheltenham, GLOUCESTER, A417, A47, A48, Haresfield Beacon, Woodchester Park, Minchinhampton and Rodborough Commons, Stroud, M5, Newark Park, Dyrham Park, Westbury Court Garden, Ashleworth Tithe Barn, A40, A433, Cirencester

Ascott

Wing, near Leighton Buzzard,
Buckinghamshire LU7 0PR

🏠 ❀ 1949

This 'Old English' half-timbered manor house,
transformed by the Rothschilds towards the
end of the 19th century, houses an exceptional
collection of paintings, fine furniture and
superb oriental porcelain. The extensive
gardens are an attractive mix of formal and
natural, with specimen trees, shrubs and
beautiful herbaceous borders.

**Trees line an avenue at Ascott in Buckinghamshire,
above, and 'The "Fries" Madonna' by Andrea del Sarto,
below, one of the exceptional collection of paintings**

Eat, shop, stay: tea-room offering light
lunches, afternoon tea, ice-cream and a
selection of hot and cold drinks. Shop selling
Ascott souvenirs, guide books, calendars,
postcards, gifts, plants, flowers and kitchen
garden produce (when in season).

Things to see and do: guide book for the
house and gardens available at kiosk, as well
as booklet showing key points of interest.
Dogs: assistance dogs only.

Access: 🅿️🚻♿🎫🚹📶 Building ♿♿♿
Grounds ♿♿♿
Parking: 220 yards.

Find out more: 01296 688242 or
ascott@nationaltrust.org.uk

Ascott			M	T	W	T	F	S	S
21 Mar–17 Sep	2–6*		·	T	W	T	F	S	S

Open Bank Holiday Mondays. *House closes at 5, tea-room
and shop open at 1 and close at 5:30. Gardens open in
aid of National Gardens Scheme, 1 May and 28 August
(£5 entry, including members); house closed on NGS days.

Ashleworth Tithe Barn

Ashleworth, Gloucestershire GL19 4JA

🏠 1956

Barn, with immense stone-tiled roof,
picturesquely situated close to the
River Severn. **Note**: sorry no toilet.

Find out more: 01452 814213 or
ashleworth@nationaltrust.org.uk

Badbury Hill

Coleshill, near Swindon

2011

Numerous easy circular walks criss-cross the former plantation woodland of Badbury Hill near Swindon

This former plantation woodland is criss-crossed with easy circular walks, offering stunning views over the Upper Thames Valley. A spread of snowdrops heralds spring, followed by a carpet of bluebells. A copse of military-straight beech trees defines the Iron Age hill fort, currently under archaeological investigation.

Eat, shop, stay: four holiday cottages on the Buscot and Coleshill Estates.

Things to see and do: perfect woodland for family adventures and den-building. New natural play area with a large fallen tree to climb on. Great Coxwell Barn nearby. **Dogs**: under close control.

Access:
Sat Nav: use SN7 7NJ.
Parking: at countryside car park.

Find out more: 01793 762209 or badburyhill@nationaltrust.org.uk

Boarstall Duck Decoy

Boarstall, near Bicester,
Buckinghamshire HP18 9UX

1980

One of the very few remaining decoys in the country, providing fascinating insights into a rare aspect of rural life. **Note**: open Monday and weekends, 11 March to 29 October, 11 to 5 (and Good Friday).

Find out more: 01280 817156 or boarstalldecoy@nationaltrust.org.uk

Boarstall Tower

Boarstall, near Bicester,
Buckinghamshire HP18 9UX

1943

Charming 14th-century moated gatehouse set in beautiful gardens, retaining original fortified appearance. Grade I listed. **Note**: access to upper levels is via a spiral staircase. Restricted opening due to building and restoration works, call for details before visiting.

Find out more: 01280 817156 or boarstalltower@nationaltrust.org.uk

Buckingham Chantry Chapel

Market Hill, Buckingham,
Buckinghamshire MK18 1JX

1912

Atmospheric 15th-century chapel, restored by Sir Gilbert Scott in 1875. Today it is a thriving coffee shop and second-hand bookshop. **Note**: open Tuesday, Friday and Saturday, 3 January to 30 December, 10 to 3 (to 4 on Saturdays).

Volunteer-run, opening is subject to availability (please contact property before visiting).

Find out more: 01280 817156 or buckinghamchantry@nationaltrust.org.uk

The Buscot and Coleshill Estates

Coleshill, near Swindon

✝ 🖼 🍷 ❖ 💪 🛏 | 1956 |

These countryside estates on the western border of Oxfordshire include the attractive, unspoilt villages of Buscot and Coleshill, each with a thriving tea-room. There are circular walks of differing lengths and a series of footpaths criss-crossing the estates, with breathtaking countryside and wildlife at Buscot Lock and Badbury Hill. **Note**: toilets in Coleshill Estate office yard and next to village shop and tea-room in Buscot.

Children explore the breathtaking countryside on The Buscot and Coleshill Estates near Swindon

Eat, shop, stay: Buscot tea-room offering lunches and afternoon tea. Locally sourced produce served at Coleshill shop and tea-room and The Radnor Arms (none National Trust). Four holiday cottages.

Things to see and do: guided walks throughout the year, including tours of the Second World War bunker. See the restored watermill in action and visit the replica Operations Base on special open afternoons. **Dogs**: on leads near livestock and under close control at all times.

Access: 🔊
Sat Nav: use SN6 7PT. **Parking**: at Buscot village and by Coleshill Estate office.

Find out more: 01793 762209 or buscotandcoleshill@nationaltrust.org.uk

The Buscot and Coleshill Estates
Coleshill Watermill open second Sunday of the month: April to October, 2 to 5.

Buscot Old Parsonage

Buscot, Faringdon, Oxfordshire SN7 8DQ

🏛 ❖ | 1949 |

Beautiful early 18th-century house with small walled garden, on the banks of the Thames. **Note**: sorry no toilets. Open Wednesday, 5 April to 25 October, 2 to 6. Admission by written appointment with tenant (please mark envelope 'National Trust booking').

Find out more: 01793 762209 or buscot@nationaltrust.org.uk

Buscot Park

Faringdon, Oxfordshire SN7 8BU

🏛 ❖ 💪 | 1949 |

Lord Faringdon's family live in the house, maintain its interior, curate its contents on behalf of the Trustees of The Faringdon Collection and manage and develop the grounds and gardens. This unusual arrangement for a National Trust property gives it an idiosyncratic air and a different take on taste and presentation. As a result the whole entity becomes more fluid and more surprising.

Find out more: 01367 240932 (Infoline).
01367 240786 or
buscotpark@nationaltrust.org.uk
buscotpark.com

Buscot Park		M	T	W	T	F	S	S
House, grounds and tea-room								
5 Apr–29 Sep	2–6	·	·	**W**	**T**	**F**	·	·
Grounds only								
3 Apr–26 Sep	2–6	**M**	**T**	·	·	·	·	·

Weekend openings: 1/2, 15/16, 29/30 April, 13/14, 27/28 May,
10/11, 24/25 June, 8/9, 22/23 July, 12/13, 26/27 August,
9/10, 23/24 September, 2 to 6 (tea-room open 2 to 5:30).
Last admission to house one hour before closing.
Open Bank Holiday Mondays.

Chastleton House

Chastleton, near Moreton-in-Marsh,
Oxfordshire GL56 0SU

⬚ ⬚ 1991

A collection of dressmakers' dummies mesmerise
young visitors at Chastleton House in Oxfordshire

Jacobean country house and garden built in
the early 17th century by Walter Jones as an
impressive statement of wealth and power. The
house has remained essentially unchanged for
400 years, as the family who owned it until
1991 struggled financially, leaving a unique and
fascinating time capsule. **Note**: last entry one
hour before closing (timed tickets on arrival).

Tall clipped hedges and sculpture characterise the
elegant water garden at Buscot Park in Oxfordshire

New works of art mingle with the old within
the house, and new alleys and vistas stride
out within the grounds. Paintings, statuary
and objects by contemporary artists
reinvigorate the whole – refreshing the spirit.
Note: access to house may be limited due
to major conservation work on the roof.

Eat, shop, stay: tea-room (not National Trust),
serving cream teas, cakes, ice-cream and a
selection of hot and cold drinks. Local honey
and cider, peppermints, plants and kitchen
garden produce (when available). Ice-cream
also available in ticket office. Picnic area.

Things to see and do: occasional events in
grounds and theatre (available for hire).
Dogs: in Paddock (overflow car park) only.

Eat, shop, stay: plants and home-grown seasonal garden produce for sale. Honey from our hives and local ice-cream. Stables second-hand books. Light refreshments available in the local church (not National Trust), Wednesday to Saturday. Sunday tea and cake from Chastleton Brewhouse.

Things to see and do: **Indoors** Conservation in action and Family Explorer packs available throughout the season. Christmas-themed weekends in December. **Outdoors** Introductory video, croquet on the lawn, garden tours and Garden Explorer packs. **Dogs**: on leads in car park and Dovecote Field. Assistance dogs only in garden.

Access: 🅿️♿️🕃🎨🔲🎫📶 ⠿
Building 📷 Garden 📷
Sat Nav: misleading, follow brown signs.
Parking: 270 yards (steep path to house).

Find out more: 01494 755560 (Infoline). 01608 674981 or chastleton@nationaltrust.org.uk

Chastleton House		M	T	W	T	F	S	S
1 Mar–29 Oct	12:30–5*			W	T	F	S	S
2 Dec–17 Dec	11–3						S	S

*House opens at 1, March to October. Last entry one hour before closing. Timed-ticket system on arrival during peak times.

Chedworth Roman Villa

Yanworth, near Cheltenham, Gloucestershire GL54 3LJ

🏛️ 1924

Cradled in a beautiful wooded valley and fed by a natural spring, this high-status Roman villa saw imperial fashions and local spirits living side by side. Nature took over and hid the magnificent mosaics, intricate hypocaust systems, bathhouses and ancient water-shrine for more than 1,500 years until Victorian gamekeepers rediscovered the site. The National Trust has, in turn, looked after Chedworth's Roman treasures and Victorian legacy for nearly a century, providing its modern villa guests with new facilities, as well as astonishing

Uncovering magnificent Roman mosaics at Chedworth Roman Villa in Gloucestershire

archaeology to enjoy. It remains a hidden place of natural beauty and continual discovery.

Eat, shop, stay: café serving sandwiches, soup, jacket potatoes, cakes, snacks, hot and cold drinks and ice-cream. You can find Roman-themed souvenirs, books and games, seasonal plants and National Trust gifts in the shop.

Things to see and do: **Indoors** Updated guidebook and audio guides. Activities, including Roman dressing-up for children. Costumed interpreters and living history events. **Outdoors** Family activities and trails (Bank Holiday weekends and school holidays). **Dogs**: assistance dogs only.

Access: 🅿️♿️🕃🔲🎨📶📱 Reception 📷♿️
West Range 📷🔲♿️ Grounds 📷📷➡️♿️
Parking: on lane at entrance, plus woodland overflow (March to October).

Find out more: 01242 890256 or chedworth@nationaltrust.org.uk

Chedworth Roman Villa		M	T	W	T	F	S	S
11 Feb–25 Mar	10–4	M	T	W	T	F	S	S
26 Mar–28 Oct	10–5	M	T	W	T	F	S	S
29 Oct–26 Nov	10–4	M	T	W	T	F	S	S

Claydon

Middle Claydon, near Buckingham,
Buckinghamshire MK18 2EY

🏠✝🏵🛏🔔🍷 1956

Nestled in peaceful parkland, this Georgian exterior hides a lavish interior filled with oddities. The collection encompasses the unique and wonderful, as well as stunning carvings and portraits of interesting characters from 300 years of Verney family history. An inspirational place, where Florence Nightingale, Lady Verney's sister, spent her summers. **Note**: garden entry charges apply (including members).

Eat, shop, stay: second-hand bookshop, courtyard shops, galleries and tea-room (not National Trust). Picnics welcome.

Things to see and do: Indoors Historical costume exhibition. Children's activities, trails and dressing-up. **Outdoors** The classic English garden opened by the Verney family. **Dogs**: welcome on leads in the park.

Access: 🅿♿♿♿♿♿📷📹♿:::
House 🔥♿🔥 Grounds 🔥♿➡🔥
Parking: on site.

Find out more: 01296 730349 or claydon@nationaltrust.org.uk

Claydon		M	T	W	T	F	S	S
11 Mar–5 Nov	11–5	M	T	W	.	.	S	S

Gardens and tea-rooms open as house (telephone 01296 730252 for details). Open Good Friday.

Claydon in Buckinghamshire: sitting within peaceful parkland, the Georgian house is fronted by a lake

Cliveden

Cliveden Road, Taplow, Maidenhead,
Buckinghamshire SL1 8NS

🏠🏵🛏🖼 1942

Majestic woodlands and far-reaching views make Cliveden in Buckinghamshire irresistible to all

High above the River Thames with panoramic views over the Berkshire countryside, these gardens capture the grandeur of a bygone age. Over the course of 350 years, each family added their own extravagant touch, creating a series of distinct gardens. From carpets of spring bulbs and vibrant floral displays on the elaborate Parterre, to the intimate Rose Garden and rich autumn colour in the oriental Water Garden, each area is designed purely for enjoyment, and all echo Cliveden's rich history of politics, passion and pleasure. Miles of walks meander through majestic woodlands and along riverbank paths, while a giant yew-tree maze, storybook-themed play area and acres of space to run around in, make this a great place to play. **Note**: mooring charge on Cliveden Reach, £10 per 24 hours (including members), does not include entry.

Eat, shop, stay: Dovecote Coffee Shop serving morning coffee and afternoon tea. Breakfast, lunch (12 to 2:30) and snacks available at the Orangery Café. Doll's House Café beside play area designed especially with families in mind. Shop, including plant sales. Picnic areas.

Things to see and do: **Indoors** Short guided tour of part of the house (now a hotel) on certain days. Introductory film. Greys Court and Hughenden nearby. **Outdoors** More than 30,000 plants create striking displays on the Parterre in spring and summer, with thousands more flowers filling the Long Garden each season. The Rose Garden blooms from late June. Walking and fitness trails. Highlights for families include a play area, maze, free seasonal trails, woodland play trail and den-building area. Events include open-air theatre, family fun days, guided garden walks and workshops. Boat trips on the Thames, April to October (additional charge including members). **Dogs**: welcome under close control in woodlands only.

Access: ⃞⃞⃞⃞⃞⃞⃞⃞
House (hotel) ⃞⃞⃞⃞⃞ **Garden** ⃞⃞⃞⃞⃞
Sat Nav: for gardens use Cliveden Road and SL1 8NS. For woodlands use SL6 0HJ.
Parking: on site.

Find out more: 01628 605069 or cliveden@nationaltrust.org.uk

Cliveden		M	T	W	T	F	S	S
Garden, shop, café and woodland*								
1 Jan–10 Feb	10–4**	M	T	W	T	F	S	S
11 Feb–31 Dec	10–5:30**	M	T	W	T	F	S	S
House (part) and chapel								
2 Apr–29 Oct	3–5				T			S

*Café last orders 30 minutes before closing. **Closes dusk if earlier. Property closed 24 and 25 December. Admission to house by timed ticket only from Information Centre.

The Water Garden, with its ornate Japanese pagoda, is just one of the many distinct gardens at Cliveden

Coombe Hill

Butler's Cross, near Wendover, Buckinghamshire

🏛️ 🅿️ ♿ 🚻 1918

Nationally important chalk grassland site and the highest viewpoint in the Chilterns. Stunning views over the Aylesbury Vale. **Note**: picnic area and play trail. Sorry no toilet. For Sat Nav use HP17 0UR.

Find out more: 01494 755573 (Hughenden Estate Office) or coombehill@nationaltrust.org.uk

Crickley Hill

Birdlip, Gloucestershire

♿ 1935

Sitting high on the Cotswold escarpment with views towards the Welsh hills, Crickley Hill overlooks Gloucester and Cheltenham. **Note**: car park and visitor centre not National Trust. For Sat Nav use GL4 8JY. Parking charges (including members).

Find out more: 01452 814213 or crickleyhill@nationaltrust.org.uk

Dorneywood Garden

Dorneywood, Dorney Wood Road, Burnham, Buckinghamshire SL1 8PY

✳️ 1942

Ministerial residence with country garden. Afternoon teas. Open selected afternoons (dates may change at short notice). **Note**: no photography. Visitor details recorded for security

reasons. Open daily, 8 to 19 July, 2 to 4:30; garden only open, Wednesday and Thursday, 26 April to 29 June, 17 to 24 August and 6 to 14 September, 2 to 4. Booking essential.

Find out more: dorneywood@nationaltrust.org.uk

Dyrham Park

Dyrham, near Bath, South Gloucestershire SN14 8ER

🏛️ ✝️ ✳️ ♿ 1961

Dyrham is a place of exploration. Parkland adventurers can savour far-reaching views towards the Welsh hills or encounter the resident herd of majestic fallow deer, while in the garden we are creating a haven of tranquillity and inspiration. Sumptuous planting in the pool garden contrasts with the Dutch formality of the avenue and parterre, as well as with the wilder wooded terraces. The house is an intimate encounter with the 17th century. There are treasures gathered from across the world, reflecting an age of exploration and empire and revealing the personal passions of William Blathwayt – Secretary at War to William III. The house interior will be evolving throughout 2017, as we develop new ways of revealing Dyrham's stories.

Among the treasures at Dyrham Park in South Gloucestershire are this pair of precious pyramid Delftware tulip vases, right. Opposite, a couple enjoy one of the park's glorious views

Eat, shop, stay: tea-room serving lunch, cakes and refreshments. Courtyard and garden kiosks (with outdoor seating) offering drinks, ice-cream and snacks on busy days. Shop selling plants, books, local products and gifts. Second-hand bookshop. Indoor and outdoor picnic tables at Old Lodge.

Level paths in the elegant formal garden at Dyrham Park make it easily accessible

Things to see and do: **Indoors** Events and activities all year, including behind-the-scenes tours. **Outdoors** Guided tours of the park and garden. Family trail through the park, with natural play zones and fun things to discover along the way. Play area at Old Lodge. Borrow a Tracker Pack to help explore nature. The Cotswold Way passes next to Dyrham Park, linking into longer walks. Nearby Prior Park Landscape Garden offers great views and access to the Bath Skyline, where you can enjoy a 6-mile circular walk through beautiful woodlands, meadows and historic features.
Dogs: welcome in Whitefield next to car park.

Access:
House **Grounds**
Sat Nav: use SN14 8HY and enter via A46.
Parking: 20 yards from visitor centre.

Find out more: 0117 937 2501 or dyrhampark@nationaltrust.org.uk

Dyrham Park		M	T	W	T	F	S	S
House								
4 Mar–29 Oct	11-5	M	T	W	T	F	S	S
Park, garden, shop, tea-room and basement								
1 Jan–10 Feb	10-4	M	T	W	T	F	S	S
11 Feb–28 Oct	10-5	M	T	W	T	F	S	S
29 Oct–31 Dec*	10-4	M	T	W	T	F	S	S

Last admission one hour before closing. Whole place closed until 1 on 6 and 20 September, 1, 8, 15, 22 and 29 November, plus 6 December. Guided tours of the house available in winter. *Except 24 and 25 December.

Great Coxwell Barn

Great Coxwell, Faringdon, Oxfordshire SN7 7LZ

1956

Former 13th-century monastic barn, a favourite of William Morris, who would regularly bring his guests to wonder at its structure.
Note: sorry no toilet; narrow access lanes leading to property. Open daily, dawn to dusk.

Find out more: 01793 762209 or greatcoxwellbarn@nationaltrust.org.uk

Greys Court

Rotherfield Greys, Henley-on-Thames, Oxfordshire RG9 4PG

1969

Set in the rolling hills of the Chilterns, Greys Court is a picturesque Tudor manor house surrounded by layers of history, intimate walled gardens and glorious wooded parkland. The house is warm and welcoming, unfurling the memories of the Brunner family through the rooms of their comfortable home.
Across the perfect lawn, a medieval tower and patchwork of mellow brick buildings conceal an English country garden. Through an ancient arch, seasonal blooms are revealed, from bright bulbs through clematis and wisteria to glorious peonies and roses in the summer. Winter walks in the woodland are a must.

Picturesque Tudor Greys Court in Oxfordshire

Lavender lines a stone path in one of the intimate walled gardens at Greys Court

Eat, shop, stay: tea-room serving morning coffee, afternoon tea, lunches and snacks. Shop selling books, gifts, souvenirs and plants. Seasonal organic produce and plants from the gardens (when available).

Things to see and do: **Indoors** Enjoy the elegant, comfortable rooms of the Brunner family home. **Outdoors** Discover many 'rooms' in the walled gardens and rambling woodland walks. Visit Nuffield Place nearby. **Dogs**: welcome on leads (excluding the walled gardens and children's play area).

Access: ⓟ♿♿♿♿♿♿♿♿
House ♿ Tea-room ♿ Grounds ♿♿
Parking: 220 yards.

Find out more: 01491 628529 or greyscourt@nationaltrust.org.uk

Greys Court		M	T	W	T	F	S	S
Garden, tea-room and shop								
Open all year	10–5*	M	T	W	T	F	S	S
House guided tours**								
1 Jan–28 Feb	11–3†	M	T	W	T	F	S	S
1 Mar–31 Oct	11–12	M	T	W	T	F	S	S
1 Nov–30 Nov	11–3†	M	T	W	T	F	S	S
House								
1 Mar–31 Oct	1–5	M	T	W	T	F	S	S
1 Dec–31 Dec	1–5	M	T	W	T	F	S	S

*Close dusk if earlier. Closed 24 and 25 December.
**House tickets available from visitor reception (places limited). †Weekend tours in January, February and November at 11 and 12; free-flow from 1. Whole property opens at 12 on 3 September for annual village fête.

Haresfield Beacon

near Stroud, Gloucestershire

🏛♿ 1931

Haresfield Beacon in Gloucestershire offers views towards the Forest of Dean and Brecon Beacons

Prominently positioned on three spurs of the Cotswold escarpment. Views across the Severn Estuary towards the Forest of Dean and Brecon Beacons. The wildlife is some of the best in the Cotswolds and there's a wealth of archaeological features, including long and round barrows, a hill fort and cross dyke. **Note**: Cotswold Way National Trail runs through estate.

Eat, shop, stay: pubs in Randwick and Haresfield (not National Trust). Ice-cream vendor (not Trust) in Shortwood car park on sunny days. Picnics welcome.

Things to see and do: bluebells and butterflies to spot and woods to explore – there are superb veteran beech trees on the slopes of Shortwood. Great place to fly a kite, watch buzzards and kestrels. **Dogs**: welcome on lead near livestock. Dog bins available in Shortwood car park.

Access: 🐕
Sat Nav: use GL6 6PP for Shortwood car park.
Parking: at Shortwood.

Find out more: 01452 814213 or haresfieldbeacon@nationaltrust.org.uk

Hartwell House Hotel, Restaurant and Spa

Oxford Road, near Aylesbury,
Buckinghamshire HP17 8NR

🏠 ❄ ♨ 🛏 🔔 🍸 2008

Elegant Grade I listed stately home, having
both Jacobean and Georgian façades, contains
magnificent main hall with rococo ceiling and
elegant drawing-rooms serving morning coffee
or afternoon tea. Set in beautifully landscaped
grounds, including ruined Gothic church, lake,
bridge and 36 hectares (90 acres) of parkland.
Only one hour from central London.
Note: access is for paying guests of the
hotel, including for luncheon, afternoon
tea and dinner. Children over the age of
six welcome. Held on a long lease from
the Ernest Cook Trust.

Find out more: 01296 747444. 01296 747450
(fax) or info@hartwell-house.com
hartwell-house.com

Eat, shop, stay: Barn Café, plus
Winthrop's Café and conservatory.
Largest Trust plant centre. Shop selling
exclusive Hidcote souvenirs.

Things to see and do: themed activities
and workshops. You can play croquet on the
Great Lawn, or tennis on the new all-weather
court using period wooden racquets.
Dogs: assistance dogs only.

Hidcote

Hidcote Bartrim, near Chipping Campden,
Gloucestershire GL55 6LR

❄ 🔔 🍸 1948

This world-famous Arts and Crafts garden
nestles in a north Cotswolds hamlet. Created
by the talented and wealthy American
horticulturist Major Lawrence Johnston,
Hidcote's colourful and intricately designed
outdoor 'rooms' are full of surprises, which
change in harmony with the seasons. Many of
the unusual plants found growing in the garden
were collected from Johnston's plant-hunting
trips to faraway places. Wandering through
the maze of narrow paved pathways, you
come across secret gardens, unexpected
views and plants that burst with colour.
The Wilderness with its secluded stretch
of tall trees is just right for a picnic.

Access: 🅿️♿🚻♿📷📖📷🔍
Visitor reception ♿🔽 **Grounds** ♿➡️🔽🔽
Parking: 100 yards.

Find out more: 01386 438333 or
hidcote@nationaltrust.org.uk

Hidcote		M	T	W	T	F	S	S
Garden, shop and Winthrop's Café								
11 Feb–19 Feb	11–4	M	T	W	T	F	S	S
25 Feb–26 Feb	11–4	·	·	·	·	·	S	S
4 Mar–7 Apr	10–5	M	T	W	T	F	S	S
8 Apr–1 Oct	10–6	M	T	W	T	F	S	S
2 Oct–29 Oct	10–5	M	T	W	T	F	S	S
4 Nov–17 Dec	11–4	·	·	·	·	·	S	S
Plant centre and Barn Café*								
4 Mar–7 Apr	10–5	M	T	W	T	F	S	S
8 Apr–1 Oct	10–6	M	T	W	T	F	S	S
2 Oct–29 Oct	10–5	M	T	W	T	F	S	S

Last admission to garden one hour before closing.
*Barn Café closes one hour earlier; March and October
only open at weekends.

**Soaking up the sun at Hidcote in Gloucestershire, left.
The Pillar Garden, below, is just one 'room' within
this world-famous Arts and Crafts garden. Intricately
designed, there are surprises around every corner**

Hughenden

High Wycombe, Buckinghamshire HP14 4LA

🏠✝️❄️♿ 1947

It's hardly surprising that the unconventional
Victorian Prime Minister Benjamin Disraeli so
loved Hughenden (above). His handsome
home, set in an unspoiled Chiltern valley with
its views of ancient woods and rolling hills, is
full of the fascinating personal memorabilia
of this charismatic and colourful statesman.
Disraeli's hillside retreat later became the
headquarters for a top-secret, Second World
War operation that put Hughenden high on
Hitler's target list. The basement exhibition,
1940s living-room and ice house bunker bring
wartime Britain to life. The estate also offers a
variety of walks, rewarding visitors with perfect
views of the Chiltern Hills.

Eat, shop, stay: Stableyard café serving hot
meals, sandwiches, cakes and drinks. Dizzy's
tea-room serving sandwiches, cakes and
drinks, weekends only. Shop stocks local
produce, ales and honey, as well as Disraeli and
'Hillside' memorabilia. Second-hand bookshop,
plants and estate produce also available.

Things to see and do: **Indoors** Historical introductory talks throughout the day.
Outdoors Woodland walks, children's trails in Walled Garden and woodland play at the top of the picnic orchard. **Dogs**: welcome in orchard, park and woodland. Assistance dogs only in formal and walled gardens.

Access: 🄿♿🄳♿🖼♿📶♿🖐♿🎨💻♿♿🄰♿🅾️
Manor ♿♿🚻♿ **Grounds** ♿♿➡️♿
Parking: on site.

Find out more: 01494 755565 (Infoline).
01494 755573 or
hughenden@nationaltrust.org.uk

Hughenden	
Open every day all year	10–5*

*Closes dusk if earlier. Shop opens at 11. Manor: 5 January to 10 February, opens at 12 weekdays, 11 weekends; 11 February to 31 December, opens from 11. Closed 24 and 25 December.

The monument to Isaac Disraeli, father of Benjamin, at Hughenden in Buckinghamshire, above. Visitors explore the garden, below

King's Head

King's Head Passage, Market Square,
Aylesbury, Buckinghamshire HP20 2RW

🏠🍺 1925

Historic public house dating back to 1455, with a pleasant family atmosphere. This is one of England's best-preserved coaching inns. **Note**: Farmers' Bar leased by Chiltern Brewery. Open Monday to Saturday, 11 to 11, and Sundays, 12 to 10:30. Open Bank Holiday Mondays and other public holidays, 12 to 10:30. Closed 25 December.

Find out more: 01296 718812 (Farmers' Bar).
01280 817156 (National Trust) or
kingshead@nationaltrust.org.uk

Lodge Park and Sherborne Estate

Aldsworth, near Cheltenham,
Gloucestershire GL54 3PP

🏠🍽️🛏️🎫🍷 1983

Within the tranquil Sherborne Estate sits England's only surviving 17th-century deer-coursing grandstand. Lodge Park was built in 1634 to satisfy John 'Crump' Dutton's love of gambling and entertaining. Now an enchanting place to explore, discover, picnic and play. Don't miss the dramatic views from the roof. **Note**: toilets at Lodge Park only.

Eat, shop, stay: tea, cake, ice-cream and plants for sale at Lodge Park, when open. Tea-room and shop in Sherborne village (not National Trust). Nearby holiday cottages: Deer Park Lodge at Lodge Park, West Lodge in Sherborne and 9 Arlington Row in Bibury.

Things to see and do: living history, family events, children's quizzes, lawn games, historic shepherd's hut, woodland play trail and beautiful walks in Bridgeman landscape at Lodge Park. Country walks across the wider estate.

Lodge Park and Sherborne Estate in Gloucestershire

Dogs: on leads in Lodge Park grounds and near livestock. Under control at all times.

Access: 🅿️ 🅿️ ⬚ ⬚ ⬚ ⬚ Lodge ⬚ ⬚ ⬚
Sat Nav: for Lodge Park use GL54 3PP; for Sherborne Estate use GL54 3DT (Ewe Pen Barn) or GL54 3DL (Water Meadows).
Parking: on site for Lodge Park. For Sherborne Estate use either Ewe Pen Barn or Water Meadows car parks.

Find out more: 01451 844130 or lodgepark@nationaltrust.org.uk

Lodge Park and Sherborne Estate		M	T	W	T	F	S	S
Lodge Park								
11 Feb–19 Feb	11–4	·	·	·	·	·	S	S
3 Mar–28 May	11–4	·	·	·	·	F	S	S
2 Jun–1 Oct*	11–4	M	·	·	·	F	·	S
6 Oct–29 Oct	11–4	·	·	·	·	F	S	S
Sherborne Estate								
Open all year	Dawn–dusk	M	T	W	T	F	S	S

Open Bank Holiday Mondays. *June to September, Monday entry may be by tour (bookable). Lodge Park occasionally closes for private functions (telephone to check openings).

Long Crendon Courthouse

Long Crendon, Aylesbury, Buckinghamshire HP18 9AN

 1900

Superb example of a 14th-century courthouse with a wealth of local history – the second building acquired by the National Trust.

Note: extremely steep stairs. Sorry no toilet. Parking limited. Open Wednesday and weekends, 11 March to 29 October, 11 to 5. Volunteer-run, so opening subject to availability (please check before visiting). Open all public and Bank Holidays.

Find out more: 01280 817156 or longcrendon@nationaltrust.org.uk

Minchinhampton and Rodborough Commons

near Stroud, Gloucestershire

🏛️ 🔧 1913

Historic Minchinhampton and Rodborough Commons in Gloucestershire offer rare flowers and ancient remains

These historic Cotswold commons, traditionally grazed, are famed for rare flowers and butterflies, prehistoric remains and far-reaching views. Minchinhampton Common contains a nationally important complex of Neolithic and Bronze Age burial mounds, while Rodborough Common's limestone grasslands have abundant wild flowers, including rare pasqueflowers and many varieties of orchid.

Eat, shop, stay: many great picnic spots (no tables). The historic Winstones ice-cream factory is on Rodborough Common; ice-cream vans usually found in Reservoir car park in summer. Several pubs around the edge of both commons (none National Trust). Two holiday cottages nearby.

Things to see and do: the commons are great places to walk, picnic, spot butterflies or fly a kite, and there are events throughout the year. Downloadable Rodborough Common butterfly walk available. **Dogs**: welcome everywhere (under close control near livestock). Dog bins in car parks.

Access: ♿
Sat Nav: use GL5 5BJ for Minchinhampton; GL5 5BP Rodborough. **Parking**: at Reservoir car park on Minchinhampton Common; Rodborough Fort car park on Rodborough Common.

Find out more: 01452 814213 or minchinhampton@nationaltrust.org.uk

Newark Park

Ozleworth, Wotton-under-Edge, Gloucestershire GL12 7PZ

🏠 ❀ ♨ ⛺ 1949

The Tudor house at the heart of Newark Park, Gloucestershire, has had a dramatic, chequered history

With splendid views from the Cotswold escarpment, Newark Park is a secluded estate with a historic country home at its heart. From Tudor beginnings to dramatic rescue by a 20th-century Texan, the house has many stories to tell. The informal garden and estate provide space to play, explore and contemplate. **Note**: toilets in car park (accessible toilet in house).

Eat, shop, stay: plants for sale at visitor reception. Shop on first floor of Newark House selling gifts and souvenirs. Pavilion Café in garden serving light lunches, cakes, drinks and ice-cream. Outdoor seating provided, with indoor seating available in Newark House.

Things to see and do: waymarked walks and geocaching on estate. Open-air theatre events and croquet on the lawn, with peacocks for company. Exhibitions in Newark House. Seasonal garden specials include snowdrops and wild garlic. **Dogs**: welcome on leads in the garden and estate (please mind peacocks and grazing livestock).

Access: 🐕♿ 🅿️ 📶 ♨ ⬛ ⬛
Building ♿ ♿ Grounds ♿
Sat Nav: only works when approaching from north; if approaching from south follow brown signs from Wotton-under-Edge and A46.
Parking: 100 yards.

Find out more: 01453 842644 or newarkpark@nationaltrust.org.uk

Newark Park		M	T	W	T	F	S	S
4 Feb–5 Feb	11–4	·	·	·	·	·	S	S
11 Feb–27 Feb	11–4	M	·	W	T	F	S	S
1 Mar–30 Oct	11–5	M	·	W	T	F	S	S
4 Nov–10 Dec	11–4	·	·	·	·	·	S	S

Estate walks open daily dawn to dusk (weather permitting). Reduced car-park opening in winter.

Nuffield Place

Huntercombe, near Henley-on-Thames, Oxfordshire RG9 5RY

🏠 ❀ 2011

Though he left school at 15, William Morris went on to become an international figure and one of the richest men in the world.

Despite their wealth, Lord and Lady Nuffield preferred a simple life, as Nuffield Place in Oxfordshire shows

Find out more: 01491 641224 or nuffieldplace@nationaltrust.org.uk

Nuffield Place		M	T	W	T	F	S	S
27 Feb–5 Nov	10–5*	**M**	**T**	**W**	**T**	**F**	**S**	**S**

Closed 9 April, 25 June and 11 July. ***House: entry by guided tour between 11 and 12; free-flow access between 1 and 5, timed tickets may be used on busy days.** Both guided tour and timed tickets available from visitor reception (places limited). Closes dusk if earlier.

As founder of Morris Motors he changed not only the industrial, but social landscape with his philanthropic benefactions. Despite his great wealth, Morris, later Lord Nuffield, lived in a pleasant but unostentatious home in the Oxfordshire countryside. Perched on the Ridgeway, this house and garden typify early 20th-century taste and thrift, and reveal the home life of a couple who, with a fortune behind them, still enjoyed the simpler things in life.

Eat, shop, stay: tea-room serving light lunches and afternoon tea. Shop selling unique Nuffield Place mementoes, gifts, books and postcards. Seasonal produce and plants grown in the garden (when available).

Things to see and do: **Indoors** Immerse yourself in the wonderful storytelling of our passionate volunteers. **Outdoors** Charming Arts and Crafts-style gardens with interesting details that are being beautifully restored. Greys Court nearby. **Dogs**: welcome on leads in the gardens and woodlands.

Pitstone Windmill

Ivinghoe, Buckinghamshire LU7 9EJ

⚒ 🏚 1937

Believed to be the oldest postmill in England. Stunning views of the Chilterns. **Note**: access to windmill 262 yards via a grassy field track. Sorry no facilities. Limited parking. Open Sundays, 28 May to 27 August, 2 to 5:30 (also open Mondays, 29 May and 28 August).

Find out more: 01442 851227 or pitstonemill@nationaltrust.org.uk

Priory Cottages

1 Mill Street, Steventon, Abingdon, Oxfordshire OX13 6SP

🏠 1939

Now converted into two houses, these former monastic buildings were gifted to the National Trust by the famous Ferguson's Gang. **Note**: Priory Cottage South only open. Administered by a tenant. Sorry no toilet. Open Tuesday, 4 April to 26 September, 2 to 6 (Great Hall only open). Admission by written appointment with the tenant.

Find out more: 01793 762209 or priorycottages@nationaltrust.org.uk

Snowshill Manor and Garden

Snowshill, near Broadway,
Gloucestershire WR12 7JU

🏛️ ✿ ⚓ 1951

Charles Wade had a passion. From the age of
seven, he collected and restored beautiful and
interesting objects, living his whole life according
to his motto 'Let nothing perish'. Seeing the true
value of craftsmanship, colour and design, he
housed his curious and unlikely finds in the
Manor, and laid them out pictorially 'to inspire a
thousand fancies'. Next to the manor house is
the Priest's House, Charles Wade's humble home,
set in a beautiful terraced garden with lovely
views of the Cotswolds. Snowshill Manor and
Garden is a quirky place, a world away from
ordinary. **Note**: entry by timed ticket
(including members), places limited.

Eat, shop, stay: tea-room serving cream
teas, homemade cakes and lunches using
home-grown produce where possible.
Shop selling gifts, plants and local produce.
Second-hand bookshop. Picnic tables.
Why not stay a while longer at one of the
holiday cottages here?

Things to see and do: Indoors Family
trail, handling collection and discovery
talks. **Outdoors** Family trail, natural play
area and introductory talks.

Dogs: assistance dogs only.

Access: 🅿️ 🏛️ 🔛 🔛 🔛 🖥️ 🔛 ⬛ 🅰️
Manor 🔛 🚻 **Garden** 🔛 ♿
Sat Nav: follow signs from centre of village.
Parking: 500 yards.

Find out more: 01386 852410 or
snowshillmanor@nationaltrust.org.uk

Snowshill Manor and Garden		M	T	W	T	F	S	S
Manor								
13 Mar–29 Oct	12–5	M	T	W	T	F	S	S
4 Nov–26 Nov*	Tour	.	.	.	.	.	S	S
Garden, shop and tea-room								
13 Mar–29 Oct	11–5:30	M	T	W	T	F	S	S
4 Nov–26 Nov	10:30–3:30	.	.	.	.	.	S	S

Manor admission by non-bookable timed tickets
(may run out on busy days). Last admission one hour before
closing. *Winter weekend tours (please contact property
for details). Priest's House opens at 11.

A beautiful terraced garden surrounds Snowshill Manor
in Gloucestershire, above and below

Stowe in Buckinghamshire, offers temples, lakes and perfect views in a landscape which changes with the seasons

Stowe

Buckingham, Buckinghamshire MK18 5EQ

🏠 ❄ ⚓ 🍴 🍷 1990

The beauty of Stowe has attracted visitors since 1717. Picture-perfect views, lakeside walks and temples create a monumental landscape that changes with the seasons. Full of hidden meanings and classical references, the garden remains an earthly paradise. You will follow in the footsteps of 18th-century tourists by beginning your visit at the New Inn, now a visitor centre. From here it is a short walk or buggy-ride to the garden, where another world awaits. Our ongoing programme of works continues, as we return Stowe to its 18th-century glory. The sheer size and scale is perfect for either a steady stroll or vigorous ramble, and will leave you overwhelmed by its awe-inspiring splendour.

Eat, shop, stay: café inside New Inn serving fresh homemade food, such as light lunches, cakes, soups and scones. Shop selling local products inspired by Stowe, as well as gifts and plants. A second-hand bookshop is a must for bookworms. Picnics welcome.

Stowe		M	T	W	T	F	S	S
Gardens, shop, café and parlour rooms								
Open all year**	10–5*	M	T	W	T	F	S	S
Parkland								
Open all year	Dawn–dusk	M	T	W	T	F	S	S

*Closes dusk if earlier. Recommended last entry to gardens 90 minutes before closing. **Gardens closed 27 May (visitor centre, parkland, café and shop open). Whole property closed 24 and 25 December.

Things to see and do: **Indoors** 18th-century tavern rooms in the New Inn. Stowe House (not National Trust) – New Inn visitor centre provides details about visiting Stowe House State Rooms. New visitor centre open, includes exhibition and family-friendly activities. St Mary's church open for visits. **Outdoors** Crisp winter walks, blooming spring displays, lazy summer days and vivid autumn colour – Stowe is forever changing. Fun family activities and outdoors event programme. We are restoring paths, statues and opening new garden areas all year, so there will be more to explore on every new visit. **Dogs**: welcome on leads (downloadable dog trail available). Tie-up points and water provided.

Access: 🅿️♿🚻📷🔊🅰️
Visitor centre 🏛️🔼♿ Grounds 🏛️➡️🦽
Parking: 545 yards.

Find out more: 01280 817156 or stowe@nationaltrust.org.uk

Popular with visitors since 1717, Stowe, above and below, offers so much for visitors of all ages, with the new visitor centre organising family-friendly activities

Waddesdon Manor

Waddesdon, near Aylesbury, Buckinghamshire HP18 0JH

🏛️🍴♿🦮🔔🍷 1957

The opulent dining-room at Waddesdon Manor, Buckinghamshire, above. Visitors enjoy the Victorian gardens, right, among the finest in Britain

Baron Ferdinand de Rothschild started building Waddesdon Manor in 1874 to display his outstanding collection of art treasures and entertain fashionable society. His choice of French-château style, typical of the Loire Valley, surprises many visitors. The highest quality 18th-century French decorative arts are displayed alongside magnificent English portraits and Dutch Old Master paintings in more than 40 elegant interiors. Outside is one of the finest Victorian gardens in Britain, famous for its parterre and ornate working aviary, and enhanced with classical and contemporary sculpture. Today, the Manor continues its tradition of entertainment and hospitality with events celebrating food and wine. Visitors can explore Waddesdon's history, collections and gardens through changing exhibitions, talks and tours. **Note**: advance booking for house tickets essential for weekends and holidays for all visitors, including members.

Eat, shop, stay: two licensed restaurants for breakfasts, lunches and afternoon teas. Snacks and drinks at the Summer House or Coffee Bar. Gift shop, wine shop and old-fashioned sweet shop. Five Arrows Hotel in Waddesdon village (managed by the Rothschild Foundation charitable trust).

Things to see and do: **Indoors** Timed ticket entry to house with furnished interiors displaying the collections (booking advised for weekends, holidays and Christmas). Wide range of talks and tours on aspects of the house, collection, archive and special exhibitions with experts. Free rolling programme of films about Waddesdon, its history, collections, aviary, gardens and cellars. Daily free gardens and wine cellar tours and regular wine tastings. **Outdoors** Guided walks in the gardens and tours of the aviary. Woodland playground and den-building for children. Weekend and school holiday family events. Open-air film and theatre. Food festivals, Winter Light and Christmas fair. **Dogs**: assistance dogs only.

Access: 🅿♿♿♿♿♿♿♿♿
Building ♿♿♿ **Grounds** ♿➡♿
Parking: ¾ mile (frequent free shuttle service).

Find out more: 01296 820414 or waddesdonmanor@nationaltrust.org.uk

Waddesdon Manor		M	T	W	T	F	S	S
Gardens, aviary, playground, wine cellars, shops, restaurant								
1 Jan–2 Jan	11–6	M	·	·	·	·	·	S
7 Jan–19 Mar	11–4	·	·	·	·	·	S	S
22 Mar–5 Nov	10–5	·	·	W	T	F	S	S
8 Nov–31 Dec	11–6	·	·	W	T	F	S	S
11 Feb–19 Feb	11–4	M	T	W	T	F	S	S
1 Apr–17 Apr	10–5	M	T	W	T	F	S	S
27 May–4 Jun	10–5	M	T	W	T	F	S	S
21 Oct–29 Oct	10–5	M	T	W	T	F	S	S
House*								
22 Mar–22 Oct	12–4	·	·	W	T	F	S	S
27 May–4 Jun	12–4	M	T	W	T	F	S	S
Christmas House (partial opening)*								
8 Nov–31 Dec	11:30–6	·	·	W	T	F	S	S
Coach House Gallery								
7 Jan–19 Mar	11–4	·	·	·	·	·	S	S
13 Feb–19 Feb	11–4	M	T	W	T	F	S	S
22 Mar–22 Oct	11–5	·	·	W	T	F	S	S

House: open 11 to 4, weekends and Bank Holiday Mondays. *House: admission by timed ticket, available at waddesdon.org.uk or by calling 01296 820414 (booking fee). Advance booking of house tickets essential at busy times, especially weekends, public and school holidays. Recommended last entry 2:30; last tickets available 3:10. Closed 24, 25 and 26 December.

West Wycombe Park, Village and Hill

West Wycombe, Buckinghamshire

🏠✝♿♿ 1943

With such a nefarious creator, West Wycombe Park, Village and Hill, Buckinghamshire, cannot fail to fascinate

Alongside this historic village lies an exquisite Palladian mansion. This lavish home and serene landscape garden reflect the wealth and personality of its creator, the infamous Sir Francis Dashwood, founder of the Hellfire Club. Still home to the Dashwood family and their fine collection, it remains a busy, private estate. **Note**: opened in partnership with the Dashwood family. The Hellfire Caves and café are privately owned and National Trust members receive a discount on the admission charge.

Eat, shop, stay: refreshments available at the Hellfire Caves and café (not National Trust), where members receive a discount. Variety of shops and pubs in the National Trust village, offering refreshments and local produce (none National Trust).

Things to see and do: **Indoors** Mansion guided tours, Monday to Thursday (free-flow access Sundays). **Outdoors** Centuries-old village with historic cottages and coaching inns. West Wycombe Hill, iconic Dashwood mausoleum and church with golden ball. **Dogs**: welcome on West Wycombe Hill. Assistance dogs only in park.

Access: 🅿♿♿♿♿♿ **Building** ♿♿♿
Sat Nav: use HP14 3AJ. **Parking**: 250 yards.

Westbury Court Garden

Westbury-on-Severn, Gloucestershire GL14 1PD

1967

Originally laid out between 1696 and 1705, this is the only restored Dutch water garden in the country. There are canals, clipped hedges, working 17th-century vegetable plots and many old varieties of fruit trees.

Eat, shop, stay: light refreshments available in the local church (not National Trust) on Sunday afternoons.

Things to see and do: evening garden tours, Easter Egg trails, Apple Day.
Dogs: welcome on short leads at all times.

White Horse Hill

Uffington, Oxfordshire

1979

The White Horse at Uffington is part of an ancient landscape, steeped in history and mythology. It's the oldest chalk figure in the country, dated to the late Bronze Age about 3,000 years ago. Its linear form dominates the landscape, yet no one knows how it was made. The walls of an Iron Age hill fort are visible on the hilltop, the highest point in Oxfordshire. You can also look down on a valley known as The Manger and a natural outcrop known as Dragon Hill, where St George was said to have fought and slain the dragon.
Note: archaeological monuments under English Heritage guardianship. Sorry no toilet.

Westbury Court Garden in Gloucestershire, left, and White Horse Hill in Oxfordshire, below

White Horse Hill: the highest point in Oxfordshire with a wealth of history and mythology

Things to see and do: guided walks and events to re-chalk the White Horse. Stunning views can be enjoyed from the top of the hill. Ashdown House woodland walks nearby. **Dogs**: under close control at all times (stock grazing).

Access: 🅿️ ♿
Sat Nav: use SN7 7QJ. **Parking**: on site.

Find out more: 01793 762209 or whitehorsehill@nationaltrust.org.uk

Woodchester Park

Nympsfield, near Stroud, Gloucestershire

🏞️ 1994

This tranquil wooded valley contains a 'lost landscape': remains of an 18th- and 19th-century landscape park with a chain of five lakes. The restoration of this landscape is an ongoing project. Waymarked trails (steep in places) lead through picturesque scenery,

passing an unfinished Victorian mansion. **Note**: mansion managed by Woodchester Mansion Trust. Toilet not always available. Mansion not National Trust, admission charges apply (including members).

Eat, shop, stay: seasonal café, shop and toilet facilities available at Woodchester Mansion (not National Trust).

Things to see and do: waymarked trails through valley and popular woodland play trail for children built along shortest route, which includes rope swings, see-saw, balance beams and zip wire. Events throughout the year. **Dogs**: under close control, on leads where requested.

Access: Grounds ♿
Sat Nav: nearest GL10 3TS, then follow signs. **Parking**: accessible from Nympsfield road, 300 yards from junction with B4066.

Find out more: 01452 814213 or woodchesterpark@nationaltrust.org.uk

Within Woodchester Park in Gloucestershire lies a lost landscape

Additional countryside car parks in Gloucestershire and Buckinghamshire	
Gloucestershire	
Mayhill	GL18 1JS
Dover's Hill	GL55 6PN
Buckinghamshire	
Ivinghoe Beacon	HP4 1NF
Pulpit Wood,	
Whiteleaf Fields	HP27 0NB

Berkshire, Hampshire and the Isle of Wight

The Needles Batteries and Headland, the Isle of Wight
Competition entry from Gareth Wyre

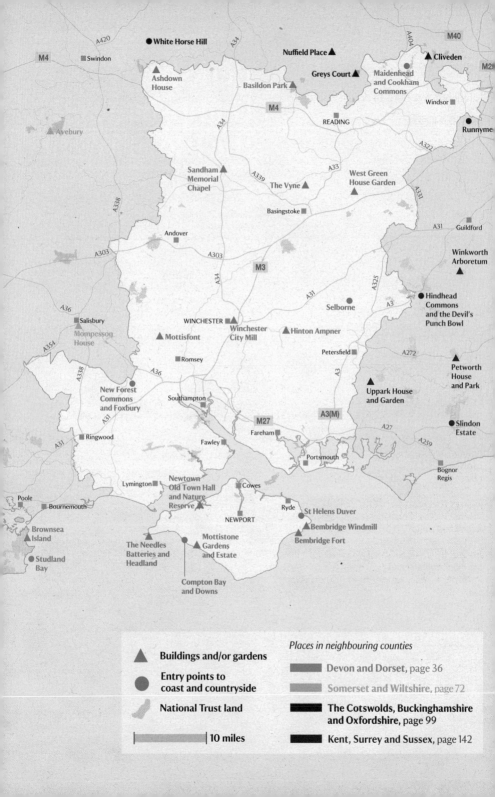

White Horse Hill

Nuffield Place ▲

Cliveden ▲

M40

M4 ■ Swindon

Ashdown House ▲

M404

Maidenhead and Cookham Commons ●

Greys Court ▲

Basildon Park ▲

Windsor ■

M4

Avebury ▲

READING

Runnyme ●

A322

A34

Sandham Memorial Chapel ▲

A339

The Vyne ▲

A33

West Green House Garden ▲

A331

A338

Basingstoke ■

Andover ■

A303

A31

Guildford ■

A303

M3

A34

Winkworth Arboretum ▲

A36

Salisbury ■

A325

Selborne ●

A3

Hindhead Commons and the Devil's Punch Bowl ●

Mompesson House

WINCHESTER ■

Winchester City Mill ▲

Hinton Ampner ▲

A354

A338

Mottisfont ▲

A272

Romsey ■

Petersfield ■

A36

Petworth House and Park ▲

New Forest Commons and Foxbury ●

Southampton

A3

Uppark House and Garden ▲

Slindon Estate ●

Ringwood ■

Fawley ■

M27

Fareham ■

A27

A259

A31

Portsmouth ■

Bognor Regis ■

Poole

Lymington

Newtown Old Town Hall and Nature Reserve ▲

Cowes ■

Ryde ■

St Helens Duver ●

Bournemouth ●

NEWPORT

Bembridge Windmill ▲

Brownsea Island ▲

The Needles Batteries and Headland ▲

Mottistone Gardens and Estate ▲

Bembridge Fort

Studland Bay ●

Compton Bay and Downs

Legend

▲ Buildings and/or gardens

● Entry points to coast and countryside

National Trust land

|——————| 10 miles

Places in neighbouring counties

Devon and Dorset, page 36

Somerset and Wiltshire, page 72

The Cotswolds, Buckinghamshire and Oxfordshire, page 99

Kent, Surrey and Sussex, page 142

Ashdown House

Lambourn, Newbury, Berkshire RG17 8RE

🏛 🏚 ❄ ⚓ 1956

The outstanding views from the roof of Ashdown House, Berkshire, stretch across three counties

Unique 17th-century chalk-block hunting lodge, with doll's-house appearance, built for the Queen of Bohemia by the Earl of Craven. The guided tour, which reveals an intriguing family history, leads up the staircase hung with fine 17th-century paintings. Outstanding rooftop views across three counties. **Note**: access to roof via 100-step staircase.

Things to see and do: guided staircase tour. White Horse Hill nearby. **Dogs**: on leads in woodland only.

Access: 🅦 🎧 🏢 Building 🔳 Grounds 🔳
Sat Nav: follow local brown signs from B4000.
Parking: in main estate car park, 437 yards.

Find out more: 01494 755569 (Infoline).
01793 762209 or
ashdownhouse@nationaltrust.org.uk

Ashdown House		M	T	W	T	F	S	S
House								
5 Apr–28 Oct	Tour*	·	·	**W**	·	·	**S**	·
Woodland								
Open all year	Dawn–dusk	**M**	**T**	**W**	**T**	·	**S**	**S**

*House: admission by guided tour only, 2:15, 3:15 and 4:15 (advance booking not necessary).

Basildon Park

Lower Basildon, Reading, Berkshire RG8 9NR

🏛 ❄ ⚓ ☕ 1978

Sitting elegantly in 162 hectares (400 acres) of historic parkland and gardens, this 18th-century house was purchased by Lord and Lady Iliffe in the 1950s, when it was de-requisitioned after the Second World War. With extraordinary vision, the Iliffes brought Basildon Park back to life, acquiring a collection of fine furnishings and carefully selected Old Masters. The wooded parkland offers glorious seasonal colour, with spring bluebells, summer buttercups and autumn leaves, while the landscape has been carefully restored to offer wonderful views, peaceful trails and picnic places, with areas for children to run and play. Winter walks are a must. **Note**: entrance to main show rooms of mansion on first floor – 21 steps from ground level.

Eat, shop, stay: mansion tea-room serves warm lunches between 12 and 2:30, with homemade cakes and cream teas available all day. The Parlour in the stableyard offers tasty treats and drinks. The shop sells books, plants, local food, ice-cream and much more.

Behind the stately portico of Basildon Park, Berkshire, lies a collection of fine furnishings and Old Masters

Bembridge Fort

Bembridge Down, near Bembridge,
Isle of Wight PO36 8QY

🏛️ ♿ 🏰 1967

In a commanding position on top of Bembridge Down, this unrestored Victorian fort is open for volunteer-run guided tours. **Note**: sorry no toilets. Not suitable for children under ten. Open Tuesday, 4 April to 24 October, 2 to 3:30.

Find out more: 01983 741020 or bembridgefort@nationaltrust.org.uk c/o Longstone Farmhouse, Strawberry Lane, Mottistone, Isle of Wight PO30 4EA

Bembridge Windmill

High Street/Mill Lane, Bembridge,
Isle of Wight PO35 5SQ

🍴 ♿ 1961

Some of the original machinery at Bembridge Windmill on the Isle of Wight

With fabulous treasures and works of art inside Basildon Park, top, and wild play areas outside, above, there is something to entertain every visitor

Things to see and do: **Indoors** Exhibition: 'At Home with Art, Treasures of the Ford Collection'. Guided house tours. **Outdoors** Woodland and parkland walks. Wild Play and family activities. **Dogs**: welcome on leads in grounds. Assistance dogs only in house.

Access: 🅿️ 🚻 ♿ 📷 📹 🎵 ♿ 📷
Mansion ♿ 🅿️ Grounds ➡️ ♿
Sat Nav: not reliable, please follow brown tourist signs. **Parking**: 400 yards.

Find out more: 01491 672382 or basildonpark@nationaltrust.org.uk

Basildon Park	
Open every day all year	10–5*

*House: free-flow from 12, access by guided tour only 11 and 11:30, tickets available from visitor reception (places limited). Closes dusk if earlier. Closed 24 and 25 December.

This little gem, the only surviving windmill on the Isle of Wight, is one of the island's most iconic images. Built *circa* 1700 and last operated in 1913, it still has most of its original machinery intact. Climb to the top and follow the milling process down its four floors.

Built around 1700, iconic Bembridge Windmill was last in operation in 1913

Compton Bay and Downs

Compton, Isle of Wight

🦽♿🏛 1961

Compton Bay offers a great day out, there's plenty of space on the sandy beach, and it's a prime site for fossil-hunting. The multi-coloured cliffs provide a wonderful backdrop, with fine views. A self-guided trail runs along part of this ridge, which is rich in wild flowers and butterflies.

Eat, shop, stay: licensed van selling hot and cold snacks, drinks and ice-cream. Two holiday cottages, Compton Farm Cottages, within walking distance – both ideally placed for exploring the coast and Downs.

Things to see and do: one of the best spots on the Isle of Wight for swimming and surfing, or just taking time out. Why not search for dinosaur foot casts in the rocks? **Dogs**: welcome on beach between Hanover Point and Brook Chine all year.

Access: Compton Bay 🦽
Sat Nav: use PO30 4HB. **Parking**: on site.

Find out more: 01983 741020 or comptonbay@nationaltrust.org.uk

Compton Bay and Downs, Isle of Wight: a prime site for fossil-hunting, the beach is backed by multi-coloured cliffs

Eat, shop, stay: the reception kiosk offers hot and cold drinks, including tea and a selection of coffees. Ice-cream, postcards, sweets, gifts and souvenirs also available. Picnic tables in grounds. Four holiday cottages nearby – Chert, Little Chert, Wydcombe and Knowles Farm cottages.

Things to see and do: walks, including the start of Culver Trail. Nature trails (school holidays). Bembridge Fort (booking essential) nearby. **Dogs**: welcome in grounds on leads. Assistance dogs only in windmill.

Access: 🅿♿🖼🖥👓 Building 🦽🚺🦽
Sat Nav: do not use, look for brown signs.
Parking: free (not National Trust), 100 yards in lay-by.

Find out more: 01983 873945 or bembridgemill@nationaltrust.org.uk

Bembridge Windmill		M	T	W	T	F	S	S
11 Mar–29 Oct	10:30–5	**M**	**T**	**W**	**T**	**F**	**S**	**S**

Closes dusk if earlier. Conducted school groups and special visits March to end October (telephone or email to book).

Hinton Ampner

Hinton Ampner, near Alresford,
Hampshire SO24 0LA

🏠 ✝ 🌼 🎑 🍵 1986

Hinton Ampner is the fulfilment of one man's vision. After a catastrophic fire in 1960, Ralph Dutton rebuilt his home in the light and airy Georgian style he loved. A passionate collector, he filled the sunny rooms with ceramics and art. Outside, Dutton designed a series of tranquil garden rooms, each with their own distinctive planting still apparent today. Geometric topiary, exotic-coloured dahlias and borders of repeat-flowering roses lead onto terraces with panoramic views across the South Downs. Extensive lawns, a park with ancient oaks and beech woodland provide plenty of space to stroll, play, relax and picnic.

Eat, shop, stay: the old social club tea-room serves seasonal dishes, homemade cakes and cream teas, made using produce grown in our walled garden. Shop sells many locally sourced products, including estate-grown plants. Second-hand bookshop. Picnics welcome.

Things to see and do: **Indoors** Conservation demonstrations throughout the year. **Outdoors** Estate walking trails and free seasonal garden walks. Children's trails and events. Uppark House and Garden and Winchester City Mill nearby. **Dogs**: welcome on leads in parkland, estate walks and tea-room courtyard (no access to formal gardens).

Access: 🅿️♿🏠🏠🏠🅿️🖥️🎧📷🅿️
Building 🏠♿ Grounds 🏠➡️♿
Sat Nav: use SO24 0NH – takes you to Hinton Arms pub, 21 yards west of main entrance. **Parking**: on site.

Find out more: 01962 771305 or hintonampner@nationaltrust.org.uk

Hinton Ampner		M	T	W	T	F	S	S
House								
9 Jan–5 Feb*	11–4	M	T	W	T	F	S	S
12 Feb–26 Nov	11–4	M	T	W	T	F	S	S
2 Dec–23 Dec	11–4	M	T	W	T	F	S	S
Gardens								
11 Feb–23 Dec	10–5**	M	T	W	T	F	S	S
Estate, shop and café								
Open all year	10–5**	M	T	W	T	F	S	S

*January: house entrance hall only open. **Close dusk if earlier. Whole property closed 24 and 25 December.

One man's vision rescued light and airy Hinton Ampner in Hampshire after a catastrophic fire in 1960

Maidenhead and Cookham Commons

near Maidenhead, Berkshire

🏛🏖 1934

The rich habitats of Maidenhead and Cookham Commons, Berkshire, make them perfect for wildlife-spotting

This chain of ancient commons offers footpaths through broadleaf woodlands, chalk downland, marshes dotted with orchids and hay meadows buzzing with insects in summer. These rich habitats are great for wildlife-spotting throughout the year – you might see emperor dragonflies, marbled white butterflies, redwings, skylarks and fieldfares.

Eat, shop, stay: numerous shops, restaurants, pubs and cafés in nearby Cookham, Cookham Dean, Golden Ball, Pinkneys Green and Maidenhead (none National Trust). Picnic on wildflower meadows.

Things to see and do: enjoy walking and horse-riding along rides and tree-lined avenues. Let your imagination run wild on family-friendly routes, with great places to try den-building and bug-hunting. **Dogs**: welcome (please be mindful of ground-nesting birds and cattle grazing).

Access: 🦽
Sat Nav: use SL6 6QD for Pinkneys Green.
Parking: numerous on site.

Find out more: 01628 605069 or maidenheadandcookham@nationaltrust.org.uk

Mottisfont

near Romsey, Hampshire SO51 0LP

🏛✦🏖 1957

Ancient trees, babbling brooks and rolling lawns frame this 18th-century house with a medieval priory at its heart. Maud Russell made Mottisfont her home in the 1930s, bringing artists here to relax and create works inspired by Mottisfont's past, including an extraordinary drawing-room painted by Rex Whistler. We continue those artistic traditions today, with a permanent 20th-century art collection and major exhibitions in our top-floor gallery. Outside, carpets of spring bulbs, a walled rose garden, rich autumn leaves and a colourful winter garden create a feast for the senses all year round. Our world-famous collection of old-fashioned roses flowers once a year in June. Winding paths meander through stately trees, with the sound of water never far away.

Eat, shop, stay: Old Kitchen in house serving hot meals on china. Coach House Café in stables offering lighter lunches on eco-friendly disposable tableware. Ice-cream parlour, additional kiosk in good weather. Shop and plant centre at Welcome Centre, second-hand bookshop in stables.

A hub for artists in the 1930s, art continues to play a central role at Mottisfont in Hampshire

The celebrated rose garden in June at Mottisfont,
left, and the joys of spring inspire one
young visitor in this garden paradise, above

Things to see and do: **Indoors** Five major
exhibitions in the art gallery every year – 2017
includes Rex Whistler, the Shell Heritage Art
Collection and The Gruffalo and Friends.
Outdoors Free daily guided walks and talks.
Family activities, including a year-round wild
play trail and seasonal activity trails in school
holidays. Open-air theatre events in summer.
Other seasonal events throughout the year.
Seasonal variety in the gardens. Wider estate
to explore on foot or by bike. **Dogs**: welcome
on short leads at all times in most of grounds,
with some restrictions.

Access: ⃣⃣⃣⃣⃣⃣⃣⃣
House and gallery ⃣⃣ Grounds ⃣⃣⃣⃣
Sat Nav: use SO51 0LN. **Parking**: on site.

Find out more: 01794 340757 or
mottisfont@nationaltrust.org.uk

Mottisfont	
Open every day all year	10–5*

*Closes dusk if earlier. House and gallery: open at 11; close at 4
from 1 November. House: closed for short period in November.
Gallery: closed for short periods in between exhibitions.
Late opening during rose season (garden only). Timed tickets
may apply at certain times. Closed 24 and 25 December.

Mottistone Gardens and Estate

Mottistone, near Brighstone,
Isle of Wight PO30 4ED

[❄ ♣ 🏛 ⌖] 1965

Set in a sheltered south-facing valley, these gardens are full of surprises, with shrub-filled banks, hidden pathways and colourful herbaceous borders. Surrounding an attractive manor house (tenanted, not open), these 20th-century gardens have a Mediterranean-style planting scheme to take advantage of its southerly location, including drought-tolerant plants from subtropical regions. Other surprises include a monocot-border, a small organic kitchen garden and a traditional tea-garden alongside The Shack, a unique cabin retreat designed as their summer drawing office by architects John Seely (2nd Lord Mottistone) and Paul Paget. There are also delightful walks across the adjoining Mottistone Estate.
Note: manor house open two days a year.

Mottistone Gardens and Estate boasts colourful borders, top, and The Shack, above, a unique cabin retreat

Things to see and do: family events and garden tours. Flowerpot trail and estate walks. Newtown Old Town Hall and The Needles Batteries and Headland nearby. **Dogs**: welcome on leads.

Access: [icons]
The Shack [icons] Garden [icons]
Parking: 50 yards.

Find out more: 01983 741302 or mottistonegardens@nationaltrust.org.uk

The attractive manor house at Mottistone Gardens and Estate on the Isle of Wight

Eat, shop, stay: shop selling gifts, books, cards, postcards and ice-cream. Plant stall. Second-hand books. Tea-garden serving hot and cold drinks, soup, sandwiches, cake, cream teas and light refreshments. Three holiday cottages nearby – Mottistone Manor Farmhouse, Longstone Cottage and Rose Cottage.

Mottistone Gardens		M	T	W	T	F	S	S
Gardens								
12 Mar–26 Oct	10:30–5	M	T	W	T	.	.	S
Shop								
2 Nov–9 Dec	11–3	.	.	.	T	F	S	.
10 Dec	11–3	.	.	.	.	.	.	S

Estate open every day all year. Gardens close dusk if earlier. House open two days only: 28 May by guided tour, 9:30 to 12 (timed ticket, available on day); free-flow 1 to 5, and 29 May, 10:30 to 5 by free-flow (additional charges apply).

The Needles Batteries and Headland

West High Down, Alum Bay,
Isle of Wight PO39 0JH

🏠♿🏛️🚪 1975

The Needles Batteries and Headland, Isle of Wight: the Old Battery was used throughout both world wars

You can walk from Freshwater Bay to The Needles Headland along Tennyson Down for stunning views of the coast. Then, perched high above The Needles, amid acres of this unspoilt countryside, is The Needles Old Battery, a Victorian fort built in 1862 and used throughout both world wars. The Parade Ground has two original guns, and the fort's fascinating military history is brought to life with displays and models, plus a series of vivid cartoons by acclaimed comic book artist Geoff Campion. An underground tunnel leads to a searchlight emplacement with dramatic views over The Needles rocks. The New Battery, further up the Headland, has an exhibition on the secret British rocket tests carried out there during the Cold War. **Note**: steep paths and uneven surfaces. Spiral staircase to tunnel. Toilet at Old Battery only.

Eat, shop, stay: clifftop 1940s-style tea-room serving soup, jacket potatoes, sandwiches, cakes, cream teas and light refreshments. Picnic tables. Gift shop selling ice-cream, confectionery and gifts. Drinks, snacks and ice-cream available at New Battery. You can stay at the Coastguard clifftop holiday cottages.

Things to see and do: **Indoors** Family activity packs. Inspector and soldier trails. **Outdoors** Clifftop walks to Tennyson Monument and beyond. **Dogs**: welcome on leads, assistance dogs only in upstairs tea-room, all dogs welcome downstairs.

Access: 🅿️🌐🏢🎢🛗🚪🅐♿
Old Battery 🦽🪑🍴♿ New Battery 🦽
Parking: no parking on site (limited disabled parking by arrangement). Nearest at Alum Bay, ¾ mile, not National Trust (minimum charge £5, including members). Freshwater Bay, 3½ miles (not National Trust), or Highdown (196:SZ325856) 2 miles.

Find out more: 01983 754772 or needles@nationaltrust.org.uk

The Needles	M	T	W	T	F	S	S
Old Battery and tea-room							
11 Mar–29 Oct 10:30–5	M	T	W	T	F	S	S
Old Battery tea-room							
7 Jan–12 Feb 11–3	.	.	.	.	.	S	S
18 Feb–26 Feb 11–3	M	T	W	T	F	S	S
4 Nov–17 Dec 11–3	.	.	.	.	.	S	S
New Battery							
11 Mar–29 Oct 11–4	M	T	W	T	F	S	S
Needles Headland							
Open all year	M	T	W	T	F	S	S

Needles Batteries close dusk if earlier and in high winds. 14 May: no disabled vehicular access due to Walk the Wight. 1 July: Old Battery early opening for Round the Island yacht race.

Inside the Old Battery searchlight emplacement, below, and taking in the views of The Needles, right

New Forest Commons and Foxbury

near East Wellow, Hampshire

 1928

Woodland, grassland, heathland, bogs and mires make up the unique landscape of the New Forest Commons, an apparent wilderness that's teeming with wildlife. The National Trust looks after commons at the following places: Bramshaw, Foxbury, Hale Purlieu, Hightown, as well as Rockford and Ibsley. Foxbury is nature's very own playground, a 150-hectare (370-acre) area of heathland restoration on the edge of the New Forest. Wide open spaces, gentle hillsides and hidden ponds are there to be discovered in this recovering landscape. This is a fragile conservation site for wildlife and we only allow access for special seasonal events.

Things to see and do: programme of events throughout the year at Foxbury focusing on the site's rich wildlife, including seasonal bird walks, volunteer tree-planting events and Wild Play Days for young children. **Dogs**: dogs on leads or under close control March to July (due to nesting birds).

Access: 🐾
Sat Nav: for Foxbury use SO51 6AQ and look out for the Omega signs; Bramshaw Commons SO51 6AQ; Hale Purlieu SP6 2QZ; Hightown Common BH24 3HH; Rockford and Ibsley Commons BH24 2NA. **Parking**: for Foxbury at Half Moon car park on Blackhill Road.

Find out more: 01425 650035 or newforest@nationaltrust.org.uk

---

New Forest Commons and Foxbury

For your safety we would not advise access to the New Forest between dusk and dawn. Foxbury is accessible for special seasonal events only.

Made up of grassland, bogs and heath, the wilderness of New Forest Commons and Foxbury, Hampshire, teems with wildlife, as well as still being home to wild ponies

Newtown Old Town Hall and Nature Reserve

Newtown, near Shalfleet,
Isle of Wight PO30 4PA

🏛️ ♿ 📷 🐿️ 1933

Wander past flower-filled hay meadows and through ancient woodlands filled with rare butterflies and red squirrels down to the picturesque harbour. Newtown is the only National Nature Reserve on the island, owned and managed by the National Trust since 1963. Tucked away in a tiny hamlet adjoining the National Nature Reserve is a small and quirky 17th-century building, the only remaining evidence of Newtown's former importance. Bought for and donated to the National Trust by Ferguson's Gang, a group of young people in the 1930s battling against the sprawling development of England. **Note**: nearest toilet in car park.

Eat, shop, stay: postcards and souvenirs available at the Town Hall. Here on the north side of the island there are two holiday cottages at Cowes – called Rosetta and East Rosetta.

Things to see and do: **Indoors** Children's quiz sheet. Exhibitions by local artists. **Outdoors** National Nature Reserve walks. Bird hide (April to September). Family activities run by Newtown Ranger from nearby Visitor Point.

Access: 🚫📷🏛️📱👁️ Building ♿
Parking: 15 yards.

Find out more: 01983 531785 (Old Town Hall). 01983 531622 (Visitor Point) or newtown@nationaltrust.org.uk

Newtown		M	T	W	T	F	S	S
Old Town Hall								
12 Mar–19 Oct	2–5	·	**T**	**W**	**T**	·	·	**S**
Nature Reserve								·
Open all year		**M**	**T**	**W**	**T**	**F**	**S**	**S**
Bird hide								
1 Apr–30 Sep	10–4	**M**	**T**	**W**	**T**	**F**	**S**	**S**

Old Town Hall, last admission 15 minutes before closing. Closes dusk if earlier.

The boardwalk at Newtown National Nature Reserve on the Isle of Wight, left, and a wonderful haven for wildlife, below

St Helens Duver

near St Helens, Isle of Wight

 1928

Sandy beaches, rock pools, sand dunes and coastal woods. The Duver itself was a Victorian golf course with royal patronage – evident from its short turf and undulating ground. Today, it's a fascinating place to look for wildlife, from burrowing digger wasps to wasp spiders and waterbirds over the harbour. **Note**: no toilets.

Eat, shop, stay: why not stay for longer at one of two charming holiday cottages close to the Duver? Old Church Lodge, a single-storey Victorian stone cottage sleeps four, while the Old Club House, an attractive wooden chalet overlooking the Duver, sleeps five.

Things to see and do: this great spot next to the beach, is ideal for exploring rock pools, taking a coastal walk, or birdwatching across the harbour. **Dogs**: welcome under close control.

Access:
Sat Nav: use PO33 1XY. **Parking**: on site.

Find out more: 01983 741020 or sthelensduver@nationaltrust.org.uk

Once a Victorian golf course, St Helens Duver on the Isle of Wight is now open for everyone to enjoy

Why not share your pictures with us? #nationaltrust

A place of quiet contemplation, Sandham Memorial Chapel, Hampshire, houses paintings by Stanley Spencer recalling his experiences in the First World War

Sandham Memorial Chapel

Harts Lane, Burghclere, near Newbury, Hampshire RG20 9JT

[†] [✿] 1947

Lose yourself in Stanley Spencer's extraordinarily powerful paintings, recollecting his First World War service as a medical orderly and soldier, housed within this tranquil space. An exhibition area gives historical context before you enter the Chapel, while the garden is somewhere to pause and reflect afterwards or perhaps to picnic.

Eat, shop, stay: small shop selling books, postcards, plants and local products. Picnics welcome.

Things to see and do: new exhibition contextualising the paintings.
Dogs: in grounds on leads only.

Access: [icons] Chapel [icon]
Visitor reception/exhibition [icon] Grounds [icons] [►]
Parking: opposite entrance to chapel.

Find out more: 01635 278394 or sandham@nationaltrust.org.uk

Sandham Memorial Chapel		M	T	W	T	F	S	S
1 Mar–29 Oct	11–4*	·	·	W	T	F	S	S
3 Nov–17 Dec	11–3	·	·	·	·	F	S	S

*6 May to 1 October: extended opening to 5, weekends only. Open Bank Holiday Mondays, 11 to 4. New car park opposite chapel available during normal opening hours. Car park locked 15 minutes after closing.

Selborne

near Alton, Hampshire GU34 3JR

[icons] 1933

These beechwood hangers and flower-filled meadows inspired the pioneering naturalist Gilbert White, and are havens for wildlife and walkers alike. **Note**: traditional management with grazing animals in operation.

Find out more: 01428 751338 or selborne@nationaltrust.org.uk

The Vyne

Vyne Road, Sherborne St John,
Basingstoke, Hampshire RG24 9HL

⌂ ✝ 🏠 🔅 ♿ 🐾 🍴 ▼ | 1956 |

Once an important Tudor palace, this
atmospheric mansion has some illustrious
connections, from Henry VIII to Jane Austen
and J. R. R. Tolkien. A major conservation
project is taking place at The Vyne. This
exciting project will bring changes to the visitor
experience throughout the year. Outside, acres
of wildlife-rich gardens, meadows and woods
create a wonderful space for relaxation and
exploration, while the play space gives children
freedom to let their imaginations take them
on fantasy adventures. Sweeping lawns offer
lakeside picnicking, and a short stroll reveals a
cosy bird hide overlooking the water meadows.

**Daffodils herald spring in the garden at
The Vyne in Hampshire, above. Indoors the piano
proves irresistible to musical visitors, below**

Note: major roof works, whole house covered in scaffold. Only ground floor open.

Eat, shop, stay: tea-room serving light lunches, soup, sandwiches, cakes and scones. Gift shop. Second-hand bookshop in house, plant sales. Picnics welcome.

Things to see and do: **Indoors** Events and activities all year. Free guided tours, exhibitions and themed days. **Outdoors** Open-air theatre. Seasonal garden tours, trails and woodland walks. Geocaching, orienteering and play areas. **Dogs**: welcome on short leads in woodlands and most of gardens.

Access: 🅿♿🎫♿♿♿🎨💻🎒♿🅰
House ♿🍴♿ Grounds 🌿♿♿➡♿
Sat Nav: not reliable, follow brown tourist signs. **Parking**: on site, limited in winter (October to April) due to ground conditions.

Find out more: 01256 883858 or thevyne@nationaltrust.org.uk

The Vyne		
Open every day all year	10–5*	

*Closes dusk if earlier. House: opens 11 for visit by tour or timed ticket (telephone for details). Shop: opens 11. Last entry one hour before closing. Closed 24 and 25 December.

West Green House Garden

West Green, Hartley Wintney, Hampshire RG27 8JB

❄ 1957

Four seasons of beauty, contrast and inspiration. Created by acclaimed garden designer and writer Marylyn Abbott. **Note**: maintained on behalf of the National Trust by Marylyn Abbott. Facilities not National Trust. Open Wednesday to Sunday, 1 March to 29 October, 11 to 4:30 and daily, 15 November to 20 December, 11 to 4. Open Bank Holiday Mondays.

Find out more: 01252 844611 or westgreenhouse@nationaltrust.org.uk

Winchester City Mill

Bridge Street, Winchester, Hampshire SO23 9BH

🏛❄🍴 1929

This restored working watermill has stood at the heart of the city of Winchester for a millennium and is probably the oldest working watermill in the UK. As the official Gateway to the South Downs National Park, City Mill provides information for visitors wishing to explore local walks and attractions. **Note**: nearest toilet 220 yards (not National Trust).

Eat, shop, stay: shop selling local produce, gifts and books, as well as our freshly milled wholemeal flour.

Things to see and do: tours, workshops and exhibitions. School holiday quizzes and trails and seasonal events for the whole family, including Easter Egg hunts. Flour-milling demonstrations every weekend and regular baking demonstrations. **Dogs**: assistance dogs only.

Access: ♿♿🎨💻🎒♿🅰 Building ♿
Sat Nav: do not use. **Parking**: at Chesil car park or park and ride, neither National Trust (charge including members).

Find out more: 01962 870057 or winchestercitymill@nationaltrust.org.uk

Winchester City Mill		M	T	W	T	F	S	S
1 Jan–24 Dec	10–4*	**M**	**T**	**W**	**T**	**F**	**S**	**S**

*20 February to 29 October, open to 5.

Winchester City Mill, Hampshire, is probably the oldest working watermill in the UK

Kent, Surrey and Sussex

Sheffield Park and Garden, East Sussex
Competition entry from John Atfield

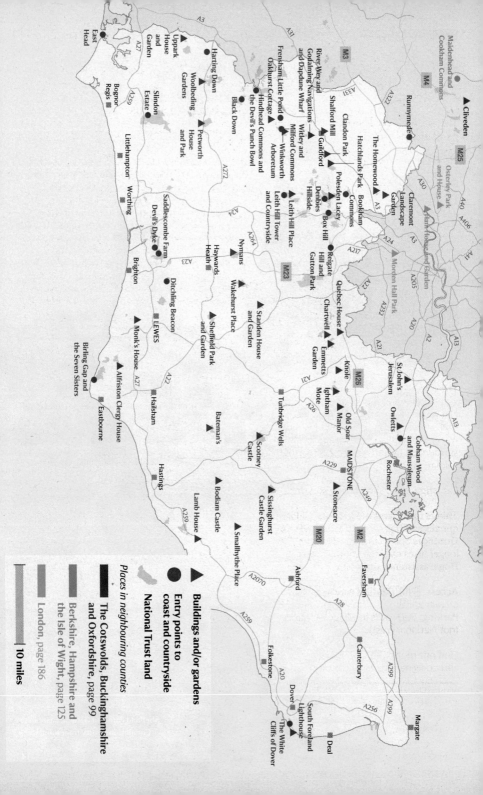

East Head

Cliveden ▲

Maidenhead and Cookham Commons

M4

M25

Osterley Park and House

Ham House and Garden

Cobham Wood and Mausoleum

Morden Hall Park

St John's Jerusalem

Owlets

Rochester

Runnymede

Claremont Landscape Garden

The Homewood

Boolham Commons

Hatchlands Park

Clandon Park

Shalford Mill

Guildford

Polesden Lacey

Denbies Hillside

Box Hill

Reigate Hill and Gatton Park

Quebec House

Chartwell

Emmetts Garden

Knole

Ightham Mote

Old Soar Manor

MAIDSTONE

Stoneacre

Sissinghurst Castle Garden

Smallhythe Place

Bodiam Castle

Scotney Castle

Batemans's

Tunbridge Wells

Lamb House

Hastings

Standen House and Garden

Sheffield Park and Garden

Wakehurst Place

Nymans

Haywards Heath

Ditchling Beacon

LEWES

Monk's House

Alfriston Clergy House

Eastbourne

Halsham

Birling Gap and the Seven Sisters

Saddlescombe Farm

Devil's Dyke

Brighton

Worthing

Littlehampton

Bognor Regis

Slindon Estate

Petworth House and Park

Woolbeding Gardens

Uppark House and Garden

Harting Down

Black Down

Hindhead Commons and the Devil's Punch Bowl

Oakhurst Cottage

Winkworth Arboretum

Witley and Milford Commons

Frensham Little Pond

River Wey and Godalming Navigations and Dapdune Wharf

Leith Hill Tower and Countryside

Leith Hill Place

Faversham

Ashford

Canterbury

Folkestone

Dover

Deal

Margate

South Foreland Lighthouse

The White Cliffs of Dover

Places in neighbouring counties

▲ Buildings and/or gardens

● Entry points to coast and countryside

National Trust land

London, page 186

Berkshire, Hampshire and the Isle of Wight, page 125

The Cotswolds, Buckinghamshire and Oxfordshire, page 99

10 miles

Alfriston Clergy House

The Tye, Alfriston, Polegate,
East Sussex BN26 5TL

🏠❄ 1896

Alfriston Clergy House, East Sussex: first Trust house

This rare 14th-century Wealden 'hall-house'
was the first building to be acquired by the
National Trust, in 1896. The thatched,
timber-framed house is in an idyllic setting,
with views across the River Cuckmere, and is
surrounded by a tranquil cottage garden full of
wildlife. **Note**: nearest toilet in village car park.

Eat, shop, stay: shop selling souvenirs.

Things to see and do: **Indoors** Children's
quizzes and trails. Varied events all year.
Outdoors Short circular walks and
longer hikes over the South Downs.
Dogs: assistance dogs only.

Access: 🅿️📷📷📷📷 Building 📷📷
Grounds 📷📷
Parking: 500 yards in village car parks
(not National Trust).

Find out more: 01323 871961 or
alfriston@nationaltrust.org.uk

Alfriston Clergy House		M	T	W	T	F	S	S
4 Mar–29 Oct	10:30–5	M	T	W	·	·	S	S
4 Nov–17 Dec	11–4	·	·	·	·	·	S	S
Open Good Friday.								

Bateman's

Bateman's Lane, Burwash,
East Sussex TN19 7DS

🏠🖼❄📷📷 1940

Rudyard Kipling loved this place; it was his
personal paradise, and somewhere he could
enjoy family life. Surrounded by the wooded
landscape of the Sussex Weald, this
17th-century house, with mullion windows,
pretty secluded garden and acres of countryside,
provided a tranquil sanctuary. The atmospheric
oak-beamed rooms remain much as he
left them. Outside, winding paths take in
manicured lawns, a wildflower meadow and
Kipling's 1928 Rolls-Royce Phantom 1, while
beside the river sits a 17th-century watermill.

Eat, shop, stay: shop selling Kipling souvenirs,
flour and plants from the garden. New Scullery
bookshop. Tea-room offering seasonal lunches
(made using fresh produce from the kitchen
garden), homemade cakes and light bites.

**Rudyard Kipling's desk at Bateman's in East Sussex:
this 17th-century house was Kipling's personal paradise**

Things to see and do: **Indoors** Children's house guide. **Outdoors** Re-enactment weekends, garden and countryside walks. Family fun days. Children's Tracker Packs, quizzes, trails and storytelling. Scotney Castle and Bodiam Castle nearby. **Dogs**: welcome in the gardens on a short lead.

Access: ⚌⚌⚌⚌⚌⚌⚌⚌⚌⚌⚌
Building ⚌⚌⚌ **Grounds** ⚌⚌⚌
Parking: 30 yards.

Find out more: 01435 882302 or batemans@nationaltrust.org.uk

Bateman's		M	T	W	T	F	S	S
House								
1 Jan–24 Feb	11–3	M	T	W	T	F	S	S
25 Feb–29 Oct	11–5*	M	T	W	T	F	S	S
30 Oct–31 Dec	11–3	M	T	W	T	F	S	S
Garden, shop and tea-room								
Open all year	10–5*	M	T	W	T	F	S	S

*Closes at dusk if earlier. Closed 24 and 25 December.

Turning the well handle at Bateman's, below. The house, bottom, sits surrounded by Sussex Weald woods

Birling Gap and the Seven Sisters

near Eastbourne, East Sussex

⚌⚌⚌⚌ 1931

Fun at Birling Gap and the Seven Sisters, East Sussex

For drama, nothing beats the point where the sheer chalk cliffs of the South Downs meet the sea. One of the south coast's longest undeveloped stretches, the Seven Sisters are truly iconic. If you venture down the steps onto the beach, you can discover fascinating rock pools and the intricate wave-cut platform. The visitor centre, with its café and shop, is a delightful place to start or end your peaceful downland walk. Before you explore the rare chalk heath and grassland, why not pick up a Tracker Pack or get some friendly advice from a volunteer in the visitor centre?

Eat, shop, stay: licensed clifftop café serving hot and cold drinks, bottled beer and wine, light lunches, cream teas and cakes. Drinks and sandwiches available to take away. Seaside shop selling gifts and seasonal items. Picnic area outside shop.

Things to see and do: **Indoors** Visitor centre. **Outdoors** Rock-pooling, countryside walks and

With the iconic and dramatic cliffs of the Seven Sisters in the background, a family enjoys exploring the beach

star-gazing. Crowlink downland, on top of the Seven Sisters, Alfriston Clergy House and Monk's House nearby. Events and activities for all ages. **Dogs**: welcome, on leads in café, shop, visitor centre and beach or near livestock.

Access: 🅿️ ♿ 🚻 🗺️ 📷 🚌
Café ♿ Shop ♿ Beach ♿
Sat Nav: use BN20 0AB. **Parking**: at Birling Gap.

Find out more: 01323 423197 or birlinggap@nationaltrust.org.uk

Birling Gap and the Seven Sisters		
Café and shop		
Open every day all year*	10–5**	

*Closed 24 and 25 December. **Closes at 4, November to Easter.

Black Down

Haslemere, Surrey

🏞️ 1944

Highest point on the South Downs with breathtaking views. The heathland and woodland offer a true sense of the wild. **Note**: sorry no toilet. For Sat Nav use GU27 3AF.

Find out more: 01428 652359 or blackdown@nationaltrust.org.uk

The strong stone walls of Bodiam Castle in East Sussex, have stood sentinel for more than 700 years

Bodiam Castle

Bodiam, near Robertsbridge,
East Sussex TN32 5UA

[icons] 1926

A brooding symbol of power for over 700 years, the strong stone walls of Bodiam Castle rise up proudly from the peaceful river valley setting. A wide moat encircles the seemingly untouched medieval exterior. Once inside, spiral stairways, tower rooms and battlements with dizzying viewpoints are ripe for exploration. The ruins of the inner rooms are brought to life through stories told by a range of medieval characters. **Note**: popular with schools. Toilets in car park only.

Eat, shop, stay: shop selling gifts, castle-themed products and local produce. Tea-room serving homemade lunches, teas, snacks and ice-cream. Seasonal coffee shop overlooking the castle.

Things to see and do: medieval character talks, trails and guided walks. Events, including Easter Egg hunt and various family activities throughout the year. **Dogs**: welcome on leads in grounds only.

Access: [icons]
Castle [icons] Grounds [icons]
Parking: 400 yards.

Find out more: 01580 830196 or
bodiamcastle@nationaltrust.org.uk

Bodiam Castle	
Open every day all year	10–5*

*Castle opens 10:30. Closes dusk if earlier.
Closed 24 and 25 December.

Bookham Commons

Church Road, Great Bookham, Surrey KT23 3LT

1923

Varied landscape, from ancient oak woods to grassland plains and tranquil ponds. Bird hide and natural play area. **Note**: no toilets.

Find out more: 01306 887485 or bookhamcommons@nationaltrust.org.uk

Box Hill

Tadworth, Surrey

1914

A great place for family adventures: exploring the woods, braving the natural play trail, finding the tower or paddling in the River Mole at the stepping stones. On a clear day you can see for miles from the top of Box Hill, so if you're hiking up, the view is well worth it.

You can pick up free walks guides from the shepherd's hut and outside the café, or find your own way along our many footpaths.

Eat, shop, stay: the Box Hill café has indoor and outdoor seating and serves light lunches, snacks and afternoon teas. Servery offers takeaway hot drinks, cakes, sandwiches and the famous 'revival' flapjack!

Things to see and do: school holiday activities and walks guides available. You can borrow a children's Tracker Pack from the shepherd's hut to explore the wild and make the most of the outdoors. **Dogs**: under close control where livestock is grazing. Assistance dogs only in café.

Access: 🅿️♿ 🚾 ♿ 📷 ♨️
Café and Discovery Zone ♿ Grounds ➡️
Sat Nav: use KT20 7LB. **Parking**: off the Box Hill Zig Zag road (short walk to café and viewpoint).

Find out more: 01306 888793.
01306 878554 (learning and events) or boxhill@nationaltrust.org.uk

Box Hill		M	T	W	T	F	S	S
Café, servery, shop and Discovery Zone*								
1 Jan–13 Apr	10–4*	M	T	W	T	F	S	S
14 Apr–29 Oct	9–5*	M	T	W	T	F	S	S
30 Oct–31 Dec**	10–4*	M	T	W	T	F	S	S

*May close early in bad weather. **Closed 25 December.

With a natural play trail, tower, woods and river, Box Hill in Surrey is a great place for a family adventure

Chartwell

Mapleton Road, Westerham, Kent TN16 1PS

[icons] 1946

Sir Winston Churchill's much-loved home, Chartwell in Kent remains much as it was when he lived here

Chartwell was a home and a place that truly inspired Sir Winston Churchill. The house has been open to visitors for more than 50 years and is still much as it was when the family lived here, with pictures, books and personal mementoes. The studio contains a large collection of Churchill's paintings and offers an insight into Churchill the painter, while the garden reflects Churchill's love of the landscape and nature, including the lakes he created. The woodland estate offers family walks, trails, den-building, a Canadian camp and opportunities to stretch your legs. You may come across our resident cat, Jock, making his daily inspection of the grounds. **Note**: house entrance by timed ticket (booking available on the Chartwell website).

Eat, shop, stay: café serving food inspired by Churchill's family cook – salads, light bites, cream teas, cakes and delicious deserts. Shop stocking Churchill memorabilia, books, garden ornaments, plants and local produce, as well as a special range of Jock the Cat items.

Things to see and do: **Indoors** Daily talks in the studio about Sir Winston's love of painting. New exhibition in winter displaying never-seen-before items. **Outdoors** Family adventure trails around the garden and estate throughout the season. Guided tours of Churchill's family garden on selected days (March to October). The woodland trail offers great views of the house and connects with the hilly 5-mile circular Weardale Walk to Emmetts Garden. Why not pick up some takeaway food from the Landemare Café and enjoy a picnic on the lower lawns by the lakes? **Dogs**: welcome on short leads in the garden and estate (except for the kitchen garden).

Access: [icons]
Building [icons] Grounds [icons]
Parking: on site.

Find out more: 01732 868381 or chartwell@nationaltrust.org.uk

Chartwell		M	T	W	T	F	S	S
House*								
25 Feb–29 Oct	11–5	M	T	W	T	F	S	S
2 Dec–17 Dec	11–3	.	.	.	.	.	S	S
Garden, exhibition, studio, shop and café								
Open all year	10–5**	M	T	W	T	F	S	S

*Entry to house by timed ticket (places limited) available from the visitor welcome centre. Last entry 45 minutes before closing. **Studio opens daily, times vary, closed in January, tours only in February. Exhibition closes for short periods to change display. Closes dusk if earlier. Whole site closed 24 and 25 December.

Statue of Clementine and Winston Churchill at Chartwell, below. The glorious setting of the house becomes apparent when seen from afar, right

Places may occasionally close for events or bad weather

Clandon Park

West Clandon, Guildford, Surrey GU4 7RQ

Until a major fire in 2015, Clandon Park was one of the country's most complete Palladian mansions. The house is currently being restored. For up-to-date information on our progress and for details on opening arrangements, please contact the property.

Find out more: 01483 222482 or clandonpark@nationaltrust.org.uk

Claremont Landscape Garden

Portsmouth Road, Esher, Surrey KT10 9JG

[❋] [1949]

Hidden in the heart of Surrey, this green oasis has always been a place to escape everyday life and enjoy simple pleasures with family and friends. For centuries the garden was a sanctuary for some of the wealthiest, most influential people in the country, however now everyone can enjoy it. The impressive turf amphitheatre offers wonderful views over the lake. Walks take in interesting features like the grotto and camellia terrace. As a child, Queen Victoria loved relaxing here, and the tradition of play continues today with nine-pin bowling, two play areas and a cottage full of toys and games. **Note**: limited parking during busy times. Please park considerately to maximise spaces available.

Eat, shop, stay: café (licensed) serving lunches and freshly baked homemade cakes, biscuits and scones. Outside terraced seating area overlooking lake. Café is outside the pay barrier and close to the car park at the main entrance. Shop area within café. Free wi-fi.

Things to see and do: events throughout the year, including children's trails, crafts and activities during school holidays. Guided walks. Belvedere Tower open on selected dates (April to October). **Dogs**: welcome on short leads between 1 October and 30 April only.

Access: [icons] Grounds [icons]
Sat Nav: unreliable, instead follow brown signs from Cobham and Esher. **Parking**: main car park at entrance. Space limited at busy times – use car park in West End Lane opposite.

Find out more: 01372 467806 or claremont@nationaltrust.org.uk

Claremont Landscape Garden		M	T	W	T	F	S	S
1 Jan–31 Jan	10–5*	M	T	W	T	F	S	S
1 Feb–31 Mar	10–5	M	T	W	T	F	S	S
1 Apr–31 Oct	10–6	M	T	W	T	F	S	S
1 Nov–31 Dec	10–5*	M	T	W	T	F	S	S

Café and shop close 30 minutes earlier than garden.
*Closes dusk if earlier (local closing times posted at property).
Closed 24 and 25 December.

The green oasis of exceptional Claremont Landscape Garden lies hidden away in the heart of Surrey

Cobham Wood and Mausoleum

near Cobham, Kent

 2014

Sitting proud in historic woodland pasture, the 18th-century Darnley Mausoleum commands stunning views across the North Kent downs. **Note**: for Sat Nav use DA12 3BS. Mausoleum and South Lodge Barn normally open first Sunday of month, April to September, and selected other dates. Mausoleum open 12:30 to 4:30; South Lodge Barn 12 to 5.

Find out more: 01732 810378 or cobham@nationaltrust.org.uk

Denbies Hillside

near Dorking, Surrey

 1963

Panoramic views from Denbies Hillside in Surrey

Denbies Hillside is a dramatic chalk escarpment with panoramic views of the Surrey countryside. It's a great place to walk, picnic and watch wildlife – you may even spot chalk downland species such as the Adonis blue and Chalkhill blue butterflies.

Eat, shop, stay: picnic area with benches in Steers Field.

Things to see and do: self-guided trail and spectacular views. Walk west along the North Downs Way to discover several Second World War pillboxes. Why not also visit nearby Hackhurst Downs? **Dogs**: welcome – please keep on leads when livestock are grazing.

Access: ♿ 🅿
Sat Nav: use RH5 6SR. **Parking**: at Ranmore West car park and Denbies Hillside.

Find out more: 01306 887485 or denbieshillside@nationaltrust.org.uk

Devil's Dyke

near Brighton, West Sussex

🍴 🏛 ♿ 1995

At nearly a mile long, the Dyke Valley is the longest, deepest and widest 'dry valley' in the UK. Legend has it that the Devil dug this chasm to drown the parishioners of the Weald. On the other hand, scientists believe it was formed naturally just over 10,000 years ago in the last ice age. The walls of the Iron Age hill fort can be seen when you walk around the hill, and there is a carpet of flowers and a myriad of colourful insects to discover in the valley.

Devil's Dyke in West Sussex is the longest, deepest and widest 'dry valley' in the UK

Ditchling Beacon

near Ditchling, Westmeston, East Sussex

🏛 ⛵ 1953

Just 7 miles north of Brighton, at 248 metres above sea level, Ditchling Beacon is the highest point in East Sussex and offers panoramic views all around the summit. To the south visitors can see the sea, while to the north you look across the Weald or east–west across the Downs. The site also has the remains of an Iron Age hill fort. Situated on the South Downs Way, it makes an excellent place to start a walk heading west towards Devil's Dyke or east towards Black Cap and Lewes.

The many bridleways at Devil's Dyke offer excellent cycling, top. There are treats in store for walkers too, with numerous far-reaching views to enjoy, above

Eat, shop, stay: Devil's Dyke pub (not National Trust) beside car park.

Things to see and do: self-guided walks leaflet, orienteering course map and family Discovery Packs available from information trailer (open April to September, weekends and some weekdays). Numerous bridleways offer great cycling.

Access: 🅿 🅳 ♿ 🚶 👪 ➡
Sat Nav: use BN1 8YJ. **Parking**: on site.

Find out more: 01273 857712 or devilsdyke@nationaltrust.org.uk

Eat, shop, stay: refreshments available from ice-cream van. Picnics welcome.

Things to see and do: great for bracing walks with amazing views on the South Downs. Traces of the rampart and ditch of the hill fort to discover. Why not visit nearby Ditchling Down? **Dogs**: welcome but must be kept on leads at all times.

Access: ♿ ♿
Sat Nav: use BN6 8XG.
Parking: off Ditchling Road.

Find out more: 01323 423197 or ditchlingbeacon@nationaltrust.org.uk

Ditchling Beacon is the highest point in East Sussex, offering southern views of the sea and northern views towards the Weald, or east–west across the Downs

East Head

near Chichester, West Sussex

🏖 ⚓ 1966

One of the last surviving areas of natural coastline in West Sussex, with unspoilt sand dunes and fabulous views.
Note: for Sat Nav use PO20 8AJ.

Find out more: 01243 814730 or easthead@nationaltrust.org.uk

Emmetts Garden

Ide Hill, Sevenoaks, Kent TN14 6BA

❀ ⚓ 1965

Emmetts is a garden to enjoy with friends and family. If you delve a little deeper, there are exotic plants collected from around the world and a host of stories to be discovered. Emmetts is known for its beautiful bluebells and amazing spring colour, summer brings the romantic rose garden, followed by vibrant autumn foliage – there is something to see all year round. It is a place where you can let off steam, play games, picnic in our meadow or simply sit back and relax. Far-reaching views across the Weald of Kent can be enjoyed from our countryside walks.

Whatever the season, there is something to delight visitors to Emmetts Garden in Kent

Eat, shop, stay: the Old Stables serving cakes, bakes and light refreshments. Shop selling a variety of gifts, including children's toys, sweets, jams and souvenirs. Venture outside to the plant area for an array of garden gifts.

Things to see and do: **Indoors** Children's activities in the Discovery Cabin. **Outdoors** Children's trails (school holidays and December) and activities in wild play area. Garden tours (selected days). Walk guides available for surrounding countryside. **Dogs**: welcome on short leads in gardens and in the wider countryside.

Access: 🅿️🏡🚾🏛️🅱️🔍 **Grounds** ♿➡️♿
Parking: 100 yards.

Find out more: 01732 751507 or emmetts@nationaltrust.org.uk

Emmetts Garden		M	T	W	T	F	S	S
25 Feb–31 Dec	10–5*	**M**	**T**	**W**	**T**	**F**	**S**	**S**

*Last entry 45 minutes before closing. Closes dusk if earlier. All winter opening weather permitting. Closed 24 and 25 December.

In August the Rock Garden at Emmetts Garden is ablaze with tiny blooms

Frensham Little Pond

Priory Lane, Frensham, Surrey GU10 3BT

🏞️ 1974

Frensham Little Pond, Surrey, dates from the 11th century

Originally created in the 11th century to supply the Bishop of Winchester with fish, the pond and surrounding area is now a sanctuary for wildlife. The heathland is a colourful mosaic of purple heathers, fragrant bright-yellow gorse and rich green bracken with many footpaths to explore. **Note**: toilet available only when café open.

Eat, shop, stay: Tern Café serving snacks, homemade sandwiches and cakes (outside seating only). Picnics welcome.

Things to see and do: bird hide and telescope next to café. **Dogs**: welcome, but on leads around café and during bird-nesting season (March to September) please.

Access: ♿
Parking: at Priory Lane corner, Frensham and Grange Road.

Find out more: 01428 681050 (Rangers) or frenshamlittlepond@nationaltrust.org.uk

Frensham Little Pond		M	T	W	T	F	S	S
Café*								
1 Jan–31 Mar	10–3*	**M**	**T**	**W**	**T**	**F**	**S**	**S**
1 Apr–31 Oct	10–5*	**M**	**T**	**W**	**T**	**F**	**S**	**S**
1 Nov–31 Dec**	10–3*	**M**	**T**	**W**	**T**	**F**	**S**	**S**

*May close in bad weather. **Closed 24 and 25 December.

Why not share your pictures with us? #nationaltrust

Harting Down

Harting Down, near South Harting,
West Sussex GU31 5PN

 1994

A tapestry of downland with scattered scrub and woodland, rich in wildlife and steeped in history. **Note**: nearest toilets at South Harting or Uppark. Sat Nav unreliable.

Find out more: 01730 816638 or
hartingdown@nationaltrust.org.uk

Hatchlands Park

East Clandon, Guildford, Surrey GU4 7RT

 1945

With open fields, ancient woodland and wildflower meadows, the parkland is perfect for relaxation and exploration. Our natural adventure area, with its tree house, balance beams, willow tunnels and bug hotel, is a great place for families to get even closer to nature. Nestled in the parkland is a Georgian country house, home to tenant Alec Cobbe and his superb collection of Old Master paintings and the Cobbe Collection, Europe's largest array

of keyboard instruments – including some which inspired such world-famous composers as J. C. Bach, Elgar and Chopin. **Note**: only six ground-floor rooms are open to the public.

Eat, shop, stay: café in the original kitchen. Gift shop. Picnic areas.

Things to see and do: **Indoors** Guided mansion tours most Thursdays. Cellar tours (selected days). Cobbe Collection concerts. **Outdoors** Children's adventure area, Sylvanian Families trail, open-air theatre. Courtyard garden. **Dogs**: welcome under close control in designated areas.

Access: 🅿️🚌♿🚽🍴🎦🎨📷👜📖
Building 🔥🔥♿ Grounds 🔥➡️🐕
Sat Nav: misleading, instead follow brown signs to main entrance on A246 (grid reference TQ06349 51580).
Parking: 300 yards.

Find out more: 01483 222482 or
hatchlands@nationaltrust.org.uk

Hatchlands Park		M	T	W	T	F	S	S
House and garden*								
2 Apr–29 Oct	2–5†	·	T	W	T	·	·	S
Shop, café and park walks								
Open all year**	10–5††	M	T	W	T	F	S	S

*Also Bank Holiday Mondays and Fridays in August.
**Closed 24 and 25 December. †Garden open 10 to 5 on house open days. ††Closes dusk if earlier.

The wildflower meadows, ancient woodland, parkland and adventure area make Hatchlands Park, Surrey, the perfect destination for a family day out

Hindhead Commons and the Devil's Punch Bowl

near Hindhead, Surrey

 1906

Spectacular views from Hindhead Commons and uninterrupted walks to the Devil's Punch Bowl make this an unforgettable place to relax and take in some of the best countryside in the South East. Since the opening of the A3 tunnel, paths, cycle routes and bridleways have been reconnected and natural contours restored. Peace and calm now reign and the glorious landscape, with its carpets of purple heather in the summer and grazing Highland cattle, is there to enjoy.

Eat, shop, stay: café with indoor and outdoor seating, serving drinks, hot food, sandwiches and cakes.

Things to see and do: walks leaflets available from the café and shepherd's hut. Borrow a children's Tracker Pack at weekends to explore the wild and make the most of your visit. **Dogs**: under close control during bird-nesting season (March to October). Assistance dogs only in café.

Access: 🅿️ 🚻 ♿ 🔉 🚶

Café and shop ♿ Grounds ➡️

Sat Nav: use GU26 6AB.

Parking: off the London Road.

Find out more: 01428 681050 (Rangers). 01428 608771 (café) or hindhead@nationaltrust.org.uk

Hindhead Commons		M	T	W	T	F	S	S
Café								
Open all year**	9–4*	M	T	W	T	F	S	S

*Extended café opening during fine weather and school holidays. **Closed 25 December.

. **Hindhead Commons and the Devil's Punch Bowl, Surrey: the perfect spot for relaxation or uninterrupted walking, cycling and riding**

The Homewood

Portsmouth Road, Esher, Surrey KT10 9JL

🏠 ✤ 1999

Patrick Gwynne's extraordinary early 20th-century family home is a masterpiece of Modernist design in the midst of a picturesque garden. **Note**: administered on behalf of the National Trust by a tenant. **Access is via minibus from Claremont Landscape Garden only**. Sorry no toilet. Additional charge for minibus and guided tour (including members). Open alternate Fridays and Saturdays (see website for details), 1 April to 29 October. 45-minute guided tours at 10:30, 11:30, 12:30, 2 and 3 (entry by booked tours only).

Find out more: 01372 476424 or thehomewood@nationaltrust.org.uk c/o Claremont Landscape Garden, Portsmouth Road, Esher, Surrey KT10 9JG

Ightham Mote

Mote Road, Ivy Hatch, Sevenoaks, Kent TN15 0NT

🏠 ✤ 🛏 🍴 1985

Hidden away in a secluded Kent valley is this perfectly preserved medieval moated manor house. Created in the natural landscape almost 700 years ago, Ightham Mote is built from Kentish ragstone and great Wealden oaks. While its architecture and decoration trace the development of the English country house, its owners provide the stories of a once-cherished family home, evoking a deep sense of history. In the tranquil gardens there are streams and lakes fed by natural springs, an orchard, flower borders and a cutting garden. The wider estate offers walks with secret glades and countryside views. **Note**: very steep slope from visitor reception – passenger buggy or lower drop-off available.

The perfectly preserved medieval moated manor house at Ightham Mote in Kent, above right, sits within tranquil gardens and is surrounded by its wider estate

Eat, shop, stay: Mote café (licensed) serving hot lunches, sandwiches, cream teas, cakes and hot and cold drinks. Seating indoors and outside. Picnic facilities available. Shop selling gifts, local produce and plants.

Things to see and do: **Indoors** Year-round events, including introductory talks and tower tours, housekeeping events and family craft days. **Outdoors** Countryside walks and family fun days. Children's natural play area and den. **Dogs**: welcome on café patio and unticketed areas; assistance dogs only in ticketed areas.

Access: 🅿️🔖🏠🐕🔊📷🚐📽️🎫🚗♿🅰️
Building 🔥🅱️♿🍴♿ Grounds ♿➡️
Parking: 200 yards.

Find out more: 01732 810378 or ighthammote@nationaltrust.org.uk

Ightham Mote		M	T	W	T	F	S	S
House								
4 Mar–29 Oct	11–5	M	T	W	T	F	S	S
30 Oct–31 Dec	11–3	M	T	W	T	F	S	S
Garden, café, exhibition and shop								
Open all year*	10–5	M	T	W	T	F	S	S

Closed 24 and 25 December. *Closes dusk if earlier.
Partial access to house and grounds in winter.

Knole

Sevenoaks, Kent TN15 0RP

🏠 ❄ 🎫 1946

Knole is a house full of hidden treasures. Built as an archbishop's palace and nestled in a medieval deer-park, the house passed through royal hands and into those of the Sackville family, who still live here 400 years on. A major conservation project is taking place at Knole, with the support of the Heritage Lottery Fund. This exciting project brings changes to the visitor experience and facilities all year. In 2017, some of our recently restored show rooms will reopen to visitors, while several others will be closed as we continue with specialist restoration work. For the first time, visitors can climb to the top of the newly restored Gatehouse Tower with incredible views across the parkland and rooftops. **Note**: some rooms are closed for restoration work.

Eat, shop, stay: Brewhouse Café, boasting rooftop terrace outdoor seating area, serving delicious hot and cold food. Grab & Go kiosk for park walkers. Gift shop and plant sales in Brewhouse Courtyard. Specialist bookshop in Green Court. Enclosed picnic area in park.

Things to see and do: **Indoors** After a year of conservation work, discover the delights of our reopened historic show rooms. See items being repaired and conserved in the newly opened Knole Conservation Studio.

Climb to the top of the Gatehouse Tower for stunning views across the park, and explore the private rooms of Eddy Sackville-West. Enjoy year-round events revealing ongoing restoration work and Knole's unique stories. **Outdoors** Ancient parkland to explore, home to a wild deer herd. Guided park walks every Saturday and Sunday at 2. Outdoor family trails available. Special entry to Lord Sackville's private garden (Tuesdays, 4 April to 26 September). **Dogs**: welcome in parkland and courtyards on leads.

Access: 🅿♿ 🚪♿ 🚻♿ 🔔 ♿ 🦮 📷 🎥 📺 🧸 📷
Show rooms ♿ 🚻 **Gatehouse Tower** ♿ 🚻
Park/garden ♿ 🏔 ➡ ♿ 🦽
Sat Nav: use TN13 1HU and follow brown signs to Sevenoaks High Street (concealed entrance opposite St Nicholas church). **Parking**: 60 yards. Additional parking in town centre.

Find out more: 01732 462100 or knole@nationaltrust.org.uk

Knole		M	T	W	T	F	S	S
Show rooms								
4 Mar–5 Nov*	12–4			T	W	T	F	S	S
Tower, Conservation Studio, café, shop, parkland**								
Open all year	10–5†	M	T	W	T	F	S	S

*Entry by guided tours, 11 to 12; free-flow from 12. Open Bank Holidays, except 26, 27 December and 2 January 2018. **Includes courtyards (visitor centre and bookshop): open 10 to 5. †November to February: closes 4. Private garden: open Tuesdays, 4 April to 26 September, 11 to 4. Property closed 24 to 25 December.

Every year, more of the vast complex palace of Knole in Kent, below, is opened for visitors to discover its hidden treasures. Meanwhile conservation work to protect these precious objects never stops, right

Lamb House

West Street, Rye, East Sussex TN31 7ES

 1950

Georgian home of writers Henry James and E. F. Benson, who depicted the property in the *Mapp and Lucia* stories. **Note**: maintained on the National Trust's behalf by a tenant. Sorry no toilet. Open Tuesday, Friday and Saturday, 18 March to 28 October, 11 to 5.

Find out more: 01580 762334 or lambhouse@nationaltrust.org.uk

Leith Hill Place

Leith Hill Lane, near Coldharbour, Dorking, Surrey RH5 6LY

 1945

Childhood home of English composer Ralph Vaughan Williams, once owned by the Wedgwood family and regularly visited by Charles Darwin. Opened to the public in 2013 for the first time in 40 years, it is a work in progress with an unusually informal atmosphere. Glorious views

Opened to the public in 2013 the first time in 40 years, Leith Hill Place in Surrey is a work in progress

over the South Downs. **Note**: parking access across sloping field (often muddy). Cash or cheques only – no credit-card facilities.

Eat, shop, stay: no café, but volunteer bakers provide freshly made cakes and cream teas by donation. Original AGA, stone-flagged dining-room and outside seating on the terrace or the courtyard garden. Camping at nearby Etherley Farm or group stay at Henman Bunkhouse.

Things to see and do: free soundscape tour (timed tickets). Play the piano, listen to music (often live). Children's trails and activities. Summer concerts. Small museum area in study with Vaughan Williams's piano on display. **Dogs**: welcome on leads in grounds and house, except kitchen, study and soundscape.

Access: ⬚⬚⬚⬚ House ⬚
Courtyard garden/south terrace ⬚⬚
Sat Nav: use RH5 6LU.
Parking: Rhododendron Wood car park, 437 yards, in Tanhurst Lane.

Find out more: 01306 711685 or leithhillplace@nationaltrust.org.uk

Leith Hill Place	M	T	W	T	F	S	S
24 Mar–29 Oct[1]	11–5					**F**	**S**	**S**
8 Dec–10 Dec*	11–3:30					**F**	**S**	**S**

Open Bank Holiday Mondays. [1]Closed Sunday, 30 July, due to RideLondon cycle race; closes at 4, Sunday 29 October. *Christmas event: ground and first floors open.

Leith Hill Tower and Countryside

near Coldharbour village, Dorking, Surrey

⬚⬚⬚ 1923

Built in 1765 by Richard Hull, the top of Leith Hill Tower is the highest point in south-east England and offers panoramic views of London to the north and the coast to the south. On a clear day it is possible to see the sea sparkling through Shoreham Gap. Visitors with a head for heights are invited to climb the staircase inside the tower and look out at the 360-degree panorama through telescopes on the rooftop.

Walking country surrounds the tower, with views of heathland, woodland and farmland landscapes. The historic rhododendron wood was created by Charles Darwin's sister. **Note**: steep spiral stairs to the top of the tower; no toilet or parking at tower.

Eat, shop, stay: hot and cold food and drinks available at Leith Hill Tower (not National Trust), or at Leith Hill Place, when house open. Picnics welcome, but no barbecues please. Self-catering accommodation at Henman Bunkhouse for up to 16 people.

Things to see and do: every season is a riot of colour – spring bluebells at Frank's Wood, early summer colour at the Rhododendron Wood or stunning displays of autumn golds and reds. Walks leaflets available. **Dogs**: on leads on heathland (April to July).

Access: 🐾
Sat Nav: for Rhododendron Wood and Starveall Corner use RH5 6LU; for Windy Gap RH5 6LX; for Landslip RH5 6HG.
Parking: for tower use car parks at foot of hill.

Find out more: 01306 712711 or leithhill@nationaltrust.org.uk

Leith Hill		M	T	W	T	F	S	S
Tower								
Open all year*	10–3**	M	T	W	T	F	S	S

*Closed 25 December **Open 9 to 5, weekends and Bank Holidays (daylight permitting).

Leith Hill Tower and Countryside, Surrey: the view over Leith Hill Place, right, and looking down from the hill, below

Monk's House

Rodmell, Lewes, East Sussex BN7 3HF

🏠 ✿ 📷 1980

The Writing Lodge at Monk's House in East Sussex

This small 17th-century weatherboarded cottage in the village of Rodmell was the country retreat of novelist Virginia Woolf and her husband Leonard and a meeting place for the Bloomsbury Group. The garden features the room where she created her best-known works and includes cottage garden borders, orchard, allotments and ponds. **Note**: no access to Rodmell from A26.

Eat, shop, stay: gift shop offering Woolf and Bloomsbury-related products. Holiday cottage studio in the garden.

Things to see and do: why not try your hand at a game of bowls? One of the favoured pastimes of the Woolfs. **Dogs**: allowed in garden on leads.

Access: 🅿♿📷♿ Building 📷🧍 Grounds 📷
Sat Nav: do not use as wrongly indicates access across railway crossing.
Parking: 100 yards (height restriction barrier).

Find out more: 01273 474760 or monkshouse@nationaltrust.org.uk

Monk's House		M	T	W	T	F	S	S
5 Apr–29 Oct	1–5	·	·	**W**	**T**	**F**	**S**	**S**

Last admission to house 15 minutes before closing. Open Bank Holiday Mondays. Admission to garden 12:30 to 5:30.

Nymans

Handcross, near Haywards Heath, West Sussex RH17 6EB

🏠 ✿ 📷 🛏 🔔 🍵 1954

One of the National Trust's premier gardens, Nymans was a country retreat for the creative Messel family, and has views stretching out across the Weald. Today you can recharge your batteries here, while exploring this beautiful place, discovering hidden corners through stone archways and walking along tree-lined avenues. From vibrantly colourful summer borders, to the tranquillity of ancient woodland, Nymans is a place of experimentation, with evolving planting designs and an unusual plant collection.
The comfortable yet elegant house, a partial ruin, reflects the personalities and stories of the talented Messel family – from the Countess of Rosse to Oliver Messel.

The garden at Nymans in West Sussex, below, is one of the finest in the care of the National Trust. The elegant and comfortable house, right, is partially ruined and has many stories to tell

Eat, shop, stay: large shop, plant and garden centre selling a collection of plants grown at Nymans. Café serving a choice of seasonal food. Grab & Go kiosk open during busy periods. Woodland craft sales. Second-hand bookshop. Holiday cottage in woods.

Things to see and do: **Indoors** Gallery with year-round exhibitions. **Outdoors** Daily guided walks. Contemporary art installation (January to May). Mobility buggy tours. Daily family activities, including trails and natural play. Gardening and creative workshops. **Dogs**: in woodland only, on leads during bird-nesting season (1 March to 31 July).

Access: ♿🅿️🏷️📷🎧🐕📷📱
House 🏠🏠🏠🏠 **Gallery** 🏠 **Garden** 🏠🏠🏠🏠
Parking: on site.

Find out more: 01444 405250 or nymans@nationaltrust.org.uk

Nymans	
Open every day all year	10–5*

Gallery closed for short periods to change exhibitions. *Closes dusk if earlier. 1 November to 28 February: house closed for winter conservation. Closed 24 and 25 December.

Oakhurst Cottage

Hambledon, near Godalming, Surrey GU8 4HF

🏠🏵️ 1952

Timber-framed home offering a rare insight into domestic life in the mid-19th century, with a traditional cottage garden to explore. **Note**: sorry no toilet. Nearest visitor facilities at Winkworth Arboretum (4 miles approximately). Open 1 April to 30 September, 2 to 5, and 1 to 29 October, 2 to 4, Wednesday, Thursday and weekends. Admission by booked guided tour only. Please call Winkworth Arboretum, 01483 208936, for tour times and to book.

Find out more: 01483 208936 or oakhurstcottage@nationaltrust.org.uk

Old Soar Manor

Plaxtol, Borough Green, Kent TN15 0QX

🏠 1947

Dating from 1290, the remaining rooms of this knight's house offer a glimpse back to the time of Edward I. **Note**: sorry no toilet or tea-room. Narrow lanes, limited off-road parking. Open Monday to Thursday and weekends, 1 April to 30 September, 10 to 6.

Find out more: 01732 810378 or oldsoarmanor@nationaltrust.org.uk

Owletts

The Street, Cobham, Gravesend,
Kent DA12 3AP

🏠 ❄ 1938

An architect's 17th-century family home with
a varied history and architectural features,
set within a relaxing, traditional garden.
Note: parking available. Open Sunday,
2 April to 24 September, 11 to 5.

Find out more: 01732 810378 or
owletts@nationaltrust.org.uk

Petworth House
and Park

Petworth, West Sussex GU28 0AE

🏠 ⛲ ⊤ 1947

Shaped by a family of collectors over the past
800 years, this 17th-century mansion inspired
countless artists, including England's greatest
landscape painter, J. M. W. Turner. The finest
collection of art and sculpture in the care of
the National Trust, including world-famous
paintings by Van Dyck, Reynolds, Blake and
Turner, is displayed in the opulent state rooms
and North Gallery. In contrast the atmospheric
servants' quarters evoke the hustle and bustle
of life 'below stairs'. Outdoors is a woodland
Pleasure Ground and acres of 'Capability'
Brown landscape deer-park with glorious
views of the South Downs National Park.
Note: additional charge may apply for some
events, including Winter Art Exhibition.

Eat, shop, stay: Servants' Hall coffee shop
serving barista-style coffee and tempting
treats. Audit Room café serving light lunches,
afternoon teas and homemade cakes. Gift
shops selling books, products inspired by
the collection and locally sourced souvenirs.

Set within its 'Capability' Brown deer-park, glorious
Petworth House and Park, West Sussex, glows in the
setting sun, right. The magnificent staircase, opposite

Things to see and do: **Indoors** Free daily
introductory talks, specialist talks and
behind-the-scenes tours (Tuesday and Thursday).
Exhibitions throughout the year. Family activities.
Outdoors 283 hectares (700 acres) of deer-park
to explore. Downloadable walks and interactive
Park Explorer guide for smart phones or tablets.
Dogs: under close control in Petworth Park.
Assistance dogs only in Pleasure Ground.

Access: 🅿️🅳♿♿🅻♿🎨🖥🅰️••🅰
Building 🅻🅰🅱
Sat Nav: use GU28 9LR. **Parking**: on A283,
700 yards. Separate car park for Petworth Park.

Find out more: 01798 342207 or
petworth@nationaltrust.org.uk

Petworth House and Park		M	T	W	T	F	S	S
House								
18 Mar–5 Nov	11–5	M	T	W	T	F	S	S
6 Nov–31 Dec	11–3	M	T	W	T	F	S	S
Pleasure Ground, shop and café								
Open all year	10–5†	M	T	W	T	F	S	S

House: 6 November to 1 December, open by guided tours
only; 2 to 31 December, decorated for Christmas.
†Closes dusk if earlier. Closed 24 and 25 December.

Kent, Surrey and Sussex

Polesden Lacey

Great Bookham, near Dorking, Surrey RH5 6BD

🏠 ❄ 🎗 ⚓ 🍽 1942

Polesden Lacey was the lavish country retreat of Mrs Greville, a voracious socialite who rubbed shoulders with the best in Edwardian high society and who liked to collect kings in her social set. The house is open daily this year with new exhibits exploring Mrs Greville's royal connections, her jet-set lifestyle and the lives of the servants who ran Polesden Lacey like clockwork. You can explore an opulent collection of Fabergé, maiolica and fine art, including a world-renowned collection of Dutch Old Master paintings. The gardens blend Edwardian splendour with the majestic beauty of the ancient woodlands on the wider 566-hectare (1,400-acre) estate. The rose garden, herbaceous borders and the long walk offer more opportunities for gentle exploration. **Note**: an additional charge may apply to certain events, including holiday trails (including members).

Eat, shop, stay: the Granary Café and Cowshed Coffee Shop offer home cooking, snacks, coffee and ice-cream. Pop-up outlets available in warmer weather. Home and giftware, souvenirs and plants available to buy, all located outside the pay perimeter. Second-hand bookshop in the grounds.

Things to see and do: **Indoors** House tours explore fascinating pieces in the collection, such as the Greville tiara, stories about Edwardian society and conservation work. Pianists play in the gold room on weekends and throughout the summer, and the halls are decked in glorious festive style for our annual Christmas event. **Outdoors** Set in an Area of Outstanding Natural Beauty, the estate offers some of the most idyllic picnic spots in Surrey. Explore Ranmore Common, a Site of Special Scientific Interest, on waymarked walks across our huge estate. Free garden tours from March until November. **Dogs**: on short leads in designated areas, under control on landscape walks, estate and farmland.

Access: 🅿 ♿ 🚻 🧸 📷 🔦 📱 💺 House 🔼 🏠 ♿ Grounds 🏠 ➡ 🐾 ♿
Sat Nav: use KT23 4PZ. **Parking**: 200 yards.

Find out more: 01372 452048 or polesdenlacey@nationaltrust.org.uk

Polesden Lacey		M	T	W	T	F	S	S
1 Jan–29 Oct	10–5*	M	T	W	T	F	S	S
30 Oct–31 Dec	10–4*	M	T	W	T	F	S	S

*House opens 11; weekday access by guided tour, 11 to 12:30, then free-flow. Admission by timed tickets at certain times. Last entry one hour before closing. Closed 24 and 25 December.

Polesden Lacey in Surrey, this page and opposite. With opulent collections, splendid gardens and ancient woodland, there is something to delight visitors of all ages

Quebec House

Quebec Square, Westerham, Kent TN16 1TD

 1918

The childhood home of General James Wolfe, Quebec House (above) retains much of its original charm and family feel. Interactive collections and objects belonging to Wolfe are used to explore Georgian family life and Wolfe's most celebrated victory at the Battle of Quebec in 1759.

Eat, shop, stay: second-hand books, souvenirs and guidebooks for sale in the Coach House, as well as hot and cold drinks and a selection of cakes.

Things to see and do: house guided tours at 12 and 12:30 (book on arrival). On Sundays we re-create Mrs Wolfe's recipes in the Georgian kitchen. Exhibition in the coach house on Wolfe's Canadian campaign. **Dogs**: welcome on short leads in the gardens.

Access:
Building Grounds
Parking: 80 yards in main town car park on A25 (not National Trust).

Find out more: 01732 868381 or quebechouse@nationaltrust.org.uk

Quebec House		M	T	W	T	F	S	S
House, garden and exhibition								
25 Feb–29 Oct	11–5*			W	T	F	S	S
4 Nov–17 Dec	1–4						S	S

*House opens at 12 (access by tour only, 12 to 1).
Open Bank Holiday Mondays. Closes dusk if earlier.

Reigate Hill and Gatton Park

near Reigate, Surrey

1912

Reigate Hill commands sweeping views across the Weald to the South Downs. It's a great spot for walking, family picnics and wildlife-watching. A short walk away is the 19th-century Reigate Fort. The complex is open every day and the fort buildings open for special events. To the east of Reigate Hill is Gatton Park, designed by Lancelot 'Capability' Brown. **Note**: areas of Gatton Park opened monthly by the Gatton Trust.

Eat, shop, stay: picnics welcome.
Tea kiosk (not National Trust) at Wray Lane.

Things to see and do: walks detailed on
noticeboards and downloadable from website.
Chalk downland species, such as the Adonis blue
butterfly, to spot, as well as mysterious military
structures on Reigate Hill. **Dogs**: welcome,
on leads when livestock grazing.

Access: 🅰️ ♿
Sat Nav: use RH2 0HX.
Parking: at Wray Lane or Margery Wood
car parks.

Find out more: 01342 843036 or
reigate@nationaltrust.org.uk

**A sweep of sky, far-reaching views
across to the South Downs
and green slopes characterise
Reigate Hill and Gatton Park in Surrey**

River Wey and Godalming Navigations and Dapdune Wharf

Navigations Office and Dapdune Wharf,
Wharf Road, Guildford, Surrey GU1 4RR

🏠 ♿ 🍴 1964

A hidden haven where you can take a boat trip,
explore a restored barge, or enjoy scenic walks.
Dapdune Wharf in Guildford brings to life
stories of this historic waterway, along 20 miles
of waterside towpath. A great place for children
to have fun – and raid our dressing-up box.
Note: boat trip charges, mooring and fishing
fees apply to members.

Eat, shop, stay: small tea-room serving
sandwiches, cakes, ice-cream and drinks.
Small shop with plant sales. Picnic areas
at Dapdune Wharf.

Things to see and do: **Indoors** Dressing-up
clothes for children. **Outdoors** Year-round
events, including activities for children at
Dapdune and guided walks along towpath and
beyond. River Festival in September. Overnight
moorings available. **Dogs**: on leads at Dapdune
Wharf and lock areas; elsewhere under control.

**River Wey and Godalming Navigations and Dapdune
Wharf, Surrey: narrowboats line up at the wharf**

Access: 🅿️♿🚻🔄📷📷🚲 **Grounds** ♿
Parking: at Dapdune Wharf.

Find out more: 01483 561389 or
riverwey@nationaltrust.org.uk

River Wey and Dapdune Wharf		M	T	W	T	F	S	S
Dapdune Wharf								
25 Mar–6 Nov	11–5	**M**	·		**T**	**F**	**S**	**S**

Open daily during local school half-term and summer
holidays. 24 October to 5 November: closes one hour
earlier. River trips from Dapdune Wharf, 11 to 4 (conditions
permitting). Access to towpath during daylight hours all year.

Runnymede

Egham, near Old Windsor, Surrey

🏠🍴♿♿ 1931

Seen by many as the birthplace of modern
democracy, this picturesque open landscape
beside the Thames was witness to King John's
historic sealing of the Magna Carta more
than 800 years ago. Today Runnymede offers
the ideal space to enjoy ancient woodlands,
countryside walks or picnics by the river,
all within easy reach of the M25. Along with
Lutyens' impressive Fairhaven Lodges, the
peaceful landscape is also home to memorials
for the Magna Carta, John F. Kennedy and
Commonwealth Air Forces, making it the
perfect place to remember and reflect
upon important moments in world history.
Note: toilets available only when tea-room
open. Mooring and fishing (during fishing
season) available for additional fee
(including members).

Runnymede in Surrey is known as the birthplace of
modern democracy. It is also a place of reflection
at The Kennedy Memorial, below, and play, above

Eat, shop, stay: tea-room and shop
serving freshly baked homemade produce,
morning coffee, light lunches and
afternoon teas. Free wi-fi.

Things to see and do: events throughout
the year. River boat trips available with
French Brothers Boat Hire (01784 439626).
Dogs: welcome, but must be on leads
near livestock.

Access: 🅿️♿🚻 **Tea-room** ♿ **Grounds** ♿♿
Sat Nav: unreliable, follow brown
Runnymede Memorial signs instead.
Parking: either side of A308. Seasonal
opening, check website for closing times.

Find out more: 01784 432891 or
runnymede@nationaltrust.org.uk

Runnymede	
Tea-room	
Open every day all year	10–5*

*Closes dusk if earlier. Car parks: locked at 7, April to
October; at dusk in winter. Closed 24 and 25 December.

Saddlescombe Farm

Saddlescombe Road, near Brighton, West Sussex BN45 7DE

[icons] 1995

Saddlescombe Farm – a gem on the South Downs Way, 5 miles from Brighton – is a unique downland farm showing a changing way of life throughout the centuries. Newtimber Hill offers the finest chalk grassland, with many varieties of downland flowers and wildlife, ancient lime trees and 19th-century graffitied beech trees. **Note**: Saddlescombe is a working farm and is fully open only on special open days.

Things to see and do: circular route to Devil's Dyke and walks up Newtimber Hill through ancient woodland. Cycling along the South Downs Way. Open days and events throughout the year. **Dogs**: welcome, on leads where livestock grazing.

Access: [icons] **Buildings** [icons]
Sat Nav: use BN45 7DE. **Parking**: at Devil's Dyke. Very limited parking in lay-by opposite farm entrance (no parking in farm).

Find out more: 01273 857712 or saddlescombe@nationaltrust.org.uk

Saddlescombe Farm, West Sussex: a hidden gem

St John's Jerusalem

Sutton-at-Hone, Dartford, Kent DA4 9HQ

[icons] 1943

Set within a secluded moated garden is this rare example of a 13th-century chapel built by the Knights Hospitaller. **Note**: private residence, maintained and managed by a tenant on behalf of the National Trust. Sorry no toilet or tea-room. Open Wednesdays, 5 April to 27 September, 2 to 6, and 4 to 25 October, 2 to 4.

Find out more: 01732 810378 or stjohnsjerusalem@nationaltrust.org.uk

Scotney Castle

Lamberhurst, Tunbridge Wells, Kent TN3 8JN

[icons] 1970

Scotney Castle, Kent, rises from its mirror-like moat

The medieval moated Old Scotney Castle lies in a peaceful wooded valley. In the 19th century its owner Edward Hussey III set about building a new house, partially demolishing the Old Castle to create a romantic folly, the centrepiece of his picturesque landscape. From the terraces of the new house, sweeps of rhododendrons and azaleas cascade down the slope in summer, followed by highlights of autumn leaf colour, mirrored in the moat.

In the house three generations have made their mark, adding possessions and character to the homely Victorian mansion which enjoys far-reaching views out across the estate.

Eat, shop, stay: the coach house tea-room offers a selection of hot meals and sandwiches, as well as homemade cakes and scones. Take home your own part of Scotney with local honey, Scotney Ale and plant sales available in the shop.

A moment for refreshments at Scotney Castle

Things to see and do: **Indoors** Children's trail around the house. Seasonal changing exhibitions and conservation demonstrations throughout the year. **Outdoors** Regular guided and self-led estate walks. Natural play and children's play areas. **Dogs**: welcome on leads in the garden and on the estate.

Access: 🅿️ 📱 🏠 🏛️ 🔄 📷 🚻 🎨
House 🏠 🏠 🏠 Grounds 🏠 ➡️ 🏠
Parking: 130 yards (limited), overflow parking 440 yards.

Find out more: 01892 893820 (Infoline). 01892 893868 or scotneycastle@nationaltrust.org.uk

Scotney Castle		M	T	W	T	F	S	S
Open all year	10–5	M	T	W	T	F	S	S

Closes dusk if earlier. House opens 11, admission by timed ticket only, including members (places limited, early sell-outs possible). 6 November to 31 December: shop and tea-room close one hour earlier; house open 11 to 3. Estate walks available every day. May close during adverse weather. Closed 24 and 25 December.

Shalford Mill

Shalford, near Guildford, Surrey GU4 8BS

🏠 1932

You can sense the evocative stories of the past in the very structure of the mill, although the machinery no longer works. The wonderful story of the Ferguson's Gang is waiting for you – eccentric young women from the 1930s, determined to save the fabric of England for the future. **Note**: sorry no toilet or refreshments.

Things to see and do: **Indoors** Regular guided tours, evening talks and children's events. **Outdoors** Geocaching kits available on Sundays. **Dogs**: assistance dogs only.

Access: 🚻 📱 **Building** 🏠
Parking: none on site, off-street parking available near church.

Find out more: 01483 561389 or shalfordmill@nationaltrust.org.uk

Shalford Mill		M	T	W	T	F	S	S
2 Apr–29 Oct	11–4:30	·	·	W	·	·	·	S

Open Bank Holiday Mondays.

Shalford Mill in Surrey boasts a proud history of dissent

Entry is still possible at most places up to 30 minutes before closing

Sheffield Park and Garden

Sheffield Park, Uckfield, East Sussex TN22 3QX

⌗ ♿ ☂ 1954

Colour, perfume and sound excite your senses as you enjoy winding paths, majestic trees, ponds and dappled glades. Falls, cascades and bridges are integral to the garden design. Planting is reflected in ponds so clear that the eye is tricked into thinking up is down. Bold and grand planting has a sculptural form in winter. Spring and summer bring vibrant blooms, fragrant arbours and splashes of colour. Autumn is a blazing kaleidoscope of greens, flame-reds, burnt oranges and bright yellows, planted for their combined display.

The encircling park and woodland provide opportunities for further adventure. Dragonflies skit across the meadows, buzzards circle in the sky and kingfishers flash across the ponds.

Eat, shop, stay: tea-room serving homemade cakes, sandwiches, hot lunches and cream teas. Takeaway kiosk open seasonally. Shops in reception building and Coach House selling gifts, local products, gardening items and plants. Second-hand bookshop in Coach House.

Things to see and do: '50 things' self-led activities for families all year, with extra events and trails in the school holidays. Natural playtrail in Ringwood Toll – try den-building, balance beams, rope swing and much more. More than 121 hectares (300 acres) of parkland, with circular walks, River Ouse, lock remains and wildlife haven. Cricket matches most summer weekends. Carpets of bluebells in spring and outstanding autumn colour display. Guided garden tours on Tuesdays and Thursdays.

Majestic trees and cascades: just some of the delights awaiting visitors to Sheffield Park and Garden, East Sussex

Water lilies embellish a lake, top, while visitors lose themselves among the lush green leaves of Giant Gunnera, above, at Sheffield Park and Garden

Pulham Falls waterfall (12 to 1, Tuesdays and Fridays). Bluebell Railway – Sheffield Park station just a short walk across the parkland (weekend bus link operates spring/summer). **Dogs**: on short leads after 1:30 in garden and anytime on parkland. Off-lead in East Park.

Access: 🅿️🅳♿️♿️♿️🔄📺♿️⚫⚫📷
Reception ♿️🅱️ Tea-room ♿️♿️
Garden ♿️♿️➡️♿️🅱️
Sat Nav: please look out for brown signs when approaching property. **Parking**: on site (overflow car park 600 yards in use when dry). Car park can become busy during May and October.

Find out more: 01825 790231 or sheffieldpark@nationaltrust.org.uk

Sheffield Park and Garden	
Garden, shop and tea-room	
Open every day all year	10–5*

Last admission to garden one hour before closing.
*November to February: closes 4 (last entry to garden 3).
Garden, shop and tea-room closed 24 and 25 December.

Sissinghurst Castle Garden

Biddenden Road, near Cranbrook, Kent TN17 2AB

🏛️🔄❄️🍴🛏️🔔🍷 1967

Sissinghurst Castle Garden sits within the ruin of a great Elizabethan house surrounded by the rich Kentish landscape of woods, streams and farmland. The famous garden, with its fairytale tower, is the result of the creative tension between the formal design of Harold Nicolson and the lavish planting of Vita Sackville-West. The colour schemes, intimacy of the different garden 'rooms' and rich herbaceous borders are the epitome of an English garden. The wider estate, which includes a vegetable garden, lakes and rich variety of wildlife, is waiting to be explored, while our regular exhibitions tell Sissinghurst's stories and show how history and landscape have combined to shape this special place. **Note**: limited access for buggies and wheelchairs.

Sissinghurst Castle Garden, Kent: the colourful Rose Garden in July, below, and the tower seen from the White Garden, right

Eat, shop, stay: restaurant serving lunch and afternoon tea made with produce from our vegetable garden and farm (hot food available until 3). The Old Dairy, offering sandwiches, cakes and drinks. Second-hand bookshop and garden shop selling plants grown in the Sissinghurst nursery.

Things to see and do: **Indoors** Exhibitions and daily talks. The Library contains the National Trust's most significant collection of 20th-century literature, and visitors can learn how we conserve it. **Outdoors** Vegetable garden tours, three-minute gardener talks, welcome talks and '50 things' activities. Packs available from visitor reception to help you explore. Acres of ancient woodland and lakes. Panoramic views across the Wealden countryside. You can see animals on our working farm. Smallhythe Place, Lamb House and Stoneacre nearby.
Dogs: welcome on leads on estate. Assistance dogs only in garden and vegetable garden.

Access:
Building **Grounds**
Parking: 315 yards.

Find out more: 01580 710700 or sissinghurst@nationaltrust.org.uk

Sissinghurst Castle Garden		M	T	W	T	F	S	S
Garden								
11 Mar–31 Oct	11–5:30	M	T	W	T	F	S	S
The South Cottage†, tower and exhibitions								
1 Jan–10 Mar	11–4	M	T	W	T	F	S	S
11 Mar–31 Dec*	11–5:30	M	T	W	T	F	S	S
Shop and restaurant								
Open all year	10–5:30**	M	T	W	T	F	S	S
Estate								
Open all year	Dawn–dusk	M	T	W	T	F	S	S

*Restricted access to garden November and December.
**Closes dusk if earlier. Last entry to garden 45 minutes before closing. For conservation reasons, no food, drink or buggies in garden (carriers provided). †South Cottage: closed June; limited timed tickets in winter.

Slindon Estate

near Arundel, West Sussex

🏠🏛🚻♿🐕⛺△ 1950

The ancient Slindon Estate is an expansive patchwork of woodland, downland, farmland and parkland, with an unspoilt Sussex village at its centre. Countless historic features cover the landscape, such as Stane Street, the Roman road from Chichester to London soldiers once marched along. Slindon has a rich and wonderfully varied wildlife, and its sun-dappled woods are filled with wild flowers, with badgers and bats hunting there at dusk. The meadows are great places to spot butterflies and downland flowers, while expansive views take in the Weald and South Downs, continuing across the coastal plain to the sea.

Eat, shop, stay: The Forge in Slindon village (tenant-run) stocks everything from locally baked bread, deli items, fruit and vegetables, to sandwiches, biscuits and cakes. Fresh coffee and tea, beer, light breakfasts, lunches and afternoon tea are also available.

Things to see and do: there are more than 25 miles of rights of way to explore on the estate, as well as the village to discover. **Dogs**: welcome under close control.

Access: ♿➡
Sat Nav: use BN18 0QY for Park Lane; BN18 0SP Duke's Road; BN18 1PH Bignor Hill. **Parking**: at Park Lane, Duke's Road and Bignor Hill.

Find out more: 01243 814730 or slindonestate@nationaltrust.org.uk

Dark stormy clouds threaten to obscure the blue summer sky above The Folly on the Slindon Estate in West Sussex

Smallhythe Place

Smallhythe, Tenterden, Kent TN30 7NG

🏠❄️🔔🍸 1939

Smallhythe Place in Kent: Victorian theatrical history

Nestled among the rolling Kent countryside, the corridors of this early 16th-century cottage resonate with the vibrant spirit of its theatrical former owner, Victorian actress Ellen Terry. Bursting with memorabilia from her life-long career on stage, visitors can see unique theatrical artefacts and attend a show in the Barn Theatre.

Eat, shop, stay: charming vintage tea-room attached to the Barn Theatre selling soup, sandwiches, cakes, as well as soft and alcoholic drinks.

Things to see and do: **Indoors** A diverse variety of plays and music performed in the Barn Theatre. **Outdoors** Open-air theatre in the garden throughout the summer. Sissinghurst Castle Garden, Lamb House and Stoneacre nearby. **Dogs**: allowed on leads in grounds.

Access: 🏷️📷🎵⛶📷 Building 🚶🏽 Grounds 🏽▶️
Parking: 50 yards (not National Trust).

Find out more: 01580 762334 or smallhytheplace@nationaltrust.org.uk

Smallhythe Place	M	T	W	T	F	S	S
1 Mar–29 Oct 11–5			**W**	**T**	**F**	**S**	**S**

Tea-room closes 30 minutes prior to closing.
Open Bank Holiday Mondays 11 to 5. Closes dusk if earlier.

South Foreland Lighthouse

The Front, St Margaret's Bay, Dover, Kent CT15 6HP

🏠🚫♿🍸 1989

This historic landmark, dramatically situated on the White Cliffs, guided ships past the infamous Goodwin Sands and has a fascinating tale to tell. It was the first lighthouse powered by electricity and the site of the first international radio transmission. **Note**: no access for cars.

Eat, shop, stay: loose-leaf tea and homemade cakes served in Mrs Knott's tea-room. Shop selling ice-cream, cold drinks and gifts.

Things to see and do: **Indoors** Tours run by knowledgeable guides. Interactive and hands-on displays. **Outdoors** Family fun with kite-flying and games. **Dogs**: in grounds only.

Access: 🏷️📷📷📷📷📷
Lighthouse 🚶🏽 Tea-room 🏽 Grounds 🏽
Parking: none on site. Nearest at White Cliffs, 2 miles, or St Margaret's, 1 mile.

Find out more: 01304 853281 or southforeland@nationaltrust.org.uk

South Foreland Lighthouse		M	T	W	T	F	S	S
Lighthouse*								
27 Mar–29 Oct	11–5:30	**M**	·	·	·	**F**	**S**	**S**
Tea-room								
1 Jan	11–3	·	·	·	·	·	·	**S**
4 Feb–26 Mar	11–3	·	·	·	·	·	**S**	**S**
27 Mar–3 Sep	11–5	**M**	**T**	**W**	**T**	**F**	**S**	**S**
4 Sep–29 Oct	11–5	**M**	·	·	·	**F**	**S**	**S**

*Also open 1 January and daily during local school holidays. 29 October: closes 3.

Looking out from South Foreland Lighthouse in Kent

Standen House and Garden

West Hoathly Road, East Grinstead,
West Sussex RH19 4NE

[icons] 1973

Nestled in the Sussex countryside with views across the High Weald, James and Margaret Beale chose an idyllic location to build their rural retreat. Designed by Philip Webb, the house is one of the finest examples of Arts and Crafts workmanship with Morris & Co. interiors and decorative art of the period. The 5-hectare (12-acre) hillside garden established by Mrs Beale are restored to its 1920s glory. Each garden room offers something for every season, from colourful spring bulbs to autumn shades. On the wider estate, footpaths lead out into the woodlands and the High Weald Area of Outstanding Beauty. **Note**: seasonal tours to top of water tower, £2 (suggested donation).

Eat, shop, stay: Barn Café serving homemade cakes, hot lunches and cream teas (wi-fi). Takeaway drinks, sandwiches and ice-cream.

**Standen House and Garden, West Sussex:
Arts and Crafts heaven in the High Weald**

Distinctive wallpaper in the Westbourne Bedroom at Standen House and Garden

Arts and Crafts-inspired gifts in shop. Plant centre, including the Standen Collection. Second-hand bookshop. Woodland craft. Kitchen-garden produce. Picnics welcome. Holiday apartment within house.

Things to see and do: **Indoors** Daily talks. Changing exhibitions. Family Christmas. **Outdoors** New for 2017: restored Rosary and Quarry Garden. 10,000 spring tulips. Estate woodland walks. Natural play area and trails (school holidays). **Dogs**: dogs welcome on short leads in formal garden and woodland estate (seasonal grazing cattle).

Access: [icons]
House [icons] Garden [icons]
Parking: 200 yards (steep hill).

Find out more: 01342 323029 or standen@nationaltrust.org.uk

Standen House and Garden		M	T	W	T	F	S	S
House, garden, café and shop*								
Open all year[1]	10–5**	M	T	W	T	F	S	S
'Behind Closed Doors' tours only								
3 Jan–31 Jan	11–3†	M	T	W	T	F		
House tours								
1 Nov–24 Nov	11–3:30†	M	T	W	T	F		

*House: February to October, open 11 to 4:30; January, November and December, open 11 to 3:30. [1]House admission by guided tour only at certain times, including weekdays, 1 February to 7 April (except 20 to 24 February), 11 to 12:55; free-flow from 1:30. **Closes one hour earlier in January, November and December. †Last tour leaves 30 minutes earlier. Closed 24 and 25 December.

Stoneacre

Otham, Maidstone, Kent ME15 8RS

🏠 ✳ 1928

Medieval farmhouse surrounded by garden, orchard, rolling meadows and woodland. Home to famous designer and critic Aymer Vallance. **Note**: maintained on National Trust's behalf by tenant. Limited parking. Open Saturday, 18 March to 23 September, 11 to 5:30 (last admission one hour before closing). Open Bank Holiday Mondays.

Find out more: 01622 861584 or stoneacre@nationaltrust.org.uk

Uppark House and Garden

South Harting, Petersfield, West Sussex GU31 5QR

🏠 ✳ ♿ 1954

Uppark House and Garden: the north front

Visitors are fascinated by a collection at Uppark House and Garden in West Sussex

Perched on its vantage point high on the South Downs ridge, Uppark commands views as far south as the English Channel. Outside, the intimate garden is being gradually restored to its original 18th-century design, with plenty of space in the adjacent meadow to play and relax with a picnic. Uppark's Georgian interiors illustrate the comfort of life 'upstairs', in contrast to the 'downstairs' world of its servants. Highlights include one of the best examples of an 18th-century doll's-house in the country.

Eat, shop, stay: shop selling local products and peat-free plants. Café (licensed) serving light lunches and cakes.

Things to see and do: **Indoors** Print room open first Wednesday of the month (March and October). **Outdoors** Garden tour Thursdays. Outdoor toy chest on South Meadow. Harting Down, Hinton Ampner and Petworth House nearby. **Dogs**: assistance dogs only.

Access: 🅿️ 🐕 🎫 🏛️ ⓘ 🎞️ ♨ 👓 📷
House ♿ 🔆 🍴 ♿ **Garden** ♿ 🏠 ➡️ ♿
Parking: 300 yards.

Find out more: 01730 825857 or uppark@nationaltrust.org.uk

Uppark House and Garden		M	T	W	T	F	S	S
Servants' quarters*								
1 Jan–17 Feb	11–3	M	T	W	T	F	S	S
18 Feb–29 Oct	11–4	M	T	W	T	F	S	S
30 Oct–26 Nov	11–3	M	T	W	T	F	S	S
2 Dec–31 Dec	11–3	M	T	W	T	F	S	S
House (ground floor only)								
4 Mar–29 Oct	12:30–4**	M	T	W	T	F	S	S
Garden, shop and café								
Open all year	10–5¹	M	T	W	T	F	S	S

*Doll's-house open as servants' quarters.
**House: open 11 to 4 on Bank Holiday Sundays and Mondays. ¹Closes dusk if earlier. Limited access to the garden in winter. Whole property closed 24 and 25 December.

Wakehurst Place

Ardingly, Haywards Heath,
West Sussex RH17 6TN

Wakehurst Place, West Sussex: the country
estate of the Royal Botanic Gardens, Kew

Wakehurst, the country estate of the Royal
Botanic Gardens, Kew, is internationally
significant for collections, scientific research
and plant conservation. The gardens, wetland
and woodland are delightful, and there is also
a nature reserve. You can also visit Kew's
unique Millennium Seed Bank to see science
and horticulture working side-by-side.
Note: funded and managed by the Royal
Botanic Gardens, Kew. **Parking charges
apply (including members)**.

Eat, shop, stay: Seed Café serving tea, coffee,
cakes, bacon sandwiches, teacakes and soup.
Redwoods Coffee Shop serving hot drinks and
fresh patisserie. Stables Restaurant offering
hot and cold food, plus cakes served all day.
Gift shop. Plant centre (not National Trust).

Things to see and do: free daily guided
tours. Seasonal festival programme.
Courses. Events all year. Willow sculpture
trail. Adventurous Journeys and natural
play areas for families. Seasonal soup and
stroll. Kingfisher/badger/bat-watching
(charges apply). **Dogs**: assistance dogs only.

Access: Buildings
Grounds
Parking: 50 yards.

Find out more: 01444 894066 or
wakehurst@kew.org. kew.org

Wakehurst Place		M	T	W	T	F	S	S
Garden								
1 Jan–28 Feb	10–4:30	M	T	W	T	F	S	S
1 Mar–31 Oct	10–6	M	T	W	T	F	S	S
1 Nov–23 Dec	10–4:30	M	T	W	T	F	S	S
26 Dec–30 Dec	10–4:30		T	W	T	F	S	

Mansion and Millennium Seed Bank: close one hour earlier.
Shop: closes at 4, 2 January to February; at 5:30, March to
October; at 5, November to 1 January 2018. Catering facilities:
available to 4, 2 January to February; to 5:15, March to
October; to 4:15, November to 1 January 2018. Property
closed 24 and 25 December. Shop closed Easter Sunday.
UK National Trust members free (reciprocal agreements
made between the Trust and other parties do not apply).

The White Cliffs of Dover

Langdon Cliffs, Dover, Kent

1968

There can be no doubt that The White Cliffs
of Dover are one of this country's most
spectacular natural features. They are an
official icon of Britain and have been a symbol
of hope for generations. You can appreciate
their beauty through the seasons by taking one
of the country's most dramatic clifftop walks,
which offer unrivalled views of the busy English
Channel while savouring the rare flora and
fauna found only on this chalk grassland.
You can also learn more about the fascinating
military history of The White Cliffs by taking
a torch-lit tour of Fan Bay Deep Shelter,
a labyrinth of forgotten Second World War
tunnels. **Note**: nearest toilets at White
Cliffs. Over twelves only in Fan Bay Shelter.

**Recognisable the world over, The White Cliffs of Dover
in Kent, right, are truly iconic. The tunnels at Fan Bay
Deep Shelter, below, bring the Second World War to life**

Eat, shop, stay: shop selling gifts and outdoor goods. Coffee shop serving lunches, homemade cakes and afternoon teas. Both with unrivalled views of the Port of Dover. Homemade cakes and loose-leaf tea available in lighthouse tea-room.

Things to see and do: spectacular viewpoints and photo opportunities everywhere. Events, talks and guided walks throughout the year. Waymarked trail to South Foreland Lighthouse (just 2 miles away). Lighthouse guided tours. Feeling adventurous? Why not pick up a timed ticket from the White Cliffs of Dover Visitor Centre for a torch-lit tour of Fan Bay Deep Shelter and the newly uncovered sound mirrors? Descend deep into the cliffs and peer into the darkness of the hidden world beneath. **Dogs**: under close control at all times (animals grazing).

Access: 🅿️🚻♿🚼🍴☕♿ Visitor centre ♿🚻
Fan Bay Deep Shelter 🚶 Countryside ♿➡️🚻
Sat Nav: use CT15 5NA. **Parking**: on site.

Find out more: 01304 202756 or whitecliffs@nationaltrust.org.uk

The White Cliffs of Dover		M	T	W	T	F	S	S
Visitor Centre								
2 Jan–26 Feb	11–4	M	T	W	T	F	S	S
27 Feb–29 Oct	10–5*	M	T	W	T	F	S	S
30 Oct–31 Dec**	11–4	M	T	W	T	F	S	S
Fan Bay Deep Shelter								
27 Mar–29 Oct	11–3:30	M	·	·	·	F	S	S

*3 July to 3 September, open to 5:30.
**Closed 24 and 25 December.

Dramatic clifftop walk at The White Cliffs of Dover

Winkworth Arboretum

Hascombe Road, Godalming, Surrey GU8 4AD

❇️🚻 1952

The National Trust's only arboretum is the result of one man's vision and passion. Dr Wilfrid Fox used the wooded valley and its lakes as a canvas to experiment with planting trees to 'paint a picture'. The fruits of his labour are now an award-winning collection of more than 1,000 varieties of trees and shrubs, offering stunning combinations of colour with every changing season. Famous for vibrant autumnal foliage and endless carpets of bluebells in spring, the azaleas, magnolias, witch hazel and snowdrops mean Winkworth is worth visiting all year for beautiful scenery, a picnic or fun family events. **Note**: some steep slopes; banks of lake and wetlands only partially fenced.

Eat, shop, stay: small tea-room offering freshly baked scones, cakes and light lunches.

Things to see and do: events and guided walks throughout the year. **Dogs**: welcome on leads.

Access: 🅿️🚻♿🍴 Grounds ♿➡️
Parking: 100 yards.

As an autumnal mist drifts in, leaves glow with golden-brown hues at Winkworth Arboretum, Surrey

Find out more: 01483 208477 or winkwortharboretum@nationaltrust.org.uk

Winkworth Arboretum		M	T	W	T	F	S	S
1 Jan–31 Jan	10–5*	M	T	W	T	F	S	S
1 Feb–31 Mar	10–5	M	T	W	T	F	S	S
1 Apr–31 Oct	10–6	M	T	W	T	F	S	S
1 Nov–31 Dec	10–5*	M	T	W	T	F	S	S

Tea-room closes 30 minutes earlier than arboretum.
*Closes at dusk if earlier; local closing times posted at the property. Car-park gates locked at closing time. Closed 24 and 25 December.

Witley and Milford Commons

Haslemere Road, Witley, Surrey GU8 5QA

[symbol] 1921

Wonderful area of great contrasts, with extensive heathland views and secluded woodland glades. Trails available from car parks. **Note**: no toilets. For Sat Nav use GU8 5QA.

Find out more: 01428 681050 or witleymilfordcommons@nationaltrust.org.uk

Woolbeding Gardens

Midhurst, West Sussex GU29 9RR

[symbol] 1956

Woolbeding delights at every turn, with distinctive garden rooms set against manicured hedges and thoughtfully composed colour-themed borders. Formal lawns melt into the rural landscape, and beyond the meadow you will find a waterfall, Gothic summerhouse and enchanting landscape garden. **Note**: access by park-and-ride minibus from Midhurst only (booking essential).

Eat, shop, stay: Orchard Café serving barista-style coffee, speciality teas, and a selection of tempting treats. Shop selling gardening books, gifts and plants.

Things to see and do: introductory talks and specialist Gardeners' Workshops. Nearby properties include Petworth House and Park, Uppark House and Garden, and Hinton Ampner. **Dogs**: assistance dogs only.

Access: [symbols] Reception [symbols] Garden [symbols]
Parking: none available.
Access by complimentary park-and-ride minibus from Midhurst only.

Find out more: 0344 249 1895 or woolbedinggardens@nationaltrust.org.uk

Woolbeding Gardens		M	T	W	T	F	S	S
20 Apr–29 Sep	10:30–4:30	·	·	·	T	F	·	·

Advance booking essential. Access by park and ride only from Midhurst.

Woolbeding Gardens, West Sussex: delights at every turn

London

2 Willow Road, Hampstead

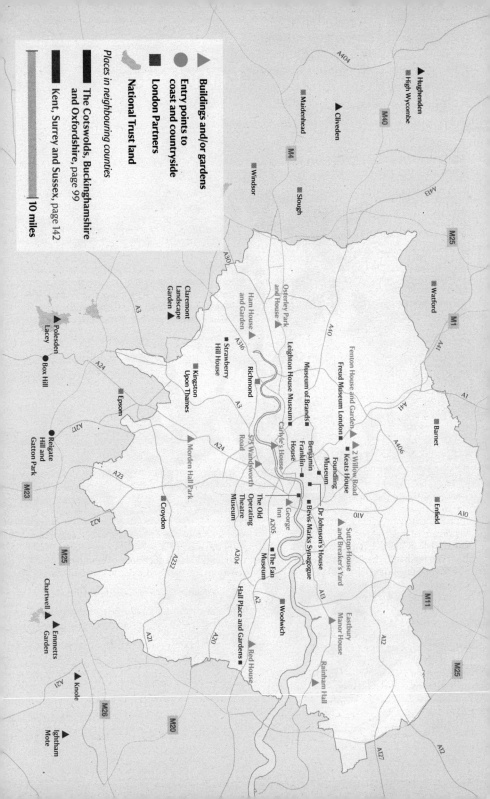

Places in neighbouring counties

■ Kent, Surrey and Sussex, page 142

■ The Cotswolds, Buckinghamshire and Oxfordshire, page 99

▶ National Trust land

■ London Partners

● Entry points to coast and countryside

▶ Buildings and/or gardens

├───────┤ 10 miles

Claremont Landscape Garden ▶

Ham House and Garden ▶

Osterley Park and House ▶

Strawberry Hill House ■

Richmond

Kingston Upon Thames ■

Polesden Lacey ▶

Box Hill ●

Epsom ■

Reigate Hill and Gatton Park ●

Morden Hall Park ▶

Croydon ■

Chartwell ▶

Emmetts Garden ▶

Knole ▶

Ightham Mote ▶

Leighton House Museum ■

Museum of Brands ■

Fenton House and Garden ▶

Freud Museum London ■

Keats House ■

2 Willow Road ▶

Foundling Museum ■

Carlyle's House ■

Benjamin Franklin House ■

Dr Johnson's House ■

Sutton House and Breaker's Yard ▶

George Inn ▶

Bevis Marks Synagogue ■

The Old Operating Theatre Museum ■

575 Wandsworth Road ▶

The Fan Museum ■

Woolwich ■

Hall Place and Gardens ▶

Eastbury Manor House ▶

Rainham Hall ▶

Red House ▶

High Wycombe ▶

Hughenden ▶

Cliveden ▶

Maidenhead ■

Windsor ■

Slough ■

Watford ■

Barnet ■

Enfield ■

Carlyle's House

24 Cheyne Row, Chelsea, London SW3 5HL

🏛️ ✺ 1936

Contemporary drawing of Carlyle's House, Chelsea

'Let no woman who values peace of soul ever dream of marrying an author!' wrote Jane Carlyle in 1837. Her amusing letters about her husband, the sage of Chelsea, their friends (including Charles Dickens), impossible servants, noisy neighbours, builders, burglars and bedbugs bring this Victorian home to hilarious life.

Access: 🗎 🏠 Building 🐾 🚻 Grounds 🐾
Parking: limited on street (metered).

Find out more: 020 7352 7087 or carlyleshouse@nationaltrust.org.uk

Carlyle's House		M	T	W	T	F	S	S
1 Mar–5 Nov	11–5			W	T	F	S	S
Open Bank Holiday Mondays.								

Eastbury Manor House

Eastbury Square, Barking IG11 9SN

🏛️ ✺ 🔔 ⊤ 1918

Elizabethan gentry house *circa* 1573. Little-altered, featuring 17th-century wall-paintings and garden with bee-boles. Tours, re-enactments, family days and crafts. **Note**: managed by London Borough of Barking and Dagenham. Some rooms are occasionally closed for functions. Independent tea-room and shop selling Tudor pottery, souvenirs and toys. Special events and activities are charged at an additional cost. Open Sunday, 26 March to 10 December, 12 to 5; Thursday and Friday, 30 March to 8 December, 10 to 4.

Find out more: 020 8227 2942 or eastburymanor@nationaltrust.org.uk

Fenton House and Garden

Hampstead Grove, Hampstead, London NW3 6SP

🏛️ ✺ ⊤ 1952

This 1686 town house, with views across London from the top of Hampstead's Holly Hill, is filled with world-class collections of ceramics, paintings, textiles and musical instruments.

Delightful Fenton House and Garden in Hampstead

Fenton House and Garden never fails to please

The ever-changing horticultural gem that is the garden, includes an orchard, kitchen garden, rose garden, terraces and lawns, and never fails to delight.

Eat, shop, stay: small shop area selling local and National Trust items, garden plants and produce.

Things to see and do: Indoors Collections talks, exhibitions and music events. **Outdoors** Garden events, including Apple Weekend. 2 Willow Road and the Freud Museum (Trust London Partner) are both nearby. **Dogs**: assistance dogs only.

Access: 🎨🖼️📷🏛️ **Building** 🚶🦽🚻 **Grounds** 🚶
Parking: none on site.

Find out more: 020 7435 3471 or fentonhouse@nationaltrust.org.uk

Fenton House and Garden		M	T	W	T	F	S	S
1 Mar–5 Nov	11–5		·	**W**	**T**	**F**	**S**	**S**

Open Bank Holiday Mondays and selected dates in December.

George Inn

The George Inn Yard, 77 Borough High Street, Southwark, London SE1 1NH

🏠 🍷 1937

This public house, dating from the 17th century, is London's last remaining galleried inn.
Note: leased to a private company. No table bookings (telephone for details). Open daily (apart from 25 and 26 December), 11 to 11.

Find out more: 020 7407 2056 or georgeinn@nationaltrust.org.uk

Ham House and Garden

Ham Street, Ham, Richmond TW10 7RS

🏠 🌸 🍷 1948

On the banks of the River Thames, Ham is one of London's treasure houses and gardens. With a substantial collection of 17th-century paintings, furniture and textiles, Ham reveals what life looked like during the reigns of Charles I and II. You can learn how later generations protected their heritage by caring for their ancestors' treasured heirlooms. The ongoing re-creation of the 17th-century garden now features a large walled kitchen garden containing a collection of trained fruit, a formal lavender garden and a woodland wilderness, full of places to be seen and to hide. **Note**: to protect fragile textiles, some rooms have low light levels.

Eat, shop, stay: the café serves lunches, teas and delicious cakes made on site using kitchen garden produce. Picnics are welcome and some tables are provided. The gift shop sells gifts for all occasions and plants, many Ham-grown.

Things to see and do: **Indoors** Art activities and trails during school holidays and weekends. **Outdoors** Garden history and architecture tours. Guided tour only in winter. **Dogs**: assistance dogs only.

Access: [icons] Café [icons]
House [icons] Garden [icons]
Sat Nav: takes you to stables on Ham Street nearby. **Parking**: none on site, nearest 380 yards (not National Trust) and on street.

Find out more: 020 8940 1950 or hamhouse@nationaltrust.org.uk

Ham House and Garden		M	T	W	T	F	S	S
House								
1 Jan–31 Mar	Tour*	M	T	W	T	F	S	S
1 Apr–31 Dec	12–4**	M	T	W	T	F	S	S
Garden, café and shop								
Open all year	10–5†	M	T	W	T	F	S	S

*Tours start at 12 (places limited). **Selected rooms only, November and December. †Closes dusk if earlier. Whole property closed 24 and 25 December.

Morden Hall Park

Morden Hall Road, Morden, London SM4 5JD

[icons] 1941

Behind the Grade II listed walls lies a 50-hectare (125-acre) urban oasis. Once a country estate attached to a mansion house, these grounds were gifted to the National Trust by a far-sighted philanthropist. The park has the River Wandle at its heart, which flows through meadows, a formal rose garden and beside tree-lined avenues. Streams trickle past a natural play area for children and alongside the National Trust's first garden centre. You can see ducks, herons and egrets as you walk through wetlands along a new boardwalk, then discover local history in our renovated Snuff Mill and Stable Yard. **Note**: parking for visitors to Morden Hall Park only (including members). Admission charges apply to some events (including members).

The portraits at Ham House and Garden in Richmond, left, are always fascinating. Morden Hall Park, right, is a serene oasis in the midst of busy South London

Eat, shop, stay: the Potting Shed Café in the former kitchen garden serves hearty fare, made with vegetables grown on site. The garden centre sells plants grown in Trust nurseries. Why not head to the Victorian Stable Yard on weekends for light refreshments?

Things to see and do: regular exhibitions in the Stable Yard Gallery and a second-hand bookshop with period features. Family events at Easter, Hallowe'en and Christmas and open-air theatre and cinema during the summer. **Dogs**: welcome on leads around buildings and mown grass, including rose garden. Within sight elsewhere.

Access: [icons]
Snuff Mill [icons] Café and garden centre [icons]
Parkland [icons]
Sat Nav: use SM4 5JD and follow signs to Morden Hall Park Garden Centre.
Parking: 25 yards, next to garden centre.

Find out more: 020 8545 6850 or mordenhallpark@nationaltrust.org.uk

Morden Hall Park
Open every day all year

Potting Shed Café open 9 to 6. Garden centre open Monday to Saturday, 9 to 6; Sunday, 10:30 to 4:30. Rose garden and Stable Yard open 8 to 6. 1 November to 1 March: all buildings and gardens close one hour earlier.

Osterley Park and House

Jersey Road, Isleworth, London TW7 4RB

🏠 ❀ ♿ ☕ 1949

A suburban palace caught between town and country, Osterley Park and House is one of the last surviving country estates in London. Past fields and grazing cattle, just around the lake the magnificent house awaits, presented as it would have been when it was redesigned by Robert Adam in the late 18th century for the Child family. A place for entertaining friends and clients, fashioned for show and entertaining, the lavish state apartments tell the story of a party palace. Recently returned family portraits and furniture now add a personal touch to grand rooms. 'Below stairs' see the contrast of the domestic quarters. Elegant pleasure gardens and hundreds of acres of parkland are perfect for whiling away a peaceful afternoon.

Eat, shop, stay: Stables Café, serving fresh seasonal dishes and homemade cakes (indoor and outdoor seating), and Brewhouse Coffee Shop (open seasonally). Gift shop, second-hand bookshop and plant sales in the Stables courtyard. Free wi-fi. Picnics welcome in the park and gardens.

Things to see and do: **Indoors** Year-round events and family activities, including free daily talks. **Outdoors** You can stroll through colourful formal gardens, with herbaceous borders, ornamental vegetable beds and a new winter garden. With meadows, woodland and a natural play trail with rope swings and stepping stones, you can let your imagination (and the children's) run wild. Why not enjoy a game of table tennis on the front lawn or, for an experience like no other, have a go at canoeing on Middle Lake (Sundays, peak season only, charges apply)? Family-friendly multipurpose paths are perfect for cycling, with trail maps and suggested routes available. **Dogs**: welcome in parkland areas, with designated on- and off-lead areas.

Osterley Park and House, Isleworth, offers grand interiors, right, and endless opportunities for fun in the extensive grounds, below

For information about getting to National Trust places, please see page 3

Access: P♿ 🅿♿ ♿ ♿WC ♿ ♿ 📷 🎦 ♿ ∴ 🖼
House ♿ 🔄 **Shop and bookshop** ♿ ♿
Garden ♿ ➡ ♿ 🔄
Sat Nav: enter Jersey Road and TW7 4RD.
Parking: 400 yards.

Find out more: 020 8232 5050 or
osterley@nationaltrust.org.uk

Osterley Park and House		M	T	W	T	F	S	S
House and shop*								
25 Feb–31 Dec[1]	11–5[2]	M	T	W	T	F	S	S
Garden and café								
Open all year	10–5†	M	T	W	T	F	S	S

*House: last entry one hour before closing. Shop: open weekends only from 7 January to 19 February and 11 to 26 November; open daily in December. [1]6 November to 31 December: basement only open for winter exhibition; principal floor open Christmas weekends. [2]6 November to 31 December: house closes 4. †Garden and café: close dusk if earlier. Property closed 25 December.

Rainham Hall

The Broadway, Rainham, London RM13 9YN

🏠 ❄ 1949

Built in 1729 for an enterprising merchant, Rainham Hall has been home to nearly 50 different inhabitants, including a scientist-vicar, a *Vogue* photographer and local children, who attended a wartime nursery. One by one, we will be bringing their stories to life, with a new exhibition planned this year.

Eat, shop, stay: the Stables Café serves seasonally inspired light lunches, freshly baked scones, cakes, barista coffee, teas and soft drinks. Gifts, guidebooks and postcards available.

Things to see and do: Indoors Regular events, including special themed late openings, family activities and seasonal festivities. **Outdoors** Nearly 1½ hectares (3 acres) of urban green space featuring local community garden projects. **Dogs:** assistance dogs only.

Access: ♿WC ♿ ♿ 📷 🎦 House ♿ 🖼
Café ♿ ⬆ Garden ♿ ➡
Parking: 300 yards (not National Trust).

Find out more: 01708 525579 or
rainhamhall@nationaltrust.org.uk

Rainham Hall		M	T	W	T	F	S	S
Stables Café and gardens								
4 Jan–31 Dec*	10–5			W	T	F	S	S
Hall								
1 Mar–29 Oct**	11–4			W	T	F	S	S
3 Nov–31 Dec	11–4					F	S	S

*Gardens close dusk if earlier. **Hall opening dates and times subject to change as exhibition is installed. Open Bank Holiday Mondays. Café and gardens closed 25 and 26 December.

Imposing Rainham Hall is a place to relax and learn about wartime stories in the new exhibition

Red House

Red House Lane, Bexleyheath DA6 8JF

🏠 ❄ 2003

Red House in Bexleyheath: home to William Morris

The only house commissioned, created and lived in by William Morris, founder of the Arts and Crafts Movement, Red House is a building of extraordinary architectural and social significance. An ongoing conservation project is gradually revealing Red House's secrets, including original Pre-Raphaelite wall-paintings and Morris's first decorative schemes.

Eat, shop, stay: William Morris shop housed in our Grade I listed Coach House. Café in original kitchen serving light lunches and a selection of cakes. Picnics welcome in the orchard.

Things to see and do: **Indoors** Exhibition of Philip Webb's personal effects. Wombat trails in school holidays. Guided tours. **Outdoors** Garden tours. Picnic area. Lawn games. **Dogs**: assistance dogs only.

Access: 🅿♿🏠🎦🔃 Building 🔃 Grounds ♿➡
Sat Nav: use DA6 8HL – Danson Park car park.
Parking: at Danson Park, just over ½ mile. Charge at weekends and Bank Holidays (including members).

Find out more: 020 8304 9878 or redhouse@nationaltrust.org.uk

Red House		M	T	W	T	F	S	S
1 Mar–29 Oct	11–5		·	**W**	**T**	**F**	**S**	**S**
3 Nov–17 Dec	11–4:30		·	·	·	**F**	**S**	**S**

Admission by guided tour only at 11, 11:30, 12, 12:30 and 1 (booking essential); free-flow 1:30 to 5. Last admission 45 minutes before closing. Tea-room: last serving 4:30 (4 in winter). Open Bank Holiday Mondays.

Sutton House and Breaker's Yard

2 and 4 Homerton High Street, Hackney, London E9 6JQ

🏠 ❄ 🔔 ☕ 1938

Transport yourself from buzzing Hackney into a 500-year-old country house full of twists and surprises. Fine oak-panelled chambers, a great hall, cellars, Tudor, Georgian, Victorian and squatter rooms are all arranged around a tranquil courtyard. Our new garden playfully celebrates its industrial past as a car-breaker's yard.

Eat, shop, stay: treat yourself to tea and cake, served on vintage crockery in the Georgian-styled tea-room – overlooked by prints of Hogarth's *A Harlot's Progress* – or in the courtyard, bookshop or among upcycled vehicles of the Breaker's Yard garden.

Leave modern Hackney behind and step back 500 years at Sutton House and Breaker's Yard

Things to see and do: **Indoors** Toy treasure chests playfully reveal secret, adventurous and refined stories. Panels open to show hidden features, such as 500-year-old graffiti. **Outdoors** Breaker's Yard playground. Seasonal events. **Dogs**: assistance dogs only.

Access: 🅿♿🏠🎦📷🔃🔃♿🔲 Building ♿♿
Sat Nav: use E9 6JQ. **Parking**: none on site and very limited nearby (not National Trust, charge including members).

Find out more: 020 8986 2264 or suttonhouse@nationaltrust.org.uk

Sutton House	M	T	W	T	F	S	S
1 Feb–17 Dec	12–5			**W**	**T**	**F**	**S**	**S**

Open daily summer school holidays. Open Bank Holiday Mondays and Good Friday (excluding December and January). Many local community groups, schools and events in house. If you would like to visit during quieter times please call. Many late openings for events, contact property for details.

575 Wandsworth Road

575 Wandsworth Road, Lambeth, London SW8 3JD

 2010

The kitchen at 575 Wandsworth Road in Lambeth

Khadambi Asalache (1935–2006) turned this modest Grade II listed Georgian terraced house into a work of art. Featuring hand-carved fretwork throughout, the house and collections continue to inspire all who visit. **Note**: sorry no toilets or café. Access by booked guided tour only.

Access: House 🦽 🚹
Parking: none on site.

Find out more: 0844 249 1895 (bookings). 020 7720 9459 (enquiries) or 575wandsworthroad@nationaltrust.org.uk

575 Wandsworth Road	M	T	W	T	F	S	S
2 Mar–29 Oct	Tour*				**T**	**F**	**S**	**S**

*House closed last Sunday of month. Admission by booked guided tour only, booking essential (places limited). Tours on Thursdays at 6:30, Fridays at 1:30 and 3:30 and weekends at 11, 1:30 and 3:30.

2 Willow Road

Hampstead, London NW3 1TH

🏠 🍴 1994

This late 1930s house, an architect's vision of the future, paints a vivid picture of the creative and social circles in which Ernö and Ursula Goldfinger moved. Today you can explore the intimate and evocative interiors, innovative designs, intriguing personal possessions and impressive 20th-century art collection. **Note**: sorry no toilet.

Eat, shop, stay: a small table in the entrance hall has property-related items available for sale.

Things to see and do: events, including late openings and tours. Fenton House and Freud Museum (London Partner) nearby. **Dogs**: assistance dogs only.

Access: 🅿️ 🅿️ 🗐 🖻 🖩 🔅 📷 Building 🦽 🚹
Parking: very limited, metered on-street parking nearby (not National Trust).

Find out more: 020 7435 6166 or 2willowroad@nationaltrust.org.uk

2 Willow Road	M	T	W	T	F	S	S
1 Mar–5 Nov	11–5*			**W**	**T**	**F**	**S**	**S**

*Entry by one-hour guided tour only, 11, 12, 1 and 2 (places limited, tickets available on day at door only). Wednesday to Friday, tours at 11 occasionally booked by groups. 3 to 5, self-guided viewing (timed entry when busy). Open Bank Holiday Mondays.

Willow Road, Hampstead: an architect's vision made real

National Trust
Partner

London partners

'National Trust Partner' is an exciting venture between the National Trust and a selection of small, independent heritage attractions and museums within London. The Partnership aims to bring enhanced benefits to National Trust members living in London or for those visiting the capital for a day out, helping to provide increased opportunities to explore our rich and diverse heritage.

Entry charges: 50 per cent discount for members on presentation of a valid membership card. For full visiting information (and access), please see individual National Trust Partner websites.

Benjamin Franklin House

The world's only remaining home of Benjamin Franklin, featuring a unique 'Historical Experience'.

Underground: Charing Cross or Embankment.
Train: Charing Cross.

Find out more: 020 7925 1405 or benjaminfranklinhouse.org

Bevis Marks Synagogue

Dated 1701, Britain's oldest surviving synagogue contains Cromwellian and Queen Anne furniture.

Underground: Liverpool Street or Aldgate.
Train: Liverpool Street.

Find out more: 020 7626 1274 or bevismarks.org.uk

Dr Johnson's House

Late 17th-century town house, once home to lexicographer and wit Samuel Johnson.

Underground: Chancery Lane or Blackfriars.
Train: Blackfriars.

Find out more: 020 7353 3745 or drjohnsonshouse.org

Foundling Museum

Nationally important collection of 18th-century art, interiors, social history and music.

Underground: Russell Square, King's Cross St Pancras or Euston. **Train**: King's Cross, St Pancras or Euston.

Find out more: 020 7841 3600 or foundlingmuseum.org.uk

The Fan Museum

Unique collection of more than 4,000 fans, housed in elegant Georgian buildings.

Train: Cutty Sark (DLR) or Greenwich.

Find out more: 020 8305 1441 or thefanmuseum.org.uk

Freud Museum London

The final home of pioneering psychoanalysts Sigmund Freud and his daughter Anna.

Underground: Finchley Road.
Overground Finchley Road & Frognal.

Find out more: 020 7435 2002 or freud.org.uk

Hall Place and Gardens

Stunning Tudor house with magnificent gardens.

Train: Bexley.

Find out more: 01322 526574 or hallplace.org.uk

Leighton House Museum

Restored home of Victorian painter Lord Leighton, with priceless Islamic tile collection.

Underground: High Street Kensington or Holland Park.

Find out more: 020 7602 3316 or leightonhouse.co.uk

Keats House

Elegant Regency villa where the Romantic poet John Keats wrote his best-loved poems.

Underground: Hampstead or Belsize Park.
Overground: Hampstead Heath.

Find out more: 020 7332 3868 or keatshouse@cityoflondon.gov.uk

Museum of Brands

Intense experience of consumer culture: journey from Victorian times to your childhood.

Underground: Ladbroke Grove.

Find out more: 020 7243 9611 or museumofbrands.com

The Old Operating Theatre Museum

Unique, atmospheric museum, hidden in the timbered Herb Garret of St Thomas's church.

Underground: London Bridge.
Train: London Bridge.

Find out more: 020 7188 2679 or thegarret.org.uk

National Trust *Partner*

Strawberry Hill House

Horace Walpole's beautifully restored Gothic-revival castle by the Thames in Twickenham.

Train: Strawberry Hill.

Find out more: 020 8744 1241 or strawberryhillhouse.org.uk

London partners

Entry charges: 50 per cent discount for members on presentation of a valid membership card. For full visiting information (and access), please see individual National Trust Partner websites.

Anglesey Abbey, Gardens and Lode Mill, Cambridgeshire
Competition entry from Steve Haydon

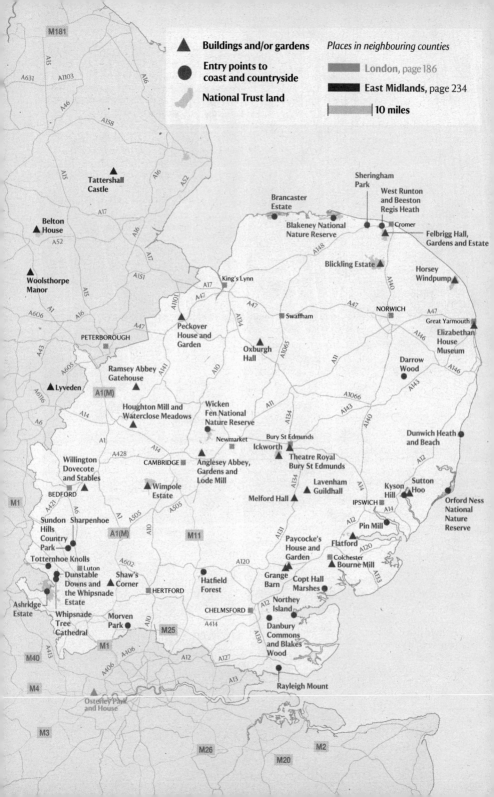

Buildings and/or gardens

Entry points to coast and countryside

National Trust land

Places in neighbouring counties

London, page 186

East Midlands, page 234

10 miles

M181

Tattershall Castle

Belton House

Woolsthorpe Manor

Lyveden

Peckover House and Garden

PETERBOROUGH

Ramsey Abbey Gatehouse

A1(M)

Houghton Mill and Watercloose Meadows

Willington Dovecote and Stables

BEDFORD

Wimpole Estate

Sundon Hills Country Park

Sharpenhoe

Totternhoe Knolls

Luton

Dunstable Downs and the Whipsnade Estate

Shaw's Corner

HERTFORD

Ashridge Estate

Whipsnade Tree Cathedral

Morven Park

CHELMSFORD

M25

M1

M40

M4

M3

Osterley Park and House

Brancaster Estate

Sheringham Park

West Runton and Beeston Regis Heath

Blakeney National Nature Reserve

Cromer

Felbrigg Hall, Gardens and Estate

King's Lynn

Blickling Estate

Horsey Windpump

Swaffham

NORWICH

Great Yarmouth

Elizabethan House Museum

Oxburgh Hall

Darrow Wood

Wicken Fen National Nature Reserve

Newmarket

Bury St Edmunds

Ickworth

Theatre Royal Bury St Edmunds

CAMBRIDGE

Anglesey Abbey, Gardens and Lode Mill

Lavenham Guildhall

Dunwich Heath and Beach

Melford Hall

Kyson Hill

Sutton Hoo

IPSWICH

Orford Ness National Nature Reserve

Pin Hill

Paycocke's House and Garden

Flatford

Colchester

Bourne Mill

Grange Barn

Copt Hall Marshes

Hatfield Forest

Northey Island

Danbury Commons and Blakes Wood

Rayleigh Mount

M11

M1

M26

M20

M2

Anglesey Abbey, Gardens and Lode Mill

Quy Road, Lode, Cambridge,
Cambridgeshire CB25 9EJ

🏠 🖼 ❄ 1966

Journey back to a golden age of country-house living at Anglesey Abbey, Gardens and Lode Mill, Cambridgeshire

When you step into this elegant home, you journey back to a golden age of country-house living. The Domestic Wing shows how the staff serving the meticulous Lord Fairhaven ran his household like clockwork. The celebrated garden, with its sweeping avenues, classical statuary and flower borders, offers captivating views, vibrant colours and delicious scents whatever the season. Children can play, explore and discover nature in the Wildlife Discovery Area. A visit to the historic working watermill and famous Winter Garden will complete your day.

Eat, shop, stay: Redwoods restaurant serving sandwiches, hot meals, teas, cakes, hot drinks. Light refreshments and snacks in gardens during peak times. Shop and plant centre selling local products and gifts. Freshly milled wholemeal flour available from the historic watermill. Second-hand bookshop.

Things to see and do: **Indoors** Hands-on activities and demonstrations in Domestic Wing (Thursday and Friday). **Outdoors** Self-led family activities, geocaching. Weekday garden tours. Winter Lights – special event lighting the gardens at night (December weekends). **Dogs**: assistance dogs only. Downloadable dog walk in local area available.

Access: 🅿♿♿♿♿♿♿♿♿
Abbey and Lode Mill ♿♿ **Grounds** ♿➡♿♿
Parking: 50 yards.

Find out more: 01223 810080 or angleseyabbey@nationaltrust.org.uk

Anglesey Abbey		M	T	W	T	F	S	S
Garden, restaurant, shop and plant centre								
1 Jan–25 Mar	10–4:30	M	T	W	T	F	S	S
26 Mar–28 Oct	10–5:30	M	T	W	T	F	S	S
29 Oct–31 Dec	10–4:30	M	T	W	T	F	S	S
House								
29 Mar–29 Oct	11–5	·	·	W	T	F	S	S
Lode Mill								
Open all year	11–3:30	·	·	W	T	F	S	S

Snowdrop season: 23 January to 26 February.
Domestic Wing: open daily, March to October. House and Lode Mill: open Bank Holiday Mondays and daily in school holidays. House: last entry one hour before closing; tours 29 March to 29 October. Closed 24 to 26 December.

Scented narcissi delight a young visitor at Anglesey Abbey, Gardens and Lode Mill

With wide open spaces and rich wildlife habitats, Ashridge Estate, Hertfordshire, is heaven for walkers and nature lovers

Ashridge Estate

near Berkhamsted, Hertfordshire

[🎿][🏛][🏊][1926]

This special place has been enjoyed for centuries by everyone from pilgrims to picnickers. With its rich wildlife, diverse habitats and varied history, there is plenty to uncover at Ashridge. From the scent of the bluebells in spring, glorious birdsong and spectacular views from the chalk downland of the Pitstone Hills in summer, the rutting fallow deer in autumn and crisp walks on swathes of open common in winter, Ashridge has a landscape for every season. Waymarked trails and walks leaflets from the visitor centre. Wildwood Den natural play area for children. Climb the Bridgewater Monument for fantastic views. **Note**: toilets available only when café open.

Eat, shop, stay: our shop offers an ever-changing array of local and seasonal gifts, maps and books. The Brownlow Café (concession) serves homemade meals and snacks to eat in our outdoor courtyard.

Things to see and do: events and children's activities throughout the year. Why not visit Pitstone Windmill, also part of the Ashridge Estate, open Sundays and Bank Holiday Mondays from 28 May to 28 August? **Dogs**: under close control at all times for the safety of wildlife and visitors.

Access: [P♿][♿][♿][♿][♿] Visitor centre [♿] Grounds [♿][➡][♿]
Sat Nav: use HP4 1LT for the visitor centre and Bridgewater Monument (points to the end of the drive). **Parking**: at the visitor centre, Ivinghoe Beacon and many other parts of the estate.

Find out more: 01442 851227 or ashridge@nationaltrust.org.uk

Ashridge Estate		M	T	W	T	F	S	S
Estate								
Open all year	Dawn–dusk	M	T	W	T	F	S	S
Visitor centre, Brownlow Café and shop*								
1 Jan–28 Feb	10–4	M	T	W	T	F	S	S
1 Mar–31 Oct	10–5	M	T	W	T	F	S	S
1 Nov–31 Dec	10–4	M	T	W	T	F	S	S
Bridgewater Monument (weather dependent)								
1 Apr–29 Oct	12–4	M	T	W	T	F	S	S

*Visitor centre and shop closed 24 and 25 December. Café: March to October, opens 8 and closes 6; November to February, closes 4; closed 25 December. Estate may close in very high winds.

Blakeney National Nature Reserve

near Morston, Norfolk

⌂ 🏛 ♿ 🏄 🐕 🚻 1912

At the heart of the Norfolk Coast Area of Outstanding Natural Beauty, Blakeney National Nature Reserve boasts wide open spaces and uninterrupted views of the beautiful North Norfolk coastline. The 4-mile long shingle spit of Blakeney Point offers protection for Blakeney Harbour and provides a perfect habitat for the vast array of residential and migratory wildlife. Spectacular displays of the summer breeding tern colony and winter breeding grey seals will delight visitors all year round. Great for walkers, sightseers and wildlife enthusiasts alike, the internationally important reserve guarantees an inspiring and memorable visit no matter the season. **Note**: nearest toilet at Morston Quay and Blakeney Quay.

Eat, shop, stay: takeaway snacks, drinks and tasty treats available from our refreshment kiosk at Morston Quay. Nearby pubs and hotels (not National Trust) offering locally themed menus.

Our holiday cottage, a simple lodge by Blakeney village, offers a romantic getaway for two.

Things to see and do: information centres at Morston Quay and Lifeboat House on Blakeney Point. Extensive coastal walks on the Norfolk Coast Path. Guided walks available. Ferry trips (not National Trust) to Blakeney Point. **Dogs**: some restrictions apply (particularly Blakeney Point), 1 April to 15 August.

Access: 🚐 🆚 Information centre ♿ 🦽
Lifeboat House ♿ 🦽
Sat Nav: use NR25 7BH for Morston Quay.
Parking: at Green Way Stiffkey Saltmarshes, Morston Quay and Blakeney Quay.

Find out more: 01263 740241 or blakeneypoint@nationaltrust.org.uk

Blakeney		M	T	W	T	F	S	S
Refreshment kiosk (Morston Quay)								
7 Jan–12 Feb	11–2						S	S
13 Feb–19 Feb	11–2	M	T	W	T	F	S	S
25 Feb–12 Mar	11–2						S	S
13 Mar–29 Oct	10–4	M	T	W	T	F	S	S
4 Nov–31 Dec	11–2						S	S
Lifeboat House (Blakeney Point)								
3 Apr–29 Sep	Dawn–dusk	M	T	W	T	F	S	S

Morston Information Centre open around the tides.
Nature Reserve open all year.

The sun sets over peaceful Blakeney National Nature Reserve in Norfolk

East of England

Blickling Estate

Blickling, Aylsham, Norfolk NR11 6NF

⌂ ✝ 🍴 ❀ 🛏 🚶 1940

'Why are you here?' You'll never forget your first sight of Blickling, as the breathtaking Jacobean mansion comes into view, flanked by the welcoming, outstretched arms of its magnificent yew hedging. This gift to the nation was bequeathed by the grace of its visionary owner, Philip Kerr. Kerr knew that the preservation of his special place, as well as others like it, depended upon it finding a home in the heart of the nation. Today we explore this story by opening the house and gardens as they would have been; a place of hospitality, of life, with period music and personal insights into the lives of those who made Blickling's 1,821-hectare (4,500-acre) estate a place worth saving. **Note**: additional charges apply for some special events.

Eat, shop, stay: three cafés and a pub offering bed and breakfast (not National Trust). Large second-hand bookshop, stamp shop with extensive stock for collectors (donations welcome), gift shop, plant and garden centre and exhibition gallery. Nine holiday cottages on the estate.

Things to see and do: **Indoors** Nearly 400 years of history brought to life through sounds, stories and personal insights. Nationally important book collection in the Long Gallery. Tours change daily: social history, behind-the-scenes, conservation, gardening. Hobart Gallery with local artists' work. Family games and trails. Living history performances. RAF museum. **Outdoors** Magnificent garden offering three centuries of inspired planting. Walled garden regeneration project under way. Park offers cycling and walking along waymarked routes (free guides available). Pyramid mausoleum. Permit fishing June to March. Events throughout year, including open-air cinema, summer music concerts, special days leading up to Christmas. Felbrigg Hall and Sheringham Park nearby.
Dogs: welcome on leads in park and outside farmyard café. Assistance dogs only elsewhere.

Access:
House **Gardens**
Parking: 400 yards.

Find out more: 01263 738030 or blickling@nationaltrust.org.uk

Blickling Estate		M	T	W	T	F	S	S
House*								
6 Mar–29 Oct†	12–5	**M**	**T**	**W**	**T**	**F**	**S**	**S**
4 Nov–26 Nov	12–4	·	·	·	·	·	**S**	**S**
1 Dec–10 Dec	12–6	·	·	·	·	**F**	**S**	**S**
Garden, shops and cafés*								
1 Jan–5 Mar	11–4	**M**	**T**	**W**	**T**	**F**	**S**	**S**
6 Mar–29 Oct	10–5:30	**M**	**T**	**W**	**T**	**F**	**S**	**S**
30 Oct–30 Nov	11–4	**M**	**T**	**W**	**T**	**F**	**S**	**S**
1 Dec–23 Dec**	11–4**	**M**	**T**	**W**	**T**	**F**	**S**	**S**
26 Dec–31 Dec	11–4	·	**T**	**W**	**T**	**F**	**S**	**S**
Park								
Open all year	Dawn–dusk	**M**	**T**	**W**	**T**	**F**	**S**	**S**

*House and garden: last entry one hour before closing. †Tuesdays: special focus on caring for our collection (shorter house route). **Christmas: 1 to 10 December, Friday, Saturday and Sunday, open until 7. Plant shop, RAF Museum and stamp shop: check times before visit.

Blickling Estate, Norfolk, clockwise from left: the breathtaking Jacobean mansion, cycling on one of the waymarked routes, and examining books in the Long Gallery

Bourne Mill

Bourne Road, Colchester, Essex CO2 8RT

🏛 1936

**Picturesque Bourne Mill in Essex
still has a fully functioning waterwheel**

Picturesque watermill with working waterwheel in tranquil grounds. A delightful piece of late Elizabethan playfulness, used at different times for banqueting, milling flour and 'fulling' wool cloth. Large millpond, Tudor Physic Garden, wildlife area with ponds and babbling stream. Pond-dipping and garden games. Special events and family activities.

Eat, shop, stay: light refreshments available. Pond-side seating area. Shop selling locally designed and produced goods.

Things to see and do: you can view the mill's workings, then explore the wildlife area and see how many '50 things' activities you can tick off. **Dogs**: welcome on leads.

Access: 🅿♿🏷🅿♿ 🖺🎵 •• Building 🚶♿ .
Grounds 🚶♿
Parking: on site (limited), or on street.

Find out more: 01206 549799 or bournemill@nationaltrust.org.uk

Bourne Mill		M	T	W	T	F	S	S
15 Mar–29 Oct	10–5	·	·	**W**	**T**	**F**	**S**	**S**

Open Bank Holiday Mondays, March to October. Closes 4 from 24 September.

Brancaster Estate

near Brancaster, Norfolk

🏛♿🏷♿🖺 1923

The Brancaster Estate comprises the beautiful endless sandy Brancaster Beach, perfect for summer sandcastles and winter walks, the intriguing Branodunum Roman Fort site and the traditional fishing harbour of Brancaster Staithe. The area is rich in wildlife and offers a memorable visit regardless of the time of year. **Note**: beach car park (not National Trust). Toilets at beach and harbour. Parking charges apply at Brancaster Beach (including members). Weekly and seasonal passes available.

Eat, shop, stay: stay at Brancaster Activity Centre, perfect for a large group and family getaways. Self-catering accommodation sleeping up to 48 in dorm-style bedrooms with *en-suite* facilities.

Things to see and do: walk along the Norfolk Coast Path and explore the coastline, taking in the panoramic views of the saltmarsh across to Brancaster Harbour and Scolt Head Island National Nature Reserve beyond.

The long sandy beach at Brancaster Estate in Norfolk

Dogs: responsible dog owners welcome. Restrictions apply on Brancaster Beach (May to August).

Access: 🚾
Sat Nav: use PE31 8AX (Beach Road); PE31 8BW (Brancaster Staithe). **Parking**: Beach Road, Brancaster (not National Trust), charge including members. Limited parking at Harbour Way, Brancaster Staithe. Both subject to tidal flooding.

Find out more: 01263 740241 or brancaster@nationaltrust.org.uk

Copt Hall Marshes

near Little Wigborough, Essex

🕇 ⛴ ♿ 🚲 🐾 1989

Working farm on the remote and beautiful Blackwater Estuary – a fantastic birdwatching spot, important for overwintering species. **Note**: for Sat Nav use CO5 7RD.

Find out more: 01376 565450 or copthall@nationaltrust.org.uk

Danbury Commons and Blakes Wood

near Danbury, Essex

🏠 ♿ 🐾 1953

Varied countryside, ranging from the lowland heath of Danbury Common to ancient woodland with stunning spring flowers at Blakes Wood. **Note**: sorry no toilets. Sat Nav: for Danbury Commons use CM3 4JH and for Blakes Wood use CM3 4AU. Danbury Commons main car park closes dusk.

Find out more: 01245 227662 or danbury@nationaltrust.org.uk

Darrow Wood

Darrow Green Road, Denton, Harleston, Norfolk IP20 0AY

🏠 🏠 ♿ 1990

Darrow Wood is a small, hedge-enclosed, lightly wooded pasture field containing earthworks, including a compact motte-and-bailey castle. **Note**: very limited roadside parking. Sorry no toilet.

Find out more: 01728 648020 (Dunwich Heath) or darrowwood@nationaltrust.org.uk

Dunstable Downs and the Whipsnade Estate

near Dunstable, Bedfordshire

🏠 ♿ 🐾 🍴 1928

The Downs have so much to offer all year round. The best kite-flying and picnicking site for miles around. A haven for wildlife; home to orchids, butterflies, birds and much more. Enjoy the ever-changing view from the Chilterns Gateway Centre with a refreshing drink or delicious meal. **Note**: Chilterns Gateway Centre is owned by Central Bedfordshire Council and managed by the National Trust.

Dunstable Downs and the Whipsnade Estate, Bedfordshire

Dunstable Downs and the Whipsnade Estate: as well as astounding views, the Downs offer the best kite-flying sites for miles around

Eat, shop, stay: shop selling a wide range of kites, homemade fudge and Dunstable Downs branded products. The View Café serves light lunches, snacks, hot and cold drinks with the option to eat in or take away.

Things to see and do: events, including the annual Kite Festival in July. Nature trail and playscape in Chute Wood. Waymarked routes. History to discover and wildlife to spot.
Dogs: under close control, on leads in car parks, near livestock and ground-nesting birds.

Access: ⬚⬚⬚⬚⬚⬚
Chilterns Gateway Centre ⬚⬚
Dunstable Downs ⬚➡⬚
Sat Nav: use LU6 2GY (or LU6 2TA for older equipment). **Parking**: at Dunstable Downs, off B4541, and Bison Hill off the B4540.

Find out more: 01582 500920 or dunstabledowns@nationaltrust.org.uk

Dunstable Downs		M	T	W	T	F	S	S
Chilterns Gateway Centre								
1 Jan–12 Feb	9:30–4	M	T	W	T	F	S	S
13 Feb–29 Oct	9:30–5	M	T	W	T	F	S	S
30 Oct–31 Dec	9:30–4	M	T	W	T	F	S	S
Closed 24 and 25 December.								

Dunwich Heath and Beach

Dunwich, Saxmundham, Suffolk

🏊⛺🦆🛏️ 1968

A precious landscape on the Suffolk coast, Dunwich Heath offers a true sense of being at one with nature. Set in the very middle of an Area of Outstanding Natural Beauty, there is an abundance of wildlife to discover, including rare birds such as the Dartford warbler and nightjar. With a network of footpaths to explore, a walk on Dunwich Heath will rejuvenate you any time of the year. Deepen your understanding of this special place by joining an event or Ranger-led activity. Download our free app to help you make the most of your visit – search 'Dunwich Heath'.

Eat, shop, stay: clifftop tea-room serving breakfast, lunch, cream teas, homemade cakes, scones and ice-cream. Enjoy views from the lookout or warm yourself by the log burner. Gift shop selling local products, National Trust bestsellers and Dunwich-branded items.

Things to see and do: self-guided and guided walks. Family activities, including bug-hunting and nature trails. Heath Barn discovery area and family beach. Quarterly Sconeathon (there are dozens of flavours to try). **Dogs**: welcome, including in tea-room (*Woof* guide available). On leads, 1 March to 31 August.

Access: 🅿️ 🅿️ 🅿️ 🅿️ 🅿️ **Grounds** ➡️ 🅿️
Sat Nav: use IP17 3DJ. **Parking**: on site.

Find out more: 01728 648501 or
dunwichheath@nationaltrust.org.uk

Dunwich Heath and Beach		M	T	W	T	F	S	S
Tea-room and shop								
1 Jan–5 Feb	10:30–3	·	·	·	·	·	S	S
11 Feb–19 Feb	10:30–4	M	T	W	T	F	S	S
25 Feb–26 Feb	10:30–4	·	·	·	·	·	S	S
4 Mar–31 Mar	10–4	M	T	W	T	F	S	S
1 Apr–1 Oct	10–5	M	T	W	T	F	S	S
2 Oct–31 Oct	10–4	M	T	W	T	F	S	S
4 Nov–17 Dec	10:30–3	·	·	·	·	·	S	S
26 Dec–31 Dec	10:30–3	·	T	W	T	F	S	S

Information centre open as tea-room and shop.
Visitor facility openings dependent on weather conditions.

Dunwich Heath and Beach in Suffolk, left and below, is in the very centre of an Area of Outstanding Natural Beauty

Elizabethan House Museum

4 South Quay, Great Yarmouth,
Norfolk NR30 2QH

🏠 🔺 🍷 1943

A 16th-century quayside home, set out to reflect day-to-day domestic life from Tudor to Victorian times. **Note**: managed by Norfolk Museums Service. Open Monday to Friday and Sundays, 2 April to 29 October, 10 to 4.

Find out more: 01493 855746 or
elizabethanhouse@nationaltrust.org.uk

Felbrigg Hall, Gardens and Estate

Felbrigg, Norwich, Norfolk NR11 8PR

🏠 ✝️ 🐾 🛏️ 📷 1969

Felbrigg Hall is a surprising mixture of opulence and homeliness, where the stories of its owners unfold through the completeness of its original contents. Why not pick up some inspiration from the Walled Garden? Once it provided fruit and vegetables for the kitchens, now it provides flowers for the Hall and is a tranquil place to escape and relax. The rolling landscape park, with a lake, ancient woodland and miles of waymarked trails, is a great place to explore nature, spot wildlife, or just to get away from it all.

Felbrigg Hall, Gardens and Estate in Norfolk

Felbrigg Hall, Gardens and Estate:
a strange mix of opulence and homeliness

Eat, shop, stay: relax indoors and out at Squire's Pantry (licensed) with a wide choice of hot and cold food and drink. The gift shop and second-hand bookshop offer a selection of goods, plants and books. Stay in one of our holiday cottages.

Things to see and do: **Indoors** Attics and cellars tours on selected days. Children's trails. **Outdoors** Natural play area in Walled Garden. Events, including Chilli Fiesta, 'Made in Norfolk' and Christmas event. **Dogs**: on leads in parkland when stock grazing, under close control in woodland.

Access: ⓟ ⓓ 🏛 ⛪ 🔄 ◉ 🅿 Hall ♿ 🔄
Gardens ♿ ➡ ♿ 🔄
Sat Nav: use NR11 8PP. **Parking**: 100 yards.

Find out more: 01263 837444 or felbrigg@nationaltrust.org.uk

Felbrigg Hall		M	T	W	T	F	S	S
Shop and tea-room								
1 Jan–8 Jan	11–3	M	T	W	T	F	S	S
14 Jan–5 Feb	11–3	·	·	·	·	·	S	S
House								
11 Feb–19 Feb	11–3	M	T	W	T	F	S	S
20 Feb–22 Mar	11–3	M	T	W	·	·	S	S
25 Mar–18 Oct*	11–5	M	T	W	·	·	S	S
20 Oct–29 Oct	11–4	M	T	W	T	F	S	S
Garden, shop and tea-room								
11 Feb–19 Feb	11–4	M	T	W	T	F	S	S
20 Feb–19 Oct	11–5	M	T	W	T	F	S	S
20 Oct–29 Oct	11–4	M	T	W	T	F	S	S
2 Nov–24 Dec	11–3	·	·	·	T	F	S	S
26 Dec–31 Dec	11–3	·	T	W	T	F	S	S

House open daily in local school holidays (February to October). *24 July to 5 September: access to some areas of house may be limited on Thursdays and Fridays. Parkland: open every day all year, dawn to dusk. Gardens close 30 minutes after house, 25 March and 19 October.

Flatford

East Bergholt, Suffolk CO7 6UL

🏛 ⛴ 1943

Flatford lies in the heart of the beautiful Dedham Vale. This charming hamlet was the inspiration for some of John Constable's most famous paintings, including *The Hay Wain*, *Boatbuilding* and *Flatford Mill*. While wandering beside the River Stour or looking at Flatford Mill and Willy Lott's House, you can feel as if you are actually walking through one of his paintings. Our informative exhibition will give you an insight into Constable's life at Flatford. While you are here, enjoy exploring the countryside on one of our circular walks or hire a boat and row along the river. **Note**: no public access inside Flatford Mill, Valley Farm and Willy Lott's House.

Eat, shop, stay: riverside tea-room serving homemade cakes and light lunches. Shop selling plants, gifts and souvenirs.

Things to see and do: volunteer guides offer tours sharing their passion for Constable and show some of the locations he used. Waymarked circular walks and family trails around Flatford. **Dogs**: welcome, but please be aware of livestock in fields.

Access: ⬚⬚⬚⬚⬚⬚⬚⬚⬚⬚
Bridge Cottage ⬚⬚ Grounds ⬚⬚⬚
Parking: 100 yards.

Find out more: 01206 298260 or flatford@nationaltrust.org.uk

Flatford		M	T	W	T	F	S	S
7 Jan–12 Feb	10:30–3:30	·	·	·	·	·	S	S
15 Feb–26 Mar	10–4:30	·	·	W	T	F	S	S
27 Mar–30 Jun	10–5	M	T	W	T	F	S	S
1 Jul–31 Aug	10–5:30	M	T	W	T	F	S	S
1 Sep–1 Oct	10–5	M	T	W	T	F	S	S
2 Oct–29 Oct	10–4:30	M	T	W	T	F	S	S
1 Nov–17 Dec	10:30–3:30	·	·	W	T	F	S	S
29 Dec–31 Dec	10:30–2:30	·	·	·	·	F	S	S

The River Stour runs through the charming hamlet of Flatford in Suffolk, which lies at the very heart of the beautiful Dedham Vale – John Constable country

Grange Barn

Grange Hill, Coggeshall, Colchester, Essex CO6 1RE

🏠🔔🍷 1989

Oak pillars soar up to a cathedral-like roof at Grange Barn in Essex

One of Europe's oldest timber-framed buildings, Grange Barn stands as a lasting reminder of the once-powerful Coggeshall Abbey. With oak pillars soaring up to a cathedral-like roof, bearing the weight of centuries, it was saved and restored in the 1980s. This 13th-century building has truly stood the test of time.

Eat, shop, stay: honey from Grange Barn's beehives is available to buy, alongside a limited range of souvenirs, second-hand books, takeaway refreshments and ice-cream. Coffee shop at nearby Paycocke's House and Garden. Picnics welcome.

Things to see and do: exhibition on the life and work of local woodcarver Bryan Saunders. Events during the year, including our annual Beer Festival. Circular walk taking in Paycocke's House and Garden nearby. **Dogs**: welcome on leads in grounds.

Access: ⬚⬚ Building ⬚ Grounds ⬚
Parking: on site.

Find out more: 01376 562226 or grangebarncoggeshall@nationaltrust.org.uk

Grange Barn		M	T	W	T	F	S	S
18 Mar–1 Oct	11–4	M	T	W	T	F	S	S
2 Oct–29 Oct	11–3	M	T	W	T	F	S	S

Closes occasionally for private events.

Ancient Hatfield Forest in Essex:
once a Royal hunting forest, it is now
managed using traditional techniques

Hatfield Forest

near Bishop's Stortford, Essex

[icons] 1924

When Henry I established a Royal Hunting Forest here in 1100, he could little have guessed that almost a millennium later it would be the best survivor of its kind in the world. The ancient trees are managed using traditional techniques and the forest is home to more than 3,500 species of wildlife, including fallow deer descended from the original herd. Explore the wide open plains, grazed by Red Poll cows, or enjoy the shade of the coppice woodland. With over 405 hectares (1,000 acres), there are many places for imaginative play or a spot of quiet relaxation.

Eat, shop, stay: café (outdoor-only dining area) serving hot and cold refreshments, ice-cream and drinks. Shop selling gifts, guidebook and maps, plus Hatfield Forest venison and Red Poll beef (when in season).

Things to see and do: events, including open-air theatre and WoodFest. Rowing boat hire available in the summer. Family activities in the summer holidays. **Dogs**: welcome under close control. On leads in lake area, boardwalk and near livestock.

Access: [icons]
Shell House [icons] **Forest** [icons]
Sat Nav: use CM22 6NE.
Parking: on site (limited in winter).

Find out more: 01279 874040 (Infoline).
01279 870678 or
hatfieldforest@nationaltrust.org.uk

Hatfield Forest		M	T	W	T	F	S	S
Café								
1 Jan–17 Mar	10–3:30	M	T	W	T	F	S	S
18 Mar–29 Oct	9–5	M	T	W	T	F	S	S
30 Oct–31 Dec	10–3:30	M	T	W	T	F	S	S

Entrance car park open daily; Shell House and Elgin's car parks open 20 March to 29 October, 10 to 4:30, Monday to Friday, and 9 to 4:30, Saturday and Sunday (conditions permitting). Café closed 25 December.

Horsey Windpump

Horsey, Great Yarmouth, Norfolk NR29 4EF

⚔ ♨ 📷 🏠 🚻 1948

This summer Horsey Windpump reopens with a fully restored cap and set of historic pattern sails and, once again, standing proud over the Broadland landscape and Horsey Mere. Horsey Windpump is an iconic building with a fascinating past and the perfect place to experience the connection between man and nature. **Note**: surrounded by Horsey Estate – managed by the Buxton family. Horsey Gap car park, not National Trust (charge including members).

Eat, shop, stay: shop and tea-room (next to Horsey Windpump) serving snacks, drinks, tasty treats and small range of gifts. Stay in one of our converted barn holiday cottages nearby in Horsey village. Perfectly placed for exploring the Broads and Norfolk coast.

Things to see and do: Horsey Windpump is a great starting point for accessing the outdoors with walking routes to Horsey Mere and the beach. Boat trips (not National Trust) across Horsey Mere (May to September). **Dogs**: welcome (on leads near wildlife and livestock).

Access: 🅿 ⛴ 🏠 🔼 🔼 🗐 🖼
Windpump 🔼 🔼 🔼 Grounds 🔼 ▶
Parking: on site. Alternatively, at Horsey Gap car park, 1 mile, not National Trust (charge including members).

This year, Horsey Windpump in Norfolk gets its sails back

Find out more: 01263 740241 or horseywindpump@nationaltrust.org.uk

Horsey Windpump		M	T	W	T	F	S	S
Shop and tea-room								
27 Feb–5 Nov	10–4:30	M	T	W	T	F	S	S
Windpump								
1 Jul–5 Nov	10–4:30	M	T	W	T	F	S	S

Car park and toilets open all year, dawn to dusk. Windpump undergoing restoration and may be subject to closure.

Houghton Mill and Waterclose Meadows

Houghton, near Huntingdon, Cambridgeshire PE28 2AZ

🏠 ♨ ⛺ 🔔 1939

Children enjoy hands-on activities at Houghton Mill and Waterclose Meadows in Cambridgeshire

In a stunning riverside setting, surrounded by meadow walks, Houghton Mill is the oldest working watermill on the Great Ouse. There are hands-on activities for all the family, as well as milling demonstrations. You can buy our flour, ground in the traditional way by our French burr millstones.

Eat, shop, stay: Riverside tea-room serving snacks, cakes and scones made with our traditional stoneground flour. Freshly ground flour and gifts for sale in our mill shop. Come and stay at our tranquil riverside camp/caravan site.

Things to see and do: **Indoors** Milling demonstrations (Sundays) and baking days. Family events. **Outdoors** Open-air theatre.

Children's trails, activities and summer holiday events. Access to surrounding meadows via public footpaths. **Dogs**: assistance dogs only please in mill; all dogs welcome in grounds on leads.

Access: 🅿️🌫️♿🐕🏷️📷📹🚻
Mill ♿🅗 Tea-room ♿ Grounds ➡️
Sat Nav: use PE28 2AZ. **Parking**: on site.

Find out more: 01480 301494 or houghtonmill@nationaltrust.org.uk

Houghton Mill		M	T	W	T	F	S	S
Tea-room								
7 Jan–12 Mar	10:30–3:30	·	·	·	·	·	S	S
18 Mar–29 Sep	10:30–5	M	T	W	T	F	S	S
30 Sep–25 Oct	10:30–5	M	T	W	·	·	S	S
28 Oct–30 Dec	10:30–3:30	·	·	·	·	·	S	S
Mill								
18 Mar–29 Oct	11–5	·	·	·	·	·	S	S
20 Mar–19 Jul	1–5	M	T	W	·	·	·	
24 Jul–1 Sep	1–5	M	T	W	T	F	·	
4 Sep–25 Oct	1–5	M	T	W	·	·	·	

Open Bank Holiday Mondays and Good Friday, 11 to 5. Waterclose Meadows Caravan and Campsite: National Trust, open 17 March to 30 October (01480 466716). Car park: closes 8 or dusk if earlier.

Ickworth

The Rotunda, Horringer, Bury St Edmunds, Suffolk IP29 5QE

🏠✝️🍴❄️👥♿ 1956

An Italian vision brought to Suffolk. The Ickworth Estate reflects the Hervey family's passion for everything Italian. The Rotunda is a Neo-classical showcase, intended by the 4th Earl of Bristol to display his impressive treasures. The Rotunda houses one of the finest silver collections by Huguenot silversmiths, and family portraits by artists such as Gainsborough and Reynolds. In the basement, 1930s domestic service is brought to life through the memories of former staff. The Italianate Garden mirrors the house architecture, with clipped hedges and Mediterranean planting, while an idiosyncratic Victorian stumpery, planted with shade-loving ferns, creates an air of mystery.

The impressive Rotunda at Ickworth in Suffolk

The numerous parkland walks at Ickworth offer space and freedom to everyone, from dog-walkers to joggers

Extensive parkland walks and cycle routes offer space and freedom to discover personal pathways and inspiring views. **Note**: accommodation provided at The Ickworth hotel (part of the Luxury Family Hotel Group), 01284 735350.

Eat, shop, stay: West Wing Café serving seasonal lunches all year. Porter's Lodge outdoor café. Court Café open peak times. Gift shop, plant and garden shop and second-hand bookshop offer a wide range of local goods. Five stunning holiday cottages across the estate.

Things to see and do: Indoors Tours daily, house exhibitions, 1930s Living History days and children's crafts in the Gallery. Basement servants' quarters, an extensive silver collection, Regency furniture, historic books and Italian porcelain, as well as paintings by Titian, Vigée Le Brun and Kaufmann. **Outdoors** Events and activities all year, including Easter Egg trails, open-air theatre, wildlife days, summer Wool Fair, autumn Wood and Country Craft Fair and family Christmas weekends. Seasonal highlights include snowdrops, lambing and Walled Garden seasonal flower meadow. Extensive guided tours, waymarked walks, cycle routes (all year), Hervey family church,

den-building, children's play area and trim trail. **Dogs**: welcome on leads at all times. Assistance dogs only in the Italianate Garden.

Access: ⓟⓓ🖼️🖼️🖼️🖼️🖼️🖼️🖼️🖼️
House 🖼️🖼️↕️🖼️♿ **West Wing** 🖼️🖼️↕️🖼️♿
Gardens/parkland 🖼️➡️🖼️♿
Sat Nav: may not direct you to main entrance. Access to Ickworth is through Horringer village.
Parking: on site.

Find out more: 01284 735270 or ickworth@nationaltrust.org.uk

Ickworth		M	T	W	T	F	S	S
House								
4 Mar–29 Oct*	11–5	M	T		T	F	S	S
30 Oct–31 Dec**	11–3	M	T	W	T	F	S	S
Gift shop and West Wing café†								
1 Jan–3 Mar	10:30–4	M	T	W	T	F	S	S
4 Mar–29 Oct	10:30–5	M	T	W	T	F	S	S
30 Oct–31 Dec	10:30–4	M	T	W	T	F	S	S
Porter's Lodge outdoor café								
1 Jan–26 Feb	11–4						S	S
4 Mar–29 Oct	10–5	M	T	W	T	F	S	S
4 Nov–31 Dec	11–4						S	S
Plant and garden shop								
4 Mar–29 Oct	10–5	M	T	W	T	F	S	S
4 Nov–31 Dec	12–3						S	S

*Tours only 11 to 12 and 4 to 5; free-flow 12 to 4.
**Tours only weekdays; basement free-flow only weekends.
†West Wing reception open as gift shop and café.
House: open additional Wednesdays in Suffolk school holidays; last entry 45 minutes before closing. Italianate garden, parkland, woods and children's playground: open daily, 9 to 5:30 (closes dusk if earlier). Plant and garden shop may close earlier in winter. Porter's Lodge outdoor café may close in adverse weather. Closed 24 and 25 December.

Kyson Hill

Broomheath, Woodbridge, Suffolk

🖼️🖼️ 1934

Diminutive Kyson Hill, with its grassy slopes, specimen trees and estuarine views, is a favourite destination for walking or relaxation. **Note**: sorry no toilet. Broomheath public car park, 546 yards (not National Trust). For Sat Nav use IP12 4DL. OS map reference is 197/212:TM264478.

Find out more: 01394 389700 (Sutton Hoo) or kysonhill@nationaltrust.org.uk

Lavenham Guildhall

Market Place, Lavenham, Sudbury,
Suffolk CO10 9QZ

🏠 ❖ 1951

Set in the lovely village of Lavenham, the
Guildhall of Corpus Christi tells the story of one
of the best-preserved and wealthiest towns in
Tudor England. When you step inside this fine
timber-framed building, you'll feel the centuries
melt away. You can discover the stories of the
people who have used the Guildhall through
almost 500 years at the heart of its community,
and learn about the men and women who
have shaped the fortunes of this unique village.
Then you can explore the picturesque streets
of Lavenham, lined with shops, galleries and
more than 320 buildings of historic interest.

Timber-framed Lavenham Guildhall in Suffolk,
above and below, has stood at the
heart of its community for almost 500 years

Eat, shop, stay: tea-room serving light lunches, cream teas and hot and cold drinks. Shop selling local gifts, souvenirs, books and plants.

Things to see and do: **Indoors** Children's trails and dressing-up costumes. Changing exhibitions. **Outdoors** Guided walks and talks in summer.

Access: [icons] Guildhall [icons] Garden [icons]
Parking: in village (free) – no National Trust parking. Nearest car parks at Prentice Street (200 yards, 24 spaces), use CO10 9RD, and main car park Church Street (800 yards, 86 spaces), use CO10 9SA.

Find out more: 01787 247646 or lavenhamguildhall@nationaltrust.org.uk

Lavenham Guildhall		M	T	W	T	F	S	S
7 Jan–26 Feb*	11–4						S	S
1 Mar–29 Oct	11–5	M	T	W	T	F	S	S
2 Nov–24 Dec	11–4				T	F	S	S

*Open for guided tours only, on the hour 11 to 3.
1 to 3 December: Lavenham Christmas fair (admission free).

Melford Hall

Long Melford, Sudbury, Suffolk CO10 9AA

[icons] 1960

There are many stories to discover in this eclectic family home. Melford Hall has had its fair share of trials and tribulations, from being ransacked during the Civil War to being devastated by fire in 1942. It is thanks to the many generations who have left their mark that it continues to survive. It remains the Hyde Parkers' much-loved family home and it is their stories of family life, from naval exploits to visits from their cousin Beatrix Potter, which makes this house more than mere bricks and mortar.

Eat, shop, stay: small tea-room or Park Room serving sandwiches and cream teas. Gatehouse shop selling souvenirs, gifts, books, souvenir story books and plants.

Things to see and do: **Indoors** Talks. Spot-it quiz for children under eight and Spy Catcher trail for older children (up to 13).

Outdoors Garden games. Walks, talks and family events. **Dogs**: welcome on leads in car park and park walk only.

Access: ⬚⬚⬚⬚⬚⬚⬚⬚⬚
Building ⬚⬚⬚⬚⬚ Grounds ⬚⬚
Parking: on site.

Find out more: 01787 376395 (Infoline).
01787 379228 or melford@nationaltrust.org.uk

Melford Hall			M	T	W	T	F	S	S
29 Mar–29 Oct*	12–5			·	W	T	F	S	S

*Closed Saturday 6 May. Open Bank Holiday Mondays.
12 to 1: entry to house by short taster tour only.

Morven Park

Great North Road, Potters Bar, Hertfordshire

⬚ 1928

On the site of the original Potters Bar, these 8 hectares (20 acres) of parkland are over 150 years old. **Note**: sorry no toilet. For Sat Nav use EN6 1HS.

Find out more: 01582 873663 or morvenpark@nationaltrust.org.uk

Northey Island

near Maldon, Essex

⬚⬚⬚⬚ 1978

A peaceful retreat in the Blackwater Estuary, important for overwintering birds, Northey is also the oldest recorded battlefield in Britain. **Note**: causeway access is restricted by tides. Telephone in advance to arrange your visit. For Sat Nav use CM9 6PP (CM9 5JQ for parking).

Find out more: 01621 853142 or northeyisland@nationaltrust.org.uk

Despite its peaceful appearance, Melford Hall in Suffolk has suffered more than its fair share of trials and tribulations. Now it is a much-loved family home

Orford Ness National Nature Reserve

Orford Quay, Orford, Woodbridge, Suffolk IP12 2NU

⌂ ♿ 🖼 🚻 1993

Orford Ness National Nature Reserve, Suffolk: rare and fragile wildlife thrives where weapons were once tested

This is Suffolk's secret coast, only reached by National Trust ferry. Wild, remote and exposed, the 'Island' contains the ruined remnants of a disturbing past. Ranked among the most important shingle features in the world, rare and fragile wildlife thrives where weapons, including atomic bombs, were once tested and perfected. **Note**: limited tickets. Steep, slippery steps, long distances. Hazardous debris. Limited access: 'pagodas' only on tours. Charge for ferry crossing (including members).

Eat, shop, stay: shops, cafés and pubs in village (none National Trust). Fresh fish available at quay. Local smokehouses.

Things to see and do: walk the trails through coastal grazing marsh and vegetated shingle habitats to the sea, taking in wildlife, ex-military testing areas, buildings and displays. Events and booked guided tours available. **Dogs**: assistance dogs only.

Access: 🅿♿🖼🏛 Buildings ♿🚻 Trails ♿🅿
Parking: at Riverside car park, Quay Street, not National Trust (charge including members), 150 yards to Trust Orford Quay office to buy ferry ticket.

Find out more: 01728 648024 (Infoline). 01394 450900 (tour bookings) or orfordness@nationaltrust.org.uk

Orford Ness		M	T	W	T	F	S	S
15 Apr–24 Jun	10–2							S
27 Jun–30 Sep	10–2			T	W	T	F	S
7 Oct–28 Oct	10–2							S

Access by National Trust ferry from Orford Quay. Boats cross every 20 minutes, 10 to 2 only, returning regularly through day (last ferry departs 5). Tickets limited, only available on day. Main visitor trail (Red Route) always available, other routes open seasonally.

Oxburgh Hall

Oxborough, near Swaffham, Norfolk PE33 9PS

⌂ ✝ ♣ ♿ 🖼 🍴 1952

No one forgets their first sight of Oxburgh. Built in 1482 by the Catholic Bedingfeld family, it is the enduring legacy of their survival through turbulent times. There are 500 years of history to explore and hidden doors, rooftop views and a secret priest's hole to discover.

Victorian Gothic interiors reflect a romantic view of Oxburgh's medieval past. The collections include embroideries worked by Mary, Queen of Scots, and colourful wallpapers from the mid-19th century. The moated hall is surrounded by nearly 28 hectares (70 acres), containing gardens with seasonal interest, streams and woodland walks.

Eat, shop, stay: tea-room in old Kitchen and Servants' Hall. The Pantry is a seasonal kiosk serving light refreshments. Picnic in the grounds or the area by the car park. Gift shop selling gifts, games and local products. Plant sales. Second-hand bookshop.

Things to see and do: Indoors Introductory talks most days, March to October. Family trails. **Outdoors** Daily guided garden tours, March to October. Winter weekend snowdrop walks. Children's activities, including woodland den-building area. Year-round events.
Dogs: on short leads in the gardens and countryside. Assistance dogs only indoors.

Moated Oxburgh Hall in Norfolk is a house of secrets, with hidden doors and a priest's hole. Among its many collections are embroideries worked on by Mary, Queen of Scots

Access: 🏷️🖐️🧏🔄🎧📷📺📶♿
Hall ♿🪜🚻♿ Chapel 🪜 Garden ♿➡️♿
Parking: on site.

Find out more: 01366 328258 or oxburghhall@nationaltrust.org.uk

Oxburgh Hall		M	T	W	T	F	S	S
House								
11 Feb–10 Mar	12–3	M	T	W	T	F	S	S
11 Mar–1 Oct	11–5	M	T	W	T	F	S	S
2 Oct–29 Oct	11–4	M	T	W	T	F	S	S
Garden, shop and tea-room								
1 Jan–12 Feb	11–4	·	·	·	·	·	S	S
13 Feb–10 Mar	11–4	M	T	W	T	F	S	S
11 Mar–1 Oct	10:30–5	M	T	W	T	F	S	S
2 Oct–29 Oct	10:30–4	M	T	W	T	F	S	S
4 Nov–23 Dec	11–4	·	·	·	·	·	S	S

Paycocke's House and Garden

25 West Street, Coggeshall, Colchester, Essex CO6 1NS

🏠✳️ 1924

Exquisitely carved half-timbered Tudor cloth merchant's house, with a beautiful and tranquil cottage garden. Visitors can follow the house's changing fortune, see how it was saved from demolition and restored to its former glory. You can admire carved timbers, architectural features and discover details about Coggeshall White cloth. **Note**: toilet on first floor only.

Paycocke's House and Garden, Essex: Tudor cloth merchant's house

Paycocke's House and Garden: once facing demolition, it has now been restored to its former glory

Eat, shop, stay: coffee shop serving cream teas, coffee, cakes and soft drinks (courtyard and garden). Picnics welcome. Ice-cream available. Shop selling gifts and local products. Plants for sale at our garden stall. Second-hand bookshop.

Things to see and do: Indoors Events all year, including annual exhibition. Children's dressing-up costumes. **Outdoors** Relax or play garden games. Why not combine with visit to nearby Grange Barn and enjoy the circular walk? **Dogs**: welcome in garden only on a lead; assistance dogs only in house.

Access: ⬚⬚⬚⬚⬚ Building ⬚ Grounds ⬚⬚
Parking: at Coggeshall Grange Barn, ½ mile, or at Stoneham Street car park, ¼ mile (not National Trust). Limited roadside parking.

Find out more: 01376 561305 or paycockes@nationaltrust.org.uk

Paycocke's		M	T	W	T	F	S	S
House								
18 Mar–1 Oct	11–5	M	T	W	T	F	S	S
2 Oct–29 Oct	11–4	M	T	W	T	F	S	S

Garden: open 10:30 to house closing time; not open winter. House: limited areas open from 30 October due to conservation. Closed 25 to 29 December.

Peckover House and Garden

North Brink, Wisbech, Cambridgeshire PE13 1JR

⬚⬚⬚⬚⬚ 1943

While its riverside setting at Wisbech was popular among merchants, imposing Peckover House stood apart as an oasis of calm, reflecting the Quaker way of life. As you wander through the intimate rooms, you can imagine the family reading in the library and talking with friends in the drawing-room. The Peckovers were bankers and added a specially designed wing to the house; an exhibition tells its story. They also

loved their garden, and you can discover its delights as you explore the unexpected 0.8 hectare (2 acres), discovering borders, summerhouses, an orangery and 60 varieties of rose. **Note**: Octavia Hill's Birthplace House open opposite (not National Trust).

Eat, shop, stay: the Reed Barn is the ideal place for a light lunch or afternoon tea. Browse our gift shop, second-hand bookshop and our plant trolley. Stay a little longer in one of our holiday cottages – Wainman House or Coach House Loft.

Things to see and do: **Indoors** Grand piano to play. Behind-the-scenes tours. Handling collection and children's trails. Ever-changing exhibitions. Octavia Hill's Birthplace House opposite. **Outdoors** Free garden tours. Croquet and lawn games (summer). **Dogs**: assistance dogs only.

Access: ▯▯▯▯▯▯▯
House ▯▯ Garden ▯▯▯
Sat Nav: use PE13 1RG or PE13 2RA for nearest car parks. **Parking**: nearest at Chapel Road or Somers Road, 500 yards (not National Trust). Car parks occasionally used for town events and may not be in use – please check before journey.

Find out more: 01945 583463 or peckover@nationaltrust.org.uk

Peckover House and Garden		M	T	W	T	F	S	S
14 Jan–19 Feb	12–4*	·	·	·	·	·	S	S
25 Feb–2 Apr	11–4**	M	T	W	T	·	S	S
3 Apr–16 Apr	11–5[1]	M	T	W	T	F	S	S
17 Apr–25 Jun	11–5[1]	M	T	W	T	·	S	S
26 Jun–2 Jul	11–5[1]	M	T	W	T	F	S	S
3 Jul–22 Oct	11–5[1]	M	T	W	T	·	S	S
23 Oct–29 Oct	11–4[1]	M	T	W	T	F	S	S
4 Nov–19 Nov	11–4**	·	·	·	·	·	S	S
9 Dec–17 Dec[2]	11–4	M	T	W	T	F	S	S

*House: open for conservation talk at 2 only (limited spaces, booking advisable). **House open by timed tours only. [1]House open 12 to 4. Closed 1 June for wedding. [2]Christmas Celebration.

A flush of brilliant pink-red roses covers an arch at Peckover House and Garden in Cambridgeshire, left, contrasting with the cool blues and greys of the gracious drawing-room, below

Pin Mill

near Chelmondiston, Suffolk

 1978

A woodland and heathland restoration site. A number of footpaths from the village with panoramic views over the River Orwell. **Note**: for Sat Nav use IP9 1JW. Parking in Pin Mill village, not National Trust (charge including members), or Chelmondiston.

Find out more: 01206 298260 or pinmill@nationaltrust.org.uk

Ramsey Abbey Gatehouse

Hollow Lane, Ramsey, Huntingdon, Cambridgeshire PE26 1DH

 1952

This fascinating medieval gatehouse, along with the Lady Chapel, are all that remain of the great Benedictine abbey at Ramsey. **Note**: in school grounds so no public access except on open days. Gatehouse and Lady Chapel open first Sunday of the month, April to September, 1 to 5.

Find out more: 01480 301494 or ramseyabbey@nationaltrust.org.uk

Rayleigh Mount

Rayleigh, Essex

 1923

Medieval motte-and-bailey castle site, with adjacent windmill housing historical exhibition. **Note**: exhibition in windmill operated by Rochford District Council. For Sat Nav use SS6 7ED. Parking at Bellingham Lane –

adjacent to main entrance (not National Trust). Opening times may vary, telephone 01268 775328 to check.

Find out more: 01284 747500 or rayleighmount@nationaltrust.org.uk

Sharpenhoe

Sharpenhoe Road, Streatley, Bedfordshire

1939

Dominating the landscape, this steep chalk escarpment is crowned with beech woodland and at the northern end traces of an Iron Age hill fort. Managed as a nature reserve, there is wildlife to discover all year around. **Note**: sorry no toilets.

Access:
Sat Nav: use LU3 3PR.
Parking: on Sharpenhoe Road, Streatley.

Find out more: 01582 873663 or sharpenhoe@nationaltrust.org.uk

Shaw's Corner

Ayot St Lawrence, near Welwyn, Hertfordshire AL6 9BX

1944

George Bernard Shaw's tranquil rural home shows what inspired this great philosopher playwright. Pictures and sculpture reflect his wide circle of friends in theatre and the arts. See the secluded writing hut where he created plays which won the Nobel Prize, an Oscar and the hearts of millions of admirers. **Note**: access roads very narrow.

Eat, shop, stay: small gift shop. Second-hand bookshop. Ice-cream and soft drinks available in garden. Pre-1950s varieties of plants for sale.

Things to see and do: events, including open-air performances of George Bernard Shaw's plays (summer). **Dogs**: assistance dogs only.

Shaw's Corner in Hertfordshire:
George Bernard Shaw's tranquil rural home

Access: [icons]
House [icons] Grounds [icons]
Sat Nav: use AL6 9BX (some routes might take you through a ford and a route not signposted to Shaw's Corner). **Parking:** very limited (not suitable for large vehicles).

Find out more: 01438 821968 (Infoline).
01438 820307 or
shawscorner@nationaltrust.org.uk

Shaw's Corner		M	T	W	T	F	S	S
25 Mar–29 Oct	12–5		·	**W**	**T**	**F**	**S**	**S**

Open Bank Holiday Mondays. Garden closes 5:30.

Sheringham Park

Upper Sheringham, Norfolk NR26 8TL

[icons] 1987

Using the undulating landscape laid down by glaciers 430,000 years ago, Humphry Repton created views of the North Norfolk coast that can still be enjoyed today. His 1812 design stated 'Sheringham Park had more natural beauty and advantages than any place he had ever seen'. The Upcher family added an extensive rhododendron collection to Repton's design, bringing an array of colour to the wild garden in the spring. A walk may be interrupted by the drumming of a woodpecker, the song of skylarks as they spiral above you, or the sound of a steam train travelling through the park.
Note: Sheringham Hall is privately occupied. April to September: limited access by written appointment with leaseholder.

Eat, shop, stay: gift shop selling guidebooks, local gifts and souvenirs. Peat-free plant sales. Courtyard Café serving soup, sandwiches, cake and ice-cream. A range of gluten-free food also available. Picnics welcome. Five holiday cottages on site.

Sheringham Park in Norfolk: Humphry Repton used the natural undulating landscape as the basis of his design

Views from Sheringham Park towards the distant sea, top, while above, visitors are entranced by colourful blooms

Things to see and do: self-guided trails and guided walks (suggested routes downloadable from website). Climb to top of Gazebo tower to see coastal views enjoyed since Napoleonic times. Free use of children's Tracker Packs. **Dogs**: welcome under control. Please keep on leads near livestock and visitor facilities.

Access: 🅿️ 🖼️ 🎭 🔔 🖼️ ♿ 📷 📷
Building ♿ ♿ **Grounds** ♿ ➡️ 🔆 ♿
Parking: 60 yards.

Find out more: 01263 820550 or sheringhampark@nationaltrust.org.uk

Sheringham Park		M	T	W	T	F	S	S
Park								
Open all year	Dawn–dusk	M	T	W	T	F	S	S
Visitor Centre and Courtyard Café*								
7 Jan–5 Mar	11–4						S	S
11 Mar–29 Oct	10–5	M	T	W	T	F	S	S
4 Nov–31 Dec	11–4						S	S

*Courtyard Café opens 8:45 and Visitor Centre 9:30 every Saturday. Visitor Centre and Courtyard Café open daily, 10 to 5, 11 to 19 February, 11 to 4, 27 to 31 December; open until 6, 14 to 17 April, and until 7, 19 May, 26 May to 2 June and 9 June. Closed 24 December.

Sundon Hills Country Park

Harlington Road, Upper Sundon, Bedfordshire

♿ 🐾 2000

Wildlife-rich chalk grassland, beech woodland, open meadows and a picnic site with views north towards the Greensand Ridge.
Note: sorry no toilets. For Sat Nav use LU3 3PE.

Find out more: 01582 873663 or sundonhills@nationaltrust.org.uk

Sutton Hoo

Tranmer House, Sutton Hoo, Woodbridge, Suffolk IP12 3DJ

🏠 🏛️ ♿ 🛏️ 🍴 1998

Shortly before the outbreak of the Second World War, the ship burial of an Anglo-Saxon king and his extraordinary treasures were unearthed by archaeologist Basil Brown. These ancient graves kept their secrets for 1,300 years, but what was found here changed our perceptions of the past for ever. The atmospheric burial mounds, breathtaking replica treasures, original finds and reconstruction of the king's burial chamber bring this fascinating story to life. Edith Pretty's country house takes you back to that remarkable discovery, while relaxing in true 1930s style. Walks across this Anglo-Saxon landscape offer stunning views over the River Deben.

Eat, shop, stay: café serving hot meals, snacks and cream teas with views of the River Deben. Range of gifts in our shop. Second-hand bookshop. Stay in one of our three spacious apartments in an impressive house in a unique and atmospheric location.

Things to see and do: **Indoors** Exhibition – introductory video, information panels, audio recordings, dressing-up, replica treasures, burial reconstruction. House – 1930s decoration, gramophone, children's quiz, Basil's workshop. **Outdoors** Burial mound tours, circular walks. Children's play area. **Dogs**: welcome on leads in reception, shop, café terrace and countryside only.

Access: 🅿️♿👓🦻📷🎧🎵📶
Buildings 🏠♿ **Grounds** 🏠➡️♿♿
Parking: on site.

Find out more: 01394 389700 or suttonhoo@nationaltrust.org.uk

Sutton Hoo		M	T	W	T	F	S	S
1 Jan–5 Feb	10:30–4						S	S
11 Feb–29 Oct	10:30–5	M	T	W	T	F	S	S
4 Nov–17 Dec	10:30–4						S	S
27 Dec–31 Dec	10:30–4			W	T	F	S	S

Estate walks open daily, 9 to 6 (except some Thursdays, November to end December).

Ancient graves are lit by a misty early morning sun at Sutton Hoo in Suffolk. The discoveries unearthed at this remarkable site changed our views of the past for ever

Theatre Royal Bury St Edmunds

Westgate Street, Bury St Edmunds, Suffolk IP33 1QR

🏠🔔🍴 1974

Grade I listed theatre, one of the country's most significant theatre buildings and the only surviving Regency playhouse in Britain. **Note**: managed by Bury St Edmunds Theatre Management Ltd. Admission charges apply to live shows and selected guided tours (including members). Please call before visiting, as opening times may vary due to performances.

Find out more: 01284 769505 or theatreroyal@nationaltrust.org.uk

Totternhoe Knolls

Castle Hill Road, Totternhoe, Bedfordshire

🏛️♿👤 2000

The dramatic earthworks of a Norman castle rise from important chalk grassland habitat, sitting high above the surrounding landscape. **Note**: sorry no toilets. For Sat Nav use LU6 1RG.

Find out more: 01582 873663 or totternhoeknolls@nationaltrust.org.uk

West Runton and Beeston Regis Heath

near West Runton, Norfolk

🏛️♿ 1925

A lovely place to walk among heath and woods, with fine views of the North Norfolk coast. **Note**: sorry no toilets. For Sat Nav use NR27 9ND.

Find out more: 01263 820550 or westrunton@nationaltrust.org.uk

Whipsnade Tree Cathedral

Whipsnade, Dunstable, Bedfordshire

♿ 1960

Peaceful place with trees planted in shape of medieval cathedral. Created after the First World War to commemorate fallen comrades. **Note**: dogs allowed under control. Annual service second Sunday, June. Car park open 9 to 4 (winter); 9 to 7 (summer). For Sat Nav use LU6 2LQ. Donations welcome.

Find out more: 01582 872406 or whipsnadetc@nationaltrust.org.uk

Wicken Fen National Nature Reserve

Lode Lane, Wicken, Ely, Cambridgeshire

♿♿👤 1899

With vast skies above flowering meadows, sedge and reed-beds, Wicken Fen is a window onto a lost fenland landscape. A wealth of wildlife is at home in this important wetland, including rarities such as hen harriers and bitterns, numerous dragonflies, moths and wildfowl. The landscape feels wild, though people have managed it for years, as revealed by the fenman's yard, windpump and cottage. The Wicken Fen Vision, an ambitious landscape-scale conservation project, is opening up new areas for wildlife and for you to explore. Grazing herds of Highland cattle and Konik ponies help create a diverse range of new habitats. **Note**: some paths may be subject to seasonal closure.

Eat, shop, stay: shop in the visitor centre selling wildlife and outdoor books, local food and crafts. Café serving light lunches and afternoon teas. Picnics welcome.

Wicken Fen National Nature Reserve in Cambridgeshire, below and right: a window onto a lost fenland landscape

Things to see and do: explore the heart of the Fen on foot, via the Boardwalk and longer paths. Seasonal boat trips available. Cycle across the wider reserve; we hire bikes, or bring your own. **Dogs**: welcome on leads on reserve and in visitor centre.

Access:
Building **Grounds**
Sat Nav: use CB7 5XP. **Parking**: 120 yards.

Find out more: 01353 720274 or wickenfen@nationaltrust.org.uk

Wicken Fen		M	T	W	T	F	S	S
Reserve, visitor centre and shop								
Open all year	10-5*	**M**	**T**	**W**	**T**	**F**	**S**	**S**
Café								
1 Jan–12 Feb	10–4:30	·	·	**W**	**T**	**F**	**S**	**S**
13 Feb–29 Oct	10–5	**M**	**T**	**W**	**T**	**F**	**S**	**S**
30 Oct–31 Dec	10–4:30	**M**	**T**	**W**	**T**	**F**	**S**	**S**

*Access to reserve dawn to dusk; visitor centre closes dusk in winter. Closed 25 December.

Willington Dovecote and Stables

Willington, Church End, near Bedford, Bedfordshire MK44 3PX

1914

A hidden gem in a tranquil setting; were these magnificent Tudor stone buildings built for Henry VIII's 1541 visit? **Note**: admission by appointment with the volunteer team, contact Mrs J. Endersby, 21 Chapel Lane, Willington MK44 3QG (01234 838278).

Find out more: 01480 301494 or willingtondovecote@nationaltrust.org.uk

Wimpole Estate

Arrington, Royston, Cambridgeshire SG8 0BW

🏠✝🏛️♿♻️⚓🔔🍽️ 1976

Fun on the farm at Wimpole Estate in Cambridgeshire

A unique working estate, with an impressive mansion at its heart. Discover Wimpole's acres of parkland, miles of walks, vibrant Walled Kitchen Garden and active Home Farm. Explore the hall, where intimate rooms contrast with beautiful Georgian interiors. With its various owners driven by passions and purposeful agendas, Wimpole is both a place to escape to and a place to get involved. We continue the 3rd Earl of Hardwicke's passion for trail-blazing food production and design, celebrating the estate's past magnificence and echoing Elsie Bambridge's 20th-century revival. As owners changed, a roll-call of ingenious architects, artists and landscape designers cultivated magnificence. Wimpole is an 'all-year-round' place to visit, reflecting the changing seasons, with something to captivate and inspire all visitors.

Eat, shop, stay: choose from the Old Rectory Restaurant, Farm Café and Stables Café, serving produce from the Walled Garden and Home Farm. Stable shop with gifts and plants, Wimpole rare-breed meat, flour, apple juice and eggs. Second-hand bookshop, toy shop.

Things to see and do: **Indoors** Explore the Hall at your own pace or try a bookable basement tour. Discover our contemporary art display. Pop into the Gardener's Cottage to uncover our garden history.

Entry is still possible at most places up to 30 minutes before closing

Outdoors Seasonal spectaculars, including daffodils, spring blossom, summer parterre, herbaceous borders and autumn trees. Free guided walks in the parkland, and geocaching. Daily farm activities: grooming the donkey, meeting the Shire horse, rabbits, feeding the pigs and milking the cow. Lambing time. History festival, open-air theatre, literary festival, '50 things to do before you're 11¾' and Christmas events. Sporting activities, including running and walking groups, cycle and running trails. **Dogs**: welcome on leads in park and near livestock.

Access: 🅿 ♿ 🚻 ♿ ♿ 🌀 🖼 🎫 📷
Hall 🅻 ♿ Farm 🅰 ♿ Gardens 🅰 ➡ 🚿 ♿
Sat Nav: entrance via A603, not A1198.
Parking: 275 yards.

Find out more: 01223 206000 or wimpole@nationaltrust.org.uk

Wimpole Estate		M	T	W	T	F	S	S
Garden, Old Rectory Restaurant and stable block								
1 Jan–10 Feb	11–4	M	T	W	T	F	S	S
11 Feb–29 Oct	10–5	M	T	W	T	F	S	S
30 Oct–31 Dec	11–4	M	T	W	T	F	S	S
Home Farm and Farm Café								
1 Jan–5 Feb	11–4						S	S
11 Feb–29 Oct	10:30–5	M	T	W	T	F	S	S
4 Nov–31 Dec	11–4						S	S
Hall								
11 Feb–29 Oct	11–5	M	T	W	T	F	S	S
Hall (guided basement tour)								
4 Nov–26 Nov	11–3						S	S

Park: open daily all year dawn to dusk. Home Farm: open 1 to 4 January and 27 to 31 December, 11 to 4. Estate: closed 25 and 26 December, however park and stable block (café and gift shops) open 26 December, 11 to 4. Bookshop: as shop, but closed Monday mornings. Car park: open 7:30 to 6:30.

The lavish interiors at Wimpole Estate, left, match the impressive exterior of this magnificent mansion, below

East Midlands

Ilam Park, Dovedale and the White Peak, Derbyshire
Competition entry from Roy Kennie

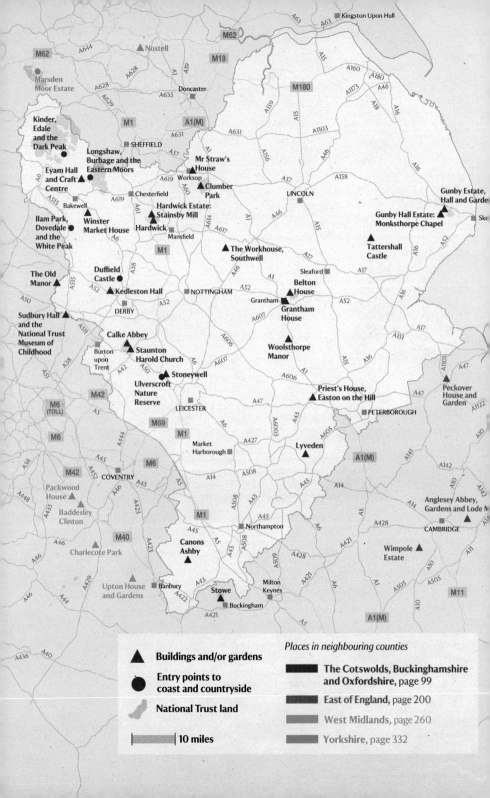

Kingston Upon Hull

M62

Nostell

M18

Marsden
Moor Estate

Doncaster

M180

Kinder,
Edale
and the
Dark Peak

SHEFFIELD

Longshaw,
Burbage and the
Eastern Moors

Mr Straw's
House

Gunby Estate,
Hall and Garde

Eyam Hall
and Craft
Centre

Chesterfield

Worksop

Clumber
Park

LINCOLN

Gunby Hall Estate:
Monksthorpe Chapel

Ske

Bakewell

Hardwick Estate:
Stainsby Mill

Ilam Park,
Dovedale
and the
White Peak

Winster
Market House

Hardwick

Mansfield

Tattershall
Castle

The Old
Manor

Duffield
Castle

The Workhouse,
Southwell

Sleaford

Kedleston Hall

NOTTINGHAM

Belton
House

DERBY

Grantham

Grantham
House

Sudbury Hall
and the
National Trust
Museum of
Childhood

Calke Abbey

Burton
upon
Trent

Staunton
Harold Church

Woolsthorpe
Manor

Stoneywell

Ulverscroft
Nature
Reserve

LEICESTER

Priest's House,
Easton on the Hill

PETERBOROUGH

M6
(TOLL)

M6

M42

M69

M1

Market
Harborough

Lyveden

A1(M)

M42

COVENTRY

Peckover
House and
Garden

Packwood
House

Baddesley
Clinton

M6

Anglesey Abbey,
Gardens and Lode M

M1

Northampton

CAMBRIDGE

M40

Charlecote Park

Canons
Ashby

Wimpole
Estate

Upton House
and Gardens

Banbury

Stowe

Milton
Keynes

M11

Buckingham

A1(M)

Buildings and/or gardens

Entry points to
coast and countryside

National Trust land

10 miles

Places in neighbouring counties

The Cotswolds, Buckinghamshire
and Oxfordshire, page 99

East of England, page 200

West Midlands, page 260

Yorkshire, page 332

The fine furnishings and opulent décor of Belton House in Lincolnshire are matched by elegant formal gardens

Belton House

Grantham, Lincolnshire NG32 2LS

🏠 ✝ ❀ ♿ 🔔 ⅄ 1984

Sitting elegantly in formal gardens with views across pleasure grounds and an ancient deer-park, Belton is often cited as being the perfect example of an English country-house estate. Although built on a modest scale, it has a fine collection of porcelain and silver, a world-renowned library and architectural finesse that reflects the continued wealth and cultured tastes of its former owners, the

Brownlow family. In more recent times, Belton has become a popular destination for families in search of outdoor fun, with seasonal trails and the National Trust's largest open-air adventure playground. **Note**: restoration work due to start on Stables late this year. Whole property closed 9/10 January.

Eat, shop, stay: Stables Café serving hot meals (between 12 and 2), including Belton's award-winning venison (in season). Snacks and light meals served in Ride Play Café and outdoor playground kiosk. Two shops selling gifts, plants and local produce. Large second-hand bookshop.

Things to see and do: Indoors You can enjoy the mansion show rooms at your own pace, with no set visitor route. Learn more about the house with themed interpretation and guided tours. The 'below stairs' servant areas are open all year, by guided tour. For young families there's an indoor adventure play café, and a discovery centre for weekend and school holiday activities.

Outdoors Downloadable walks and seasonal trails. Open-air cinema and theatre in the summer. Extensive outdoor adventure playground. Family-focused events during the school holidays. Christmas lights and events. Woolsthorpe Manor, home of Sir Isaac Newton, is nearby. **Dogs**: welcome in parkland and stableyard on leads. Assistance dogs only in gardens, playground and mansion.

Access: 🅿️🚐♿🚾📷🖼️🎦♿🔄
House 🔽♿🔽 Grounds ♿➡️🔄🔽
Sat Nav: use NG32 2LW. **Parking**: on site.

Find out more: 01476 566116 or belton@nationaltrust.org.uk

Belton House		M	T	W	T	F	S	S
House								
4 Mar–5 Nov	12:30–5	·	·	**W**	**T**	**F**	**S**	**S**
Shops, restaurant, Ride Play Café, adventure playground*								
Open all year	9:30–5:30	**M**	**T**	**W**	**T**	**F**	**S**	**S**
Basement**								
Open all year†	Tour	**M**	**T**	**W**	**T**	**F**	**S**	**S**

*Close at 4 in winter. **Tours 11 to 3; last tour at 2 in winter.
†Volunteer-led tours (subject to availability).
Park and gardens: open as shops and restaurant.
Bellmount Woods: open daily (access from separate car park).
Whole property closed 9, 10 January and 25 December.

The richly furnished Hondecoeter Room at Belton House, above, hints at the lavish hospitality which the house was once famous for. Below, children explore the boathouse

Despite the grand façade, Calke Abbey in Derbyshire tells the tale of a country house and estate in crisis

Calke Abbey

Ticknall, Derby, Derbyshire DE73 7LE

🏠➕🔥❄️🎔👕🦽🍽️ 1985

Calke Abbey tells the story of the dramatic decline of the Harpur Crewe's once-grand country estate. This year we reveal more of the hidden objects, curiosities and stories about this once forbidden and intriguing estate. The house and stables have been preserved as found in the 1980s, with grand rooms crammed full of collections – from art to natural history. These contrast with abandoned rooms and objects no longer used. You can explore the overgrown stable courtyards, with their peeling paintwork and faded garden buildings, such as the Orangery, which hint at former fortunes. Beyond the garden, the historic and fragile habitats of Calke Park and its National Nature Reserve await discovery, together with the limeyards, wetlands, ancient trees and ponds. **Note**: everyone requires admission tickets for house and garden (including members). House admission by timed ticket.

Eat, shop, stay: restaurant meals include dishes made with estate-reared meat. Café open every weekend and at peak times. Estate-reared burgers on offer from our barbecue (peak times). Large gift shop selling seasonal gifts, plants and local food. Five estate cottages.

Things to see and do: Indoors Family activities in Squirt's Stable at weekends and during school holidays (February to October).

The abandoned stables at Calke Abbey, above, contrast strangely with the splendour of the saloon, left

Park play map available from the ticket office. Tramway cycling and walking circuit suitable for all the family. **Dogs**: welcome on leads in parkland and stableyards; assistance dogs only in the house and garden.

Access: 🅿♿🚼🔆🔍📷🎥📹🎵♿
House ♿♿♿ Stables ♿♿ Grounds ♿♿➡
Sat Nav: use DE73 7JF. **Parking**: on site.

Find out more: 01332 863822 or calkeabbey@nationaltrust.org.uk

Calke Abbey		M	T	W	T	F	S	S
Calke Park National Nature Reserve†								
Open all year	7:30–7:30	M	T	W	T	F	S	S
House*								
4 Mar–31 Oct	11–5	M	T	W	T	F	S	S
Garden								
4 Feb–31 Oct	10–5	M	T	W	T	F	S	S
Stables, restaurant and shop**								
Open all year	10–5	M	T	W	T	F	S	S

†Closes dusk if earlier; closed 25 December. *House: ground-floor taster visit between 11 and 12:30; house opens fully 12:30 (admission by timed ticket). **Stables, restaurant and shop: close at 5 when house is open, March to October; at 4 all other times. Whole property closed 25 December.

Garden outbuildings to peek into, as well as tunnels in the house, garden and lime yards. **Outdoors** Events all year, whatever the weather, including guided park and garden walks, Fine Food and Vintage Fairs, open-air cinema, summer outdoor natural play and autumnal favourites, such as Apple Day and the Pumpkin Party. Children's play areas.

Canons Ashby

near Daventry, Northamptonshire NN11 3SD

🏠 ✝ 🏛 ♿ ❄ 🐾 | 1981 |

Ancient and peaceful, Canons Ashby is far removed from today's bustling lifestyle. Medieval canons built their priory near the little village of Ashby, but the dissolution left a curiously truncated church, and the village was lost, leaving nothing but mounds in the landscape. Nearby, the Elizabethan Dryden family built their home, making few changes over their 450 years of occupation. Victorian Sir Henry Dryden's curiosity led him to record the detail of the mansion, with its quirky blend of architectural styles, mysterious wall-paintings, plasterwork and fine furnishings. Outside, lush gardens, parkland, lakes and ancient church offer space for tranquil contemplation. **Note**: admission by timed tickets on busy days.

Eat, shop, stay: Stables tea-room and pretty tea-garden offering light meals and freshly baked treats. Coach House shop selling home and garden gifts and Canons Ashby home-grown plants. Well-stocked second-hand bookshop (donations welcome).

Things to see and do: **Indoors** Discovery trails for families in the house and church. **Outdoors** Parkland and garden walks all year. Open-air theatre and croquet in summer. Family activities during school holidays. **Dogs**: welcome on leads in car park, paddock, tea-garden and parkland only.

Built on the remains of a medieval priory, Canons Ashby in Northamptonshire, left, remains virtually unaltered since 1710. It contains such gems as Elizabethan murals, above

Access: 🅿 ♿ &c ♿ &c 📷 🏠 🚻 &c 🚻
Building 🏠 🚻 Church 🏠 Grounds 🏠 ♿
Parking: 218 yards.

Find out more: 01327 861900 or canonsashby@nationaltrust.org.uk

Canons Ashby		M	T	W	T	F	S	S
Tea-room, shop, gardens, priory church and parkland*								
11 Feb–10 Mar	10–3:30	M	T	W	T	F	S	S
11 Mar–29 Oct	10–5	M	T	W	T	F	S	S
30 Oct–22 Dec	10–3:30	M	T	W	T	F	S	S
27 Dec–31 Dec	10–3	·	·	W	T	F	S	S
House*								
11 Feb–10 Mar	11–3	M	T	W	·	F	S	S
11 Mar–29 Oct†	1–5†	M	T	W	·	F	S	S
4 Nov–3 Dec	11–3	·	·	·	·	·	S	S
9 Dec–17 Dec	11–3	M	T	W	T	F	S	S

†House taster tours: 11 to 1 (30 minutes, three rooms), book on arrival. *For conservation work some parts of garden and house may be closed during winter. Tea-room, shop, gardens, church, parkland: also open 1 to 5 January 2018.

Clumber Park

Worksop, Nottinghamshire S80 3BE

† ❀ ♨ ▲ ⊤ 1946

Clumber Park, Nottinghamshire: the Walled Kitchen Garden, above, and lake with Gothic Revival chapel, right

Carved out of the ancient forest of Sherwood, a space of playfulness and pleasure on a grand scale was created by the Dukes of Newcastle. Clumber Park is true to its spirit as a place of recreation, with 20 miles of cycle routes and 1,537 hectares (3,800 acres) of parkland, woodland and heathland to explore. The beauty of the Gothic Revival chapel, with its original stained-glass windows, reveal a rich historic past. The Pleasure Grounds frame the magnificent lake, making a perfect place to stroll or picnic. The Walled Kitchen Garden, with its National Collection of Rhubarb, provides a variety of fruit and vegetables to the café and colourful herbaceous borders during the summer.

Eat, shop, stay: café and garden tea house serving hot meals, snacks, cream teas and a children's menu. Barbecue at peak times. Large gift shop and plant sales. Second-hand bookshop; cycle hire, servicing and sales. Picnics welcome and designated barbecue site.

Things to see and do: Indoors Year-round activities for all ages and interests, including art, history and wildlife exhibitions at the Discovery Centre. The glasshouse and Museum of Gardening Tools at the Walled Kitchen Garden, Clumber chapel – a cathedral in miniature – The Burrow play area for under-threes and Willow Tree Farm exhibition. **Outdoors** Seasonal highlights include the spring bluebells, rhododendrons and apple blossom, late-summer-flowering heathers and autumn tree colour. During your visit, tick off some of the '50 things to do before you're 11¾'. There are many downloadable walks, woodland play areas, a cycle hire centre and many outdoor events. **Dogs**: welcome, some restrictions apply. An indoor refreshment area for dog walkers. Downloadable *Woof* guide.

Access:
Buildings **Grounds**
Parking: 250 yards.

Find out more: 01909 544917 or clumberpark@nationaltrust.org.uk

Clumber Park		M	T	W	T	F	S	S
Visitor facilities and Walled Kitchen Garden*								
1 Jan–25 Mar	10–4	M	T	W	T	F	S	S
26 Mar–28 Oct	10–5	M	T	W	T	F	S	S
29 Oct–31 Dec	10–4	M	T	W	T	F	S	S

*Walled Kitchen Garden: closes at 3:30, January to 25 March and 29 October to 31 December. Visitor facilities: close at 6 at the weekend, 26 March to 28 October (facilities include café, shop, Walled Kitchen Garden, cycle hire, chapel, Discovery Centre and woodland play park). Open daily, except 25 December. Café: open daily at 9. Tea House: open weekends, 11 to 4 and daily, 10 to 4, in school summer holidays. Chapel: closed 12 January to end March.

With 20 miles of cycle routes, the whole family can get active and enjoy a day exploring Clumber Park's beautiful and historic parkland, woods and heaths

Duffield Castle

Duffield, Derbyshire

[符][血] 1899

One of England's largest 13th-century castles – today you can see its foundations, imagine the stories and savour the views. **Note**: sorry no toilets. Steep steps. For Sat Nav use DE56 4DW.

Find out more: 01332 842191 or duffieldcastle@nationaltrust.org.uk

Eyam Hall and Craft Centre

Main Street, Eyam, Derbyshire S32 5QW

[符][❄][🍴] 2013

Eyam Hall and Craft Centre, Derbyshire: this unspoilt Jacobean house sits within a walled garden

Eyam Hall is an unspoilt example of a gritstone Jacobean manor house, set within a walled garden. Completed in 1672, it was home to the Wright family for 11 generations. Explore the legendary plague history of the village and the surrounding Peak District countryside.

Eat, shop, stay: gift and craft shops. Refreshments available.

Things to see and do: **Indoors** Seasonal events and themed workshops. **Outdoors** 'Thought walks', exploring some of the village stories and plague history, and guided walks. Hardwick Hall nearby. **Dogs**: welcome on 'thought walks'. Assistance dogs only in house and walled gardens.

The warm and welcoming library at Eyam Hall

Access: [icons] Building [icons]
Parking: 43 yards.

Find out more: 01433 639565 or eyam@nationaltrust.org.uk

Eyam Hall and Craft Centre		M	T	W	T	F	S	S
Craft Centre								
Open all year*	10:30–4:30		T	W	T	F	S	S
Hall								
11 Feb–29 Oct	10:30–4:30			W	T	F	S	S
4 Nov–12 Nov	10:30–3:30						S	S
18 Nov–17 Dec**	10:30–3:30			W	T	F	S	S

Independent craft shops and refreshments opening hours may vary from National Trust. *Open Bank Holidays, April to August. **Reduced number of rooms available to view in December.

Grantham House

Castlegate, Grantham, Lincolnshire NG31 6SS

[符][❄] 1944

Handsome town house, one of the oldest buildings in Grantham, with riverside walled garden. **Note**: leased by the National Trust and the lessee is responsible for arrangements and facilities. Open by appointment only with lessee, Wednesdays and Thursdays, April to October, 2 to 5 (appointments not required in June).

Find out more: 01476 564705 or granthamhouse@nationaltrust.org.uk

Gunby Estate, Hall and Gardens

Gunby, Spilsby, Lincolnshire PE23 5SS

🏠 ✚ 🏛 ❀ 🐾 🛏 🔔 1944

The Massingberd family home from 1700 until 1967, Gunby Hall still feels cherished and lived-in. Exploring three floors; you can easily imagine you'll bump into one of the family at any moment. Enjoy garden colour whatever the season: abundant spring flowers, summer roses, autumn borders and plentiful fruit and vegetables.

Eat, shop, stay: courtyard tea-room offering cakes, sweet treats, and savoury snacks. Well-stocked second-hand bookshop. Gifts, seasonal plants and produce for sale. Choose from three holiday cottages: The Old Rectory and Whitegates Cottage in Bratoft or Orchard Cottage, nestled in the Gunby gardens.

Things to see and do: events throughout year, from open-air theatre to Regency re-enactments and Apple Days. Public footpaths run across the wider historic park and estate: ask for directions and maps in the tea-room.
Dogs: welcome on leads in the gardens, courtyard tea-room terrace and grounds.

Access: 📷📶 House 🦽🎫♿ Grounds 🏞♿
Sat Nav: may misdirect – entrance is off roundabout (not beyond or before).
Parking: on site.

Find out more: 01754 890102 or gunbyhall@nationaltrust.org.uk

Much-cherished Gunby Estate, Hall and Gardens in Lincolnshire, is surrounded by immaculate lawns

Gunby Estate		M	T	W	T	F	S	S
House*								
18 Mar–29 Oct	11–5	M	T	W	·	·	S	S
25 Nov–10 Dec	11–3	·	·	·	·	·	S	S
Gardens and tea-room								
18 Mar–29 Oct**	11–5	M	T	W	T	F	S	S
25 Nov–10 Dec	11–3	·	·	·	·	·	S	S
Parkland†								
Open all year	11–5	M	T	W	T	F	S	S

*House: last admission one hour before closing (on busy days admission to the house may be by timed ticket).
**Tea-room: last service 4:30. May close dusk or earlier.
†Car park open as parkland.

Gunby Hall Estate: Monksthorpe Chapel

Monksthorpe, near Spilsby, Lincolnshire PE23 5PP

✚ 2000

Monksthorpe Chapel, dated 1701, was made to look like a barn to avoid detection and features a rare open-air baptistry. **Note**: chapel open daily, 18 March to 29 October, 11 to 5, and weekends, 25 November to 10 December, 11 to 3. Access by key, obtained from Gunby Hall tea-room (£20 refundable deposit required). Grounds open daily, 11 to 5.

Find out more: 01754 890102 or monksthorpe@nationaltrust.org.uk

Hardwick

Doe Lea, Chesterfield, Derbyshire S44 5QJ

🏠🎔🎞️🛏️🔔☕ 1959

One of the many treasures at Hardwick, Derbyshire

The Hardwick Estate is made up of stunning houses and beautiful landscapes that have been created by a cast of thousands. It was the formidable Bess of Hardwick who first built Hardwick Hall in the late 16th century, and in the centuries since then, gardeners, builders, decorators, embroiderers and craftsmen of all kinds have contributed and made Hardwick their creation. You can find out about the first and last ladies of Hardwick, Bess and Duchess Evelyn, and see 'Lucretia', the second of the five 'Noble Women' embroideries recently returned from conservation. Outside, why not stroll down to the newly restored ice house and duck decoy to find out how these historic features helped to feed the estate? **Note**: Old Hall owned by the National Trust and administered by English Heritage (01246 850431).

Eat, shop, stay: Great Barn Restaurant serving hot meals, seasonal specials (using garden produce) and homemade cakes. Stables shop selling gifts and souvenirs. Outdoors shop and plant sales (many propagated in Hardwick's nursery). Picnic areas. Three holiday cottages (sleeping two, six and 12).

Things to see and do: **Indoors** Seasonal events, including Easter and Christmas. **Outdoors** Open-air films during the summer and themed tours and talks. You can see the garden highlights, including the stumpery and herbaceous borders. There are also walking trails around the estate and surrounding countryside. Family woodland trail and fun family activities during all school holidays. Stainsby Mill and Eyam Hall are nearby. **Dogs**: welcome on leads in Stableyard, park and car park. Assistance dogs only in gardens.

Access: 🅿️♿🚻🔔📷🏛️📹🎵🖼️ Hall 🔦♿ Restaurant ♿ Garden ➡️♿
Sat Nav: use S44 5RW.
Parking: 600-space car park.

Find out more: 01246 850430 or hardwick@nationaltrust.org.uk

Hardwick		M	T	W	T	F	S	S
Hall								
11 Feb–29 Oct	11–5[1]		·	W	T	F	S	S
18 Nov–17 Dec	11–3[2]		·	W	T	F	S	S
Park and restaurant								
Open all year*	9–6	M	T	W	T	F	S	S
Garden and shop								
Open all year*	10–6	M	T	W	T	F	S	S

*Park, garden, restaurant and shop: close at 5, November to February, or dusk if earlier. Closed 25 December.
[1]Hall also opens Bank Holiday Mondays, April to August.
[2]Only ground and middle floors open at Christmas.

Dressing-up fun at Hardwick, below. The Hall, opposite, was built by the formidable Bess of Hardwick in the late 16th century

Hardwick Estate: Stainsby Mill

Doe Lea, Chesterfield, Derbyshire S44 5RW

1976

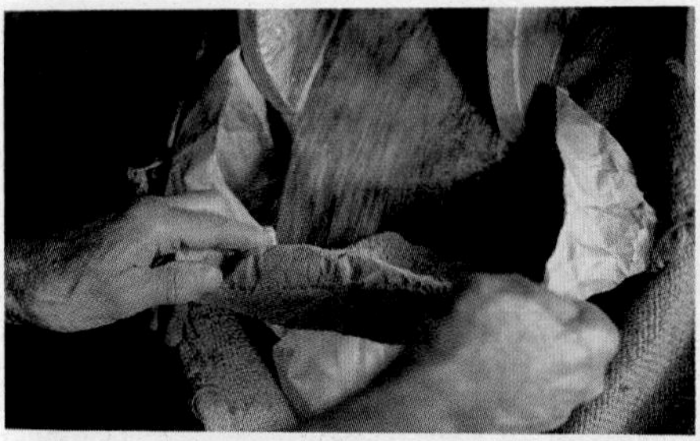

Collecting freshly ground flour at Stainsby Mill, Derbyshire

A fully operational Victorian flour mill giving an insight into the workplace of a 19th-century miller. There has been a mill on this site for hundreds of years, providing flour for the local villages and the Hardwick Estate. Flour is ground regularly showing the cogs and machinery in action. **Note**: nearest toilets and refreshments at Hardwick Hall.

Eat, shop, stay: Stainsby freshly milled flour for sale. You can learn more about the mill from our guides and pick up recipes to try at home. Restaurant and gift shop at nearby Hardwick Hall.

Things to see and do: why not start your day at Stainsby Mill, with its children's trail and activity sheets? Visitors are welcome to have a go grinding flour on the hand quern. **Dogs**: welcome on leads in Hardwick Park.

Access: **Building** **Grounds**
Parking: limited on-road parking (not National Trust).

Find out more: 01246 856522 or stainsbymill@nationaltrust.org.uk

Hardwick Estate: Stainsby Mill		M	T	W	T	F	S	S
11 Feb–29 Oct*	10–4	·	·	W	T	F	S	S

*Open Bank Holiday Mondays. 27 May to 3 September, open 10 to 5.

Ilam Park, Dovedale and the White Peak

Ilam, Ashbourne, Derbyshire

1906

The Stepping Stones at Dovedale lead to a riverside walk through a dramatic valley full of caves and pinnacles, rich in wildlife and fossils. A short walk links Dovedale and Ilam Park, a tranquil parkland nestled beneath steep-sided hills on the bank of the River Manifold. The park features a formal Italian Garden with views across to the rugged backdrop of Thorpe Cloud and Bunster Hill. Short, circular woodland and parkland routes make this a popular choice for families and dog walkers. The densely wooded Manifold Valley offers a traffic-free cycling route. **Note**: Ilam Hall is let to the Youth Hostel Association.

Eat, shop, stay: Manifold tea-room at Ilam Park, with uninterrupted views towards Dovedale, serving homemade lunches and cake. Shops at Ilam Park and Dovedale Barn offering postcard-sized walk maps, gifts and information. Café at Wetton Mill (not National Trust) overlooking the River Manifold.

Things to see and do: school holiday family trails. Summer play over the river in Hinkley Hollow. See the orchard area developing next to the tea-room. Free Monday and Friday guided walks all year. **Dogs**: under close control; on leads spring and summer (ground-nesting birds), and near livestock.

Access: [icons] Ilam Park stableyard [icons]
Ilam Park grounds [icons]
Sat Nav: use DE6 2AZ. **Parking**: at Ilam Park 119:132507, also at Dovedale and Wetton Mill, not National Trust (charge including members).

Find out more: 01335 350503 or peakdistrict@nationaltrust.org.uk

Ilam Park		M	T	W	T	F	S	S
Tea-room and shop*								
1 Jan–12 Feb	10:30–4	M	T	W	T	F	S	S
13 Feb–29 Oct	10:30–5	M	T	W	T	F	S	S
30 Oct–31 Dec	10:30–4	M	T	W	T	F	S	S
Dovedale Barn								
8 Apr–1 Oct	11–5	M	T	W	T	F	S	S

*Shop opens at 11. Tea-room and shop: closed 24 and 25 December. Ilam bunkhouse: open all year (0344 335 1296). Ilam Park Caravan Site: open 24 February to 29 October (01335 350310). Darfar and Redhurst holiday cottages: available to let throughout the year (0344 800 2070). Ilam Hall: available for overnight accommodation via the Youth Hostel Association (01335 350212).

Ilam Park, Dovedale and the White Peak, Derbyshire: Dovedale's many tempting paths run through a dramatic valley full of caves, pinnacles, wildlife and fossils

Kedleston Hall

near Quarndon, Derby, Derbyshire DE22 5JH

[icons] 1987

Designed by architect Robert Adam as 'a temple of the arts', Kedleston is one of the grandest, most perfectly finished houses and locations for entertainment. Discover the grandeur of this 1760s mansion, which was designed as a show palace with lavish décor, paintings, furniture and sculpture, and lived in over the centuries by the Curzon family. Set in beautiful naturalistic parkland, blending seamlessly into the surrounding countryside, the 332 hectares (820 acres) are perfect for walks, picnics and spotting wildlife, as well as being home to more than 100 ancient trees. **Note**: medieval All Saints church, containing many family monuments, run by the Churches Conservation Trust.

Eat, shop, stay: Old Kitchen Restaurant serving hot and cold lunches, cakes, ice-cream and teas. Refreshments available from coffee shop kiosk (peak times). Gift shop, plant sales and second-hand bookshop. Luxurious Park House holiday cottage sits on the edge of Kedleston Park.

The north front of Robert Adam's Kedleston Hall, Derbyshire, below, and one of its many treasures, above

Things to see and do: **Indoors** Hall tours and children's trails. Recently restored state bed, an 18th-century masterpiece. **Outdoors** Four waymarked walks. Talks and tours. Family crafts and activities. Newly rebuilt Hermitage on long walk. **Dogs**: welcome on leads in park and pleasure grounds.

Statues and columns in the Marble Hall at Kedleston Hall: 'a temple of the arts'

Access: 🅿♿🚻🚼🏛🖼🚪📷

Ground floor ♿ **State floor** ♿ **Grounds** ♿ ➡

Sat Nav: follow brown signs.

Parking: 200 yards.

Find out more: 01332 842191 or kedlestonhall@nationaltrust.org.uk

Kedleston Hall		M	T	W	T	F	S	S
Park and Pleasure Grounds								
1 Jan–10 Feb	10–4	M	T	W	T	F	S	S
11 Feb–29 Oct	10–6	M	T	W	T	F	S	S
30 Oct–31 Dec	10–4	M	T	W	T	F	S	S
Hall*								
25 Feb–29 Oct	12–5	M	T	W	T	·	S	S
Restaurant and shop								
1 Jan–5 Feb	10:30–3:30	·	·	·	·	·	S	S
11 Feb–29 Oct	10:30–5	M	T	W	T	F	S	S
30 Oct–31 Dec	10:30–3:30	M	T	W	T	F	S	S

*Hall: Introductory talk at 11. May close early if light level is poor. Open Good Friday. Whole property occasionally closed for events and on 25 December.

Kinder, Edale and the Dark Peak

near Hope Valley, Derbyshire

🏛♿♿♿ 1936

The Dark Peak, including Kinder, the Vale of Edale and along the Snake moors to the Derwent edges, offers exhilarating walks across heather moors, high gritstone edges and monumental windswept tors. Stories and wild nature abound amid the ancient peat bogs and quiet wooded cloughs. You can follow the route of the 1932 Mass Trespass onto Kinder Scout National Nature Reserve, retracing the steps of those early champions of access to wild places. Alternatively a short climb up the 'Shivering Mountain' rewards you with panoramic views from this ancient hilltop fortress of Mam Tor. **Note**: nearest toilets in villages and visitor centres (not Trust) at Ladybower Reservoir, Edale and Castleton.

Eat, shop, stay: Penny Pot in Edale, serving cooked breakfasts, soup, sandwiches, cakes, tea and coffee. Seating and bike racks outside, sofas and log burner inside. Find us next to Edale railway station.

The breathtaking view from Mam Tor at Kinder, Edale and the Dark Peak, Derbyshire

Dog walkers enjoy the footpath at Mam Tor, an ancient hilltop fortress

Longshaw, Burbage and the Eastern Moors

Longshaw, near Sheffield, Derbyshire

🏛🏠🛏✳🎣👤 1931

A countryside haven on Sheffield's doorstep, Longshaw, Burbage and the Eastern Moors has a network of footpaths and bridleways you can explore within a typical Peak District landscape of skies and silhouettes. Here you'll find long views, with scooping shapes of rocks and hills and gorges where water tumbles through ancient woods and over mossy boulders.

Things to see and do: guided walks, Muck-in Days, downloadable walking and cycling routes. **Dogs**: on leads near livestock and throughout spring and summer (ground-nesting bird breeding season).

Access: 🅿♿🚻🚼🎦
Sat Nav: use S33 8WA. **Parking**: at Mam Nick car park 110:SK124832. Also at Edale, Castleton, Bowden Bridge, Hayfield, Sett Valley, Hayfield and Upper Derwent Valley, none National Trust (charge including members).

Find out more: 01433 670368 or peakdistrict@nationaltrust.org.uk

Kinder, Edale and the Dark Peak		M	T	W	T	F	S	S
Penny Pot Café								
1 Jan–12 Mar	10–4					F	S	S
13 Mar–29 Oct	10–4:30	M	T	W	T	F	S	S
29 Apr–24 Sep	8:30–4:30						S	S
3 Nov–31 Dec	10–4					F	S	S

Closed 24 to 26 December. Information shelters open all year: Lee Barn (110:SK096855) and Dalehead (110: SK101843) in Edale; South Head (SK060854) at Kinder; Edale End (SK161864); Grindle Barns above Ladybower Reservoir (SK189895). Mam Nick car park (SK123832) and Dalehead bunkhouse (0344 3351296) open all year.

A tricky balancing act at Longshaw, Burbage and the Eastern Moors in Derbyshire

A diverse range of wildlife lives peacefully here among abandoned millstones and packhorse routes of the past. The designed landscape around Longshaw Lodge, a former grouse-shooting estate, offers a warm and friendly starting point for your adventure. **Note**: National Trust/RSPB manage Eastern Moors for Peak District National Park Authority/Burbage for Sheffield County Council.

Eat, shop, stay: Longshaw tea-room serving soup, scones, cakes and dishes using produce plucked straight from the kitchen garden. Shop selling outdoor and wildlife-themed products, maps and guides. Outdoor seats provide views across the valley to Burbage and Higger Tor.

Exploring Longshaw, Burbage and the Eastern Moors: a countryside haven on Sheffield's doorstep

Things to see and do: woodland walks, natural play, bridleways and waymarked walks. Kitchen garden behind tea-room. Outdoor activity events and trails. Free guided walks (Wednesdays and Sundays).
Dogs: on leads near livestock and throughout spring and summer (ground-nesting bird breeding season).

Access: **Building** **Grounds**
Sat Nav: use S11 7TZ (follow brown signs).
Parking: at Woodcroft car park (110: 266800), Wooden Pole and Haywood for Longshaw and at Curbar Gap, Birchen Edge and Shillito Wood for the Eastern Moors. Additional car parks at Surprise View and Burbage, not National Trust (charge including members).

Find out more: 01433 637904 (Longshaw). 0114 289 1543 (Eastern Moors) or peakdistrict@nationaltrust.org.uk

Longshaw, Burbage, Eastern Moors		M	T	W	T	F	S	S
Tea-room and shop								
1 Jan–12 Feb	10:30–4	M	T	W	T	F	S	S
13 Feb–29 Oct	10:30–5	M	T	W	T	F	S	S
30 Oct–31 Dec	10:30–4	M	T	W	T	F	S	S

Tea-room: last orders 30 minutes before closing. Closed 24 and 25 December. White Edge Lodge: available as holiday cottage throughout year (0344 800 2070). Longshaw Lodge: not open to public.

Lyveden

Harley Way, near Oundle,
Northamptonshire PE8 5AT

1922

Tucked away in the heart of the Northamptonshire countryside lies a mysterious garden, a remarkable example of Renaissance thinking and craftsmanship. Begun by Sir Thomas Tresham in 1595 but never completed, the garden encapsulates late Tudor landscape design. There are tranquil moats, viewing terraces and an Elizabethan orchard to explore, as well as an enigmatic garden lodge covered in religious symbols. The full extent of Sir Thomas's symbolic design remains unexplained to this day. Our audio guide describes Sir Thomas's dream and how it all ended in a nightmare for the Tresham family with their involvement in the Gunpowder Plot.

Eat, shop, stay: small traditional Northamptonshire cottage tea-room, serving homemade cakes and cream teas. Ice-cream available from visitor reception. Picnics welcome.

Things to see and do: free audio guide. Children's activities available in our Family Den. Numerous countryside walks.
Dogs: welcome on leads only.

Access: 〓〓〓〓〓〓 Building 〓 Grounds 〓
Parking: 100 yards.

Find out more: 01832 205158 or lyveden@nationaltrust.org.uk

Lyveden		M	T	W	T	F	S	S
1 Jan–26 Feb	11–4						S	S
27 Feb–29 Oct	10:30–5	M	T	W	T	F	S	S
4 Nov–31 Dec	11–4						S	S

Closed 23 and 24 December. Last audio guide issued one hour before closing.

The atmospheric Lyveden, Northamptonshire: a remarkable example of Renaissance craftsmanship

Mr Straw's House

5–7 Blyth Grove, Worksop, Nottinghamshire S81 0JG

〓 〓 1990

Within the Sanderson-papered walls of this middle-class home, the family lived thriftily, installing few modern conveniences. William Straw ensured a huge collection of everyday objects and personal papers survived alongside traces of the occasional indulgence. The lovingly tended garden and orchard include a cacti collection and fruit trees.
Note: to help you enjoy your visit we operate timed tickets, please telephone or book online.

Virtually unchanged since 1923, Mr Straw's House, Nottinghamshire, is an extraordinary time capsule

Eat, shop, stay: shop selling jam, biscuits, plants, souvenirs and gifts. Tea and coffee area. Picnic benches in garden and orchard.

Things to see and do: changing exhibitions, family activities, events and guided walks all year.

Access: 〓〓〓 5 Blyth Grove 〓〓
7 Blyth Grove 〓〓 Gardens 〓
Parking: on site, in orchard opposite property.

Find out more: 01909 482380 or mrstrawshouse@nationaltrust.org.uk

Mr Straw's House		M	T	W	T	F	S	S
28 Feb–4 Nov*	Tour		T	W	T	F	S	

*Admission by timed ticket (please telephone or book online). Closed Good Friday.

The Old Manor

Norbury, Ashbourne, Derbyshire DE6 2ED

 1987

Medieval hall featuring a rare king post, Tudor door and 17th-century Flemish glass. **Note**: parking limited (cars only). Open 24 March to 20 October, open Fridays, 11 to 1 and Saturdays, 25 March to 21 October, 1 to 3.

Find out more: 01283 585337 or oldmanor@nationaltrust.org.uk

Priest's House, Easton on the Hill

38 West Street, Easton on the Hill, near Stamford, Northamptonshire PE9 3LS

 1966

Delightful small late 15th-century building, with interesting local architecture and museum exploring Easton on the Hill's industrial past. **Note**: open daily, 10 to 5. Unmanned. Access from neighbouring keyholders (details on property noticeboard).

Find out more: 01832 205158 or priestshouse2@nationaltrust.org.uk

Staunton Harold Church

Staunton Harold Estate, Ashby-de-la-Zouch, Leicestershire LE65 1RW

✝ 1954

One of the few churches built between the outbreak of the English Civil War and the Restoration period. **Note**: nearest toilet 500 yards (not National Trust). Parking not

National Trust; Staunton Harold Estate, charges apply (including members). Open 1 to 4:30, weekends, 1 April to 29 October, and Wednesday to Sunday, 7 June to 1 September.

Find out more: 01332 863822 or stauntonharold@nationaltrust.org.uk

Stoneywell

Whitcroft's Lane, Ulverscroft, Leicestershire LE67 9QE

🏠❄ 2012

Original furniture in the dining-room at Stoneywell, Leicestershire: one man's Arts and Crafts vision

Zigzagging from its rocky outcrop, Stoneywell is the realisation of one man's Arts and Crafts vision within a family home. Original furniture and family treasures fill the cottage's quirky rooms and, outside, every turn conjures childhood memories of holiday excitement – one way to the fort, another to the woods beyond. **Note**: booking essential (including members).

Eat, shop, stay: Stables tea-room (for use by booked visitors only) serving light lunches, homemade cakes and cream teas. Small range of Arts and Crafts-inspired gifts, seasonal plants and second-hand books available. Picnics welcome in grounds.

Things to see and do: **Indoors** Guided tours, events and family activities reveal stories of life at Stoneywell. **Outdoors** The garden and woodland are great for exploring, with seasonal highlights, including daffodils, bluebells and rhododendrons. **Dogs**: assistance dogs only.

Access:
Stables 🏛 **Cottage** 🏛 **Gardens** ♿ ➡
Parking: for booked visitors only.

Find out more: 01530 248040 (Infoline).
01530 248048 (bookings) or
stoneywell@nationaltrust.org.uk

Stoneywell		M	T	W	T	F	S	S
1 Feb–30 Nov	Tour	**M**	**T**	**W**	**T**	**F**	**S**	**S**

Sudbury Hall and the National Trust Museum of Childhood

Sudbury, Ashbourne, Derbyshire DE6 5HT

🏰 ✿ ♠ ⊤ 1967

The Toys Through Time gallery at Sudbury Hall and the National Trust Museum of Childhood, Derbyshire, above, and the Hall's south front, below

A complete day out, with two unique experiences in one location. The Hall has one of the most surprising, light and beautiful long galleries in England and is the result of George Vernon's aspirations to create a perfect new home.

Get a glimpse of life 'below stairs' in the kitchen and basement, and picture yourself at home in some of the smaller family rooms. The Museum is a place of fun and fascination for all ages. View childhood from the Victorian period to the present day; send your little one up a chimney, play with our hands-on toys and games and experience the Victorian Schoolroom.

Having fun in the National Trust Museum of Childhood: one visit is never enough

Eat, shop, stay: tea-room serving light lunches and homemade cakes. Additional refreshments available at peak times. Gift shop, plant sales, sweets, ice-cream and toys.

Things to see and do: **Indoors** Hands-on toys in the museum and family crafts during most school holidays. Themed Hall tours, including the chance to explore areas not normally open to visitors. **Outdoors** Trails and fun activities for all the family. Spot wildlife from the Boathouse and younger visitors can find adventure in the woodland play area.

Access: 🅿️🎧♿️🪑👐🧤📷📱📺🚹👓📠
Hall 🧏♿️ Museum ♿️🔼♿️ Grounds 🧏🚶
Parking: 500 yards.

Find out more: 01283 585337 or sudburyhall@nationaltrust.org.uk

Sudbury Hall	M	T	W	T	F	S	S
Museum, tea-room and shop*							
11 Feb–26 Mar	10:30–5	·	·	W	T	F	S	S
27 Mar–29 Oct	10:30–5	M	T	W	T	F	S	S
2 Nov–17 Dec	10:30–4	·	·	·	T	F	S	S
Hall**							
11 Feb–29 Oct	1–5	·	·	W	T	F	S	S
Hall tours							
4 Apr–24 Oct	11:30–2:30	·	T	·	·	·	·

*Museum opens at 11. **Hall: extended opening during school holidays (may close early if light level is poor). Open Bank Holiday Mondays.

Tattershall Castle

Sleaford Road, Tattershall, Lincolnshire LN4 4LR

🏚️ 🏛️ 🔔 1925

Rising proudly from the flat Lincolnshire fens, Tattershall Castle, with its huge Gothic fireplaces and church-like windows, was designed to impress. Built by Lord Ralph Cromwell, Treasurer of England, it was designed to show off his wealth, position and power. The Great Tower is one of the earliest and finest surviving examples of English medieval brickwork and was saved from exportation to America by Lord Curzon of Kedleston in 1911. You can follow the winding staircase, wander through vast echoing chambers and walk out onto the battlements, revealing the beauty of the Lincolnshire countryside. **Note**: access to the tower via a spiral staircase only (149 steps). Loose gravel paths throughout.

Designed to impress, Tattershall Castle, Lincolnshire, is a bold statement of late medieval style

Eat, shop, stay: tea-room opening this year. Guardhouse shop selling hot and cold drinks, wrapped cakes, sandwiches (limited availability), crisps, ice-cream, gifts and souvenirs. Picnics welcome.

Things to see and do: **Indoors** Take an audio guide (adult and family versions available) or a children's trail. **Outdoors** Events throughout the year, including the Easter Hunt, medieval re-enactments, open-air theatre and Christmas market. **Dogs**: welcome on leads in the grounds only.

Rising above the flat fenland, Tattershall Castle has been a defensive tower, family home and even a cattle shed

Access: [icons] Castle [icon]
Sat Nav: LN4 4LR. **Parking:** 150 yards from entrance.

Find out more: 01526 342543 or tattershallcastle@nationaltrust.org.uk

Tattershall Castle		M	T	W	T	F	S	S
11 Feb–29 Oct	11–5	M	T	W	T	F	S	S
4 Nov–19 Nov	11–3	·	·	·	·	·	S	S

Last entry one hour before closing. Last audio guides issued one hour before closing. Some areas may temporarily close for weddings (please check before visiting).

Ulverscroft Nature Reserve

near Copt Oak, Loughborough, Leicestershire

[icon] 1945

Nestled in the ancient Charnwood Forest, a rich variety of wildlife thrives in the heathland and woodland habitats of Ulverscroft. **Note:** assistance dogs only. Sorry no toilet. For Sat Nav use LE67 9QE. Limited parking along Whitcroft's Lane adjacent to the reserve. Access by permit from Leicestershire and Rutland Wildlife Trust (0116 262 9968), apply several days before visit.

Find out more: 01332 863822 or ulverscroftnaturereserve@nationaltrust.org.uk

Winster Market House

Main Street, Winster, Matlock, Derbyshire DE4 2DJ

[icon] 1906

The origins of this small Market House are in the 16th century, when cheese and cattle fairs featured prominently in the daily life of the area. An excellent example of its type, a listed building and the first Derbyshire place acquired by the Trust, at a cost of £50. **Note:** Winster Market House is unstaffed.

Things to see and do: first-floor information room with interpretation panels and a scale model of Winster village. Ilam Park and Dovedale nearby; Longshaw and Eyam Hall are about 17 miles. **Dogs:** welcome on leads.

Access: [icon]
Parking: on street or at small village car parks, not National Trust (charge including members).

Find out more: 01335 350503 or winstermarkethouse@nationaltrust.org.uk

Winster Market House		M	T	W	T	F	S	S
8 Apr–29 Oct	11–5	M	T	W	T	F	S	S

Winster Market House in Derbyshire: an early National Trust acquisition, it cost £50 in 1906

Woolsthorpe Manor

Water Lane, Woolsthorpe by Colsterworth, near Grantham, Lincolnshire NG33 5PD

[icons] 1943

Without Isaac Newton, this small manor would be just another Lincolnshire farmhouse – but in 1665 the plague sent him back here to where he was born. For 18 months Newton worked in solitude, experimenting obsessively, laying foundations for a scientific revolution which reaches from his time and into space. Here he used a prism to split white light into colours and an apple fell from a tree and inspired his theory of gravity. Newton's genius still impacts on the modern world; for over 300 years people have come here to walk in his footsteps and be inspired by his story. **Note**: potential building works early this year.

Eat, shop, stay: Newton's Barn coffee shop. Small shop in ticket office with local and Newton-specific gifts. Small second-hand bookshop.

Things to see and do: **Indoors** Hands-on Science Centre and family activities. Craft fairs and volunteer-led 'Tales from Woolsthorpe' and science talks. Film. Family events.

Outdoors Don't miss Isaac's apple tree!
Dogs: welcome in car park only.

Access: [icons] **Grounds** [icons]
House [icons] **Science Centre** [icons]
Parking: 50 yards.

Find out more: 01476 860338 or woolsthorpemanor@nationaltrust.org.uk

Woolsthorpe Manor

Please visit website for details of 2017 opening times. The manor house is closed on Tuesdays and from Tuesday to Thursday in winter.

Walk in the footsteps of genius at Woolsthorpe Manor, Lincolnshire, above and below: Sir Isaac Newton's birthplace

The Workhouse, Southwell in Nottinghamshire, above and below, is the most complete workhouse in existence. Inside this austere building, the Victorian poor sought refuge from starvation, only to endure a harsh regime

The Workhouse, Southwell

Upton Road, Southwell,
Nottinghamshire NG25 0PT

🏠 2002

Walking up the paupers' path towards The Workhouse it is easy to imagine how the Victorian poor might have felt as they sought refuge here. This austere building, the most complete workhouse in existence, was built in 1824 as a place of last resort for the destitute. Its architecture was influenced by prison design and its harsh regime became a blueprint for workhouses throughout the country. The stories of people who lived and worked here over the years help tell the history of the building's evolution and prompt reflection on how society has tackled social welfare through time. **Note**: please expect some disruption as we embark on our creative presentation and building works programme.

Eat, shop, stay: refreshment room offering hot drinks, sandwiches, cakes and snacks. Shop selling gifts, ice-cream and traditional toys. Picnic benches in the garden.

Things to see and do: **Indoors** 'Re-imagining The Workhouse' updates our story through art, music, photography and innovative technology. Regular activities, including living history days, family events and exhibitions. **Outdoors** Re-created Victorian vegetable garden. **Dogs**: assistance dogs only in house and garden. Dogs on leads in front field.

Access: ♿ 🅿️ 👶 ♿ 📷 🖥️ 📺 🎧 ♿ 🖨️
Building ♿ ♿ 🍴 ♿ **Grounds** ♿ ➡️ ♿
Sat Nav: use NG25 0QB. **Parking**: 200 yards.

Find out more: 01636 817260 or theworkhouse@nationaltrust.org.uk

The Workhouse, Southwell		M	T	W	T	F	S	S
11 Feb–5 Nov	12–5	**M**	**T**	**W**	**T**	**F**	**S**	**S**

Guided tour of the outside and other buildings at 11 (places limited, book on arrival). House open Bank Holidays from 11. Last admission one hour before closing. Property may close earlier due to light levels.

Croome, Worcestershire
Competition entry from Roger Lane

Attingham Park

Atcham, Shrewsbury, Shropshire SY4 4TP

🏛️ ❄️ ♿ 🍴 1947

Attingham inspires a sense of beauty, space and awe. The imposing entrance, glimpses of the vast mansion against silhouettes of cedars and expansive parkland, epitomise classical design and Italian influence. Its completeness of survival exemplifies the rise and decline, love and neglect of great country-house estates. Discovering the Berwicks' estate with acres of parkland, miles of walks, the huge organic walled garden, large playfield and welcoming mansion is a full day out. There's so much to see and do at Attingham – whether you're a family looking for activities, both inside and out, or simply in search of a traditional visit to a historic house and parkland. Full of life and locally loved, there's something for everyone all year round.

Gracious Attingham Park, Shropshire, above, epitomises the perfect 17th-century English country house. Inside, history comes to life in the kitchen, right

Eat, shop, stay: a variety of experiences – main café open daily, new kitchen serving hot food and extended seating from Easter, table-service afternoon tea and takeaways from Greedy Pig catering in playfield. Courtyard shopping includes Stables shop and Grooms' second-hand bookshop.

Things to see and do: **Indoors** 'Attingham Re-discovered' project of conservation and restoration continues. Themed tours. Mansion 'below-stairs' experience throughout February half-term. Attingham '1940s Christmas' daily in December. **Outdoors** Park open from 8. Summer late opening (to 7). Parkland walks. Seasonal spectaculars, including winter snowdrops, spring bluebells, summer blossom and autumn tree colour. Year-round events for all ages and interests, including daily family activities during local school holidays, open-air cinema and theatre evenings, guided walks. Sporting activities to help you get active, including regular run groups and major events/competitions. Walled Garden and Pleasure Grounds projects continue to transform and restore Attingham. Sunnycroft is nearby. **Dogs**: welcome in grounds on leads (with some identified off-lead areas). Dog walkers' guide available.

The magnificent brass 'batterie de cuisine' in the kitchen at Attingham Park, below. Laid for a banquet, the dining table, right, recalls the days of lavish hospitality

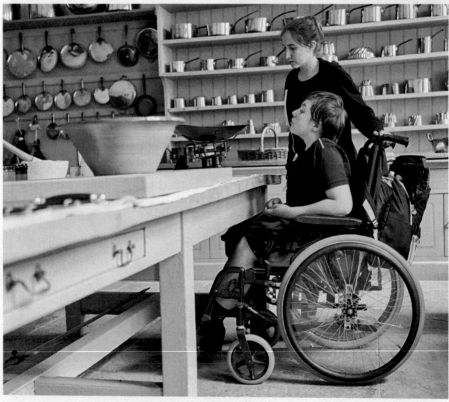

For other ways to get involved go to nationaltrust.org.uk/get-involved/volunteer

Access: ⬚⬚⬚⬚⬚⬚⬚⬚⬚
Mansion ⬚⬚⬚⬚ **Carriage House Café** ⬚
Grounds ⬚⬚⬚⬚
Parking: 25 to 200 yards.

Find out more: 01743 708123 (Infoline).
01743 708162 or attingham@nationaltrust.org.uk

Attingham Park		M	T	W	T	F	S	S
Park and playfield†								
1 Jan–26 May	8–6*	M	T	W	T	F	S	S
27 May–3 Sep	8–7	M	T	W	T	F	S	S
4 Sep–31 Dec	8–6*	M	T	W	T	F	S	S
Walled Garden and Stables Courtyard catering††								
Open all year	9–5*	M	T	W	T	F	S	S
Mansion								
4 Mar–5 Nov	11–5:30**	M	T	W	T	F	S	S
2 Dec–23 Dec	10–4**	M	T	W	T	F	S	S
Mansion winter tours								
6 Jan–12 Feb	11–3					F	S	S
Mansion 'below-stairs' experience and upstairs tours								
18 Feb–26 Feb	11–3	M	T	W	T	F	S	S
Lady Berwick's Luncheons and Afternoon Tea								
4 Mar–5 Nov	1–4						S	S
2 Dec–23 Dec	12–3						S	S

†Visitor reception open as park and playfield. *Park, playfield, walled garden: January, February, November and December, closes 5 or dusk if earlier. ††Stables Courtyard catering: January, February, November, December closes one hour before park. **Mansion: last admission one hour before closing. Playfield catering: open from 11 weekends, daily during Shropshire school holidays (weather permitting). Stables shops: open daily from 10. 24 December: mansion closed; catering and retail outlets and walled garden close at 2, property closes at 3. Property closed 25 December.

Attingham Park Estate: Cronkhill

near Atcham, Shrewsbury, Shropshire SY5 6JP

⬚⬚ 1947

Delightful picturesque Italianate hillside villa designed by Regency architect John Nash, with beautiful views across the Attingham Estate. **Note**: 'Cronkhill Restored' project. House ground floor, garden and stables open as part of visit. Property contents belong to tenant. Open Friday and Sunday, 5 and 7 May, 21 and 23 July, and 15 and 17 September, 11 to 4.

Find out more: 01743 708162 or cronkhill@nationaltrust.org.uk

Attingham Park Estate: Town Walls Tower

Shrewsbury, Shropshire SY1 1TN

 1930

This last remaining 14th-century watchtower sits on what were once the medieval fortified, defensive walls of Shrewsbury. **Note**: sorry no toilet or car parking and 40 extremely steep, narrow steps to top floor. Open weekends, 10/11 June, 12/13 August and 7/8 October, 11 to 3.

Find out more: 01743 708162 or townwallstower@nationaltrust.org.uk

Baddesley Clinton

Rising Lane, Baddesley Clinton, Warwickshire B93 0DQ

⬚⬚⬚⬚⬚ 1980

Discovering the magic of Baddesley Clinton, Warwickshire: a sanctuary since the 15th century

The magic of Baddesley Clinton comes from its secluded, timeless setting deep within its own parkland. From refuge to haven, this atmospheric moated manor house has been a sanctuary since the 15th century. Discover Baddesley's late medieval, Tudor and 20th-century history, from hiding persecuted Catholics in its priest holes to the history of the Ferrers family who lived at Baddesley for more than 500 years.

The peaceful gardens include fish pools, walled garden and a lakeside walk, perfect for a tranquil stroll. **Note**: house closed 3 to 29 January; part open 30 January to May (building work).

Eat, shop, stay: Barn Restaurant serving hot meals, drinks and snacks and The Stables offering light refreshments. Picnics welcome. Shop selling seasonal gifts, local foods and plants. Second-hand bookshop.

Things to see and do: **Indoors** Discover Baddesley's story, from medieval farmstead to modest Georgian status symbol and Victorian retreat. Take your own portrait in the Moat Room and enjoy seasonal children's trails. House dressed for Christmas throughout most of December. **Outdoors** Playful Journeys around the estate all year. Outdoor games in school holidays. Welcome talks and garden tours, plus walking trails around the estate and surrounding countryside. Packwood House and Coughton Court nearby. **Dogs**: welcome on leads in car park and estate public footpaths. Assistance dogs only beyond visitor reception.

The Great Hall at Baddesley Clinton, above. Wisteria blooms in the courtyard, main picture, and the colourful mopheads of dahlias delight visitors on a sunny day in the garden

Benthall Hall

Broseley, Shropshire TF12 5RX

🏠 ✝ ❀ ♿ 1958

Within this fine stone house, discover the history of the Benthall family from the Saxon period to the present day. Outside, the garden includes a beautiful Restoration church, a restored plantsman's garden with pretty crocus displays in spring and autumn, and an old kitchen garden.

Eat, shop, stay: tea-room serving drinks, cakes and ice-cream.

Things to see and do: **Indoors** Informative guides, children's trail. **Outdoors** Elizabethan skittle alley. Circular walks through the park and woodland. **Dogs**: in park and woodland only.

Access: 🅿️ 🔔 🎫 🥄 🎵 📷 🧷
House 🦽 🪜 Church 🦽
Parking: 100 yards.

Find out more: 01952 882159 or benthall@nationaltrust.org.uk

Benthall Hall		M	T	W	T	F	S	S
4 Feb–26 Feb	1–4*						S	S
28 Feb–29 Oct	1–5*			T	W		S	S

Open Bank Holiday Mondays and Good Friday. Tea-room: last orders 30 minutes before house closes. *Garden and church: open and close 30 minutes earlier and later than stated times, apart from February when opens at 1.

Exploring Benthall Hall in Shropshire

Access: 🅿️ 🔔 🎫 🥄 🎵 📷 📖 🧷
Building 🦽 🪜 ♿ Grounds 🪜 ➡️ ♿
Parking: 100 yards.

Find out more: 01564 783294 or baddesleyclinton@nationaltrust.org.uk

Baddesley Clinton		M	T	W	T	F	S	S
1 Jan–17 Feb	9–4*	M	T	W	T	F	S	S
18 Feb–29 Oct	9–5*	M	T	W	T	F	S	S
30 Oct–31 Dec	9–4*	M	T	W	T	F	S	S

Good Friday to Easter Monday admission by booked tickets only, limited (including members). *House: opens 11, admission by timed ticket (available from reception, not bookable); closed 3 to 29 January; part open 30 January to May (building work). Closed 24 and 25 December.

Berrington Hall

near Leominster, Herefordshire HR6 0DW

🏠❄️🐾🛏️🍽️ 1957

Standing proud and strong, this fine Georgian mansion sits within 'Capability' Brown's final garden and landscape. This year, supported by internationally renowned artists Heather and Ivan Morison, we begin the planning and showcasing of our Walled Garden and Pleasure Grounds Restoration Project. In the parkland, you can explore Brown's work with Red Earth's 'Genius Loci' exhibition. In the house, discover jewel-like interiors, designed by Henry Holland and home to the Harley, Rodney and Cawley families. Experience some of the extremes of the 18th century in the wig and bum shop and discover the hidden 'below stairs'.

Eat, shop, stay: shop selling gifts, local products and preserves made from our fruit. Tea-room serving light lunches, afternoon tea and cakes, using produce from the garden. New this year, stables café. Triumphal Arch holiday cottage.

The magnificent staircase hall, above, at Berrington Hall in Herefordshire. Below, visitors explore 'Capability' Brown's final garden and landscape

Things to see and do: Indoors Exhibitions. Costume collection on view. Family trails, games and dressing-up. Servants' quarters to explore. **Outdoors** Stables and walled garden to discover. Natural play area. Waymarked estate walks. **Dogs**: welcome on leads in parkland and in parts of garden.

Access: 🅿️🐕♿🚽♿📷🎧♿
Building 🦽♿ Grounds 🦽➡️♿♿
Parking: 30 yards.

Find out more: 01568 615721 or berrington@nationaltrust.org.uk

Berrington Hall		M	T	W	T	F	S	S
1 Jan	10–4	·	·	·	·	·	·	S
7 Jan–5 Feb	10–4	·	·	·	·	·	S	S
11 Feb–5 Nov	10–5	M	T	W	T	F	S	S
11 Nov–10 Dec	10–4	·	·	·	·	·	S	S
16 Dec–23 Dec	10–4	M	T	W	T	F	S	S
27 Dec–31 Dec	10–4	·	·	W	T	F	S	S

Mansion and shop open at 11. Last admission one hour before closing.

Biddulph Grange Garden

Grange Road, Biddulph, Staffordshire ST8 7SD

⊞ 1988

Biddulph Grange Garden is a remarkable survival, a formal Victorian horticultural masterpiece and a quirky, playful paradise full of intrigue and surprise. Created by its visionary owner, James Bateman, its design expresses and attempts to reconcile both his religious convictions and his passion for botany, plant collecting and geology. His plant collection comes from all over the world – a visit takes you on a journey from an Italian terrace to an Egyptian pyramid, via a Himalayan glen and Chinese-inspired garden, hidden by tunnels, high hedges and rockwork. The collection includes rhododendrons, dahlias, Wellingtonias and the oldest golden larch in Britain. **Note**: there are 400 steps throughout the garden. The Geological Gallery is open, but under restoration.

Eat, shop, stay: self-service tea-room. Gift shop. Plant centre. Picnics in the paddock area adjacent to the car park.

Things to see and do: talks, guided tours, events and children's trails all year. Summer activities. **Dogs**: assistance dogs only in garden.

Access: 🅿️ ♿ 👓 🗺️ 🏠 ⠿ Garden ♿
Parking: 50 yards.

Find out more: 01782 517999 or biddulphgrange@nationaltrust.org.uk

Biddulph Grange Garden		M	T	W	T	F	S	S
1 Jan–17 Feb	11–3:30	M	T	W	T	F	S	S
18 Feb–12 Mar	11–4	M	T	W	T	F	S	S
13 Mar–20 Oct	10:30–5:30	M	T	W	T	F	S	S
21 Oct–29 Oct	11–4	M	T	W	T	F	S	S
30 Oct–24 Dec	11–3:30	M	T	W	T	F	S	S
27 Dec–31 Dec	11–3:30			W	T	F	S	S

Open Bank Holiday Mondays. Closes dusk if earlier. Closed 25 and 26 December.

Living green buttresses line the glorious Dahlia Walk at Biddulph Grange Garden in Staffordshire: a formal Victorian horticultural masterpiece

Birmingham Back to Backs

55-63 Hurst Street/50-54 Inge Street, Birmingham, West Midlands B5 4TE

🏠 ⇦ 2004

The Birmingham Back to Backs in the West Midlands

Immerse yourself in the life of residents at Birmingham's last surviving court of back to backs. The evocative guided tour will give you an insight into how people lived from the 1840s to 1970s. With privies, coal fires, candlelight and cramped spaces, you'll get a real taste of back-to-back life. **Note**: booking essential. Eight flights of steep, winding stairs. Ground-floor tours available by booking.

Eat, shop, stay: traditional sweetshop and small shop selling pocket-money treats. Vintage holiday cottages (booked via National Trust Holidays).

Things to see and do: events all year.

Access: 🅿️♿🅿️🎦📷📹🖐️👓 Building 🦽♿🚹
Parking: nearest at Arcadian Centre, Bromsgrove Street (not National Trust).

Find out more: 0121 666 7671 (booking line). 0121 622 2442 (office) or backtobacks@nationaltrust.org.uk

Birmingham Back to Backs		M	T	W	T	F	S	S
31 Jan–10 Sep	Tour		·	T	W	T	F	S	S
16 Sep–21 Dec	Tour		·	T	W	T	F	S	S

Admission by timed, guided tour only (booking essential).
Open Bank Holiday Mondays (but closed next day). Term-time tours run from 1, Tuesdays, Wednesdays and Thursdays. Last tour times vary in winter due to low light levels. Closed 11 to 15 September.

Brockhampton Estate

Bringsty, near Bromyard, Herefordshire WR6 5TB

🏠 ✝ 📷 ❀ 🎫 ⇦ 1946

This medieval moated manor house sits at the heart of a 688-hectare (1,700-acre) ancient rural estate. The timber-framed house and romantic chapel ruins lie in unspoilt parkland redesigned in the 19th century. The manor house, entered through a charming timber-framed gatehouse, is a place to discover the people of Brockhampton, families who lived here and their lives, from 1425 to today. Estate walks run through traditional orchards, working farmland and wild woodlands and offer countryside views and a glimpse into rural Herefordshire life. You can also spot wildlife, climb, balance and build as you play on the nature trail.

Eat, shop, stay: Granary shop and refreshment kiosk near the manor house is open all year round, serving sandwiches, soups, one-pot meals, cakes and refreshments. Priority seating on the ground floor or relax upstairs. Gifts and award-winning local produce. Second-hand bookshop.

Brockhampton Estate, Herefordshire: the medieval timber-framed house, below, with its simple kitchen, above right, sits within unspoilt parkland

Things to see and do: **Indoors** Year-round family activities, demonstrations, exhibitions and historical re-enactments. **Outdoors** Countryside event days, family trails and games. Natural play trail and geocaching. Waymarked walks and orienteering routes. Picnics welcome. **Dogs**: welcome on leads in grounds, woods and parkland. Dog waste bins in car parks.

Access: 🅿️🅳🏢🧗📷🎨📷🚶
Building 🦽🧷♿ **Grounds** 🦽➡️♿
Parking: 100 yards and 1 mile.

Find out more: 01885 482077 (Infoline) or brockhampton@nationaltrust.org.uk

Brockhampton Estate		M	T	W	T	F	S	S
Estate								
Open all year	10–5	M	T	W	T	F	S	S
House*								
1 Jan–12 Feb	11–4	.	.	.	.	.	S	S
13 Feb–29 Oct	11–5	M	T	W	T	F	S	S
4 Nov–31 Dec	11–4	.	.	.	.	.	S	S
Granary shop and kiosk*								
1 Jan–12 Feb	10–4	.	.	.	.	.	S	S
13 Feb–13 Apr	10–5	M	T	W	T	F	S	S
14 Apr–29 Oct	11–5	M	T	W	T	F	S	S
4 Nov–31 Dec	10–4	.	.	.	.	.	S	S
Old Apple Store tea-room*								
11 Feb–19 Feb	10–5	M	T	W	T	F	S	S
25 Feb–9 Apr	10–5	.	.	.	.	.	S	S
14 Apr–29 Oct	10–5	M	T	W	T	F	S	S

*House, grounds, Granary shop, kiosk and tea-room close 30 minutes before rest of property.
Closed 24 and 25 December.

Carding Mill Valley and the Long Mynd

Church Stretton, Shropshire

🏛️🍴♿🚶🍴 1965

At Carding Mill Valley you are suddenly in the heart of wild countryside. Here families can enjoy playing in the stream, a variety of walks and exploring. From the valley, head up to the top of the Long Mynd and be rewarded with views of Shropshire and beyond.

Eat, shop, stay: Chalet Pavilion tea-room and roof terrace in Carding Mill Valley serving hot lunches, afternoon teas, drinks and ice-cream. Shop selling gifts, souvenirs, maps and pond nets.

Carding Mill Valley and the Long Mynd in Shropshire

Things to see and do: courses and family-friendly events all year. Free walks cards available in Carding Mill Valley.
Dogs: under close control and in sight (grazing livestock and ground-nesting birds).

Access: [icons] Building [icon]
Sat Nav: use SY6 6JG. **Parking**: 50 yards.

Find out more: 01694 725000 or cardingmill@nationaltrust.org.uk

Carding Mill Valley		M	T	W	T	F	S	S
Tea-room								
1 Jan–17 Feb	10–4	M	T	W	T	F	S	S
18 Feb–29 Oct	10–5	M	T	W	T	F	S	S
30 Oct–31 Dec*	10–4	M	T	W	T	F	S	S
Shop**								
1 Jan	11–4	·	·	·	·	·	·	S
7 Jan–29 Jan	10–4	·	·	·	·	·	S	S
4 Feb–17 Feb	11–4	M	T	W	T	F	S	S
18 Feb–29 Oct	11–5	M	T	W	T	F	S	S
30 Oct–31 Dec*	11–4	M	T	W	T	F	S	S

*Tea-room and shop: closed 25 December. **Shop: opens 10 at weekends. Toilets and Information Hut: open 9 to 7, March to October; 9 to 4:15, November to February.

Charlecote Park

Wellesbourne, Warwick,
Warwickshire CV35 9ER

[icons] 1946

The scene of Shakespeare's reputed poaching exploits, Charlecote Park was already in its middle age by the time Elizabeth I arrived, along the carriage drive through the Gatehouse and on to the welcoming red-brick mansion.

Generations of the Lucy family have left their mark on the buildings, gardens and parkland where visitors are intrigued to this day by the family's continuing presence. Charlecote presents a picture of peace and repose, protected by the rivers Dene and Avon and by its distinctive cleft-oak paling fences. It is a park where people picnic, play, walk and wander. Look out for the Jacob sheep and fallow deer which still roam across the 'Capability' Brown landscape.

Eat, shop, stay: The Orangery serves a range of meals and light snacks. The Servants' Hall gift shop and Pantry shop sell a range of Charlecote specific and locally sourced produce. Picnics welcome. Stay at The Turret holiday flat (sleeps six).

Things to see and do: **Indoors** Introductory Gatehouse room. Hands-on activities bring the Victorian kitchen and outbuildings to life. The house is festively decorated during December.
Outdoors Activities throughout the year, including guided park walks, talks and trails.
Dogs: assistance dogs only.

Access: [icons]
Building [icons] Grounds [icons]
Parking: 300 yards.

Find out more: 01789 470277 or charlecotepark@nationaltrust.org.uk

Charlecote Park		M	T	W	T	F	S	S
Grounds, shop and tea-room								
1 Jan–17 Feb	10–4*	M	T	W	T	F	S	S
18 Feb–5 Nov†	10–5*	M	T	W	T	F	S	S
6 Nov–31 Dec	10–4*	M	T	W	T	F	S	S
House								
18 Feb–24 Mar	11:30–3:30¹	M	T	W	T	F	S	S
25 Mar–5 Nov	11–4¹	M	T	W	T	F	S	S
11 Nov–17 Dec	11:30–3	·	·	·	·	·	S	S
18 Dec–24 Dec	11:30–3	M	T	W	T	F	S	S
Guided tours								
1 Jan–17 Feb	12–2	M	T	W	T	F	S	S
6 Nov–15 Dec	12–2	M	T	W	T	F	·	·
26 Dec–31 Dec	12–2	·	T	W	T	F	S	S

Whole property closed 25 and 26 January and 25 December. ¹House: Wednesdays by guided tours only. *Shop and tea-room: open at 10:30, close at 5, 18 February to 5 November. †Grounds: close at 6, 18 February to 5 November, or dusk if earlier.

With its turrets and warm red brick, the mansion, right, at Charlecote Park in Warwickshire, is intriguing and welcoming in equal measure. The gardens, left, and park offer space and peace, perfect for play and picnics

West Midlands

Clent Hills

near Romsley, Worcestershire

🏛️ ♿ 1959

A snowy day in the Clent Hills, Worcestershire. This oasis on the edge of Birmingham offers panoramic views

Set on the edge of Birmingham and the Black Country, this green oasis with panoramic views is the perfect place for a refreshing walk or a picnic on a sunny day. Families can create their own adventures – building dens, hunting for geocaches or simply getting closer to nature. **Note**: nearest facilities at Nimmings Wood entrance.

Eat, shop, stay: café (not National Trust) at Nimmings Wood car park serving light meals and refreshments.

Things to see and do: regular guided rambles and family activities. Natural play area and play trail. **Dogs**: welcome, but please be considerate to other visitors.

Access: 🅿️♿🚶➡️
Sat Nav: use B62 0NL for Nimmings Wood entrance. **Parking**: at Nimmings Wood; additional parking at Adam's Hill and Walton Hill.

Find out more: 01562 712822 or clenthills@nationaltrust.org.uk

Clent Hills

Nimmings Wood car park: gates open 8:30 to 5. Closed 25 December.

Coughton Court

Alcester, Warwickshire B49 5JA

🏠 ✝️ ❀ 🔔 🍷 1946

Coughton has been home to the Throckmorton family for 600 years. Facing persecution for their Catholic faith, they were willing to risk everything. You can discover their story and find out about a family's ingenuity, resilience and resolve, including their link to the infamous Gunpowder Plot. Coughton is very much a family home with an intimate feel. The Throckmorton family still live here and they created and manage the gardens, including a riverside walk, bog garden and beautiful display of roses in the walled garden.

Eat, shop, stay: Coughton Kitchen café serving lunch and teas. Drinks and ice-cream available from the Stables coffee bar. Coach House shop selling local food and seasonal gifts. Throckmorton family plant sales. Second-hand bookshop.

The Throckmorton family home for 600 years, Coughton Court in Warwickshire has an intimate feel

Why not share your pictures with us? #nationaltrust

Things to see and do: **Indoors** Morning taster tours and welcome talks. Children's trail. **Outdoors** Walking trails around the estate and surrounding countryside. Natural Play and outdoor games. Baddesley Clinton and Packwood nearby. **Dogs**: welcome on leads in car park and public footpaths. Assistance dogs only in gardens.

Access:
House **Grounds**
Parking: 150 yards.

Find out more: 01789 400777 or coughtoncourt@nationaltrust.org.uk

Coughton Court		M	T	W	T	F	S	S
House, shop and café*								
2 Mar–26 Mar	11–5	·	·	·	**T**	**F**	**S**	**S**
House, shop, café and grounds**								
29 Mar–1 Oct	11–5	·	·	**W**	**T**	**F**	**S**	**S**
5 Oct–29 Oct	11–5	·	·	·	**T**	**F**	**S**	**S**
House, shop and café†								
25 Nov–3 Dec	11–5	**M**	**T**	**W**	**T**	**F**	**S**	**S**

Good Friday to Easter Monday: admission by bookable tickets only, subject to availability (including members). *Grounds closed. Closed 24/25 June and 15 July. Open Bank Holiday Mondays. Admission to house and walled garden by timed ticket on weekends and busy days. **Walled garden opens at 12. Taster Tours, not bookable, subject to availability. †Coughton Winter Festival, grounds closed.

Croft Castle and Parkland

Yarpole, near Leominster, Herefordshire HR6 9PW

1957

This intimate house became the Croft family home before the Domesday Book. There are many compelling 20th-century stories to uncover, including the impact of the First World War. This year we share the story of Croft in the 1950s. You can discover the changes inside the castle, gardens and parkland and what life was like at Croft 60 years ago. Explore the walled garden, its working vineyard and historic glasshouse. Stroll into the picturesque Fishpool Valley or go in search of Croft Ambrey, the Iron Age hill fort, exploring the historic wood pasture and many ancient trees along the way.

There are many compelling stories to discover at Croft Castle and Parkland in Herefordshire

Eat, shop, stay: tea-room (licensed) serving food made using fresh garden produce – hot lunches, cakes and ice-cream. Children's lunchboxes and half portions. Shop selling gifts, plants, home and garden products. Second-hand bookshop. Picnic area. Garden and Ambrey holiday cottages for a longer stay.

Things to see and do: **Indoors** Games, interactive memorabilia and dressing-up. **Outdoors** Family activities, living history, open-air theatre, seasonal events. Natural and castle-inspired play areas. Walks, dog-walking, birdhide, information barn and orienteering. **Dogs**: welcome, on leads in gardens, parkland and glazed area of tea-room only.

Access: ⬚⬚⬚⬚⬚⬚⬚⬚
Castle ⬚⬚⬚ **Grounds** ⬚⬚⬚⬚
Sat Nav: use HR6 0BL. **Parking**: 100 yards.

Find out more: 01568 780246 or croftcastle@nationaltrust.org.uk

Croft Castle and Parkland		M	T	W	T	F	S	S
Tea-room, garden, shop and parkland								
1 Jan–5 Feb	10–4						S	S
27 Dec–31 Dec	10–4			W	T	F	S	S
Castle, tea-room, garden, shop and parkland								
11 Feb–5 Nov	10–5	M	T	W	T	F	S	S
11 Nov–17 Dec	10–4						S	S

Castle and shop: open 11. Play area: open as parkland.

A family explores the gardens at Croft Castle and Parkland on a beautiful sunny autumn day

Croome

near High Green, Worcester, Worcestershire WR8 9DW

⬚⬚⬚⬚⬚ 1996

The meadow at Croome in Worcestershire, above, delights as much today as when it was created. Inside Croome Court, right, all is light and calm

There's more than meets the eye at Croome. A secret wartime airbase, now a visitor centre, was once a hub of activity for thousands of people. Outside is the grandest of English landscapes, 'Capability' Brown's masterful first commission, with commanding views over the Malverns. The parkland, nearly lost but now restored, is great for walks and adventures with a surprise around every corner. At the heart of the park lies Croome Court, once home to the Earls of Coventry. The 6th Earl was an 18th-century trendsetter, and today Croome follows his lead using artists and crafts-people to tell the story of its eclectic past in inventive ways. Explore four floors of the mansion, perfect for making new discoveries.

Eat, shop, stay: 1940s-style restaurant, Gingkos shop, Gardeners' Bothy plant shop and second-hand bookshop at the visitor centre. 1940s tea-car serving snacks on busy days. Kitty Fisher's Coffee House serving light lunches in Croome Court's basement.

Things to see and do: **Indoors** Contemporary exhibitions, including the return of the collection, the lost Croome tapestries and other creative installations. All four floors of the house are open, some areas by guided tour.

Time Explorers game for older children around the house. RAF Defford Museum at the visitor centre. **Outdoors** Walled Garden (privately owned with admission fee towards its restoration) open days through the year. Regular guided tours of the park and outer eye-catcher open days. Special family trails around park every school holiday. RAF-themed playground and natural play area close to the visitor centre. **Dogs**: welcome on leads. Assistance dogs only in house, RAF museum, restaurant and shop.

Access: 🅿♿🏔♿🐕🖼🅰♿🄰
House 🏔♿♿ **Park** ➡♿♿
Sat Nav: follow signs from main road, not Sat Nav. **Parking**: on site.

Find out more: 01905 371006 or croome@nationaltrust.org.uk
Croome National Trust Visitor Centre, near High Green, Severn Stoke WR8 9DW

Croome		M	T	W	T	F	S	S
House								
1 Jan–10 Feb	11–4	M	T	W	T	F	S	S
11 Feb–5 Nov	11–4:30	M	T	W	T	F	S	S
6 Nov–23 Dec	11–4	M	T	W	T	F	S	S
26 Dec–31 Dec*	Tour		T	W	T	F	S	S
Park, restaurant and shop								
1 Jan–10 Feb	10–4	M	T	W	T	F	S	S
11 Feb–5 Nov**	9–5	M	T	W	T	F	S	S
6 Nov–23 Dec	10–4	M	T	W	T	F	S	S
26 Dec–31 Dec	10–4		T	W	T	F	S	S

*House: open for timed tours only. **Shop: opens at 10.

Cwmmau Farmhouse

Brilley, Whitney-on-Wye,
Herefordshire HR3 6JP

🏠❄♿➤ 1965

Located on the Herefordshire and Welsh border with stunning views, this 17th-century timbered farmhouse has many original features to explore. **Note**: 16 to 22 June, open daily, 1 to 5.

Find out more: 01568 780246 or cwmmaufarmhouse@nationaltrust.org.uk

Downs Banks

Washdale Lane, Oulton Heath,
near Stone, Staffordshire

♿ 1950

A little wilderness of woodlands and heath, with easy access walks, in the heart of the Midlands. **Note**: sorry no toilets. Some steep paths.

Find out more: 01889 882825 or downsbanks@nationaltrust.org.uk

Dudmaston

Quatt, near Bridgnorth, Shropshire WV15 6QN

🏠❄♿➤ 1978

Dudmaston, Shropshire: a corner of the sweeping garden

Rooted in the south Shropshire countryside, Dudmaston remains today what it has been for 875 years: a much-loved and lived-in family home. But for its ancient heritage, there's an equal measure of modern thinking, tastes and culture which continue to shape the estate today. Wooded parkland and a sweeping garden are steeped in history but with a twist. Discover modern sculptures, a woodland playground, go exploring or simply find a tranquil spot and take in the amazing views. Soak up the family history in the Hall and the contrasting Modern Art Galleries, created by the last owner, Lady Labouchere. **Note**: the family home of Mr and Mrs Mark Hamilton-Russell.

Seen from across the peaceful lake, the Hall at Dudmaston sits proudly within its glorious wooded parkland

Eat, shop, stay: Orchard tea-room offering lunches and a selection of freshly made cakes. Also a seasonal ice-cream parlour and Apple Store Snacks café. Shop selling seasonal gifts, locally sourced items and plants. Second-hand bookshop. Holiday cottage and bunkhouse available for rent.

Things to see and do: **Indoors** Explore ancient and modern collections in the Hall. **Outdoors** Walks map. Garden or Discovery tours. Let off steam in the woodland playground, then follow a '50 things' trail. **Dogs**: welcome on leads in parkland and orchard only.

Access: [icons] Building [icons] Grounds [icons]
Parking: on site or at The Old Sawmill and Hampton Loade.

Find out more: 01746 780866 or dudmaston@nationaltrust.org.uk

Dudmaston		M	T	W	T	F	S	S
Park, tea-room and shop								
18 Feb–26 Feb**	12–4						S	S
19 Mar–30 Mar	11:30–5	M	T	W	T			S
2 Apr–28 Sep	11–5:30	M	T	W	T			S
1 Oct–31 Oct	11:30–5	M	T	W	T			S
4 Nov–10 Dec**	11:30–4						S	S
Galleries								
19 Mar–30 Mar	1–5	M	T	W	T			S
1 Oct–31 Oct	1–5	M	T	W	T			S
Hall and galleries*								
2 Apr–28 Sep	1–5	M	T	W	T			S
Garden and second-hand bookshop								
19 Mar–30 Mar	12–5	M	T	W	T			S
2 Apr–28 Sep	12–5:30	M	T	W	T			S
1 Oct–31 Oct	12–5	M	T	W	T			S

No entry to the car park before opening time. *Hall and galleries: open at 2 on Sundays. **Restricted park access – Dingle walks only. Closed Good Friday.

Farnborough Hall

Farnborough, near Banbury, Warwickshire OX17 1DU

[icons] 1960

Honey-coloured stone house with library and treasures collected during the Grand Tour. Set in landscape gardens with panoramic parkland views. **Note**: occupied and administered by the Holbech family. Open Wednesday and Saturday, 1 April to 30 September, 2 to 5:30; also open Sunday and Bank Holiday Monday, 30 April and 1 May.

Find out more: 01295 690002 (Farnborough Hall). 01295 670266 (Upton House) or farnboroughhall@nationaltrust.org.uk

The Fleece Inn

Bretforton, near Evesham, Worcestershire WR11 7JE

[icons] 1978

Medieval half-timbered longhouse, now a traditional village inn, with barn and orchard. Known for folk music, Morris dancing and asparagus. **Note**: open daily, 10 to 11 (reduced opening 25 December).

Find out more: 01386 831173 or fleeceinn@nationaltrust.org.uk

Greyfriars' House and Garden

Friar Street, Worcester,
Worcestershire WR1 2LZ

🏛️ 🌸 🔔 1966

Tranquil Greyfriars' House and Garden in Worcestershire

Set in the heart of historic Worcester, Greyfriars is a charming timber-framed house – perfect for getting away from the hustle and bustle. This unique property was rescued by two extraordinary people in the 20th century with a vision to revive this medieval gem and create a peaceful home and garden.

Eat, shop, stay: light refreshments served in the walled garden or in Elsie's tea-room (in house) in colder weather. Small retail shop, including plants and a selection of second-hand books.

Things to see and do: **Indoors** Themed events throughout the year, including house tours. Children's trails. **Outdoors** Garden games and geocaching. **Dogs**: welcome in garden.

Access: 🖥️ 🎬 🔵 House 🚻 ♿ 🚹 🚻
Parking: none on site. Nearest at Corn Market, King Street and Cathedral Plaza, not National Trust (charge including members).

Find out more: 01905 23571 or greyfriars@nationaltrust.org.uk

Greyfriars		M	T	W	T	F	S	S
14 Feb–25 Mar	11–4*	·	T	W	T	F	S	·
28 Mar–28 Oct	11–5*	·	T	W	T	F	S	·
31 Oct–16 Dec	11–4*	·	T	W	T	F	S	·

*House taster tours only from 11 to 1 (last tour at 12:30), tour places allocated on arrival. Free-flow access from 1. Open Bank Holiday Mondays.

Hanbury Hall

School Road, Hanbury, Droitwich Spa,
Worcestershire WR9 7EA

🏛️ 🌸 🛶 🏡 🍽️ 1953

A country retreat in the heart of Worcestershire. The house and garden, originally a stage-set for summer parties, offer a glimpse into life at the turn of the 18th century. Don't miss the original wall-paintings by Sir James Thornhill. Full of drama and politics, they show the birth of Georgian society. The original formal gardens, designed by George London, have been faithfully re-created and complement the relaxed later gardens, with orangery, orchards and walled garden. If you venture further afield, our walks leaflet will help you find George London's visionary Semicircle in the parkland – the beginning of the landscape movement.

Eat, shop, stay: Servants' Hall tea-room serving meals and cakes made using seasonal Hanbury-grown produce. Chambers tea-room serving traditional afternoon teas. Plants and produce

from the walled garden for sale. Make Hanbury a home from home in one of two holiday cottages.

Things to see and do: spend perfect days picnicking and playing on sweeping lawns, surrounded by rolling Worcestershire countryside. Open-air theatre, November fayres and art exhibitions. **Dogs**: on leads in parkland and in stableyard. Assistance dogs only in gardens.

Access: [icons]
Building [icons] **Grounds** [icons]
Parking: 150 yards.

Find out more: 01527 821214 or hanburyhall@nationaltrust.org.uk

Two views of the garden at Hanbury Hall, Worcestershire

Hanbury Hall		M	T	W	T	F	S	S
1 Jan–26 Feb	11–4**	M	T	W	T	F	S	S
27 Feb–29 Oct	10–5*	M	T	W	T	F	S	S
30 Oct–31 Dec†	10–4**	M	T	W	T	F	S	S

*Tours only 10:30 to 1; free-flow 1 to 5. **Tours only 11 to 3 (free-flow from 1 during February half-term). †27 November to 31 December, free-flow access. Closed 25, 26 January, and 24, 25 December. Entrance by timed ticket on busy days.

Hawford Dovecote

Hawford, Worcestershire WR3 7SG

[icon] 1973

Picturesque dovecote, which has survived virtually unaltered since the late 16th century, retaining many nesting boxes. **Note**: sorry no toilet or tea-room. Please park carefully to one side of lane. Open daily, dawn to dusk.

Find out more: 01527 821214 or hawforddovecote@nationaltrust.org.uk

Kinver Edge and the Rock Houses

Holy Austin Rock Houses, Compton Road, Kinver, near Stourbridge, Staffordshire DY7 6DL

[icons] 1917

The Holy Austin Rock Houses, inhabited until the 1960s, have no equivalent in the whole of England. Discover how a few extraordinary people carved themselves homes in this imposing sandstone ridge. A walk in the surrounding woodland of Kinver Edge leads to open heath with dramatic views across three counties.

Eat, shop, stay: tea-room inside restored Rock House serving drinks, cakes and snacks, including our famous rock cakes.

Things to see and do: **Indoors** Traditional games and range. **Outdoors** Natural play trail. Guided walks and family activities all year. **Dogs**: welcome on leads within grounds of Rock Houses.

The Holy Austin Rock Houses at Kinver Edge and the Rock Houses, Staffordshire, were inhabited until the 1960s

Access: P🅿 D🅳 🅿 🎵 ♿ 📷
Building 🔥 Grounds 🔥
Parking: by Warden's Lodge, Comber Road, for the Edge, and Compton Road or Kingsford Lane overflow car park for the Rock Houses.

Find out more: 01384 872553 or kinveredge@nationaltrust.org.uk

Kinver Edge and the Rock Houses	M	T	W	T	F	S	S
18 Feb–7 Apr*	11–4				T	F	S	S
8 Apr–23 Apr	11–4	M	T	W	T	F	S	S
27 Apr–23 Jul*	11–4				T	F	S	S
26 Jul–4 Sep	11–4	M	T	W	T	F	S	S
7 Sep–29 Oct*	11–4				T	F	S	S
4 Nov–10 Dec	11–4						S	S

Rock House gardens and tea-room: open 10:30 to 4:30.
*Rock Houses grounds and tea-room: open daily during Staffordshire school half-term holidays.

Kinwarton Dovecote

Kinwarton, near Alcester,
Warwickshire B49 6HB

🏠 1958

Rare 14th-century circular dovecote with metre-thick walls, hundreds of nesting holes and original rotating ladder. **Note**: stock may be grazing. Sorry no toilet. Limited parking (not National Trust). Open daily, 2 March to 29 October, 9 to 6.

Find out more: 01789 400777 or kinwartondovecote@nationaltrust.org.uk

Knowles Mill

Dowles Brook, Bewdley,
Worcestershire DY12 2LX

🏠 1938

Dating from the 18th century, the mill retains much of its machinery, including the frames of an overshot waterwheel. **Note**: Mill Cottage not open to visitors (please respect the resident's privacy). Sorry no toilets or tea-room. No parking at Mill Cottage. Open daily, dawn to dusk.

Find out more: 01527 821214 or knowlesmill@nationaltrust.org.uk

Letocetum Roman Baths and Museum

Watling Street, Wall, near Lichfield,
Staffordshire WS14 0AW

🏠 🏛 1934

Remains of a once-important Roman staging post and settlement, including *mansio* (Roman inn) and bathhouse. **Note**: in the guardianship of English Heritage. Baths open every day all year, 9 to 5. Museum open last weekend of month, March to October (additional openings during August and for some Bank Holidays).

Find out more: 0370 333 1181 (English Heritage) or letocetum@nationaltrust.org.uk

Middle Littleton Tithe Barn

Middle Littleton, Evesham,
Worcestershire WR11 8LN

🏚 1975

The largest and finest restored 13th-century tithe barn in the country. **Note**: sorry no toilets. Open daily, 1 April to 31 October, 2 to 5.

Find out more: 01905 371006 or middlelittleton@nationaltrust.org.uk

Morville Hall

Morville, near Bridgnorth,
Shropshire WV16 5NB

🏚 ✿ 🌳 1965

Elizabethan gem with a Georgian makeover. Enchanting gardens spill down to the Mor Brook against the backdrop of Shropshire hills. **Note**: property contents are a mix of items on loan and tenant's own. Open 12 and 13 May, 9 and 10 June, 14 and 15 July, 8 and 9 September, 12 to 5. Dower House gardens opened independently (telephone 01746 714407 for details).

Find out more: 01746 780866 (Dudmaston Hall) or morvillehall@nationaltrust.org.uk

Moseley Old Hall

Moseley Old Hall Lane, Fordhouses,
Wolverhampton, Staffordshire WV10 7HY

🏚 ⭐ ✿ 🌳 1962

This atmospheric 17th-century farmhouse holds many secrets. Charles II hid here after escaping the 1651 Battle of Worcester. Inside a log fire crackles and Elizabethan domestic life

surrounds you. Outside, you can explore the walled garden, containing herbs and vegetables, the orchard and knot garden. Beyond is King's Walk Wood.

Eat, shop, stay: tea-room serving soup, one-pots and seasonal specials. Cakes and scones are baked here throughout the day. Shop selling gifts and plants. Second-hand bookshop.

History comes to life at Moseley Old Hall, Staffordshire: an atmospheric farmhouse with many secrets

Things to see and do: **Indoors** Guided tours, have-a-go sessions and re-creations of 17th-century life all year. **Outdoors** Children's activities, including two-level tree-house, den-building, rope swings, trails and activity packs. Wightwick Manor nearby. **Dogs**: welcome on leads in garden and grounds.

Access: 🅿️🔈🦽🔔🎧🚻🪑🔼🎫♿
House 🦽🦼 Garden and woodlands 🦽🦼➡️🦼
Parking: on site.

Find out more: 01902 782808 or moseleyoldhall@nationaltrust.org.uk

Moseley Old Hall		M	T	W	T	F	S	S
17 Feb–17 Mar	10:30–4	M	T	W	.	F	S	S
18 Mar–29 Oct	10:30–5	M	T	W	.	F	S	S
4 Nov–17 Dec	10:30–4	.	.	.	.	.	S	S
18 Dec–22 Dec	11–3	M	T	W	.	F	.	.

House: open from 11:30; 11 on Bank Holidays. Entry on Bank Holiday weekends and very busy times by timed ticket. February, March, November and December: access to top floor may be limited for safety. Last entry to house one hour before closing.

Packwood House

Packwood Lane, Lapworth,
Warwickshire B94 6AT

🏚 ❖ ♨ ⊺ 1941

Surrounded by beautiful gardens and countryside, Packwood was described by a guest in the 1930s as 'a house to dream of, a garden to dream in'. Lovingly restored at the beginning of the 20th century by Graham Baron Ash, you can discover the detail behind the man, his passion for collecting and his collection. The gardens include brightly coloured, 'mingled style' herbaceous borders, famous sculpted yews and an 18th-century gentleman's kitchen garden.

Eat, shop, stay: Garden Kitchen café serving hot food, soup, salads, sandwiches, cakes and snacks. Shop selling seasonal gifts, local foods and plants, many grown in our own nursery. Picnics welcome by the lakeside and in the picnic area by the car park.

Things to see and do: **Indoors** Children's trail. **Outdoors** Welcome and garden talks, countryside walks and Natural Play. Baddesley Clinton and Coughton Court nearby. Areas of the gardens may be closed, please call before travelling. **Dogs**: welcome in car park, park footpaths and café terrace. Assistance dogs only in gardens.

Access: 🅿🅿♿🦽📷📷
House 🦽♿♿ **Grounds** 🦽♿♿
Parking: 150 yards.

Find out more: 01564 782024 or packwood@nationaltrust.org.uk

Packwood House		M	T	W	T	F	S	S
House, grounds, shop and café								
1 Jan–17 Feb	9–4*		T	W	T	F	S	S
18 Feb–29 Oct	9–5*	M	T	W	T	F	S	S
30 Oct–31 Dec	9–4*	M	T	W	T	F	S	S
House and grounds tours**								
1 Jan–17 Feb	11–3		T	W	T	F	S	S
30 Oct–31 Dec	11–3	M	T	W	T	F	S	S

Good Friday to Easter Monday: admission by bookable tickets only, subject to availability (including members). *House, formal gardens and gift shop open at 11. Admission to the house by timed ticket (not bookable). **Tours run at intervals throughout day, subject to availability. Closed 24 and 25 December.

'A house to dream of, a garden to dream in': lovingly restored Packwood House in Warwickshire, above and below, offers so much, both indoors and out

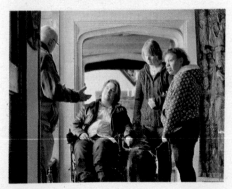

Rosedene

Victoria Road, Dodford, near Bromsgrove, Worcestershire B61 9BU

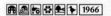 1997

Restored 1840s cottage with an organic garden and orchard, illustrating the mid-19th century Chartist Movement. **Note**: available to hire as a 'back to basics' holiday cottage. Admission by guided tour (first Sunday of month), 5 March to 3 December (booking essential). March to October tours at 10, 11:30, 2 and 3:30; November and December tours at 10, 11:30, 1 and 2:30.

Find out more: 01527 821214 or rosedene@nationaltrust.org.uk

Shugborough Estate

Milford, near Stafford, Staffordshire ST17 0XB

1966

Join us on a journey into uncharted territory as the Shugborough Estate returns to the care of the National Trust this year. Home to the Anson family since 1624, a legacy of exploration and innovation, it was once described as 'a perfect paradise'. You can explore sweeping parkland, ancient woodland and a landscape peppered with monuments, then discover Park Farm, created at the cutting-edge of agricultural reforms. In the Georgian mansion, unearth unusual treasures and experience life 'below stairs', then enter a world of glamour and royalty in the apartments of Patrick Lichfield, 5th Earl and fashion photographer.

Eat, shop, stay: delicious treats and meals on offer at the mansion and Park Farm, made with local and Walled Garden produce. Why not visit the shop and pick up the perfect gift?

Things to see and do: **Indoors** There are stories of adventure, travels and triumphs to discover in the mansion. **Outdoors** New estate walks to explore and wonderful views from the Triumphal Arch to enjoy. **Dogs**: on leads in formal gardens and parkland.

Access:
Building **Grounds**
Parking: 25 yards from reception.

Shugborough Estate, Staffordshire: back in our care

A cherub rises above the early morning mist in the garden at Shugborough Estate

Eat, shop, stay: small tea-room in house, with doors leading onto the veranda, serving light lunches, cakes, ice-cream and drinks. Picnics welcome on lawn. Shop in the historic kitchen selling gifts, seasonal plants, produce and second-hand books.

Things to see and do: **Indoors** See the house gradually transformed back to 1997, as we celebrate Sunnycroft's last owner, Joan Lander. Guided tours and children's trails. **Outdoors** Family trails, garden games and seasonal events. **Dogs**: welcome on leads in grounds only.

Find out more: 01889 881388 or shugborough@nationaltrust.org.uk

Shugborough Estate		M	T	W	T	F	S	S
Park, gardens and Park Farm†								
21 Mar–4 Nov*	10–5	M	T	W	T	F	S	S
5 Nov–31 Dec	10–4	M	T	W	T	F	S	S
Park Farm Café								
21 Mar–4 Nov	10–4:30	M	T	W	T	F	S	S
5 Nov–31 Dec	10:30–3:30	M	T	W	T	F	S	S
Mansion and servants' quarters								
21 Mar–5 Nov**	11–4	M	T	W	T	F	S	S
2 Dec–23 Dec	11–3	M	T	W	T	F	S	S
Mansion tea-room and shop								
21 Mar–5 Nov	11–4	M	T	W	T	F	S	S
11 Nov–26 Nov	11–3:30	.	.	.	.	.	S	S
2 Dec–24 Dec	11–3:30	M	T	W	T	F	S	S
30 Dec–31 Dec	11–3:30	.	.	.	.	.	S	S

†Walled Garden and visitor reception: open as park and gardens. *Iron Man event, 16 to 19 June: whole site closed (contact property for information). **Some areas of mansion accessible by timed ticket or booking only. Christmas shop: open 6 November to 31 December, 11 to 3:30. Closed 25 December.

Roses in bloom at Sunnycroft in Shropshire: a mini estate in the middle of suburbia

Access: [icons] Building [icon] Grounds [icons]
Sat Nav: use TF1 2DP (exit 7 from M54).
Parking: 150 yards from front of house.

Find out more: 01952 242884 or sunnycroft@nationaltrust.org.uk

Sunnycroft

200 Holyhead Road, Wellington, Telford, Shropshire TF1 2DR

 1999

Hidden down an avenue of towering redwoods is an oasis in the middle of suburbia. Designed to emulate the upper classes, this rare middle-class Victorian survival is a mini estate. Built to last, little was thrown away and the life of a family home envelopes you as you enter.

Sunnycroft		M	T	W	T	F	S	S
7 Jan–12 Feb	10:30–3	.	.	.	.	.	S	S
18 Feb–26 Feb	10:30–4	M	T	.	.	F	S	S
3 Mar–26 May*	10:30–5	M	.	.	.	F	S	S
27 May–29 Aug	10:30–5	M	T	.	.	F	S	S
1 Sep–30 Oct*	10:30–5	M	.	.	.	F	S	S
1 Dec–23 Dec	10:30–4	M	T	.	.	F	S	S

*Open Tuesdays during Easter holidays and October half-term. Last admission one hour before closing. Entry by timed tickets with optional ten-minute introductory talk, then free-flow. Daily guided tours available in main season (not bookable).

Upton House and Gardens

near Banbury, Warwickshire OX15 6HT

🏠 ✣ ▦ ♠ ⊤ 1948

Sold! This year you are invited to a very special house viewing. Purchased in 1927 by the 2nd Viscount Bearsted, Upton had great potential, but needed modernisation. You can follow the renovations and witness the 'before' and 'after', as the Bearsteds fashioned a made-to-measure family home, fit to showcase a world-class art collection, including works by Bosch, Stubbs, El Greco, as well as fine porcelain. Every ideal home needs a spectacular garden, and Lady Bearsted certainly created one. Her passion for plants bloomed, with early spring bulbs, lavish herbaceous planting and thriving kitchen garden, all reflected in the Mirror Pool.

Eat, shop, stay: restaurant (licensed) serving lunches and freshly baked cakes; gluten-free and vegetarian options always available. Shop selling gifts, art prints, plants and mementoes of your visit. Two holiday cottages; one with 1930s décor and one overlooking the gardens.

Things to see and do: Indoors Themed house tours, interactive displays, changing exhibitions, sewing and craft activities and design workshops. **Outdoors** Woodland adventure and games. Local walks, seasonal planting schemes. Jazz music and garden chats. **Dogs**: assistance dogs only in grounds.

Access: 🅿️🔊♿🚶♿🔊🔊📷🔊
House and gallery 🔊🔊♿ Grounds 🔊🔊♿
Sat Nav: follow brown signs to car park once you arrive at postcode location.
Parking: 300 yards.

Find out more: 01295 670266 or uptonhouse@nationaltrust.org.uk

Upton House and Gardens		M	T	W	T	F	S	S
Gardens, restaurant and shop*								
1 Jan–5 Feb	12–4						S	S
11 Feb–29 Oct	11–5	M	T	W		F	S	S
30 Oct–18 Dec	12–4	M				F	S	S
26 Dec–31 Dec	12–4		T	W	T	F	S	S
House*								
1 Jan–5 Feb	12–4						S	S
11 Feb–29 Oct	1–5	M	T	W		F	S	S
30 Oct–18 Dec	12–4	M				F	S	S

*Open daily in July and August. November to March: gardens open by winter walk only. 11 February to 29 October: themed tours 11 to 1, timed tickets available on arrival. **Timed tickets operate daily. 27 February to 22 March: house entry by guided tour only. Open daily in July and August. 27 February to 22 March: Picture Gallery closed and limited access to some rooms due to conservation and installation work.

Upton House and Gardens in Warwickshire: a family home fashioned to showcase a world-class art collection

The Weir Garden

Swainshill, Hereford, Herefordshire HR4 7QF

⚏ ✤ ⚐ 1959

A place of natural beauty, The Weir Garden, Herefordshire, is completely captivating, whatever the season

Whatever the season, the natural beauty of this riverside garden is completely captivating. During spring, the ground beneath the ancient trees is carpeted with bulbs; then, in summer, a picnic by the river while watching the wildlife is irresistible. Autumn brings an abundance of seasonal produce in the walled garden. **Note**: sturdy footwear recommended.

Eat, shop, stay: self-service tea and coffee available. Picnics welcome. Small selection of children's toys, gifts, maps and seasonal gifts available in the shop.

Things to see and do: events, including walks and talks. Historical secrets to discover, from giant fish to Roman remains. Natural play area and family trails during school holidays. **Dogs**: assistance dogs only (dogs allowed in car park).

Access: ♿ Grounds ⬆ ⬆
Parking: on site.

Find out more: 01981 590509 or theweir@nationaltrust.org.uk

The Weir Garden		M	T	W	T	F	S	S
14 Jan–22 Jan	10:30–4						S	S
28 Jan–29 Oct	10:30–4:30	M	T	W	T	F	S	S
30 Oct–5 Nov	10:30–4	M	T	W	T	F	S	S

Wichenford Dovecote

Wichenford, Worcestershire WR6 6XY

⚏ 1965

Small but striking 17th-century half-timbered dovecote at Wichenford Court. **Note**: no access to Wichenford Court (privately owned). Sorry no toilet or tea-room. Please consider local residents when parking. Open every day all year, dawn to dusk.

Find out more: 01527 821214 or wichenforddovecote@nationaltrust.org.uk

Wightwick Manor and Gardens

Bridgnorth Road, Wolverhampton, West Midlands WV6 8BN

⚏ ✤ 1937

Would you save a house that was only 50 years old? Geoffrey Mander believed his parents' home was worth preserving for the nation to enjoy, giving Wightwick to the National Trust in 1937. He then complemented the house's Old English design by filling it with Pre-Raphaelite art and William Morris furnishings. Much-loved by the people of Wolverhampton, the Mander family legacy lives on at Wightwick. The gardens of soft lawns, old yew and fragrant roses offer a place to relax and reflect. Inside, the art, textiles and designs of Rossetti, Morris, De Morgan and their friends are waiting to delight.

Eat, shop, stay: specialist shop selling William Morris and Arts and Crafts-inspired ranges and plant centre. Tea-room serving light lunches, sandwiches and sweet treats. Garden ticket required to visit shop and tea-room.

Things to see and do: Indoors World-class art collection, interactive servants' rooms, specialist talks and tours available all year. **Outdoors** Family orienteering map and trails, self-led activities. Moseley Old Hall nearby. **Dogs**: welcome on leads in garden.

Access: ⓟ♿♿♿♿♿♿♿♿♿ **Manor** ♿
♿♿ **Malthouse** ♿♿ **Gardens** ♿♿♿➡♿
Parking: entrance off A454.

Find out more: 01902 761400 (Infoline) or wightwickmanor@nationaltrust.org.uk

Wightwick Manor and Gardens		M	T	W	T	F	S	S
Manor								
1 Jan–17 Mar	12–4	M	·	W	T	F	S	S
18 Mar–30 Jun	12–5	M	·	W	T	F	S	S
1 Jul–31 Aug	12–5	M	T	W	T	F	S	S
1 Sep–29 Oct	12–5	M	·	W	T	F	S	S
30 Oct–31 Dec	12–4	M	·	W	T	F	S	S
Gardens, tea-room and shop								
1 Jan–17 Mar	11–4	M	T	W	T	F	S	S
18 Mar–29 Oct*	10:30–5	M	T	W	T	F	S	S
30 Oct–31 Dec	11–4	M	T	W	T	F	S	S

*Shop open at 11. Last entry to house one hour before closing. Closed 25 and 26 December. Reduced number of rooms open in January, February and March and from 27 December.

Making friends at Wightwick Manor and Gardens in the West Midlands, left. The house, above and below, sits within a garden of wide lawns, old yew and roses

Wilderhope Manor

Longville, Much Wenlock, Shropshire TF13 6EG

🏠♿♿♿ 1936

Charming Elizabethan manor house with commanding views across a secluded valley with many original features inside and lovely walks outside. **Note**: youth hostel, access may be restricted. Open Sundays, 8 January to 17 December, 2 to 4; additionally open Wednesdays, 2 April to 27 September, 2 to 4.

Find out more: 01694 771363 (Hostel Warden YHA) or wilderhope@nationaltrust.org.uk

North West

Little Moreton Hall, Cheshire

Buildings and/or gardens

Entry points to coast and countryside

National Trust land

Places in neighbouring counties

East Midlands, page 234
West Midlands, page 260
The Lakes, page 310
Yorkshire, page 332
Wales, page 366

10 miles

A685

A591

KENDAL
▲ Sizergh

Fell
Foot ●

A590

Ulverston ■

Arnside and Silverdale

A687

A65

Barrow-in-Furness ■

Morecambe ■

A683

Lancaster ■

Heysham Coast

Settle ■

M6

A59

A56

A629

East Riddlesden Hall ■

Blackpool ■

M55

A585

Burnley ■
Gawthorpe Hall ▲

Hardcastle Crags ●

Preston ■
A6
A59

M65

A666

A56

Todmorden ■

M62

Southport ■

Rufford Old Hall

A565

M61

M66

Rochdale ■

Formby

Wigan ■
A58

Bolton ■

M58
A570

A580

M60

LIVERPOOL

The Hardmans' House

The Beatles' Childhood Homes

A59

Salford ■

MANCHESTER

M67

M62

A57

Sale ■

Dunham Massey

Stockport ■

Kinder, Edale and the Dark Peak ●

M53

Speke Hall

A56

M56

Warrington ■

Quarry Bank ▲

Tatton Park ▲

A523

Lyme ▲

A6

Longshaw, Burbage and the Eastern Moors ●

A55

A41

Nether Alderley Mill ▲
Hare Hill ▲

Alderley Edge and Cheshire Countryside

Macclesfield ■

A537

Bakewell ■

A494

CHESTER ■

A51

A49

A530

M6

A54

Congleton ■

A52

A53

Ilam Park, Dovedale and the White Peak ●

A41

Little Moreton Hall ▲
A534

Biddulph Grange Garden

A523

A534

Crewe ■

Erddig ▲

A483

A49

A525

A53

A495

A young adventurer tackles an especially tricky challenge at Alderley Edge, Cheshire

Alderley Edge and Cheshire Countryside

Nether Alderley, Macclesfield, Cheshire

 1946

The dramatic red sandstone escarpment of Alderley Edge has far-reaching views over the Cheshire Plain and towards the Peak District. Numerous paths meander through open pasture, mature pine and beech woodland. The site, designated a Site of Special Scientific Interest for its geology and history of copper mining dating back to the Bronze Age, is also noted for its legend and *The Weirdstone of Brisingamen* novel. For similar countryside experiences, why not visit Bickerton, Bulkeley and Helsby Hills on the Sandstone Ridge, Thurstaston Common on the Wirral, and The Cloud and Mow Cop on the Staffordshire border? **Note**: toilets at Alderley Edge car park only.

Eat, shop, stay: Alderley Edge: Wizard Tea-room (Thursday to Sunday and Bank Holidays) and Wizard Inn (neither National Trust). Ice-cream vendor (when weather is fine). Picnic area close to car park.

Things to see and do: guided walks provide an insight into the industrial archaeology, geology and legends at Alderley Edge. Waymarked walking routes. Three orienteering courses. Ancient copper mine tours: Derbyshire Caving Club, twice yearly. **Dogs**: under close control. On leads near livestock and ground-nesting birds.

Access: 🅿️🚻♿ Grounds ➡️
Sat Nav: for Alderley Edge use SK10 4UB; for Mow Cop ST7 3PA; for Bickerton SY14 8LN. **Parking**: at Alderley Edge, Mow Cop ST7 3PA and Bickerton SY14 8LN (plus roadside elsewhere).

Find out more: 01625 584412 or alderleyedge@nationaltrust.org.uk

Alderley Edge		M	T	W	T	F	S	S
Car park								
Open all year	8–5*	**M**	**T**	**W**	**T**	**F**	**S**	**S**

*1 April to 31 October closes 8.

Arnside and Silverdale

near Arnside, Cumbria

🏛️🏊🚴🐾 1929

With a wildlife-rich mosaic of limestone grassland, pavement, woodland and meadows this coastal countryside offers fine views over Morecambe Bay and miles of footpaths. Arnside Knott and Eaves Wood are home to butterflies and flowers; Jack Scout's cliffs are perfect for watching the setting sun or migrant birds passing through.

Dog-walking at Arnside, Cumbria

Eat, shop, stay: variety of small shops, galleries and cafés in and around Arnside and Silverdale villages (not National Trust). Nearest National Trust café at Sizergh.

Things to see and do: toposcope viewpoint (short uphill from Arnside Knott car park). Silverdale Lots footpath to the cove perfect for strolls. Silverdale village heritage walk. **Dogs**: welcome under control (on leads where stock grazing).

Access: 🐾
Sat Nav: use LA5 0BP for Arnside Knott; LA5 0UG for Eaves Wood (Silverdale), both nearby.
Parking: at Arnside Knott (signposted from Arnside Promenade) and Eaves Wood, Silverdale. Also in Silverdale village (not National Trust).

Find out more: 01524 702815 or arnsidesilverdale@nationaltrust.org.uk

The Beatles' Childhood Homes

Woolton and Allerton, Liverpool

🏛️ 2002

A combined tour to Mendips and 20 Forthlin Road, the childhood homes of John Lennon and Paul McCartney, is your only opportunity to see inside the houses where The Beatles met, composed and rehearsed many of their earliest songs. You can walk through the back door into the kitchen and imagine John's Aunt Mimi cooking him his tea, or stand in the spot where Lennon and McCartney composed 'I Saw Her Standing There'. The custodians take you on a fascinating trip down memory lane in these two atmospheric period houses, so typical of Liverpool life in the 1950s.
Note: handbags, cameras and recording equipment must be left in secure facilities at both houses. Access to these houses is by National Trust minibus tour only from Liverpool city centre or Speke Hall (charge including members).

Eat, shop, stay: guidebooks and postcards available at both houses and Speke Hall shop.

Taking a unique trip down memory lane at The Beatles' Childhood Homes in Liverpool

The cooker where John Lennon's Aunt Mimi cooked his tea at Mendips

Speke Hall's Home Farm restaurant serving regional specialities, such as Scouse and Wet Nelly.

Things to see and do: departures from convenient pick-up points (city centre and Speke Hall). Our comfortable minibus and easy online booking service allow you to relax, as we take the strain out of visiting.

Access: 🖼️🎏🖥️🎫📱 Building 👐
Parking: numerous car parks near collection point (not National Trust) for tours from city centre, or at Speke Hall for tours departing from there.

Find out more: 0151 427 7231 (booking line) or thebeatleshomes@nationaltrust.org.uk

The Beatles' Childhood Homes		M	T	W	T	F	S	S
1 Mar–4 Jun	Tour*	·	·	W	T	F	S	S
5 Jun–29 Oct	Tour*	M	T	W	T	F	S	S
1 Nov–26 Nov	Tour*	·	·	W	T	F	S	S

*Admission by guided tour only. Times and pick-up locations vary (please visit website or call for details and tickets).

Dunham Massey

Altrincham, Cheshire WA14 4SJ

🏠✝️🏛️❀🦌🍽️ 1976

Set within a wall of warm red brick, Dunham Massey is home to more than 400 years-worth of family history, a herd of fallow deer and a garden for all seasons. 'Dunham's Lost Years' has seen the house transformed to tell a tale of love, status and scandal, which changed Dunham's history for ever. Outdoors, a 12-hectare (30-acre) garden awaits with colourful swathes of planting and a sweeping lawn at its centre – a great spot for a picnic. The stables and working mill are also close by, but for those who want to escape deeper into the park, follow one of the tree-lined avenues, spotting deer along the way.
Note: everyone (including members) requires a house and garden ticket (available from reception on the day).

Eat, shop, stay: large shop selling food, locally sourced gifts and a wide range of plants. Café with indoor and outdoor seating, the Stables Restaurant serving hot lunches and the Stables Parlour offering drinks and treats, including ice-cream (hours vary).

Things to see and do: free guided tours in the garden on weekdays. Free guided walks in the deer-park every day. Map available for walk, run and cycle routes on the wider estate.

Autumnal fun at Dunham Massey in Cheshire

For information about getting to National Trust places, please see page 3

The man-made splendour of the Great Hall at Georgian Dunham Massey, left, contrasts with the simple natural charm of the deer-park, above, outside the house

Events all year, including open-air theatre and garden parties. Family activities during school holidays. Cycling in the deer-park for under-fives only. **Dogs**: welcome under close control and on leads in deer-park.

Access: [symbols]
House [symbols] Garden and park [symbols]
Parking: 200 yards.

Find out more: 0161 942 3989 (Infoline).
0161 941 1025 or
dunhammassey@nationaltrust.org.uk

Dunham Massey		M	T	W	T	F	S	S
House and stables								
11 Feb–5 Nov*	11–5**	M	T	W	·	·	S	S
Garden, shop and café								
1 Jan–10 Feb	10:30–4†	M	T	W	T	F	S	S
11 Feb–5 Nov	10:30–5†	M	T	W	T	F	S	S
6 Nov–31 Dec	10:30–4†	M	T	W	T	F	S	S
Park								
1 Jan–10 Feb	8–6	M	T	W	T	F	S	S
11 Feb–5 Nov	8–8	M	T	W	T	F	S	S
6 Nov–31 Dec	8–6	M	T	W	T	F	S	S

*House: entry to house to 22 March by regular guided tour (booking not necessary). House: last entry one hour before closing, or dusk if earlier. **Stables: close 4. †Shop and café: open 10. Garden: closes at dusk if earlier than stated time. Mill: open 12 to 4, 11 February to 5 November. White Cottage: open last Sunday of month, March to October, 2 to 5 (booking essential, 0161 928 0075). Whole property closed 22 November and 25 December (including car park).

Formby

near Formby, Liverpool

[symbols] 1967

Making sandcastles at Formby, Liverpool

Formby's shifting sands create ever-changing dunes sculpted by the wind and squeezed by surging tides. Sea views over Liverpool Bay to the hills of North Wales can be enjoyed from the wide sandy beaches. Footprint trails 5,000 years old sometimes reappear as the sea erodes ancient mudflats. Pinewood walks with red squirrels lead to open fields and the Formby Asparagus Trail. Formby is a place for a simple family day out, for healthy exercise and relaxation and a perfect spot for a seaside picnic.

The sandy coastline of Formby offers miles of walks

Note: toilets close at 5:15 in summer, 4 in winter.

Eat, shop, stay: ice-cream, soft drinks, coffee and confectionery available from mobile vans. A favourite place for picnics. Safe barbecue area is available at the family picnic site.

Things to see and do: self-guided trails, including the Formby Asparagus Trail and the Asparagus Cycle Trail. Guided walks. Circular and longer walks linked to the Sefton Coastal Path. Orienteering and geocaching. **Dogs**: on leads on Squirrel Walk and under close control elsewhere (vulnerable wildlife).

Access: 🅿️🚻♿🚼📷🅰️ Grounds 🦽➡️
Sat Nav: use L37 1LJ. **Parking**: on site.

Find out more: 01704 878591 or formby@nationaltrust.org.uk

Formby		M	T	W	T	F	S	S
Car park								
1 Jan–5 Feb	9–4	M	T	W	T	F	S	S
6 Feb–26 Mar	9–4:45	M	T	W	T	F	S	S
27 Mar–1 Oct	9–5:15	M	T	W	T	F	S	S
2 Oct–26 Nov	9–4:45	M	T	W	T	F	S	S
27 Nov–31 Dec	9–4	M	T	W	T	F	S	S

Closed 25 December.

Gawthorpe Hall

Burnley Road, Padiham, near Burnley, Lancashire BB12 8UA

🏠♿ 1972

This imposing house, set in the heart of urban Lancashire, contains fabulously opulent interiors, created by Sir Charles Barry in the 19th century. The Hall displays textiles from the Gawthorpe Textile Collection, including needlework, lace and embroidery, while outside the grounds are popular with dog walkers. **Note**: financed and run in partnership with Lancashire County Council.

Eat, shop, stay: tea-room serving light snacks.

Things to see and do: **Indoors** Guided tours, talks and exhibitions. Events all year, including Victorian Christmas. **Outdoors** Open-air theatre in July and other events, including some for children. **Dogs**: under close control in grounds.

Access: 🅿️🚻♿📷📱🅰️ **Building** 🦽
Grounds 🦽🚶🦽➡️
Parking: 150 yards, narrow access road (passing places).

Find out more: 01282 771004 or gawthorpehall@nationaltrust.org.uk

Gawthorpe Hall		M	T	W	T	F	S	S
Hall and tea-room								
1 Apr–5 Nov	11–5*		·	·	W	T	F	S	S
Grounds								
Open all year	8–7	M	T	W	T	F	S	S

Hall and tea-room open Bank Holidays. *Hall: opens at 12, opening times subject to change.

Imposing Gawthorpe Hall in Lancashire

The Hardmans' House

59 Rodney Street, Liverpool, Merseyside L1 9ER

🏠 2003

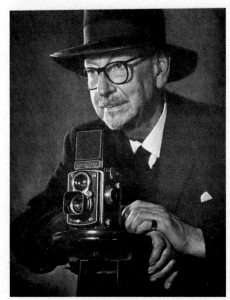

The Hardmans' House, Merseyside: E. Chambré Hardman

Step inside the sophisticated life of a 1950s society photographer in the heart of Liverpool. The former studio and home of Edward Chambré Hardman, and his talented wife Margaret, is a time capsule of Liverpool life and creativity, packed with vintage treasures and fascinating photography. **Note**: admission by guided tour only – booking advised. Entrance on Pilgrim Street at rear of property.

Eat, shop, stay: shop selling unique photographic prints, postcards, guidebooks and hot drinks. The nearest café (not National Trust) is just a short walk away at the Anglican Cathedral.

Things to see and do: tours (book your place to avoid disappointment). Family trail. Virtual tour of the house. Walking trails of Hardman's Liverpool available online.

Access: 🔲🔲🔲🔲🔲🔲 Building 🔲
Parking: none on site. Car parks at Anglican Cathedral and Slater Street, not National Trust (charge including members).

Find out more: 0151 709 6261 or thehardmanshouse@nationaltrust.org.uk

The Hardmans' House	M	T	W	T	F	S	S
15 Mar–28 Oct	11–3:30	·	·	**W**	**T**	**F**	**S**	·

Admission by timed ticket only, booking advisable (places limited). Open Bank Holiday Mondays.

Hare Hill

Over Alderley, Macclesfield, Cheshire SK10 4PY

🔲🔲 1978

Hare Hill is a place of aesthetic and spiritual refreshment set within a traditional parkland. A woodland full of twists, turns and surprises, wooden hares and hidden paths and ponds. At its heart is Colonel Brocklehurst's stunning walled White Garden offering an oasis of tranquillity and place for reflection.

A wooden hare and young fan at Hare Hill in Cheshire

A moment of peace among the rhododendrons at Hare Hill

Eat, shop, stay: external catering at weekends and Bank Holidays only. Hot drinks vending machine within the garden at all other times. Picnics welcome in the garden. Plants for sale. Small second-hand bookstall.

Things to see and do: carved hare trail throughout the woodland and bird-spotting in the hide. Why not bring a book and relax in the walled garden and explore the changing woodland in all seasons? **Dogs**: assistance dogs only in the garden and woodland.

Access: ⚙️♿👁️ Grounds ♿
Sat Nav: use SK10 4PY to take you 109 yards west of car park. **Parking**: new car park on site.

Find out more: 01625 584412 or harehill@nationaltrust.org.uk

Hare Hill		M	T	W	T	F	S	S
1 Mar–29 Oct	10:30–5	·	**T**	**W**	**T**	**F**	**S**	**S**

Open Bank Holiday Mondays. Last admission one hour before closing. Car park locked at 5.

Heysham Coast

Heysham, near Morecambe, Lancashire

✝️🏛️🌊🚂 1996

A beautiful sandstone walk in coastal grassland and peaceful woodland, leading to a unique ruined Saxon chapel and rock-cut graves. **Note**: nearest facilities in village (not National Trust); park in the main village car park. For Sat Nav use LA3 2RW.

Find out more: 01524 701178 or heysham@nationaltrust.org.uk

Little Moreton Hall

Congleton, Cheshire CW12 4SD

🏠✝️🏛️✽ 1938

While modern life rushes by on the busy road outside, Little Moreton Hall survives as a stunning Tudor fantasy, inviting the visitor back to another time and place within moments. Built to impress by craftsmen's hands over 500 years ago, the Hall continues to exude an inimitable quirky charm and homely intimacy. With its crooked walls and uneven floors, it is at once fragile and resilient. This remarkable survivor offers visitors a rare chance to pause for a moment, to take an imaginative journey back in time and reflect on the ups and downs of a simpler way of life.

Eat, shop, stay: the Little Tea Room (with outdoor orchard seating) and Mrs Dale's Tea Room serve delicious homemade food produced in the on-site bakery. Ice-cream kiosk (open on sunny days). Large shop in the car park selling gifts, refreshments and local products.

Things to see and do: **Indoors** Free guided tours and family trails. Tudor displays and activities most days. Costumes to try on. Contemporary exhibition programme.

Outdoors Theatre in the summer and Tudor festivals all year. **Dogs**: on leads in car park and front lawn only.

Access: [icons]
Hall [icons] **Reception** [icons]
Grounds [icons]
Parking: 100 yards.

Find out more: 01260 272018 or littlemoretonhall@nationaltrust.org.uk

Little Moreton Hall		M	T	W	T	F	S	S
18 Feb–26 Feb	11–5	M	T	W	T	F	S	S
1 Mar–9 Apr	11–5	·	·	W	T	F	S	S
10 Apr–23 Apr	11–5	M	T	W	T	F	S	S
26 Apr–28 May	11–5	·	·	W	T	F	S	S
29 May–4 Jun	11–5	M	T	W	T	F	S	S
7 Jun–30 Jul	11–5	·	·	W	T	F	S	S
31 Jul–28 Aug	11–5	M	T	W	T	F	S	S
30 Aug–22 Oct	11–5	·	·	W	T	F	S	S
23 Oct–29 Oct	11–5	M	T	W	T	F	S	S
1 Dec–17 Dec	11–4	·	·	·	·	F	S	S

Open Bank Holiday Mondays. Upper floors may close early if light levels are poor. Please note the building is being repainted in autumn.

Exuding an inimitable quirky charm, Little Moreton Hall in Cheshire, this page and left, allows visitors the chance to take an imaginary journey back in time

Lyme

Disley, Stockport, Cheshire SK12 2NR

🏠✝♣♨🚃 1947

Much-loved home of the Legh family for more than 600 years, Lyme sits in 570 hectares (1,400 acres) of deer-park, with glorious views across Manchester and the Cheshire Plain. Its lavish interiors reflect the life of a great estate, from its earliest beginnings to its Regency heyday, when Thomas Legh brought Lyme back to its full glory. You may recognise Lyme as 'Pemberley' from the BBC adaptation of *Pride and Prejudice*, starring Colin Firth, and the 'Big House' in series two of *The Village*. Lyme's ever-changing gardens, with the Reflection Lake, Orangery and Rose Garden, are an ideal place to relax and stroll.
Note: owned and managed by the National Trust, but partly financed by Stockport Metropolitan Borough Council.

Eat, shop, stay: choice of café and tea-rooms serving light snacks, lunches and desserts. Salting Room Tea Parlour and Garden offering full afternoon tea (booking essential). Gift, book and plant shop. East Lodge holiday cottage in deer-park with stunning views.

Things to see and do: **Indoors** Activities such as reading in the Library, home to the 15th-century *Lyme Missal* – a rare Caxton prayer book, dressing-up in Regency costume, experiencing the beautiful sounds of recently returned Regency musical instruments or discovering more about Thomas Legh, Lyme's very own Indiana Jones. **Outdoors** Regular Saturday park runs, family orienteering course (changes every month), self-led woodland and moorland walks, adventurous play in Crow Wood Playscape for five- to twelve-year-olds. Park trail and sensory play area in garden for under-fives. Events, including Easter trails, summer holiday activities, Hallowe'en and Christmas celebrations. **Dogs**: under close control in park; leads near livestock and vehicles; selected days in garden.

Access: 🅿️🔧♿🚻👶🍼📷📺🚼📍🏪
House 🔧♿🅶 Garden 🔧♿🏠➡🅶
Sat Nav: use SK12 2NR. **Parking**: 200 yards.

Find out more: 01663 762023 or lyme@nationaltrust.org.uk

Lyme in Cheshire, left, is everything a grand country house should be. With lavish interiors, top, and glorious grounds, above, Lyme is a unique treasure that all will enjoy

Lyme		M	T	W	T	F	S	S
House*								
11 Feb–5 Nov	11–5	M	T	·	·	F	S	S
24 Nov–24 Dec**	11–3	M	·	·	·	F	S	S
Garden, shop and tea-room†								
1 Jan–5 Feb	11–3	·	·	·	·	·	S	S
11 Feb–5 Nov	11–5	M	T	W	T	F	S	S
11 Nov–31 Dec¹	11–3	·	·	·	·	·	S	S
Deer-park††								
Open all year	8–6	M	T	W	T	F	S	S
Timber Yard shop and café								
1 Jan–25 Mar	10–4	M	T	W	T	F	S	S
26 Mar–5 Nov	10–5	M	T	W	T	F	S	S
6 Nov–31 Dec¹	10–4	M	T	W	T	F	S	S

*House: open Thursdays, 27 July to 31 August; 11 February to 5 November, last entry one hour before closing. **Parts of house open for Regency Christmas events only. †Garden opens 10:30; shop closed January. ††Gates: locked at closing. Deer-park: opens 8 to 8, 26 March to 5 November. ¹Lyme closed 25 December.

Nether Alderley Mill

Congleton Road, Nether Alderley, Macclesfield, Cheshire SK10 4TW

🏠 1950

Concealed under the long sloping roof of this medieval building is a fully restored, working corn mill. Inside, as the waterwheels turn, huge millstones grind the flour. On the guided tours, centuries-old graffiti can be spotted and you can discover more about the life of a miller. **Note**: view by guided tour only. Uneven floor, steep stairs and low ceilings throughout. Limited parking.

Eat, shop, stay: small range of souvenirs available. Sorry no toilets or food outlets at this property. Nearest National Trust facilities at nearby Alderley Edge.

Things to see and do: at nearby Quarry Bank, you can continue your industrial adventures at one of England's earliest cotton mills, experiencing the lives of the apprentices and workers who powered the Industrial Revolution.

Access: 🅿️📷📹 Mill 🏛️🚻
Parking: limited.

Find out more: 01625 527468 or netheralderleymill@nationaltrust.org.uk

Nether Alderley Mill		M	T	W	T	F	S	S
15 Apr–1 Oct	1–4:30	·	·	·	·	·	S	S

Access by guided tour only. Last tour 3:45. Also open for booked visits on weekdays (call 01625 445890 to book).

Nether Alderley Mill in Cheshire: within this medieval building is a fully restored, working corn mill

Quarry Bank

Styal, Wilmslow, Cheshire SK9 4LA

🏛️ ✳️ ♿ 🔔 🍽️ 1939

As the Industrial Revolution dawned, the tranquillity of the river valley at Quarry Bank gave way to the clatter and bustle of Samuel Greg's cotton mill at work. Among the shaking, hissing machinery, men, women and children toiled six days a week to earn their meagre living. This summer, our major Heritage Lottery-funded project will bring the different worlds of the mill workers and their masters to life, as a worker's cottage in Styal village and the Greg family home are opened to the public for the very first time. An exhibition in Quarry Bank House will explore the intellectual society that Samuel's wife Hannah gathered around her, in sharp contrast to the stark realities faced by the workers. **Note**: car-park improvements taking place all year. Building works in mill planned from November.

Eat, shop, stay: mill shop selling gifts, including fabric and glass cloths produced in the mill. Mill café serving hot lunches and afternoon tea. New shop and café open in the Upper Garden. Drinks and ice-cream available from the Pantry. Picnic areas.

Things to see and do: Indoors You can take a tour of the Apprentice House to see how the younger workers at the mill lived, ate and learned. A programme of interactive exhibitions,

installations and events throughout the year delves deeper into the stories of Quarry Bank, revealing unexpected insights into the lives of the people who lived and worked here.
Outdoors Thanks to your donations, the newly restored curvilinear glasshouse will be open from this spring in our peaceful and picturesque garden. Children can try out some of the '50 things to do before you're 11¾' in the meadow and woods. **Dogs**: welcome under close control on estate. On leads in garden, mill yard and meadow.

Access: 🅿️🚻♿🔄🔛🔊🧏♿.🔵🖼️
Mill 🔋♿♿🍽️♿ **Apprentice House** ♿🖼️
Grounds ♿♿➡️🔄

Parking: steep hill with 61 steps from car park. Car-park improvements all year (expect minor disruptions). No height restrictions in car park.

Find out more: 01625 527468 or quarrybankmill@nationaltrust.org.uk

Quarry Bank		M	T	W	T	F	S	S
Mill, café and shop								
1 Jan–10 Feb	10:30–4*	·	·	W	T	F	S	S
11 Feb–5 Nov	10:30–5*	M	T	W	T	F	S	S
8 Nov–31 Dec†	10:30–4*	·	·	W	T	F	S	S
Garden, café and shop								
11 Feb–5 Nov	10:30–5**	M	T	W	T	F	S	S
11 Nov–31 Dec	10:30–4**	·	·	·	·	·	S	S
Estate								
1 Jan–10 Feb	8–6	M	T	W	T	F	S	S
11 Feb–5 Nov	8–8	M	T	W	T	F	S	S
6 Nov–31 Dec	8–6	M	T	W	T	F	S	S

Whole property closed 9 to 20 January for maintenance. Closed 25 December, open 26 December to 7 January 2018. *Café: opens at 10. **Garden: closes dusk if earlier. †Building works in mill planned from November (mill closure likely); rest of property remains open. Please ring or check website for information.

Quarry Bank, Cheshire: while all was tranquillity in the picturesque garden, left and right, the mill, above, was a place of never-ending activity and fearsome noise

Rufford Old Hall

200 Liverpool Road, Rufford, near Ormskirk, Lancashire L40 1SG

🏠 ✣ ⌂ 1936

Set in the low-lying lands of south-west Lancashire, Rufford Old Hall has over 500 years of family history to tell. Step back in time to the timber-framed Tudor Great Hall where the 'moveable' oak screen has witnessed theatrical productions in Shakespeare's time and seven generations of Hesketh family history. Our daily house and garden talks will satisfy your curiosity, while our wild art and bug-hunting kits will keep the children entertained. You can relax and unwind in the 5.6 hectares (14 acres) of stunning gardens and grounds – with spring bulbs, autumn colour and views over the Leeds to Liverpool canal.

Eat, shop, stay: you can experience local tastes with Lancashire tea in the Victorian tea-room. The shop offers special treats, including Lancashire sauce, Lancashire crisps and plenty of gifts to keep memories of Rufford Old Hall fresh.

Things to see and do: **Indoors** Daily house talks and seasonal children's trail. Christmas experience with Santa's Grotto. **Outdoors** Guided garden tours. Events, including open-air theatre. Seasonal children's trails and Tudor and Victorian games. **Dogs**: on leads in courtyard and woodland only.

Whether you fancy a day as a knight, above, or want to find out more, top, Rufford Old Hall in Lancashire offers opportunities galore. Outside, stunning grounds and the garden, left, are a delight whatever the season

Access: 🅿️ 🚗 ♿ 🚻 ⬆️ 📷 🎦 📖 ♿ 🅿️
Building 🔥 ♿ ♿ 🚻 ♿ **Grounds** 🔥 ♿ ♿ ➡️ ♿
Parking: on site.

Find out more: 01704 821254 or ruffordoldhall@nationaltrust.org.uk

Rufford Old Hall		M	T	W	T	F	S	S
11 Feb–2 Apr	11–4	M	T	W	·	·	S	S
3 Apr–23 Apr	11–5	M	T	W	T	F	S	S
24 Apr–28 May	11–5	M	T	W	·	·	S	S
29 May–4 Jun	11–5	M	T	W	T	F	S	S
5 Jun–2 Jul	11–5	M	T	W	·	·	S	S
3 Jul–30 Jul*	10:30–5	M	T	W	·	·	S	S
31 Jul–3 Sep*	10:30–5	M	T	W	T	F	S	S
4 Sep–1 Oct	11–5	M	T	W	·	·	S	S
2 Oct–22 Oct	11–4	M	T	W	·	·	S	S
23 Oct–29 Oct	11–4	M	T	W	T	F	S	S
30 Oct–5 Nov	11–4	M	T	W	·	·	S	S
11 Nov–17 Dec	11–4	·	·	·	·	·	S	S

*House: opens 11. Car park: closes 30 minutes after times above. Tudor Great Hall: occasionally closed until 1 for weddings.

Speke Hall

Speke, Liverpool L24 1XD

🏠 ❀ ♿ 👶 ⛪ T 1944

Speke Hall is a cherished Tudor mansion – an oasis of beauty, atmosphere and surprise. Built by the Catholic Norris family during the unsettled Tudor period, the house has several hidden security features, including a priest's hole and eavesdrop. Following years of neglect (including a spell when it was used as a cowshed), interiors were revived in a cosy Arts and Crafts-style during the Victorian push for improvement. Today you can relax in inviting gardens and woodland, with seasonal displays of rhododendrons and bluebells – a tranquil escape from modern life.

The adjacent coastal reserve, along the shore of the River Mersey, is perfect for bracing strolls and wildlife walks. Families can explore and enjoy our play areas and trails.

Eat, shop, stay: Home Farm Restaurant serving regional specialities, including Scouse and Wet Nelly, Stable tea-room offering hot drinks and homemade cakes. Locally sourced gifts, as well as plants and books available in the gift shop.

Things to see and do: **Indoors** Costumed guided tours, Victorian billiards to play. A tricky trail to solve. Hallowe'en, Tudor and Victorian Christmas events. **Outdoors** Formal and recently restored kitchen gardens. The coastal and woodland walks are great to explore whatever the weather. Why not lose yourself in the Victorian maze, get stuck into building a den or riding the zip wire in the woodland play area or exploring the Giant Childe of Hale play trail?

An oasis of beauty, atmospheric Speke Hall, Liverpool, is guaranteed to surprise and delight visitors of all ages

Exciting range of sports activities for all abilities. Easter Egg hunts, May Day celebrations and open-air theatre in the summer.
Dogs: welcome on leads in the woodland and on signed estate walks.

Access: ⬚⬚⬚⬚⬚⬚⬚⬚⬚⬚⬚
Hall ⬚⬚⬚ **Grounds** ⬚⬚⬚⬚
Parking: on site.

Find out more: 0151 427 7231 or
spekehall@nationaltrust.org.uk

Speke Hall		M	T	W	T	F	S	S
House*								
11 Feb–23 Jul	11–5	·	·	W	T	F	S	S
25 Jul–3 Sep	10:30–5	·	T	W	T	F	S	S
6 Sep–5 Nov	11–5	·	·	W	T	F	S	S
24 Nov–10 Dec	11–4	·	·	·	·	F	S	S
Gardens, catering and retail**								
11 Feb–5 Nov	10:30–5	M	T	W	T	F	S	S
6 Nov–31 Dec†	10:30–4	M	T	W	T	F	S	S

*House: entry before 12:30 by guided tour only (places limited), tickets available from reception on day; free-flow from 12:30. **Shop opens at 11. †Closed 24 to 26 December. Access and closing times subject to change in February and March. Car park: closes 30 minutes after all times stated.

There are more than 400 years of turbulent history and many hidden secrets to uncover at Speke Hall, above and below. Costumed guides help bring the story of this Tudor manor house to life

Tatton Park

Knutsford, Cheshire WA16 6QN

🏠🕐♻️⛲🚶🅿️🔔☕ 1960

Tatton means so many different things to so many people. Set in 400 hectares (1,000 acres) of parkland, the former Egerton family home is open for you to witness contrasting upstairs and downstairs lifestyles in the mansion. You can wander through impressive formal gardens and meet rare-breed animals at the working farm. The parkland provides the perfect setting for picnics, sailing, horse-riding or relaxing country walks. The Old Hall has special open days when you can uncover centuries of history. There are over 100 events each year, ranging from festivals and fairs, to family shows and learning activities. **Note:** managed/financed by Cheshire East Council. For tours, RHS show, Christmas and other events supplementary charges may apply (including members). Park car entry charge, £6 (including members).

Eat, shop, stay: visit the historic Stableyard and enjoy the Stables self-service restaurant and Gardener's Cottage table-service tea-room. Speciality shops include the Housekeeper's Store for the best in local speciality food and drink, gift shop, garden shop and tuck shop.

Things to see and do: **Indoors** Mansion and Tudor Old Hall. Activities at the farm. Shopping and dining. Many learning activities and events. **Outdoors** Gardens, parkland and adventure playground. Numerous events and learning activities. **Dogs**: on leads at farm and under close control in park only.

Access: 🅿️♿🐕🚻🧺🖼️🖼️♿😊⚠️
Building 🔲🔲🔲🔲 Grounds 🔲🔲➡️♿
Sat Nav: use WA16 6SG. **Parking**: park car entry charge, £6 (including members).

Find out more: 01625 374435 (Infoline). 01625 374400 or tatton@cheshireeast.gov.uk
tattonpark.org.uk

Tatton Park		M	T	W	T	F	S	S
Parkland, gardens and restaurant								
1 Jan–24 Mar*	10–5	·	T	W	T	F	S	S
25 Mar–29 Oct*	10–7	M	T	W	T	F	S	S
31 Oct–31 Dec*	10–5	·	T	W	T	F	S	S
Mansion								
25 Mar–1 Oct	1–5	·	T	W	T	F	S	S
3 Oct–29 Oct	12–4	·	T	W	T	F	S	S
Farm								
1 Jan–19 Mar	11–4	·	·	·	·	·	S	S
25 Mar–29 Oct	12–5	·	T	W	T	F	S	S
4 Nov–31 Dec	11–4	·	·	·	·	·	S	S
Shops								
1 Jan–24 Mar	12–4	·	T	W	T	F	S	S
25 Mar–29 Oct	11–5	M	T	W	T	F	S	S
31 Oct–31 Dec	12–4	·	T	W	T	F	S	S

*Gardens and restaurant: close one hour earlier. Open Bank Holiday Mondays. Parkland, mansion, farm and garden: last admission one hour before closing. Guided mansion tours at 12, Tuesday to Sunday, 25 March to 1 October (timed ticket, places limited), small charge including members. Old Hall special opening arrangements and charge. Mansion open for Christmas event. Tatton Park closed 25 December.

Seen from above, the full splendour of Tatton Park in Cheshire becomes apparent

Additional coastal and countryside car parks in the North West

Coast	
Arnside Knott	LA5 0BP
Eaves Wood (Silverdale)	LA5 0UG

Cheshire countryside	
Mow Cop	ST7 3PA
Bickerton	SY14 8LN

The Lakes

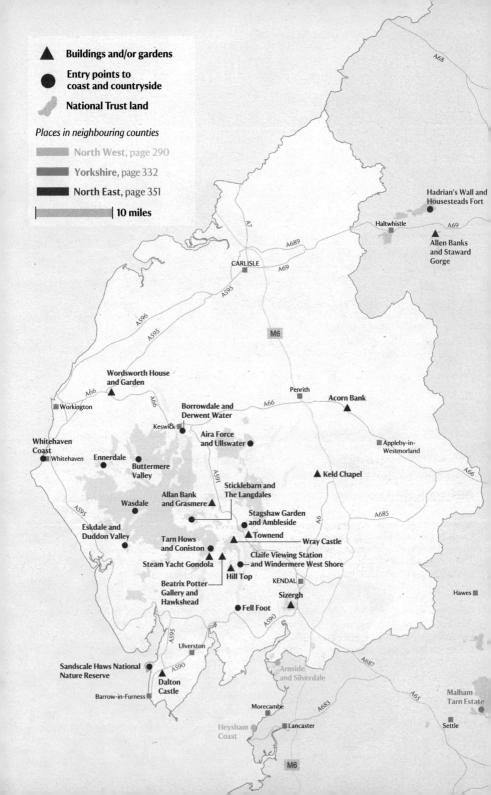

Buildings and/or gardens

Entry points to coast and countryside

National Trust land

Places in neighbouring counties

North West, page 290

Yorkshire, page 332

North East, page 351

10 miles

A68

Hadrian's Wall and Housesteads Fort

Haltwhistle

A69

Allen Banks and Staward Gorge

A7

A689

A69

CARLISLE

A69

A595

M6

A596

A595

Wordsworth House and Garden

A66

Penrith

A66

Acorn Bank

Workington

Borrowdale and Derwent Water

Keswick

Aira Force and Ullswater

Appleby-in-Westmorland

A66

Whitehaven Coast

Whitehaven

Ennerdale

Buttermere Valley

Keld Chapel

A591

Allan Bank and Grasmere

Sticklebarn and The Langdales

A685

Wasdale

Stagshaw Garden and Ambleside

A595

Eskdale and Duddon Valley

Tarn Hows and Coniston

Townend

Wray Castle

A6

Steam Yacht Gondola

Claife Viewing Station and Windermere West Shore

Hill Top

Beatrix Potter Gallery and Hawkshead

KENDAL

Hawes

Sizergh

Fell Foot

Ulverston

A595

A590

Sandscale Haws National Nature Reserve

Dalton Castle

Arnside and Silverdale

A687

Barrow-in-Furness

A590

Morecambe

A683

A65

Malham Tarn Estate

Heysham Coast

Lancaster

Settle

M6

The partially open sandstone manor house at Acorn Bank in Cumbria sits within a tranquil estate

Acorn Bank

Temple Sowerby, near Penrith,
Cumbria CA10 1SP

🏚️🏛️❀♿🚻 1950

At the heart of the Eden Valley, with spectacular views to the Lake District, Acorn Bank is a tranquil haven with a rich and diverse history. The walled gardens shelter a medicinal herb garden and traditional orchards. Woodland walks, famous for springtime daffodils, reveal a half-hidden story of gypsum mining and a working watermill with a medieval past. In the midst of this beautiful estate sits a 17th-century sandstone manor house, once owned by the indomitable author and poet, Dorothy Una Ratcliffe. This unfurnished manor is now partially open to our visitors while under restoration. **Note**: access to fragile grass paths may be restricted after wet weather. Members pay on Apple Day, 8 October (opening arrangements differ on that day, see note in table for details).

Eat, shop, stay: tea-room, using garden produce and flour from the mill (outside tables in courtyard). Shop, selling plants, watermill flour and national products. Sandwath and Bank Wood, spacious holiday apartments (sleeping two to three), allow you to enjoy the estate after hours.

Things to see and do: watermill machinery operates most weekend afternoons. Wild play area in the woods and secret places for children to discover. Apple Day is a great family day out. **Dogs**: welcome on leads on woodland walks and garden courtyard. Apple Day: assistance dogs only.

Access: 🅿️♿♿♿♿📷📱📷 **Watermill** 👟♿ **House** 👟♿♿ **Grounds** 👟♿♿➡️♿♿ **Parking**: large car park.

Find out more: 017683 61893 or acornbank@nationaltrust.org.uk

Acorn Bank		M	T	W	T	F	S	S
18 Feb–5 Mar	11–4						S	S
11 Mar–29 Oct	10–5*	M		W	T	F	S	S
4 Nov–23 Dec	11–4						S	S

*Tea-room open 10:30 to 4:30. Apple Day: Sunday 8 October, access for event only.

Aira Force and Ullswater

near Watermillock, Penrith, Cumbria

 1906

Aira Force is a showcase for the power and beauty of nature; it's a place to escape the ordinary. For 300 years visitors have been drawn here, where rainwater runs from the fells into Aira Beck and thunders in one 65-foot leap over the falls. Yet, Aira Force is much more than an impressive waterfall. A network of trails weaves its way from Ullswater lakeshore to Gowbarrow summit, passing towering Himalayan firs, rare red squirrels, woodland glades, picnic spots and views out across Ullswater. You can start your day in Glenridding and arrive by boat, taking in the sights of Ullswater Valley along the way, then stroll back to Glenridding through Glencoyne Park and along the lakeshore. **Note**: boat rides on Ullswater operated by Ullswater 'Steamers' (not National Trust).

The waterfall at Aira Force and Ullswater in Cumbria

Paddling in the gentle waters of Ullswater

Eat, shop, stay: tea-room serving light lunches, cakes, ice-cream and hot and cold drinks. Shop selling gifts, ice-cream and souvenirs. Takeaway kiosk serving hot and cold drinks, and snacks. Picnics welcome.

Things to see and do: Aira Force guide available to buy at the shop for walking trails, history and points of interest. Children can follow the red squirrel trail, play at the natural play area, or try pebble skimming at Aira Green. You can stroll through ancient woodland and landscaped glades or venture further, with walks from Aira Force to Glenridding or to Gowbarrow summit, the best spot for panoramic views across the Lakeland fells. Why not take to the water and launch a canoe at Glencoyne Bay, or take a boat ride with Ullswater 'Steamers'? Wordsworth's daffodils on Ullswater lakeshore in spring. **Dogs**: under close control (stock grazing).

Access: 🅿️ 🚻 ⛵ 🚶 Grounds 🐾
Sat Nav: use CA11 0JS for Aira Force; CA11 0NQ for Glencoyne Bay. **Parking**: at Aira Force, Aira Force High Cascades, Aira Force Park Brow and Glencoyne Bay.

Find out more: 017684 82067 or ullswater@nationaltrust.org.uk

Aira Force and Ullswater		M	T	W	T	F	S	S
Tea-room and shop								
Open all year	10:30–4:30*	M	T	W	T	F	S	S
Kiosk								
10 Apr–1 Oct	9–4:30	M	T	W	T	F	S	S

*Shop opens at 10. Tea-room and shop closed 25 December. Opening times may vary during low season.

Allan Bank and Grasmere

near Ambleside, Cumbria LA22 9QB

🏠 🏚 ✿ ♿ 1920

Make yourself at home at Allan Bank, where Grasmere's valley unfolds from the picture windows and woodland grounds. Once home to National Trust founder Canon Rawnsley and only partially decorated, this isn't a typical National Trust experience. Secret hideaways, such as the Victorian viewing tunnel, create an air of mystery. You could have something to eat in the homely kitchen, help yourself to a cup of tea, watch red squirrels as you read by the fire, or picnic on the lawn, paint or draw. William Wordsworth was inspired here – and there's even more to discover today. **Note**: designated parking only on site. Follow directions from Miller Howe Café in centre of village.

Eat, shop, stay: at Allan Bank, snacks and tasty cakes are available from the kitchen. Picnics welcome in the gardens. Church Stile shop in Grasmere selling unusual gifts, local books and maps.

Things to see and do: **Indoors** Drawing and painting, board games and children's activities. Mountaineering books in the Mountain Heritage Library. **Outdoors** Deckchairs, kitchen garden, woodland trail and wild play area. **Dogs**: welcome indoors and out, on a lead.

Access: 🅿️ 🚾 ♿ 🏛️ ♿
Allan Bank 🚶 ♿ ♿ Countryside 🚶 ♿
Sat Nav: use LA22 9TA for nearest car park.
Parking: nearest in village, not National Trust (charge including members).

Find out more: 015394 35143 or allanbank@nationaltrust.org.uk

Allan Bank and Grasmere		M	T	W	T	F	S	S
Allan Bank								
11 Feb–26 Feb	10:30–4	M	T	W	T	F	S	S
3 Mar–31 Mar	10:30–4	·	·	·	·	F	S	S
1 Apr–29 Oct	10–5	M	T	W	T	F	S	S
3 Nov–17 Dec	10:30–4	·	·	·	·	F	S	S
Grasmere shop								
1 Jan–5 Feb	11–4	·	·	·	·	·	S	S
11 Feb–29 Oct	10–5	M	T	W	T	F	S	S
30 Oct–31 Dec*	11–4	M	T	·	·	F	S	S

*Grasmere shop closed 25 and 26 December.

A young artist, above, at Allan Bank and Grasmere, Cumbria. There is plenty to do in the garden, below

Beatrix Potter Gallery and Hawkshead, Cumbria: you can view original artwork, then explore the characterful village

Beatrix Potter Gallery and Hawkshead

Main Street, Hawkshead, Cumbria LA22 0NS

⌂ 1944

The Beatrix Potter Gallery displays original items from our collection in this year's exhibition 'That Corner of the Lake District'. For anyone who has ever been enchanted by Beatrix's endearing characters, the gallery is the place to go to marvel at these miniature masterpieces. This unique space occupies a 17th-century building which served as the office of Beatrix's solicitor husband. For a perfect day out, why not follow in Beatrix Potter's footsteps to Hill Top, then spend time outdoors? Hawkshead village is an excellent base for exploring the countryside that inspired Beatrix and many other artists, authors and poets. **Note**: nearest toilet 300 yards in main village car park (not National Trust).

Eat, shop, stay: small gallery shop selling a variety of Beatrix Potter items. Hawkshead corner shop stocks more local products and gifts. You can stay nearby in our unique holiday cottages, such as Summer House and Rose Castle, or camp at Low Wray.

Things to see and do: **Indoors** Original Beatrix Potter artwork on display. **Outdoors** Miles of walking: to Hill Top, Tarn Hows and Wray Castle. The nearby Courthouse has an interesting history (collect key from shop). **Dogs**: assistance dogs only.

Access: ⌂ 🅿 ♿ 🔍 Gallery ♿ 🚻
Parking: 300 yards, not National Trust (charge including members).

Find out more: 015394 36355 (gallery). 015394 36471 (shop) or beatrixpottergallery@nationaltrust.org.uk

Beatrix Potter Gallery/Hawkshead		M	T	W	T	F	S	S
Gallery								
18 Feb–25 May	10–4	M	T	W	T	.	S	S
27 May–3 Sep	10–5	M	T	W	T	F	S	S
4 Sep–29 Oct	10–4	M	T	W	T	.	S	S
Shop								
18 Feb–26 May	10–4	M	T	W	T	F	S	S
27 May–3 Sep	10–5	M	T	W	T	F	S	S
4 Sep–31 Dec*	10–4	M	T	W	T	F	S	S

At busy periods, timed entry system in operation.
Hawkshead Courthouse open: 1 April to 29 October (access by key from National Trust shop in Hawkshead).
*Closed 24 to 26 December.

Borrowdale and Derwent Water

near Keswick, Cumbria

🏠🍴🎞️⚓♿ 1902

Derwent Water is often called the 'Queen of the Lakes', and as you canoe between the islands with your picnic at the ready it's easy to see why. The boardwalk across the wetlands completes the 10-mile circular lake walk (now waymarked from Keswick), and the jewel in the crown is Derwent Island House, open to visitors for five special days each year. As Borrowdale winds the 7 miles from Keswick to Seathwaite, there are eight car parks from which you can start your adventure into the fells. Leaflets for iconic routes, such as Cat Bells, are available in our shop. **Note**: charges apply to members on Force Crag Mine and Derwent Island House open days.

Eat, shop, stay: Keswick lakeside shop and visitor centre offering local knowledge to help you plan your visit, plus souvenirs, cold drinks and ice-cream. Tenant-run cafés serving local treats. Watendlath Bothy (sleeps 6) and Millbeck Towers (sleeps 12) provide perfect holiday hideaways.

Things to see and do: five days a year, you can don a hard-hat for a guided tour of Force Crag Mine processing mill. Windswept and atmospheric, it's a fascinating glimpse into Lakeland's industrial heritage.

Dogs: very welcome, please keep them under close control at lambing time.

Access: 🔟🔟 Derwent Island 🔟
Force Crag Mine 🔟🔟 Derwent Water foreshore 🔟➡️
Sat Nav: use CA12 5DJ for Keswick lakeside shop and CA12 5XN for Seatoller (at foot of Honister Pass). **Parking**: at Great Wood, Ashness Bridge, Surprise View, Watendlath, Kettlewell, Bowder Stone, Rosthwaite, Seatoller and Honister Pass.

Find out more: 017687 74649 or borrowdale@nationaltrust.org.uk

Borrowdale and Derwent Water		M	T	W	T	F	S	S
Shop and visitor centre								
11 Feb–31 Oct	10–5	M	T	W	T	F	S	S
3 Nov–1 Dec	10–4	M	·	·	·	F	S	S
2 Dec–31 Dec	10–4	·	·	·	·	·	S	S

Shop: open weekends 6 January to 10 February 2018.
Check 'What's On' listing online for open days at Derwent Island House and Force Crag Mine.

Borrowdale and Derwent Water, Cumbria: Force Crag Mine, above, and walking on the shore of Derwent Water, below

Buttermere Valley

near Cockermouth, Cumbria

🏕️🏛️🏊‍♀️🚶‍♀️⛺ 1935

The view over Buttermere Valley, Cumbria

Whether you start your day at Buttermere, Crummock Water or Loweswater, the Buttermere Valley offers low-level lakeshore walks on accessible footpaths. The high fell ridges around Red Pike and cascading waterfalls make for seriously impressive backdrops to your holiday snaps and some satisfyingly adventurous ridgeline walking. **Note**: toilets at Buttermere only.

Eat, shop, stay: pubs and cafés in hamlets of Buttermere and Loweswater (none National Trust). Watergate Farm (sleeps six) – a comfortable Lakeland farmhouse with views of the Loweswater fells. Fishing, swimming and walking from your doorstep will make your holiday unforgettable.

Things to see and do: Holmewood Bothy is a unique place for a camping holiday. In the heart of the woodland and right on Loweswater lakeshore, this is really getting away from it all. **Dogs**: welcome throughout the valley (please keep them under close control at lambing time).

Access: 🅿️ Lakeshore path ➡️
Sat Nav: use CA13 9UZ for Buttermere; CA13 0RT for Crummock Water; CA13 0RU for Loweswater. **Parking**: at Honister Pass, Buttermere village, Rannerdale, Cinderdale, Lanthwaite Green, Lanthwaite Wood near Crummock Water and Maggies Bridge at Loweswater.

Find out more: 017687 74649 or buttermere@nationaltrust.org.uk

Claife Viewing Station and Windermere West Shore

near Far Sawrey, Cumbria LA22 0LW

🏛️🏊‍♀️🚶‍♀️🚶‍♀️ 1962

Why not take to the water on the ferry from Bowness and explore the newly restored Claife Viewing Station and its courtyard, just as early 18th-century tourists to the Lakes did? The first-floor platform in the Viewing Station gives impressive panoramic views of Windermere and the Lakeland fells that have been hidden for years. With 4 miles of lakeshore path towards Wray Castle to explore on bike or on foot, the western shore of Windermere is perfect for a car-free adventure. You can walk from here through the landscape that inspired Beatrix Potter, to Hill Top house and Hawkshead village. **Note**: toilets at nearby Ferry House, none at the Viewing Station. Bike Boat (not National Trust) run by Windermere Lake Cruises, summer season only.

Eat, shop, stay: cosy café in the courtyard at Claife Viewing Station serving coffee and cakes. Picnics welcome anywhere along the lakeshore. You can stay at High and Low Strawberry Gardens – holiday cottages with England's largest lake on your doorstep.

Things to see and do: why not stroll up to the Viewing Station and let the coloured glass inspire you? Share your photos using #claife, then walk along the lakeshore or take to the water. **Dogs**: allowed in countryside, under close control.

Claife Viewing Station and Windermere West Shore, Cumbria

Looking out on Windermere from the Viewing Station

Access: Viewing Station ⬚ Café ⬚ ⬚
Sat Nav: use LA22 0LP for Ash Landing;
LA22 0LR Harrowslack; LA22 0JH Red Nab
(all nearby). **Parking**: at Ash Landing and
Harrowslack, near Windermere lakeshore,
for Claife Viewing Station and at Red Nab.

Find out more: 015394 41456 or
claife@nationaltrust.org.uk

Dalton Castle

Market Place, Dalton-in-Furness,
Cumbria LA15 8AX

⬚ 1965

Formerly the manorial courthouse of Furness
Abbey, this eye-catching 14th-century tower
was built to assert the Abbot's authority.
Note: opened on behalf of the National Trust
by the Friends of Dalton Castle. Parking in
Dalton town centre (not National Trust).
Open Saturday, 15 April to 30 September, 2 to 5.

Find out more: 015395 60951 or
daltoncastle@nationaltrust.org.uk

Ennerdale

Cleator, Cumbria

⬚⬚⬚ 1927

Home of the Wild Ennerdale partnership with
30 miles of traffic-free tracks and paths – the
quiet side of Lakeland. **Note**: nearest toilets at
Ennerdale Bridge. For Sat Nav use CA23 3BA
for Ennerdale Bridge, CA23 3AS for Bleach
Green and CA23 3AU for Bowness Knott.

Find out more: 017687 74649 or
ennerdale@nationaltrust.org.uk

Eskdale and
Duddon Valley

Eskdale, near Ravenglass; Duddon Valley,
near Broughton in Furness, Cumbria

⬚⬚⬚⬚⬚⬚⬚ 1926

Cycling at Eskdale and Duddon Valley in Cumbria

Eskdale is a valley of contrasts, with upper
Eskdale leading to the high mountains,
including Scafell. On the valley floor are
meandering riverside and woodland paths,
including the Eskdale Trail, for walkers and
cyclists. Across high mountain passes lies the
Duddon Valley, with wildflower meadows,
woodlands, mountains, hill-farms and rivers.

Eat, shop, stay: pubs at Eskdale Green, Boot and Seathwaite. Shops at Eskdale Green, Boot and Ulpha, café and shop at Dalegarth station (none National Trust). Bird How and Thrang – cosy, rustic, remote cottages to hire with spectacular walks from the door.

Things to see and do: Hardknott Roman Fort to explore. Eskdale Cycle Trail. Walks from the La'al Ratty railway running through Eskdale. Woodland paths in Duddon Valley. Upland walks to Harter Fell and Seathwaite Tarn. **Dogs**: well-behaved dogs welcome. Please follow local and seasonal guidance.

Access:
Parking: in lay-bys, along roadsides and at some small village car parks (not National Trust).

Find out more: 019467 26064 or eskdaleandduddon@nationaltrust.org.uk

Fell Foot

Newby Bridge, Windermere, Cumbria

🏠🚻🍴 1948

Sitting on the southern tip of Lake Windermere with views across the water to the mountains above, this family-friendly park has green lawns sloping down to the lakeshore that are a great place for playing, a picnic or barbecue. It offers the perfect opportunity to get outdoors, stroll along the lakeshore or explore, and is one of the best spots to soak up Windermere in all its beauty. With easy lake access, the park is ideal for paddling, swimming and boating. If you want to take to the water, then boats can be hired from the Boathouse Café. **Note**: building works are possible throughout the year. Launch/slipway facilities available for a wide variety of craft, charges apply (including members).

Eat, shop, stay: Boathouse Café serving hot and cold drinks, soup and snacks, homemade cakes and pastries. A small selection of children's toys, gifts, maps, picnic rugs and seasonal goods available in the shop. Picnics welcome.

Things to see and do: seasonal rowing boat hire, April to October (weather permitting).

Whatever activities you enjoy, from walking to sailing and everything in between, family-friendly Fell Foot in Cumbria, above and top, has something for you

Events. Adventure playground, new Discovery Cottage and easy lake access with 'beach' for paddling. Quiet spots and easy meadow walk. **Dogs**: welcome on leads.

Access: 🅿️♿🚻♿🚻 Grounds ♿♿
Sat Nav: use LA12 8NN. **Parking**: two large car parks on site.

Find out more: 015395 31273 or fellfoot@nationaltrust.org.uk

Fell Foot		M	T	W	T	F	S	S
Park								
1 Jan–31 Mar	9–5	M	T	W	T	F	S	S
1 Apr–3 Sep	8–6*	M	T	W	T	F	S	S
4 Sep–31 Dec**	9–5	M	T	W	T	F	S	S
Café and shop								
18 Feb–26 Feb	11–4†	M	T	W	T	F	S	S
4 Mar–19 Mar	11–4†						S	S
20 Mar–3 Sep	10–5†	M	T	W	T	F	S	S
4 Sep–5 Nov	11–4	M	T	W	T	F	S	S

*Last entry at 6. **Closed 25 December.
†Café: opens 9 on Saturdays. Boat hire available daily, April to October (weather permitting).

Hill Top

Near Sawrey, Hawkshead,
Ambleside, Cumbria LA22 0LF

🏠 🍴 ✿ 1944

Beatrix Potter's beloved Hill Top is more than just the inspiration for her little white books. Full of her precious things, Hill Top encapsulates her passion that went on to dominate her life, preserving the landscape and culture of the Lakes. From traditional Lakeland furniture, to trophies for her prize-winning Herdwick sheep, Hill Top represents her legacy. The colourful garden is just as Beatrix knew it. Today, we continue in Beatrix's footsteps, working in a changing world to conserve the Lake District for ever, for everyone. The house can be very busy and visitors occasionally have to wait to enter. **Note**: timed-ticket entry system for the house. Tickets not needed for garden and shop.

Eat, shop, stay: eat in the heart of Beatrix Potter country at neighbouring Sawrey House Hotel, Tower Bank Arms (both tenant-run) or stay at nearby holiday cottages. Hill Top shop sells an expansive range of Beatrix Potter books and collectables, including exclusive items.

A new mother shows her family around Hill Top, Cumbria

The entrance hall lies at the heart of Hill Top

Things to see and do: a short walk to Moss Eccles Tarn, where Beatrix and her husband would go boating. Combine Hill Top with a visit to the Beatrix Potter Gallery to see original artwork. **Dogs**: assistance dogs only.

Access: 🅿️ 🖼 💻 👶 ⋯ 🏵
House 🔺 🏔 Shop 🔺 Garden 🔺 ➡
Parking: limited and for visitors to Hill Top only.

Find out more: 015394 36269. 015394 36801 (shop) or hilltop@nationaltrust.org.uk

Hill Top		M	T	W	T	F	S	S
18 Feb–25 May*	10–4:30	M	T	W	T		S	S
27 May–3 Sep	10–5:30	M	T	W	T	F	S	S
4 Sep–29 Oct*	10–4:30	M	T	W	T		S	S

House: entry by timed ticket (places limited).
*Shop and garden: also open Fridays; free entry to the garden during shop opening hours. Small car park.

Keld Chapel

Keld Lane, Shap, Cumbria CA10 3NW

✝ 1918

With its rustic stone floor and walls, this 16th-century chapel is thought to have been the chantry for Shap Abbey. **Note**: sorry no facilities. Access daily (for key, see the notice on chapel door). For Sat Nav use CA10 3NW. Open every day all year, dawn to dusk.

Find out more: 017683 61893 or keldchapel@nationaltrust.org.uk

Sandscale Haws National Nature Reserve

near Barrow-in-Furness, Cumbria

 1984

Home to natterjack toads, these wild, grass-covered sand dunes and beach are the perfect habitat for rare wildlife.
Note: toilets (not National Trust). Car park open all year (height restriction 2.1 metres). For Sat Nav use LA14 4QJ.

Find out more: 01229 462855 or sandscalehaws@nationaltrust.org.uk

Sizergh

Sizergh, near Kendal, Cumbria LA8 8DZ

🏠 🍽 🏛 ❖ ♿ 🚭 1950

With more than 750 years of history and centuries-old portraits sitting alongside modern family photographs, this medieval house is home to the Strickland family. It is surrounded by rich gardens and a 647-hectare (1,600-acre) estate, combining a newly created wetland, limestone pastures, orchards and semi-natural woodland, all inhabited by a rich variety of wildlife, including the rare hawfinch. There is a unique and very special limestone rock garden, where colours change with the seasons, and its timeless atmosphere makes this the perfect place to relax. Sizergh has many tales to tell and it's an ideal place to start discovering the Lakes.
Note: some opening restrictions apply. Separate admission charges may apply for tours or special events.

Eat, shop, stay: licensed café serving drinks, meals, snacks and cakes. Shop selling local products, gifts and plants. Nearby Strickland Arms pub (tenant-run). Why not stay at rustic Holeslack Farmhouse or Courtyard Cottage?

Things to see and do: **Indoors** Exhibitions, virtual and guided tours, and Elizabethan carving of international significance.
Outdoors There is a working organic kitchen garden including bees and hens. Of great horticultural significance are four National Collections of Hardy Ferns, some showcased in a new stumpery. The orchard features more than 50 varieties of apple, some rare and local. A walk through Brigsteer Wood will take you to a newly created wetland area and bird hide at Park End Moss. A network of footpaths, guided walks and orienteering are available in the wider estate. Children can enjoy a natural play trail and quizzes. **Dogs**: welcome on estate footpaths (on leads where stock grazing). House/garden: assistance dogs only.

Access: 🅿️ 🅿️ 💺 🔤 🔁 📷 📹 🚗
Building ♿ 🚻 ♿ **Grounds** ♿ ➡ ♿ ♿
Sat Nav: use LA8 8DZ. **Parking**: 250 yards.

Find out more: 015395 60951 or sizergh@nationaltrust.org.uk

Sizergh		M	T	W	T	F	S	S
House*								
1 Apr–29 Oct	12–4	·	T	W	T	F	S	S
Garden, café and shop**								
14 Jan–5 Mar	10–4	M	T	W	T	F	S	S
6 Mar–29 Oct	10–5	M	T	W	T	F	S	S
30 Oct–31 Dec	10–4	M	T	W	T	F	S	S
Estate								
Open all year	9–6†	M	T	W	T	F	S	S

*Guided house tours (excluding Saturdays or Mondays) at 11 and 11:20 (approximately 45 minutes, places limited, £1 per person; tickets available from reception at least 15 minutes before tour). House: open Bank Holiday Mondays.
**Garden: parts closed Friday and Saturday in January, February, November and December. †Closes 4:30, 1 January to 5 March and 30 October to 31 December. Car park: open as estate. Closed 25 December.

Cycling at Sizergh in Cumbria, below.
The rock garden, right, shows its autumn colours

Stagshaw Garden and Ambleside

near Windermere, Cumbria

🏠 🏛 ✿ ⚓ 1927

**Stagshaw Garden and Ambleside in Cumbria.
In spring the garden bursts into life**

Sitting on the northern tip of Lake Windermere, the town of Ambleside is surrounded by countryside. In spring, Stagshaw Garden bursts into life, with colourful displays of azaleas and rhododendrons. Skelghyll Woods are home to Cumbria's tallest trees, and Jenkyn's Field is great for a lakeshore picnic and paddle.

Things to see and do: Bridge House, Ambleside's smallest building, built on a bridge over a beck. Tall Tree Trail at Skelghyll Woods. The remains of Ambleside Roman Fort date from 2nd century. Townend nearby. **Dogs**: welcome under close control (stock grazing).

Access: Bridge House 🦽 Stagshaw Garden 🦽 🏔
Sat Nav: use LA22 0HE for Stagshaw Garden and Skelghyll Woods; LA22 9AN for Bridge House. **Parking**: small car park at Stagshaw Garden.

Find out more: 015394 46402 or stagshawgarden@nationaltrust.org.uk

Stagshaw Garden		M	T	W	T	F	S	S
Stagshaw Garden*								
Open all year	Dawn–dusk	M	T	W	T	F	S	S
Bridge House								
1 Apr–29 Oct	11:30–4:15	M	T	W	T	F	S	S

*Stagshaw Garden is at its best April to July.

Steam Yacht Gondola

Coniston Pier, Lake Road, Coniston, Cumbria LA21 8AN

♿ 🔔 🍷 1980

This steam yacht was rebuilt by the National Trust from the original 1860's *Gondola*: today's passengers can experience the nostalgia of a steam-driven cruise on Coniston Water once enjoyed by the Victorians. Based on the design of a Venetian 'Burchiello', her streamlined hull cuts silently through the water, with Sid the golden sea serpent at the bow as her majestic figurehead. You can watch the steam engine in action at close quarters and explore the whole boat, guided by the crew with a full commentary on her long history on the lake and her association with *Swallows and Amazons*. **Note**: cruises depart from Coniston Pier (subject to weather conditions). Sorry no toilet on scheduled sailings. Gondola is a historic ship and extremely costly to run. Charge for members, although a small discount is applied on scheduled round-trip cruises.

Passengers experience the nostalgia of a steam-driven cruise, above, as Steam Yacht Gondola, left, sails on Coniston Water in Cumbria

Eat, shop, stay: small shop on board selling souvenirs. Gift experiences available online. Café at Brantwood and Bluebird Café at Coniston Pier (neither National Trust). Catering available for private charters. Rose Castle Cottage above Tarn Hows is a perfect base for ramblers.

Things to see and do: 'Steam and Cream' and 'Engineer for the Day' footplate gift experiences. Themed events. Downloadable walks from Gondola's jetties. Joint tickets with partner attractions. Tickets can be bought online in advance. **Dogs**: welcome in outside areas only.

Access: 🅿️♿🏧👁️📷 Gangway ♿♿
Parking: at Coniston Pier, 50 yards, not National Trust (charge including members).

Find out more: 015394 32733 or sygondola@nationaltrust.org.uk Booking Office, The Hollens, Grasmere, Cumbria LA22 9QZ

Steam Yacht Gondola		M	T	W	T	F	S	S
Head of Lake Cruise								
3 Apr–31 Oct	11–11:45	M	T	W	T	F	·	·
3 Apr–31 Oct	12–12:45	M	T	W	T	F	·	·
1 Apr–29 Oct	1–1:45	M	T	W	T	F	S	S
1 Apr–29 Oct	2:30–3:15	·	·	·	·	·	S	S
1 Apr–29 Oct	3:30–4:15	·	·	·	·	·	S	S
Full Lake Cruise								
3 Apr–31 Oct	2:30–4:15	M	T	W	T	F	·	·
Walkers/Full Lake Cruise								
1 Apr–29 Oct	11–12:45	·	·	·	·	·	S	S

Piers at Coniston, Monk Coniston and Parkamoor, also Lake Bank and Brantwood (not National Trust). All sailings depart Coniston Pier. Cruises subject to weather conditions.

Sticklebarn and The Langdales

near Ambleside, Cumbria

🏠🏛️🛏️⛺🔼🍷 1925

Forged by fire and ice, The Langdales are dramatic to say the least. Home to the majestic Langdale Pikes and mountain tarns, this is a natural playground. Sticklebarn sits at the heart of miles of walking routes, and with hearty food, real ale and roaring fires, this is the perfect place to eat, drink and relax after a day on the fells. The ambitious can tackle the major peaks, but it's not all about high-level scrambling. The circular route around Blea Tarn is easily accessible, with views of Little and Great Langdale. High Close Estate and Arboretum, between Elterwater and Grasmere, offers 4.5 hectares (11 acres) of tranquillity, 1,000 years of fascinating history and rare trees from around the globe.

Eat, shop, stay: Sticklebarn serves hearty Lakeland food, prepared freshly on site and a range of drinks, including Cumbrian real ales. Outdoor eating on the terrace. Café at High Close. Lovely options for camping or stay at Silverthwaite cottage (sleeps eight).

Welcome refreshments after a day's hiking at Sticklebarn and The Langdales in Cumbria

Things to see and do: **Indoors** Sticklebarn is
the perfect place to relax in all weather; settle
in for a free movie, read a book by the fire,
play a board game or simply catch up over
a drink. **Outdoors** Walking and climbing in
the Lakeland fells. Guided ghyll scrambling,
guided rock-climbing and bike hire from
Great Langdale Campsite. Off-road cycle trail
from Skelwith Bridge to Sticklebarn. You can
take a riverside ramble from Elterwater or
explore the Tree Trail at High Close. Why not
finish your day on the terrace at Sticklebarn
with occasional live music? Sleep under
the stars at Great Langdale Campsite.
Dogs: welcome indoors and out, under control.

Access: Pd 🚻 ♿ **Sticklebarn** 🐾 ♿ **Grounds** 🐾 ♿
Sat Nav: use LA22 9JU for Sticklebarn,
LA22 9PG for Blea Tarn, LA22 9HP for
Elterwater, LA22 9HJ for High Close Estate.

Sticklebarn and The Langdales:
dramatic Stickle Ghyll, above

Parking: at Stickle Ghyll, Old Dungeon
Ghyll, Blea Tarn, Elterwater village and
High Close Estate.

Find out more: 015394 37356 (Sticklebarn)
or sticklebarn@nationaltrust.org.uk

Sticklebarn and The Langdales		M	T	W	T	F	S	S
Sticklebarn								
4 Feb–9 Apr	11–9*	M	T	W	T	F	S	S
10 Apr–29 Oct	11–10:30*	M	T	W	T	F	S	S
30 Oct–31 Dec	11–9*	M	T	W	T	F	S	S
Great Langdale Campsite								
Open all year**		M	T	W	T	F	S	S

*Friday and Saturday open until 11. Sticklebarn open
1 January, closed 24 and 25 December. **For detailed opening
times and bookings please visit ntlakescampsites.org.uk or
call 015394 32733.

Tarn Hows and Coniston

near Coniston, Cumbria

🏞️♿🅿️ 1943

Stunning Tarn Hows offers an accessible circular walk for all (1¾ miles) through beautiful countryside with majestic mountain views. We have off-road mobility scooters available for less-able visitors. The area around Tarn Hows and Coniston village is a great place to begin your wider Lake District adventure.

Eat, shop, stay: ice-cream van (most days), also selling hot and cold drinks. Picnics welcome. Numerous catering options nearby in Coniston and Hawkshead plus National Trust gift shop in Hawkshead. Rose Castle Cottage, with views across Tarn Hows, is the ultimate holiday hideaway.

Things to see and do: why not theme your day around water and start with a leisurely Steam Yacht Gondola cruise on Coniston Water, then walk through the grounds of Monk Coniston to Tarn Hows? **Dogs**: welcome on leads (stock grazing).

Access: 🅿️♿🅿️ Grounds ♿⛷️
Sat Nav: use LA22 0PP for Tarn Hows or LA21 8DP for Glen Mary (both nearby).
Parking: on site at Tarn Hows, also at Glen Mary nearby. Parking available in Coniston (not National Trust).

Accessible walk at Tarn Hows and Coniston, Cumbria

Find out more: 015394 41456 or tarnhows@nationaltrust.org.uk

Tarn Hows and Coniston	M	T	W	T	F	S	S
Hoathwaite Campsite*							
31 Mar–24 Sep	**M**	**T**	**W**	**T**	**F**	**S**	**S**

*For detailed opening times and bookings please visit ntlakescampsites.org.uk or call 015394 32733.

Townend

Troutbeck, Windermere, Cumbria LA23 1LB

🏠❄️ 1948

Preparing an 18th-century meal at Townend, Cumbria

The Brownes of Townend were a simple farming family, but their home and belongings bring to life more than 400 years of extraordinary stories. The farmhouse kitchen has a real fire burning most afternoons and a quirky collection of domestic tools. Throughout the house, intricately carved furniture provides a window into the personality of George Browne. The library contains the family's well-used collection of books, including 45 that are the only remaining copies in the world. Outside, the colourful cottage-style garden is a lovely place to while away some time among the flowers.

Eat, shop, stay: picnics welcome. Tea-room in Troutbeck village (not National Trust).

Things to see and do: **Indoors** Guided tours at 11 and 12 (places limited). 'A Taste of Townend', living-history cooking demonstrations on Thursdays. Children's trail. **Outdoors** Garden trail for children. Traditional games.

Access: [P] [D] [□] [:] [⊘] **Building** [🏠] **Grounds** [🏠]
Parking: 300 yards.

Find out more: 015394 32628 or townend@nationaltrust.org.uk

Townend		M	T	W	T	F	S	S
18 Mar–29 Oct	1–5*				**W**	**T**	**F**	**S**	**S**

*11 to 1: entry by guided tour only at 11 and 12 (places limited). Open Bank Holiday Mondays. May close early due to poor light.

Wasdale

near Gosforth, Cumbria

 [1920]

The birthplace of British mountaineering and it's easy to see why. Wasdale Head lies beneath towering mountains, including England's highest – Scafell Pike. People have lived in the valley since earliest times, and the intricate network of walled fields is testimony to the long history of farming in this area. Here too lies England's deepest lake, Wastwater, with the Screes sweeping down from the top of Illgill Head to the lake below, creating ever-changing images on the surface of the water. Towards the southern end of the lake and Nether Wasdale, there are natural woodlands with winding paths. **Note**: limited toilet facilities (we are planning improvements and raising money towards this project).

Eat, shop, stay: with numerous camping options – tents, campervans, pods, Nordic tipis and cosy cottages – Wasdale is a perfect place for digital detox holidays. Campsite shop. Pub and shop at Wasdale Head; pubs in Nether Wasdale and Santon Bridge (none National Trust).

Things to see and do: walking and climbing in England's highest mountains. Lakeside, riverbank and woodland rambles. Wild swimming and paddling in Wastwater and rivers. Herdwick sheep graze in fields and on fells. **Dogs**: well-behaved dogs welcome. Please follow local and seasonal guidance.

Access: [🏠]
Sat Nav: use CA20 1EX. **Parking**: at Lake Head CA20 1EX; Overbeck CA20 1EX (limited space); Nether Wasdale CA20 1ET (limited space).

Find out more: 019467 26064 or wasdale@nationaltrust.org.uk

Wasdale	M	T	W	T	F	S	S
Wasdale Campsite*							
Open all year	**M**	**T**	**W**	**T**	**F**	**S**	**S**

*For detailed opening times and bookings please visit ntlakescampsites.org.uk or call 015394 32733.

Wasdale, Cumbria: a peaceful moment at Wastwater, below. Stay longer in a Nordic tepi, pod or tent, above

Whitehaven Coast

Whitehaven, Cumbria

🍷📷

This post-industrial coastline holds hidden gems with clifftop walks from the Georgian harbour and views to the Isle of Man. **Note**: sorry no toilets. For Sat Nav use CA28 9BG for clifftop car park and CA28 7LY for Whitehaven Harbour.

Find out more: 017687 74649 or whitehavencoast@nationaltrust.org.uk

Wordsworth House and Garden

Main Street, Cockermouth, Cumbria CA13 9RX

🏠✿🔔🍴 1938

Step back to the 1770s at the childhood home and garden that inspired William to become a poet. Hands-on rooms give a real feel for middle-class Georgian life – there's even a rope bed to try. Costumed servants cook in the kitchen, gossip and tell tales on selected days in term-time and throughout school holidays. Guided and audio tours reveal the happiness and heartache experienced by the Wordsworths and other occupants, while, in the cellar, the household's ghosts share their stories. New this year, a series of exhibitions celebrate the power of landscape to inspire generations of writers, artists and photographers.

Eat, shop, stay: browse through Wordsworth and local souvenirs in the shop. A light lunch or cream tea in the cosy café makes the perfect end to a visit. Takeaway option available and picnics welcome. Second-hand books.

Things to see and do: family games and art cart. Replica costume and toys. Holiday storytelling and activities. The garden is the ideal place to relax. Poetry in summerhouse. Heritage fruit trees, vegetables and flowers.

The 1770s come to life at Wordsworth House and Garden, Cumbria, top. Above, vegetables and flowers in the garden

Dogs: on leads in front garden only.

Access: 🅿️♿♿♿🧷📷♿♿♿
Building ♿♿♿ Grounds ♿♿
Parking: in town centre car parks, none National Trust (charge including members). Please note long-stay car park signposted as coach park, 300 yards, Wakefield Road.

Find out more: 01900 820884 (Infoline). 01900 824805 or wordsworthhouse@nationaltrust.org.uk

Wordsworth House and Garden		M	T	W	T	F	S	S
11 Mar–29 Oct	11–5*	M	T	W	T		S	S

*Café: open 10:30 to 4:30. Last entry to house one hour before closing (timed tickets may operate on busy days). Open selected Fridays in holidays (please telephone for information).

Wray Castle

Low Wray, Ambleside, Cumbria LA22 0JA

[icons] 1929

Boarding a regular lake cruise from Ambleside allows you to arrive at Wray Castle in style. A gentle walk or cycle here also make a perfect start to your visit. This unusual and exciting National Trust castle is a place for all the family to explore and enjoy. We don't have any of the original castle contents, so it is more informal and child-friendly. Our Peter Rabbit Adventure is the perfect spot for creative play for our youngest visitors, while older children might like dressing-up or building their own castle. To find out more about this fascinating building, why not join one of our guided tours, which run for most of the year? Plus, there's loads to do outdoors. **Note**: please use 'green ways' to get here: boat, bike, bus or boot. Limited car parking.

Eat, shop, stay: drinks and snacks available, but don't expect china crockery here! Picnics welcome in the grounds. Shop stocking wooden swords, archery kits, gifts and souvenirs. Why not camp or glamp at Low Wray just a short walk away from the castle.

Waiting for a boat at the jetty at Wray Castle, Cumbria

Wray Castle: plenty to spark children's imagination

Things to see and do: **Indoors** Enjoy the informal atmosphere and family-friendly activities, including crafts, dressing-up, castle-building, games and discover the castle your way. Guided tours unearth the castle's hidden past and help you learn more about this quirky building. **Outdoors** Arrive in style by boat. Miles of lakeside walks and trails, as well as an exciting adventure play area with tree house and rope swings. Holiday activities, such as tree-climbing and den-building. Wray Castle makes the perfect stop on a walk or cycle ride along the lakeshore path from Claife Viewing Station, or the new path from Hawkshead. **Dogs**: welcome in grounds on leads, assistance dogs only in castle.

Access: [icons] Castle [icons]
Parking: restricted car parking.
Please come by boat to avoid disappointment.

Find out more: 015394 33250 or wraycastle@nationaltrust.org.uk

Wray Castle		M	T	W	T	F	S	S
Castle*								
18 Feb–26 Feb	10–4	M	T	W	T	F	S	S
18 Mar–26 Mar	10–4						S	S
1 Apr–26 May	10–5	M	T	W	T	F	S	S
27 May–3 Sep	10–5:30	M	T	W	T	F	S	S
4 Sep–29 Oct	10–5	M	T	W	T	F	S	S
4 Nov–26 Nov	10–4						S	S
Grounds								
Open all year	8–8	M	T	W	T	F	S	S
Low Wray Campsite**								
17 Mar–29 Oct		M	T	W	T	F	S	S

*Last entry one hour before closing.
**For detailed opening times and bookings please visit ntlakescampsites.org.uk or call 01539432733.

Why not leave the car behind and arrive at Wray Castle by bike, boat, bus or boot?

Additional countryside car parks in The Lakes

Borrowdale and Derwent Water		Buttermere Valley		The Langdales	
Great Wood	CA12 5UP	Honister Pass	CA12 5XJ	Blea Tarn	LA22 9PG
Kettlewell	CA12 5UN	Lanthwaite Wood	CA13 0RT	Old Dungeon Ghyll	LA22 9JY
Ashness Bridge	CA12 5UN	**Ullswater**		Stickle Ghyll	LA22 9JU
Surprise View	CA12 5UU	Glencoyne Bay	CA11 0NQ	Elterwater	LA22 9HP
Watendlath	CA12 5UW	High Cascades	CA11 0JY	High Close	LA22 9HJ
Bowderstone	CA12 5XA	Park Brow	CA11 0JY	**Coniston**	
Rosthwaite	CA12 5XB	**Wasdale**		Glen Mary	LA21 8DP
Seatoller	CA12 5XN	Lake Head	CA20 1EX	**Windermere West Shore**	
		Overbeck	CA20 1EX	Red Nab	LA22 0JH
		Nether Wasdale	CA20 1ET	Harrowslack	LA22 0LR
				Ash Landing	LA22 0LP

Yorkshire

Marsden Moor Estate, West Yorkshire

A692
A1
A68
A691
A1(M)
A19
A688
A689
A66
Barnard
Castle
MIDDLESBROUGH
Ormesby Hall
Darlington
Roseberry Topping
Moulton
Hall
Stokesley
Whitby
Mount
Grace
Priory
A172
Richmond
Bridestones,
Crossliff
and Blakey
Topping
Yorkshire Coast
A171
NORTHALLERTON
A1
Braithwaite Hall
A1(M)
Rievaulx
Terrace
Scarborough
Thirsk
Pickering
A170
Filey
A168
Nunnington Hall
A165
A19
Fountains
Abbey and
Studley Royal
Water Garden
Ripon
Upper
Wharfedale
Bridlington
A64
Malham
Tarn
Estate
Brimham
Rocks
Beningbrough Hall,
Gallery and Gardens
Settle
A166
Harrogate
Treasurer's House, York
A59
Goddards
House and
Garden
YORK
Skipton
A658
Wetherby
Middlethorpe
Hall Hotel,
Restaurant
and Spa
A1079
A614
East Riddlesden Hall
Leeds
A64
Beverley
Keighley
Burnley
Hardcastle
Crags
Bradford
A63
Selby
A64
Kingston Upon Hull
M621
Halifax
A56
M62
M62
A1041
Maister
House
Wakefield
Pontefract
Rochdale
Huddersfield
M62
Nostell
A15
M18
M62
Marsden
Moor Estate
M1
M180
Doncaster
A180
BARNSLEY
A635
A159
A173
A18
A629
A15
A46
A16
M60
M61
A1(M)
A1103
A57
A6
Kinder,
Edale
and the
Dark Peak
Sheffield
A631
A158
A523
A537
Lyme
A537
A515
Longshaw,
Burbage and the
Eastern Moors
Worksop
A60
Clumber Park
M6
Hardwick
A61
A614
A46
A15
M1
A617
A17
A52
A1
A15

Buildings and/or gardens

**Entry points to
coast and countryside**

National Trust land

H **Historic House Hotel**

Places in neighbouring counties

East Midlands, page 234

North West, page 290

10 miles

Beningbrough Hall, Gallery and Gardens, North Yorkshire: architectural grandeur combined with art treasures

Beningbrough Hall, Gallery and Gardens

Beningbrough, York,
North Yorkshire YO30 1DD

🏛 ❄ ♿ ⇌ ☂ 1958

Built in the 18th century, this Italian-style baroque house has been shaped by its numerous occupants. It has an intriguing story to tell, beginning with the wealthy teenager who built the mansion to its occupation by the RAF in the Second World War to the re-invention as a country-house gallery, in partnership with the National Portrait Gallery. Today, the architectural grandeur of the rooms is a perfect setting for many 18th-century portraits featuring people who have influenced British history and its culture. In the garden, the story continues with numerous sections showing Italian, Victorian and even horse-racing influences: traditional herbaceous borders contrast with sweeping lawns, formal gardens and beds, wildlife areas, and the restored working walled garden.

Eat, shop, stay: the Walled Garden Restaurant serves hot lunches, sandwiches and snacks. You can choose from plants and extensive home and garden ranges in the shop. The Victorian Laundry holiday flat provides exclusive out-of-hours access to the gardens.

Beningbrough Hall		M	T	W	T	F	S	S
House, gardens, interactive galleries, shop and restaurant								
4 Mar–30 Jun	10:30–5*		T	W	T	F	S	S
1 Jul–31 Aug	10:30–5*	M	T	W	T	F	S	S
1 Sep–5 Nov	10:30–5*		T	W	T	F	S	S
Interactive galleries, gardens, shop and restaurant								
1 Jan–19 Feb	11–3:30**						S	S
21 Feb–26 Feb	11–3:30**		T	W	T	F	S	S
11 Nov–17 Dec	11–3:30**						S	S
30 Dec–31 Dec	11–3:30**						S	S

*House, interactive galleries and shop open 12.
**Interactive galleries open 11:30. Open Bank Holiday Mondays and 26 December.

Things to see and do: **Indoors** Get creative in the hands-on interactive galleries, and discover history and portraiture from a new perspective, including sitting for your own virtual 18th-century portrait which you can email to friends and family. A glimpse of servant life can be found in the Victorian laundry. A programme of family activities is on offer throughout the year. **Outdoors** Got a little more time to spare? Then why not get off the beaten track on riverside paths, and enjoy the easily accessible garden and pause to enjoy the parkland views? Families can let off steam in the wilderness play area. **Dogs**: welcome on leads in parkland. Assistance dogs only in gardens and buildings.

Access: [icons]
Mansion [icons] Stable block [icons]
Grounds [icons]
Parking: free, on site.

Find out more: 01904 472027 or beningbrough@nationaltrust.org.uk

Visitors enjoy some of the extensive collection of paintings at Beningbrough Hall, Gallery and Gardens, left and below. The delightful gardens, bottom, provide the opportunity to sit and contemplate natural beauty

Braithwaite Hall

East Witton, Leyburn, North Yorkshire DL8 4SY

 1941

This beautiful 17th-century tenanted farmhouse lies in the heart of Coverdale. Explore the surrounding woodland and River Cover. **Note**: please contact the tenant to arrange a visit. Sorry, no toilet. Parts of the Hall are open in June, July and August (by arrangement in advance with the tenant).

Find out more: 01969 640287 or braithwaitehall@nationaltrust.org.uk

Bridestones, Crosscliff and Blakey Topping

near Pickering, North Yorkshire

 1944

Spectacular all year, the Bridestones are a geological wonder – with rock formations, moorland vistas, woodland walks and grassy valleys. **Note**: nearest toilets at Low Staindale car park. For Sat Nav use YO18 7LR. Dalby Forest drive starting 2½ miles north of Thornton le Dale – toll charges (including members).

Find out more: 01723 870423 or bridestones@nationaltrust.org.uk

Brimham Rocks

Summerbridge, Harrogate, North Yorkshire HG3 4DW

 1970

These rock formations tower over heather moorland, offering panoramic views across Nidderdale. Dating back 320 million years,

the site is now a haven for climbers, walkers, picnickers and nature spotters and is a natural playground for families. For magical photographs, visit all year and see this landscape through the seasons. **Note**: beware of cliff edges. Nearest toilets 600 yards from car park.

Eat, shop, stay: shop selling books, gifts and the popular locally made bilberry jam. Hot and cold refreshments and ice-cream available from kiosk. Picnic tables with views of the rocks and option of seating inside the visitor centre.

Things to see and do: regular guided walks, events, family activities and climbing days. Visitor centre exhibition space reveals the story of the rocks, conservation work and views to the Vale of York. **Dogs**: welcome on leads.

Access: 🅿️ 🅰️ 🐕 ♿ 🔎 ♿
Visitor centre/shop 🔎 ♿ Countryside ➡️ ♿
Parking: on site.

Find out more: 01423 780688 or brimhamrocks@nationaltrust.org.uk

Brimham Rocks		M	T	W	T	F	S	S
Visitor centre, shop and kiosk*								
1 Jan–2 Jan	10:30–4	M	·	·	·	·	·	S
18 Feb–26 Feb	10:30–4:30	M	T	W	T	F	S	S
4 Mar–9 Apr	11–5	·	·	·	·	·	S	S
10 Apr–23 Apr	11–5	M	T	W	T	F	S	S
29 Apr–28 May**	11–5	·	·	·	·	·	S	S
29 May–1 Oct	11–5	M	T	W	T	F	S	S
7 Oct–22 Oct	11–5	·	·	·	·	·	S	S
23 Oct–29 Oct	10:30–4:30	M	T	W	T	F	S	S
4 Nov–17 Dec	10:30–4	·	·	·	·	·	S	S

Main gate locked at 9, or dusk if earlier. *Also open Bank Holidays, 1 May, 26, 30, 31 December and 1 January 2018. **Kiosk also open Monday to Friday, weather permitting.

Brimham Rocks in North Yorkshire offer panoramic views

East Riddlesden Hall

Bradford Road, Riddlesden, Keighley,
West Yorkshire BD20 5EL

[icons] 1934

This 17th-century manor house, once a hive
of farming activity, is a peaceful green space
in an otherwise urban area, with plenty of
unexpected places to explore. Discover the
hidden secrets of the Great Barn, one of the
North's finest tithe barns. The land, stretching
down to the River Aire, includes meadows,
traditional cattle breeds and a riverside walk.
Nearer the atmospheric house, there is a herb
garden, a wild garden and a more formal
garden to relax in, while inside there are
wonderful ceramics, textiles and furniture
collections. More than enough to keep
you busy for half a day.

Eat, shop, stay: a converted bothy is home
to a shop selling gifts, books, homeware,
gardenware, plants and ice-cream. On the first
floor is a characterful tea-room selling seasonal
light meals, sandwiches, cakes and drinks.
There's an accessible table on the ground floor.

Three views of 17th-century East Riddlesden Hall,
West Yorkshire. The atmospheric house, meadows
and gardens offer an antidote to urban stress

Things to see and do: **Indoors** Great Barn and
house to explore. Trails, family activities and
dressing-up. **Outdoors** Walks, bird hide, natural
playground and children's Discovery garden.
Dogs: welcome on the meadows and riverside.
Assistance dogs only in house and gardens.

Access: [icons]
House, shop and tea-room [icons] Gardens [icons]
Parking: 250 yards.

Find out more: 01535 607075 or
eastriddlesden@nationaltrust.org.uk

East Riddlesden Hall		M	T	W	T	F	S	S
18 Feb–26 Feb	10:30–4:30	M	T	W	·	·	S	S
4 Mar–12 Mar	10:30–4:30	·	·	·	·	·	S	S
18 Mar–5 Nov	10:30–4:30	M	T	W	·	·	S	S
11 Nov–17 Dec*	10:30–3:30	·	·	·	·	·	S	S

*House: limited access in November and December due to
winter conservation work, low light levels and Christmas
event. Tea-room: last entry 15 minutes before closing.
Open Good Friday.

Fountains Abbey and Studley Royal Water Garden

near Ripon, North Yorkshire HG4 3DY

🏠➕🏰📷❄️♿🚻♿🍴🍷 1983

Hidden in the secluded valley of the River Skell, you'll find breathtaking landscapes and the awe-inspiring ruins of Fountains Abbey at this World Heritage Site. Established by Cistercian monks in 1132, the walls echo with the stories of this atmospheric place. A riverside walk leads to the spectacular Studley Royal Georgian Water Garden, created by the socially ambitious John Aislabie in the 18th century. You can while away hours wandering among the mirror-like ponds and canals, taking in statues, follies and rushing

Fountains Abbey and Studley Royal Water Garden, North Yorkshire: exploring the Abbey ruins, below, and savouring the peace of the Water Garden, right

cascades. The High Ride path leads to surprise views and the chance to admire the picturesque Abbey ruins across the valley. Beyond the lake lies Studley Royal deer-park, with its ancient lime avenues and red, fallow and sika deer. **Note**: cared for in partnership with English Heritage.

Eat, shop, stay: restaurant serving breakfast, daily specials and Sunday lunch. Lighter bites at Abbey and Studley tea-rooms, with lake views/terrace. Picnics welcome. Large shop and plant stall. Stay in a cosy cottage, grand house in the park or the Jacobean Fountains Hall.

Things to see and do: **Indoors** You can uncover the ancient Abbey's history in the Porter's Lodge, then see the mill created by the skilful monks, step into the Jacobean Fountains Hall and admire St Mary's church, a Victorian Gothic masterpiece in the deer-park. **Outdoors** Families can have fun at Swanley Grange, with a new vegetable garden, sheep, hens, beehives and crafts, as well as a new play area. There are miles of walks in the deer-park and Water Garden to explore and a herb garden to enjoy. Free guided tours.
Dogs: welcome on leads. Fresh water bowls and dog-friendly eating areas outside restaurant and tea-rooms.

Looking down on the ruins of Fountains Abbey, with the graceful curve of the River Skell in the foreground

Access: [icons]
Fountains Abbey [icons]
Fountains Hall [icon]
Water Garden [icons]
Parking: on site at visitor centre
(accessible parking at West Gate)
and Studley Lakeside (pay and display).

Find out more: 01765 608888 or
fountainsabbey@nationaltrust.org.uk

Fountains Abbey		M	T	W	T	F	S	S
Abbey and Water Garden, Visitor Centre restaurant, shop								
1 Jan–24 Mar*	10–5†	M	T	W	T	F	S	S
25 Mar–29 Oct	10–6†	M	T	W	T	F	S	S
30 Oct–31 Dec**	10–5†	M	T	W	T	.	S	S
Deer-park								
Open all year	6–6	M	T	W	T	F	S	S

Last admission one hour before closing. *Closed Fridays
in January. **Closed 24 and 25 December. †Visitor Centre
restaurant and shop close one hour earlier. Check opening
times before visit for hall, mill, tea-rooms, Studley Royal shop
and St Mary's church.

Please display your current sticker for free parking

Goddards House and Garden

27 Tadcaster Road, Dringhouses, York, North Yorkshire YO24 1GG

🏠 ✿ 🍵 1984

Relaxing on the lawn at Goddards House and Garden, North Yorkshire: an Arts and Crafts gem

Celebrate 250 years of Terry's confectionery history (think Chocolate Orange) at the family's former house. In this warm Arts and Crafts building, full of memories, you can sit in the drawing-room, pour yourself a sherry and feel at home. Meander through garden 'rooms', discovering fragrant borders and hidden corners.

Eat, shop, stay: lunch served in the Terry's dining-room. You can take coffee in the drawing-room. Afternoon tea – or even Pimm's or G and T – also served there, or on the lavender terrace, enjoying views of the Arts and Crafts garden.

Things to see and do: **Indoors** Curl up by the fire on chilly days. Family trails and nostalgic displays of chocolate boxes, remembering old favourites. **Outdoors** Beautifully restored Arts and Crafts garden with outdoor games. **Dogs**: welcome on leads in garden.

Access: 🅿️ 🦽 🖼️ ⚙️ 📷
House 🦽 🪑 👟 Grounds 🦽 ➡️
Sat Nav: enter 27 Tadcaster Road, Dringhouses, York, not postcode.

Parking: disabled parking only on site (car park used by regional office staff). Please use city centre car parks (1 to 2 miles) or park on nearby Knavesmire Road (off A1036) by York racecourse.

Find out more: 01904 771930 or goddards@nationaltrust.org.uk

Goddards		M	T	W	T	F	S	S
12 Apr–5 Nov	10:30–5			**W**	**T**	**F**	**S**	**S**
17 Nov–17 Dec	10:30–4					**F**	**S**	**S**

Open spring and summer Bank Holiday Mondays.

Hardcastle Crags

near Hebden Bridge, West Yorkshire

🏞️ 🚲 🛏️ 🔔 🍵 1950

This enchanted valley in the South Pennines with its deep ravines, tumbling streams, glorious waterfalls and mature woodland is a walker's paradise. There are 25 miles of footpaths to be explored, and the area is rich in wildlife and changes dramatically through the seasons – with carpets of bluebells in late spring and golden leaves in autumn. At its heart is Gibson Mill, a former cotton mill and a successful Edwardian entertainment emporium, which offers the chance for refreshment and to explore the building and discover its history, as well as what it means to be 'Off The Grid'.

Hardcastle Crags, West Yorkshire: Gibson Mill

Occasional exhibitions. **Outdoors** Walking trails, guided walks, special interest walks, picnics, wildlife, family activities.
Dogs: under close control at all times.

Access: [icons]
Mill [icons] Countryside [icons]
Sat Nav: for Midgehole car park use HX7 7AA; Clough Hole car park HX7 7AZ. **Parking**: at Midgehole car park, 1 mile to Gibson Mill, or Clough Hole car park, ¾ mile (steep walk).

Find out more: 01422 844518 (weekdays). 01422 846236 (weekends) or hardcastlecrags@nationaltrust.org.uk

Hardcastle Crags		M	T	W	T	F	S	S
Gibson Mill and Weaving Shed Café								
7 Jan–12 Mar	11–3						S	S
18 Mar–5 Nov*	11–4	M	T	W	T	F	S	S
11 Nov–17 Dec	11–3						S	S

*Gibson Mill closed Fridays.

With woodland, glorious waterfalls, top, stepping stones across tumbling streams, above, and miles of footpaths, Hardcastle Crags is a walkers' paradise

Note: steep paths and rough terrain. Nearest toilets at Gibson Mill, 1 mile from car parks.

Eat, shop, stay: Weaving Shed Café serves drinks, sandwiches, soup, ice-cream and cakes – around a log fire in chillier weather. Shop selling books, gifts, sweets. Stay longer at Victorian Lodge (at the site's entrance), or the converted Widdop Gate Barn overlooking the valley.

Things to see and do: **Indoors** Learn about the fascinating history of the mill, surrounding area and 'Off The Grid' technology.

Maister House

160 High Street, Hull, East Yorkshire HU1 1NL

[icon] 1966

A merchant family's tale of fortune and tragedy is intertwined with the intriguing history of the 18th-century Maister House. **Note**: staircase and entrance hall only on show. Sorry no toilet. Due to a change in circumstances we are unable to confirm opening arrangements at the time of going to print. Please visit website for opening details.

Find out more: 01904 472027 or maisterhouse@nationaltrust.org.uk

Malham Tarn Estate

Waterhouses, Settle, North Yorkshire

[icons] 1946

High up in the Dales, with views across rolling fields, limestone pavements and the tarn, this National Nature Reserve is the perfect place to

Striding out on Malham Tarn Estate, North Yorkshire

enjoy the peace of the great outdoors.
With walking and cycle routes and a 'Tramper'
(scooter) for hire, you can stroll or have a
family adventure. **Note**: nearest toilet at
Malham National Park Centre car park or
Orchid House learning centre.

Eat, shop, stay: tea-rooms, pubs and facilities
in Malham village (none National Trust). To stay
longer, Darnbook Cottage (sleeps five) has fine
views of the surrounding dales of Malham
Moor and stands at the base of Fountains Fell.
Picnics welcome.

Things to see and do: guided walks and family
events during holidays. Accessible boardwalk.
Cycle trails. Exhibitions at Orchid House and
Town Head Barn. Walking routes for all abilities.
Dogs: welcome on leads (livestock roaming).

Access: Town Head Barn 🖼 Grounds 🖼 ➡ 🚾
Sat Nav: use BD24 9PT. **Parking**: off-road
at Waterhouses and at Watersinks car park,
south side of Malham Tarn.

Find out more: 01729 830416 or
malhamtarn@nationaltrust.org.uk

Marsden Moor Estate

Marsden, Huddersfield, West Yorkshire

🏛 👫 🐾 | 1955 |

The landscape and history of Marsden Moor,
within the South Pennines and Peak District
National Park, bring out the explorer in
everyone; there are acres of open moorland
and miles of footpaths. While enjoying the
stunning scenery, visitors can spot the wildlife
which inhabits this internationally important
area of conservation. **Note**: sorry, no toilet.

Eat, shop, stay: tea-rooms, restaurants and
shops in Marsden village (none National Trust).

Things to see and do: walking routes –
downloadable or paper versions – available
(OS map required) from the Exhibition Centre
at the Estate Office. Guided walks all year. Plant
sales in summer. **Dogs**: welcome on leads.

Access: Exhibition Room 🖼 Countryside 🔀
Sat Nav: use HD7 6DH for Marsden village.
Parking: at Marsden village (not National
Trust), Buckstones and Wessenden Head.

Find out more: 01484 847016 or
marsdenmoor@nationaltrust.org.uk

Marsden Moor Estate			M	T	W	T	F	S	S
Exhibition Centre									
Open all year	9–5		**M**	**T**	**W**	**T**	**F**	**S**	**S**
Closed 25 December.									

**Intrepid explorers survey the stunning
scenery on Marsden Moor Estate, West Yorkshire**

Middlethorpe Hall Hotel, Restaurant and Spa

Bishopthorpe Road, York,
North Yorkshire YO23 2GB

🏠✛♿️🏡🔔🍴 2008

William and Mary house, built in 1699, set in eight hectares (20 acres) of manicured gardens and parkland. **Note**: access is for paying guests of the hotel, including for luncheon, afternoon tea and dinner. Children over the age of six welcome.

Find out more: 01904 641241. 01904 620176 (fax) or info@middlethorpe.com middlethorpe.com

Moulton Hall

Moulton, Richmond,
North Yorkshire DL10 6QH

🏠✛ 1966

Elegant 17th-century tenanted manor house with a beautiful carved staircase. **Note**: sorry no toilet. Visit by arrangement in advance with the tenant (please give as much notice as possible).

Find out more: 01325 377227 or moultonhall@nationaltrust.org.uk

Mount Grace Priory

Staddle Bridge, Northallerton,
North Yorkshire DL6 3JG

🏠✝🏛✛ 1953

Woodland-set, best-preserved Carthusian priory in Britain. Explore ruins, reconstructed monk's cell, garden and Arts and Crafts-style manor house rooms. **Note**: operated by English Heritage; members free, except on event days. Open weekends, 1 January to 26 March and 4 November to 31 December, 10 to 4; open daily 1 April to 30 September, 10 to 6, and 1 to 31 October, 10 to 5. Closed 24 and 25 December.

Find out more: 01609 883494 or mountgracepriory@nationaltrust.org.uk

Nostell

Doncaster Road, Nostell, near Wakefield,
West Yorkshire WF4 1QE

🏠✝✛♿️🔔🍴 1954

Nostell is an architectural masterpiece. Created in the 18th century, it has been filled over the years with extraordinary pieces of craftsmanship. Discover Robert Adam interiors adorned with handmade treasures, including a world-class collection of Chippendale furniture and one of the first longcase clocks made by John Harrison. This spring, to celebrate the 300th anniversary of Harrison's clock, don't miss 'Harrison's Garden', a contemporary exhibition by Luke Jerram, comprising 2,000 ticking clocks. Families can enjoy dressing-up in the Servants' Hall and exploring the 121-hectare (300-acre) estate, which spans picturesque parkland, wildflower meadows and colourful gardens. Take in seasonal showstoppers in the kitchen garden, abundant wildlife along the lakeside paths and the secluded Menagerie Garden, once home to exotic animals.

Filled with extraordinary pieces of craftsmanship, the architectural masterpiece that is Nostell in West Yorkshire sits within swathes of picturesque parkland

Eat, shop, stay: Courtyard Café serving hot food and refreshments. Bite to Eat kiosk offering snacks and drinks at peak times. Shop selling gifts, souvenirs and plants. Picnics welcome in the park and gardens.

The impressive Tapestry Room at Nostell: opulence, splendour and beauty combined

Things to see and do: **Indoors** Year-round events, including family activities five days a week during school holidays, craft workshops and exhibitions. Regular guided walks and tours of the house, stables and grounds. Family house guide. Dressing-up and costumed character tours on selected days. Special opening in December, when house is decorated for Christmas. **Outdoors** Regular running, walking and cycling groups, all-weather track in Obelisk Park. Geocaching, den-building, children's outdoor play area. **Dogs**: under close control at all times. Assistance dogs only in gardens.

Access: 🅿️♿🐕♿♿♿♿🔊♿📷📷
House ♿♿♿ **Grounds** ♿♿➡️♿♿
Parking: 650 yards.

Find out more: 01924 863892 or nostell@nationaltrust.org.uk

Nostell		M	T	W	T	F	S	S
House*								
4 Mar–29 Oct	1–5			W	T	F	S	S
2 Dec–17 Dec	10–4						S	S
Gardens, shop and café*								
1 Jan–3 Mar	10–4	M	T	W	T	F	S	S
4 Mar–29 Oct	10–5	M	T	W	T	F	S	S
30 Oct–31 Dec	10–4	M	T	W	T	F	S	S
Parkland†								
Open all year	7–7	M	T	W	T	F	S	S

*House: open 11 to 12 for guided tours (places limited, allocated on arrival). Last admission 45 minutes before closing. Open Bank Holidays, 11 to 5 (no tours).
**Rose Garden: may close for private functions.
†Parkland: closes dusk if earlier. Closed 25 December.

Nunnington Hall

Nunnington, near York,
North Yorkshire YO62 5UY

🏠❄️ 1953

Whatever the weather, whatever the season, a trip to Nunnington Hall offers a perfect day out for all the family. This welcoming and friendly home, with its enchanting house and gardens, is within easy reach of York and Scarborough. You can learn about the Fife family, owners of the Hall in the 1920s and, if you're brave enough, hear the Hall's ghostly tales! In spring, the beautiful wildflower meadows in the organic gardens bloom. In summer, the lawn is perfect for relaxing, or you could picnic by the meandering River Rye. In autumn the orchards are bountiful with produce.

Eat, shop, stay: atmospheric, licensed waitress-service tea-room in the house, serving homemade lunch, cakes and cream teas.

Outdoor garden kiosk (available during peak times) with seating next to the River Rye. Shop on the third floor, selling gifts and souvenirs.

Things to see and do: **Indoors** Carlisle collection of 22 miniature rooms, art exhibitions, family activities, music concerts and seasonal events. **Outdoors** Garden games, mud-pie kitchen, bird-spotting, quoits, pooh-sticks, giant chess and croquet. **Dogs**: welcome on leads in the garden.

Access: ♿🅿️♿♿ **Building** ♿♿♿ **Grounds** ♿♿
Parking: on site.

Find out more: 01439 748283 or nunningtonhall@nationaltrust.org.uk

Nunnington Hall		M	T	W	T	F	S	S
11 Feb–31 Mar	10:30–4	·	T	W	T	F	S	S
1 Apr–23 Jul	10:30–5	·	T	W	T	F	S	S
24 Jul–3 Sep	10:30–5	M	T	W	T	F	S	S
5 Sep–5 Nov	10:30–5	·	T	W	T	F	S	S
11 Nov–17 Dec	10:30–4	·	·	·	·	·	S	S

Last admission 45 minutes before closing. Open all Mondays during school holidays and Bank Holiday Mondays.

Welcoming and friendly Nunnington Hall, North Yorkshire

Ormesby Hall

Ladgate Lane, Ormesby, near Middlesbrough, Redcar & Cleveland TS3 0SR

🏠🌸♿🅰️🍴 1962

Hidden in Middlesbrough, this Georgian mansion was home to the Pennyman family for over 400 years. Uncover the family's stories from 'Wicked' Sir James to Colonel Jim, survivor of the First World War, and the theatrical exploits of his wife Ruth. Colourful, Victorian formal garden and walks through the parkland.

Ormesby Hall, Redcar & Cleveland: a Georgian gem

Eat, shop, stay: second-hand bookshop. Gift shop also sells hot and cold drinks, sandwiches, cakes and ice-cream. Picnics welcome in the garden.

Things to see and do: **Indoors** Hands-on activities in the mansion. Model railway layouts on the first floor. Family Room. Children's trails. Costumed event days. **Outdoors** Seasonal colours and scents in the garden. Garden games. **Dogs**: welcome on leads in the parkland. Assistance dogs only in the house and garden.

Access: 🅿️♿♿♿♿♿♿♿♿♿
House ♿♿ **Grounds** ♿➡️♿
Parking: 200 yards.

Find out more: 01642 324188 or ormesbyhall@nationaltrust.org.uk. Church Lane, Ormesby, Middlesbrough TS7 9AS

Ormesby Hall		M	T	W	T	F	S	S
12 Feb–29 Mar	11–4*	M	T	W	·	·	·	S
2 Apr–1 Nov	11–5*	M	T	W	·	·	·	S
2 Dec–17 Dec	11–4*	·	·	·	·	·	S	S

Last entry 45 minutes before closing. Additionally open for model railway weekends. Closed on 14 May for Brides Up North WEDFEST17.

Rievaulx Terrace

Rievaulx, Helmsley, North Yorkshire YO62 5LJ

⬚ ⬚ ⬚ 1972

Created by the Duncombe family and finished *circa* 1757, Rievaulx Terrace was designed primarily for promenading and dining in style. It maintains this unique feeling of grandeur and tranquillity today. The woods are a perfect start to your visit, giving tantalising glimpses of the terrace and the views beyond, as well as opportunities to enjoy nature and wildlife. When you leave the woods and walk down the terrace, spectacular views of Rievaulx Abbey and the valley beyond are revealed through man-made vistas. Finally you'll find the Ionic Temple, where the family dined under the magnificent painted ceiling. **Note**: no access to Rievaulx Abbey (English Heritage).

Eat, shop, stay: pre-packed snacks, ice-cream and cold drinks available. Picnics welcome. Shop selling gifts and souvenirs.

Things to see and do: Ionic Temple opens at intervals throughout the day. Woodland natural play area for children including den-building, rope swing, balance beam, log-scotch, quoits and stepping stones. Family trails and activities. **Dogs**: welcome on leads.

Access: ⬚ ⬚ ⬚ ⬚ ⬚ **Visitor centre** ⬚
Temples ⬚ **Grounds** ⬚ ⬚ ⬚ ⬚
Parking: 100 yards.

The elegant Ionic Temple at Rievaulx Terrace

Find out more: 01439 798340 (summer). 01439 748283 (winter) or rievaulxterrace@nationaltrust.org.uk

Rievaulx Terrace		M	T	W	T	F	S	S
11 Feb–31 Mar	10–4	M	T	W	T	F	S	S
1 Apr–30 Sep	10–5	M	T	W	T	F	S	S
1 Oct–5 Nov	10–4	M	T	W	T	F	S	S

Last admission one hour before closing.

Soaring columns at Rievaulx Terrace, North Yorkshire

Roseberry Topping

near Newton-under-Roseberry, North Yorkshire

⬚ ⬚ ⬚ 1985

Affectionately known as 'Yorkshire's Matterhorn', layers of geological history have shaped this iconic hill. Stunning views, woodland walks and wildlife. **Note**: nearest parking at Newton-under-Roseberry, not National Trust (charge including members). Nearest toilets also in this car park. For Sat Nav use TS9 6QR.

Find out more: 01723 870423 or roseberrytopping@nationaltrust.org.uk

Treasurer's House, York

Minster Yard, York, North Yorkshire YO1 7JL

🏠 ❋ 🖼 🍴 1930

Tucked behind York Minster, Treasurer's House is not as it first appears. In 1897, Frank Green (the grandson of a wealthy industrialist) bought the property and created a lavish show home, grand enough to impress Edward VII during his visit. He was passionate about history and indulged this by saving this and other buildings in York. Frank Green built a large collection of fine antiques, art and furniture, and this was the first house given to the National Trust, complete with its collection. The award-winning garden is an oasis of calm, so relax and enjoy unrivalled views of the Minster.

There is much to fascinate both parents and children inside Treasurer's House, York

Access: 🅿 🗊 🖼 🎧 ⠿ 🖼
House 🖼 🖼 🚹 Garden 🖼
Parking: nearest at Lord Mayor's Walk (not National Trust). Park and ride from city outskirts recommended.

Find out more: 01904 624247 or treasurershouse@nationaltrust.org.uk

Treasurer's House		M	T	W	T	F	S	S
1 Mar–5 Nov	11–4:30	M	T	W	T	F	S	S
16 Nov–17 Dec	11–4:30	·	·	·	T	F	S	S

Gracious Treasurer's House, York, North Yorkshire

Eat, shop, stay: the Below Stairs Café serves morning coffee, lunch and afternoon tea. Around the corner, on Goodramgate, is the Trust's large high-street shop selling a wide selection of gifts. Stay a little longer in the York city centre holiday apartment.

Things to see and do: **Indoors** Family trails. Hard-hat tour (eight years and older) to the cellar to revisit the site of Treasurer's most famous ghost story. **Outdoors** Games (during the school holidays). **Dogs**: welcome in garden on a lead.

Upper Wharfedale

near Buckden, North Yorkshire

🖼 🖼 🖼 1989

This Dales landscape, with fields of sheep and cows, the wildflower meadows in early summer and characteristic drystone walls and barns, is a wonderful place to relax and enjoy the great outdoors. Explore the river and woodland valleys by foot or by bike.

Crook Gill waterfall in Upper Wharfdale, North Yorkshire

Eat, shop, stay: village tea-rooms, shops, pubs and farm shops (not National Trust). Nestling in the heart of Buckden, The Old Smithy holiday cottage (sleeps two) and Town Head Bunkhouse (sleeps 13).

Things to see and do: guided walks, events, workshops and activities. Family events during school holidays. Exhibition at Town Head Barn in Buckden. **Dogs**: welcome on leads due to livestock.

Access: 🅿♿ Town Head Barn ♿ Grounds ➡
Sat Nav: use BD23 5JA. **Parking**: in Kettlewell and Buckden, pay and display, not National Trust (charge including members).

Find out more: 01729 830416 or upperwharfedale@nationaltrust.org.uk

Yorkshire Coast

near Ravenscar, North Yorkshire

🏛♿♿🐕🛏 1976

The coastline from Saltburn to Filey is breathtakingly dramatic, with sea views, clifftop walks, cycling routes and sandy bays with excellent rock-pooling and fossil-hunting. Ravenscar Visitor Centre will give you lots of ideas and there's also a coastal exhibition at the Old Coastguard Station, Robin Hood's Bay.

Eat, shop, stay: Old Coastguard Station shop selling gifts, books, maps and toys. Ravenscar Visitor Centre offering a limited selection of drinks and snacks. Two holiday cottages at Ravenscar and one at Robin Hood's Bay, all with stunning sea views.

Things to see and do: Indoors Exhibitions at the Old Coastguard Station. **Outdoors** Family events, geocaching, wildlife activities and guided walks from Ravenscar and the Old Coastguard Station. **Dogs**: welcome on lead at most events. Assistance dogs only in Old Coastguard Station.

Access: ♿♿🐕🅿 Old Coastguard Station ♿
Sat Nav: for Ravenscar use YO13 0NE.
Parking: on roadside at Ravenscar. Pay and display at Saltburn, Runswick Bay and Robin Hood's Bay, not National Trust (charge including members).

Find out more: 01723 870423 or yorkshirecoast@nationaltrust.org.uk

Yorkshire Coast		M	T	W	T	F	S	S
Old Coastguard Station								
1 Jan–12 Feb	10–4	·	·	·	·	·	S	S
18 Feb–26 Feb	10–4	M	T	W	T	F	S	S
4 Mar–2 Apr	10–4	·	·	·	·	·	S	S
8 Apr–29 Oct	10–5	M	T	W	T	F	S	S
4 Nov–17 Dec	10–4	·	·	·	·	·	S	S
27 Dec–31 Dec	10–4	·	·	W	T	F	S	S
Ravenscar Visitor Centre								
18 Feb–26 Feb	10–4	M	T	W	T	F	S	S
4 Mar–12 Mar	10–4	·	·	·	·	·	S	S
18 Mar–2 Oct	10–5	M	T	W	T	F	S	S
3 Oct–5 Nov	10–4	M	T	W	T	F	S	S

Yorkshire Coast, North Yorkshire: breathtakingly dramatic

North East

Seaton Delaval Hall, Northumberland

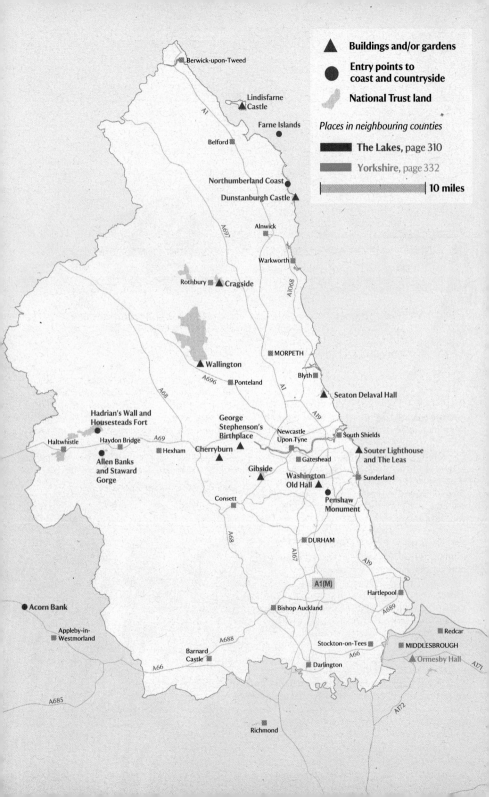

Buildings and/or gardens

Entry points to coast and countryside

National Trust land

Places in neighbouring counties

The Lakes, page 310

Yorkshire, page 332

10 miles

Berwick-upon-Tweed

Lindisfarne Castle

Farne Islands

Belford

Northumberland Coast

Dunstanburgh Castle

Alnwick

Warkworth

Rothbury ▲ Cragside

MORPETH

Blyth

▲ Wallington

Ponteland

Seaton Delaval Hall

Hadrian's Wall and Housesteads Fort

George Stephenson's Birthplace

Newcastle Upon Tyne

South Shields

Haltwhistle

Haydon Bridge

Hexham

Cherryburn

Gateshead

Souter Lighthouse and The Leas

Allen Banks and Staward Gorge

Gibside

Washington Old Hall

Sunderland

Consett

Penshaw Monument

DURHAM

A1(M)

Hartlepool

Acorn Bank

Appleby-in-Westmorland

Bishop Auckland

Redcar

Barnard Castle

Stockton-on-Tees

MIDDLESBROROUGH

Darlington

Ormesby Hall

Richmond

Hikers take a well-deserved break in the ancient woods at Allen Banks and Staward Gorge, Northumberland

Allen Banks and Staward Gorge

near Ridley Hall, Bardon Mill, Hexham,
Northumberland NE47 7BP

🏠🏚🚶‍♀️ 1942

With its deep gorge, created by the River Allen, and the largest area of ancient semi-natural woodland in Northumberland, this 250-hectare (617-acre) site provides the perfect setting for an adventure. There are many miles of waymarked walks and the picturesque, dramatic woods are home to a fantastic array of wildlife. **Note**: site suffered severe storm damage in 2015: check for open sections and routes before visiting.

Eat, shop, stay: picnics welcome at the numerous beauty spots – in the woodland and kitchen garden.

Things to see and do: events including Easter Egg hunts, woodland walks, wildlife spotting, ornamental tarn and medieval pele-tower. **Dogs**: welcome under close control.

Access: 🚻♿📷 Grounds 🦮
Sat Nav: postcode directs to Ridley Hall – turn left at Ridley Hall gates for Allen Banks car park. **Parking**: at Allen Banks.

Find out more: 01434 321888 or allenbanks@nationaltrust.org.uk

Cherryburn

Station Bank, Mickley, Stocksfield,
Northumberland NE43 7DD

🏛️🍴♿👶🍽️ 1991

This unassuming Northumbrian farmstead is the birthplace of famous artist and naturalist Thomas Bewick. Set in a tranquil garden with views across the Tyne Valley, Cherryburn is surrounded by the natural world that inspired his work. Explore the museum with Bewick's pioneering wood engravings and meet the friendly farm animals.

A sunny picnic at Cherryburn in Northumberland

Eat, shop, stay: gift shop offering books and a selection of original Bewick prints hot off the historic presses. House offers snacks, hot and cold drinks and ice-cream. Farmyard picnic area.

Things to see and do: **Indoors** Regular printing demonstrations, museum and original birthplace. **Outdoors** Family trail, mini-adventure play area and school holiday activities, following in young Tom's footsteps. Paddock walk and farmyard with seasonal animals. **Dogs**: welcome on short leads in garden and grounds (animals in farmyard).

Access: 🅿️♿🚻♿🅿️📷🚶👁️
Birthplace 🚶♿♿ Café and museum ♿♿🚻
Grounds 🚶♿♿➡️
Parking: 100 yards.

Find out more: 01661 843276 or cherryburn@nationaltrust.org.uk

Cherryburn		M	T	W	T	F	S	S
18 Feb–29 Oct	11–5	**M**	**T**	**W**	**T**	**F**	**S**	**S**

The quirky and cosy Owl Suite at Cragside: Arts and Crafts charm and comfort

Cragside

Rothbury, Morpeth, Northumberland NE65 7PX

🏠❄️♿🅿️ 1977

Trip the light fantastic to the home where modern living began. Lord and Lady Armstrong used their wealth, art and science in an ingenious way.

Visitors meet 'Douglas' at Cragside in Northumberland

Cragside was the first house in the world to be lit by hydroelectricity, making it a wonder of the Victorian age. What began as a modest country retreat became the most technologically advanced home of its time. Cleverly including every home comfort imaginable, the house evolved into an Arts and Crafts masterpiece. Outside, their passion for landscaping and gardening was equally ambitious, engineering the landscape and experimenting with plants on a spectacular scale. Combining rocky crags, tumbling water, tranquil lakes, towering North American conifers and great drifts of rhododendrons, creating changing scenes in the landscape. **Note**: challenging terrain and distances (stout footwear essential).

Eat, shop, stay: tea-room serving hot meals, sandwiches, hand-crafted treats and afternoon tea. Kiosks at the house and play area. Shop selling souvenirs, gifts, local food, crafts and plants. Two holiday cottages in the formal garden and bunkhouse sleeping up to 16 people.

Things to see and do: **Indoors** The Armstrong's vast collection of British art and furniture sits alongside items of scientific curiosity and engineering innovation.

Victorian baking demonstrations using the original range on Wednesdays, and family activities, special exhibitions and events throughout the year. **Outdoors** Six-mile estate drive through rugged woodland. Estate car parks, a vast network of paths, including lakeside trails and walks for all abilities – from family strolls to challenging hikes. Idyllic formal garden with seasonal planting and views across Northumberland. Regular guided walks and tours. Fantasy landscape, including a rhododendron labyrinth and adventure play area. Free shuttle bus between key features. **Dogs**: welcome outdoors on leads.

Access: [icons]
House [icons] **Visitor centre** [icons] **Estate** [icons]
Parking: nine car parks on estate.

Cragside: the drama of the surrounding landscape is matched by the splendour of the Victorian mansion and its astonishing technological innovations

Find out more: 01669 620333 or cragside@nationaltrust.org.uk

Cragside		M	T	W	T	F	S	S
Gardens and woodland								
18 Feb–9 Apr*	10–6		T	W	T	F	S	S
10 Apr–29 Oct*	10–6	M	T	W	T	F	S	S
3 Nov–17 Dec*	11–4					F	S	S
House								
18 Feb–9 Apr*	11–5		T	W	T	F	S	S
10 Apr–29 Oct*	11–5	M	T	W	T	F	S	S

*Last admission at the gate is 4 (3, 3 November to 17 December). Last entry to estate drive is 5:30. Last entry to house one hour before closing; entry is controlled (queueing at busy times).

Dunstanburgh Castle

Craster, Alnwick, Northumberland NE66 3TT

🏰 ⚔ 1961

Iconic castle ruin occupying a dramatic position with spectacular views of the Northumberland coastline – one-mile walk from Craster. **Note**: managed by English Heritage. National Trust members admitted free. Sorry no toilets – closest at Craster car park. Parking at Craster, pay and display, not National Trust (charge including members). Call English Heritage on 01665 576231 or visit english-heritage.org.uk for opening times. Closed 1 January and 24 to 26 December.

Find out more: 01665 576231 or dunstanburghcastle@nationaltrust.org.uk

Farne Islands

Northumberland

✝ ⚔ 🚶 1925

One of the UK's best wildlife spectacles. An exhilarating boat trip gives an unparalleled peek into the world of 23 nesting seabird species, including thousands of puffins (May to July), Arctic terns and guillemots.

Farne Islands, Northumberland: puffin paradise

In autumn, visit the grey seal colony: over 1,000 pups are born each year. **Note**: basic toilets and easy access boardwalk on Inner Farne but not Staple Island. Access by boat from Seahouses – separate charge applies (including members).

Eat, shop, stay: shop in Seahouses selling a range of gifts and local produce. Some souvenirs also available on the islands.

Things to see and do: nature-spotting paradise. Bring a hat – terns will dive-bomb! On Inner Farne: St Cuthbert's Chapel, with vibrant stained glass, Victorian lighthouse and visitor centre. Lindisfarne Castle and Northumberland Coast nearby. **Dogs**: sorry, not allowed (including assistance dogs) due to extremely sensitive nature of the colony.

Access: ♿ Grounds 🚶 ♿
Sat Nav: use NE68 7RQ.
Parking: in Seahouses, not National Trust (charge including members).

Find out more: 01665 721099. 01289 389244 (Lindisfarne Castle) or farneislands@nationaltrust.org.uk

Farne Islands		M	T	W	T	F	S	S
Inner Farne Island								
1 Apr–30 Apr	10:30–5:30	M	T	W	T	F	S	S
1 May–31 Jul	1:30–5:30	M	T	W	T	F	S	S
1 Aug–5 Nov	10:30–5:30	M	T	W	T	F	S	S
Staple Island								
1 May–31 Jul	10:30–1:30	M	T	W	T	F	S	S

Landings only on Inner Farne and Staple Islands. Seahouses information centre and shop open all year, 10 to 5.

George Stephenson's Birthplace

near Wylam, Northumberland NE41 8DS

🏠 ✿ 🚢 1949

This simple home on the idyllic banks of the Tyne was the birthplace of railway pioneer George Stephenson. Sitting beside Wylam's historic waggonway – originally 18th-century, becoming an early railway in the 19th – this tiny one-room miner's

George Stephenson's Birthplace, Northumberland: the home of a railway pioneer and visionary

cottage housed a family whose engineering legacy lives on today.

Eat, shop, stay: tea-room serving a selection of drinks, light snacks, cakes and ice-cream. You can relax and enjoy them at the garden seating.

Things to see and do: Indoors Tiny room decorated as in 1781 – the year Stephenson was born. **Outdoors** You can stroll or cycle along the route of one of the world's first steam railways. **Dogs**: welcome on leads in garden.

Access: 🖼️🦽🎧♿🔲📷 Birthplace 🔲
Café 🔲 Garden 🔲
Parking: in village, then ½ mile along Wylam Waggonway.

Find out more: 01661 843276 or georgestephensons@nationaltrust.org.uk

George Stephenson's Birthplace		M	T	W	T	F	S	S
Birthplace								
18 Feb–29 Oct	11–5				T	F	S	S
Tea-room								
18 Feb–29 Oct	11–5				T	F	S	S
4 Nov–31 Dec	11–3						S	S
Open Bank Holiday Mondays.								

Gibside

near Rowlands Gill, Gateshead,
Tyne & Wear NE16 6BG

✚🍴⚙️🔲✳️♿⛺🔔⊤ 1974

The Palladian Chapel at Gibside, Tyne & Wear

Created by coal baron George Bowes, Gibside Estate was fashioned with two things in mind: spectacular views and 'wow' moments. It is a rare example of an 18th-century designed landscape. Today, you can enjoy a welcome escape from the hustle and bustle of modern life: follow trails through woodland, countryside, riverside and gardens – looking out for wildlife. Although Gibside Hall is derelict, there are buildings such as the Palladian Chapel to explore. You can see the Walled Garden going through a transformation and discover the compelling story of the loves of wealthy heiress Mary Eleanor Bowes.

Eat, shop, stay: breakfast, lunch, drinks at Gibside café (open to 9 every Friday and Saturday). Carriage House Coffee Shop. Refreshments at the play-area cabin (weekends/holidays). Shop selling plants and gifts. Renwick's second-hand books at the Stables. Twice-monthly markets.

Things to see and do: **Indoors** Palladian chapel with unique three-tier pulpit. Gibside story and wildlife interpretation at the Stables. **Outdoors** Walled Garden and wider estate to explore. Walks and events. Play areas. **Dogs**: welcome on leads. Assistance dogs only in Strawberry Castle play area.

Access: 🅿️♿🚻🚼🛗🔔🧏🚹📷🅾️
Chapel 🧏♿🚹 Stables 🧏♿
Garden 🧏🧏🧏➡️🚹♿
Parking: 382 yards from café and shop (uphill walkway).

Find out more: 01207 541820 or gibside@nationaltrust.org.uk

Gibside		M	T	W	T	F	S	S
Garden, woodlands, shop and café/pub*								
1 Jan–31 Mar	10–4	M	T	W	T	F	S	S
1 Apr–31 Oct	10–6**	M	T	W	T	F	S	S
1 Nov–31 Dec	10–4	M	T	W	T	F	S	S
Chapel								
7 Jan–26 Mar	10–4						S	S
1 Apr–2 Sep	10–5	M	T	W	T	F	S	S
4 Nov–31 Dec	10–4						S	S

Stables: open daily, 10 to 4, 1 January to 31 March and 1 November to 31 December (excluding 24 and 25 December); open 10 to 5, 1 April to 1 October. *Garden, woodlands, café/pub and stables: open 9:30 at weekends. Café/pub: close 9, Friday and Saturday. **Garden and woodlands: close 9 on Friday and Saturday, 26 May to 2 September (last entry at 8). Shop: closes at 5, Sunday to Thursday; at 8, Friday and Saturday. Whole estate closed 24 and 25 December.

Hadrian's Wall and Housesteads Fort

near Bardon Mill, Hexham, Northumberland NE47 6NN

🏛️📷♿👶👣🐾 1930

Hadrian's Wall, an epic structure, kept the unwanted out and the welcome safe. Making use of the natural Whin Sill escarpment, this UNESCO World Heritage Site is the Roman Empire's best-maintained outpost in northern Europe. There are invigorating walks and breathtaking landscapes. The fort offers insights into Roman soldiers' lives.

Whether you relish a tricky challenge, top, or enjoy fabulous follies such as the Column for Liberty, left, Gibside has a lot to enjoy

Note: fort owned by National Trust, managed by English Heritage. ½ mile uphill from visitor centre. Parking charges (including members).

Eat, shop, stay: visitor centre offering sandwiches, snacks, ice-cream and drinks. Shop selling books, cards, gifts, souvenirs and plants. Picnics welcome. Our holiday accommodation includes a bothy, a farmhouse and a cottage: set in spectacular landscapes – ideal for walkers and star-gazers.

A spectacular run along Hadrian's Wall, Northumberland

Things to see and do: **Indoors** Museum (not National Trust) with dressing-up and video presentation. **Outdoors** Play area. Fort to explore. Walk along wall to Milecastle 37 and Sycamore Gap. Periodic activities include rock-climbing, star-gazing. **Dogs**: welcome on leads.

Access: 🅿️ 🐕 ♿ ♿ ♿ 📷 🎨
Visitor centre ♿ ♿ **Museum** ♿
Parking: at Housesteads, Steel Rigg and Cawfields, not National Trust (charge including members).

Find out more: 01434 344525 or housesteads@nationaltrust.org.uk

Hadrian's Wall and Housesteads Fort
Open daily (limited opening over Christmas and New Year).

Lindisfarne Castle

Holy Island, Berwick-upon-Tweed, Northumberland TD15 2SH

🏰 ❄️ 🖼️ 🛏️ 🔔 1944

Presiding over the tidal Holy Island, Lindisfarne Castle is one of the most iconic coastal castles in the UK. The Tudor fort was converted into a holiday home for *Country Life* editor Edward Hudson by architect Edwin Lutyens in 1903. Its position, however, makes it prey to wind, sea and salt, and this year Lindisfarne Castle is closed for vital conservation work. There's still a lot to discover with us on Holy Island: the summer-flowering garden designed by Gertrude Jekyll, the unexpected grandeur of the 19th-century industrial lime kilns, shoreline walks and a National Trust shop in the village. **Note**: castle closed this year due to conservation. No toilets. Island accessed via tidal causeway.

Rising above Holy Island, iconic Lindisfarne Castle, Northumberland, is a dramatic and unforgettable sight

With Lindisfarne Castle behind, a family explores Gertrude Jekyll's Arts and Crafts garden, which is open all year

Eat, shop, stay: National Trust shop in village with large range of home and garden wares. Two holiday cottages on the island: Lutyens-designed St Oswald's, sleeping five, on one level, looking up to the castle (dog-friendly); Glen House, sleeping two, in the village.

Things to see and do: castle closed but lime kilns, grazing and shoreline around the castle and small, but perfectly formed, garden by Lutyens-collaborator Gertrude Jekyll open. Holy Island to explore. Farne Islands nearby. **Dogs**: welcome on leads.

Access: 🅿️ ♿ Grounds ♿
Parking: at main island car park, 1 mile, not National Trust (charge including members).

Find out more: 01289 389244 or lindisfarne@nationaltrust.org.uk

Lindisfarne Castle	
Garden	
Open every day all year	

Due to conservation work, the castle is closed all year.
For access to Holy Island check tide times before visiting.

Northumberland Coast

Northumberland

🔲 ♿ 🏖️ 🚻 🅿️ 1935

From Lindisfarne to Druridge Bay, you'll find wide open skies above white sands and blue seas. This unspoilt coastline is rich in pretty fishing villages, castle silhouettes, wildlife and deserted beaches, with excellent rock pools. Look out for seals, dolphins, wading shorebirds and nesting terns at Long Nanny. **Note**: public car parks only (charge including members).

Eat, shop, stay: shops on Holy Island and in Seahouses. Cafés, pubs and shops in coastal towns and villages (none National Trust). Holiday cottages with extraordinary views: two on Holy Island; three at Low Newton, including on the green at Newton-by-the-Sea.

Things to see and do: Long Nanny little tern nesting colony (June to August), access from High Newton. Events, including guided walks, '50 things' and wildlife spotting. Dunstanburgh Castle, Farne Islands and Lindisfarne Castle nearby. **Dogs**: welcome, some local restrictions may apply.

Access: 🚻
Sat Nav: for Low Newton use NE66 3EH; Druridge Bay NE61 5EG; St Aidan's Dunes NE68 7SH. **Parking**: limited at Druridge Bay. Also at Holy Island, Seahouses, Beadnell, Newton-by-the-Sea and Craster, none National Trust (charge including members).

Find out more: 01289 389244 or northumberlandcoast@nationaltrust.org.uk

Riding out at sunset on the Northumberland Coast

Penshaw Monument

near Penshaw, Tyne & Wear DH4 7NJ

🏠 🏛 ♿ 1939

Enjoy walks and magnificent views from this iconic Wearside landmark, built as a tribute to the 1st Earl of Durham. **Note**: sorry no toilets. Walking routes nearby. Tours to the top of the monument on Saturdays, Sundays and Bank Holidays, 1 April to 24 September.

Find out more: 01207 541820 or penshaw.monument@nationaltrust.org.uk

Seaton Delaval Hall

The Avenue, Seaton Sluice,
Northumberland NE26 4QR

🏠 ❄ ♿ 2009

Enter a world where an extraordinary lifestyle was acted out in the most colourful way. This may have been one of architect Sir John Vanbrugh's smallest country houses, but it was home to the larger-than-life Delaval family. The Hall continues to bear the scars of the fierce fires which almost condemned it to ruin 200 years ago. Great theatre and drama can still be found in the house, gardens and surrounding landscape, which have served as the stage for an incredible tale of changing fortune. The story of Seaton's survival is as dramatic as any theatrical production.

Eat, shop, stay: café serving hot and cold drinks, snacks and sweet treats all year. In fine weather refreshments are served from the summerhouse. Shop in the ticket hut selling souvenirs, gifts and plants.

Seaton Delaval Hall, Northumberland: its dramatic history and survival rival any theatrical production

Seaton Delaval Hall: Vanbrugh's smallest country house

Things to see and do: **Indoors** Vanbrugh's architecture with 18th-century stables. Great Hall with fire-damaged interior and original statues. Paintings and furniture in West Wing. **Outdoors** Beautiful gardens, walks and coastal landscape. Events and activities.
Dogs: welcome on leads outdoors.

Access: ⓟ♿♿♿♿♿ Hall ♿
Stables ♿ Grounds ▶
Parking: 500 yards.

Find out more: 0191 237 9100 or
seatondelavalhall@nationaltrust.org.uk

Seaton Delaval Hall		M	T	W	T	F	S	S
Central hall, stables and gardens								
7 Jan–26 Feb*	11–3						S	S
27 Feb–29 Oct**	11–5	M	T	W			S	S
8 Apr–23 Apr**	11–5	M	T	W	T	F	S	S
27 May–4 Jun**	11–5	M	T	W	T	F	S	S
22 Jul–3 Sep**	11–5	M	T	W	T	F	S	S
21 Oct–29 Oct**	11–5	M	T	W	T	F	S	S
4 Nov–31 Dec**	11–3						S	S
West Wing								
27 Feb–29 Oct**	11–5	M	T	W			S	S

*Open Saturday to Wednesday in February half-term.
**West Wing open daily in main school holidays (as well as central hall, stables and gardens). Last admission 45 minutes before closing.

Souter Lighthouse and The Leas

Coast Road, Whitburn, Sunderland, Tyne & Wear SR6 7NH

🏠❄♿♿🍴🍽🍷 1990

Scale the heights to the top of a lighthouse which was truly modern for its time – the very first purpose-built to be lit by electricity. While you catch your breath, you can gaze out to sea, north to the Cheviot Hills and south to Roseberry Topping. The Leas is dotted with wildflower meadows where bee orchids, yellow rattle and red clover are hidden among the coastal grassland. A saunter through Whitburn Coastal Park is great for bird-spotting, and the local nature reserve provides water and rest for birds making their way across the sea and along the coast.

A trailblazer of its time, Souter Lighthouse and The Leas, Tyne & Wear, was built to run on electricity

Eat, shop, stay: Lighthouse Café serving light lunches, soup, cakes and refreshments. Local dishes Panackelty and Singin' Hinnies are a must-try. The shop stocks coastal gifts and Souter souvenirs. Extend your visit with a holiday in a Lighthouse Keeper's cottage.

Things to see and do: events and activities, including seashore safaris, bug-hunting, nature walks, birdwatching, pirate days, holiday crafts and car-boot sales. Picnic and play area. Fog-horn demonstrations, talking telescope, wildlife garden.
Dogs: all welcome on leads outdoors.

Access: ⬚⬚⬚⬚⬚⬚⬚⬚
Building ⬚⬚ Grounds ⬚⬚⬚
Parking: on site.

Find out more: 0191 529 3161 or souter@nationaltrust.org.uk

Souter Lighthouse and The Leas		M	T	W	T	F	S	S
4 Feb–29 Oct	11–5	M	T	W	T	F	S	S
30 Oct–26 Nov	11–4	M	T	W	T	F	S	S
2 Dec–17 Dec	11–4	.	.	.	.	.	S	S

Wallington

Cambo, near Morpeth,
Northumberland NE61 4AR

⬚ ⬚ ⬚ ⬚ 1941

Wallington, Northumberland: the Edwardian conservatory

Gifted to you by Sir Charles Philips Trevelyan, socialist MP and 'illogical Englishman', Wallington has something for everyone. Set within an 18th-century landscape, the house is surrounded by a huge working estate and over 20 miles of walks. The West Wood is full of wildlife and wild play spaces, the East Wood is home to towering trees and still ponds and the Walled Garden is bursting with colour, whatever the season. Further afield, you can take a circular walk to Broomhouse Farm or enjoy a stroll by the river. At the heart of the estate, the Trevelyans' informal home is full of treasured collections – make yourself at home in the impressive rooms as you find out about this unconventional family.

Eat, shop, stay: Clocktower Café serving brunch, lunch and afternoon tea. Takeaway refreshments available from the Clocktower Kiosk and the Walled Garden Kiosk (seasonal). Wide range of gifts, treats and souvenirs for sale in our shops and plant centre.

Things to see and do: Indoors You can soak up the atmosphere in the Trevelyans' home – discover Northumberland's history in the Pre-Raphaelite paintings around the Central Hall, warm up next to the AGA in the kitchen or relax on the sofas in the drawing-room.

Please display your current sticker for free parking

Regular activities, including conservation in action, cookery demonstrations, Northumbrian pipe music and December Christmas events. **Outdoors** You can enjoy heady fragrances in the Walled Garden's Edwardian conservatory. Wildlife hide, adventure playground, play train and fort. Regular guided walks and family activities during school holidays. New cycle trails across Broomhouse Farm, with far-reaching views over the estate, opening this year. **Dogs**: welcome on leads outdoors and on all walks.

Access: ⬚⬚⬚⬚⬚⬚⬚⬚
House ⬚⬚⬚⬚
Garden and grounds ⬚⬚⬚➡⬚⬚
Parking: on site.

Find out more: 01670 773600 or wallington@nationaltrust.org.uk

Wallington		M	T	W	T	F	S	S
Walled garden, woodland and estate*								
Open all year	10–6	M	T	W	T	F	S	S
House								
18 Feb–29 Oct	12–5	M	T	W	T	F	S	S
Shops and café**								
1 Jan–17 Feb	10:30–4:30	M	T	W	T	F	S	S
18 Feb–29 Oct	10:30–5:30	M	T	W	T	F	S	S
30 Oct–23 Dec	10:30–4:30	M	T	W	T	F	S	S
27 Dec–31 Dec	10:30–4:30			W	T	F	S	S

*Walled garden: closes 7 in summer; 4 in winter.
Woodland and estate: open 10 to dusk.
**Café: last orders 30 minutes before closing.

Wallington: something to delight, whatever the season

Washington Old Hall

The Avenue, Washington Village,
Washington, Tyne & Wear NE38 7LE

⬚⬚⬚⬚ 1956

Medieval Washington Old Hall in Tyne & Wear: historic manor house set within a tranquil garden

The name Washington is very important in world history. After all, the capital of the US wouldn't bear this name, if it wasn't for this little gem in North East England. You can visit the original medieval home of George Washington's ancestors at this historic manor house and tranquil garden.

Eat, shop, stay: light refreshments available in tea-room – hot and cold drinks, cakes and scones. Small seating area.

Things to see and do: **Indoors** Christmas events. **Outdoors** Wildlife-spotting in the Nuttery and school holiday nature investigator events. Fourth of July Independence Day ceremony. Open-air theatre by Pantaloons. **Dogs**: welcome on leads in garden only.

Access: ⬚⬚⬚⬚⬚⬚⬚
Building ⬚⬚ Grounds ⬚⬚➡
Parking: on site (additional unrestricted parking on The Avenue).

Find out more: 0191 416 6879 or washingtonoldhall@nationaltrust.org.uk

Washington Old Hall		M	T	W	T	F	S	S
25 Mar–24 Dec	10–4	M	T	W	T	F	S	S

Cymru Wales

Powis Castle and Garden, Powys
Competition entry from Paul Lane

Cemlyn and the North
Anglesey Coast

Holyhead

A55

LLANGEFNI

Plas Newydd House
and Gardens

Bangor

CAERNARFON

Segontium

Porthdinllaen

Craflwyn and
Beddgelert

Plas yn
Rhiw

Porthor

Porth Meudwy

Llanbedrog
Beach

Abersoch

Porth
y Swnt

Criccieth

Porthmadog

Bodysgallen
Hall Hotel,
Restaurant
and Spa

Llandudno   Conwy   Rhyl

Penrhyn
Castle

Conwy Suspension Bridge
Aberconwy House
Bodnant Garden

Ogwen Cottage

Carneddau and Glyderau

Ty Mawr Wybrnant

Hafod
y Llan

LIVERPOOL

The Beatles'
Childhood
Homes

M56

CHESTER

A494

A55

Wrexham

Erddig

Chirk Castle

Oswestry

Shrewsbury

Attingham
Park

Dolmelynllyn
Estate

DOLGELLAU

Machynlleth

A458

WELSHPOOL

Powis Castle
and Garden

Newtown

ABERYSTWYTH

A44

Llanerchaeron

Mwnt   Penbryn

Cardigan

Cilgerran Castle

St David's
Visitor
Centre
and Shop

Martin's
Haven

Marloes
Sands
and Mere

Pembroke

Tudor Merchant's
House

Colby
Woodland
Garden

CARMARTHEN

Paxton's
Tower

Dinefwr

Llanelli

SWANSEA

Stackpole

Stackpole
Outdoor
Learning
Centre

Rhossili
and South
Gower Coast

Pennard,
Pwll Du and
Bishopston
Valley

LLANDRINDOD
WELLS

Builth Wells

Dolaucothi
Estate
Woodland

Dolaucothi Gold Mines

Cwmdu

BRECON

Brecon
Beacons

Henrhyd Falls

Aberdulais
Tin Works
and Waterfall

Neath

Port Talbot

M4

Bridgend

Croft Castle
and Parkland

A456

Berrington
Hall

The Weir
Garden

HEREFORD

Skenfrith Castle

The Kymin

Merthyr
Tydfil

Tredegar House

NEWPORT

CARDIFF

Dyffryn Gardens

Chepstow

M48

M5

Places in neighbouring counties

West Midlands, page 260

North West, page 290

10 miles

Buildings and/or gardens

Entry points to
coast and countryside

National Trust land

H   Historic House Hotel

Aberconwy House

Castle Street, Conwy LL32 8AY

🏠 1934

This is the only medieval merchant's house in Conwy to have survived the turbulent history of the walled town over seven centuries. Furnished rooms and helpful volunteers bring different periods in its history alive. **Note**: nearest toilets 50 yards. Steps to all parts of property.

Eat, shop, stay: gift shop.

Things to see and do: Easter events. Father Christmas will be visiting in December. **Dogs**: assistance dogs only.

Access: 🅿 Building 🦽
Parking: none on site.

Find out more: 01492 592246 or aberconwyhouse@nationaltrust.org.uk

Aberconwy House		M	T	W	T	F	S	S
House								
8 Mar–5 Nov	10–5	M	T	W	T	F	S	S
11 Nov–24 Dec	11–4	.	.	.	.	.	S	S
Shop								
1 Jan–28 Feb	11–5	.	T	W	T	F	S	S
1 Mar–31 Dec	10–5	M	T	W	T	F	S	S

House and shop closed 25 December.

Aberconwy House, Conwy's sole surviving medieval house

Mae'r wybodaeth sydd yn y llawlyfr hwn am feddiannau'r Ymddiriedolaeth Genedlaethol yng Nghymru ar gael yn Gymraeg o Swyddfa'r Ymddiriedolaeth Genedlaethol, Tŷ Tredegar, Casnewydd, NP10 8YW, neu drwy e-bostio wa.customerenquiries@nationaltrust.org.uk

Aberdulais Tin Works and Waterfall

Aberdulais, Neath, Neath Port Talbot SA10 8EU

🏠🏛️♿🍽️ 1980

Aberdulais Tin Works and Waterfall, Neath Port Talbot: the force and power of the water never fails to fascinate

If you like archaeology, you'll love some of the secrets that have been uncovered here at Aberdulais – one of Britain's oldest tin works. As you wander through the site, you'll find yourself at the very heart of the earliest industry in Britain. You'll also discover how Aberdulais played its part in shaping the world as we know it today. If you think you've seen Aberdulais before, think again – we've made new discoveries and we're dying to share them with you. We aim to enthral and fascinate all ages... Whoever thought history could be so much fun? **Note**: waterwheel and turbine subject to water levels and conservation work.

Eat, shop, stay: Old School House tea-room serving light lunches, soup, cakes and refreshments. Gift shop and second-hand bookshop.

Things to see and do: programme of activities throughout the year, including behind the scenes and handling collections, Victorian games and Victorian Christmas.

The tin works at Aberdulais are among the very oldest in Britain

Enjoy Italianate terraces with roses, herbaceous beds and parterres, shaded shrub borders and the drama of The Dell, with its waterfalls and towering conifers. Every season brings new delights – magnolias and rhododendrons in spring, roses and water lilies in summer, rich leaf colour in autumn and frosted landscapes in winter. You can explore the Winter Garden, Old Park meadow, Yew Dell and Far End, plus the spring-opening Furnace Hill and Meadow.

Eat, shop, stay: two tea-rooms, as well as two open-air refreshment kiosks. Picnic areas. Shop. Neighbouring garden centre and craft units (not National Trust).

Things to see and do: events all year, including guided walks with a gardener, family trails and holiday activities for children. **Dogs**: welcome daily January, February, November, December. May to August, Wednesday evenings (5 to 8).

Dogs: welcome on leads and inside buildings. Assistance dogs only in the Schoolhouse tea-room.

Access: ⊞⊞⊞⊞⊞⊞⊞
Stable and Tin Exhibition ⊞⊞⊞
Turbine House ⊞⊞⊞⊞⊞
Grounds ⊞⊞⊞➡⊞
Sat Nav: follow brown signs.
Parking: 50 yards.

Find out more: 01639 636674 or aberdulais@nationaltrust.org.uk

Aberdulais		M	T	W	T	F	S	S
7 Jan–19 Feb	11–4						S	S
20 Feb–31 Mar	11–4	M	T	W	T	F	S	S
1 Apr–3 Sep	10:30–5	M	T	W	T	F	S	S
4 Sep–5 Nov	11–4	M	T	W	T	F	S	S
10 Nov–17 Dec	11–4					F	S	S

Tea-room opening times vary (contact property for details).

Access: ⊞⊞⊞⊞⊞⊞⊞⊞
Grounds ⊞➡⊞
Parking: 150 yards.

Find out more: 01492 650460 or bodnantgarden@nationaltrust.org.uk

Bodnant Garden		M	T	W	T	F	S	S
1 Jan–28 Feb	10–4	M	T	W	T	F	S	S
1 Mar–30 Apr	10–5	M	T	W	T	F	S	S
1 May–30 Jun	9–5	M	T	W	T	F	S	S
1 Jul–31 Oct	10–5	M	T	W	T	F	S	S
1 Nov–23 Dec	10–4	M	T	W	T	F	S	S
27 Dec–31 Dec	10–4			W	T	F	S	S

Garden open until 8 on Wednesdays from May to August.

One family's vision, Bodnant Garden in Conwy, right and below: horticultural styles range from the formal to pastoral, and the wild to exotic

Bodnant Garden

Tal-y-Cafn, near Colwyn Bay, Conwy LL28 5RE

⊞ ⊞ ⊞ 1949

In Snowdonia's foothills this 32-hectare (80-acre) garden features scenery, plant collections and horticultural styles from formal to pastoral, and wild to exotic. One family's vision, the garden was established in 1874 by Victorian entrepreneur Henry Pochin, who transformed the landscape with rare trees and shrubs from around the world.

Bodysgallen Hall Hotel, Restaurant and Spa

The Royal Welsh Way,
Llandudno, Conwy LL30 1RS

🏠❄️🛏️🔔🍷 2008

This Grade I listed 17th-century house, set within 89 hectares (220 acres) of parkland, has the most spectacular views towards Conwy Castle and Snowdonia. The romantic gardens, which have won awards for their restoration, include a rare parterre filled with sweet-smelling herbs, as well as several follies, cascade, walled garden and formal rose gardens. Beyond, the hotel's parkland offers miles of stunning walks and views to the coastline. **Note**: access is for paying guests of the hotel, including for luncheon, afternoon tea and dinner, and the Spa. Children over the age of six welcome.

Find out more: 01492 584466. 01492 582519 (fax) or info@bodysgallen.com bodysgallen.com

Brecon Beacons

Powys

🏠🏛️🛏️ 1936

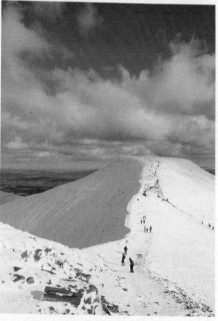

The Brecon Beacons, Sugar Loaf and Skirrid have captivated visitors for hundreds of years with their soaring mountain peaks and tranquil valleys. With lush farmland, ancient moorland and southern Britain's highest mountain, Pen y Fan, they are perfect for hill-walking and exploring hidden streams and woodlands. By contrast, Clytha Estate is a great place to have a picnic or take a short walk, meandering through parkland with views of Clytha House and Castle. In the heart of Wales you can discover the vast, remote moorlands of Abergwesyn Commons or ramble over the Begwns with panoramic views of the Brecon Beacons. **Note**: only toilets at Pont ar Daf car park in the Brecon Beacons.

From soaring mountain peaks to tranquil valleys, a trip to the Brecon Beacons, Powys, above and top, never fails to captivate and thrill visitors

Things to see and do: **Indoors** Bunkhouse near Pen y Fan. **Outdoors** Family activities throughout the year, including Wild Wednesdays at the Sugar Loaf in the school holidays. Why not visit Dinefwr or The Kymin? **Dogs**: welcome on leads.

Access: 🦽
Sat Nav: use LD3 8NL. **Parking**: main car park at Pont ar Daf, off A470; alternatives not all National Trust.

Find out more: 01874 625515 or brecon@nationaltrust.org.uk

Carneddau and Glyderau

Nant Ffrancon, Bethesda, Gwynedd

⚊📷 1951

This 8,498-hectare (21,000-acre) mountainous area includes Cwm Idwal National Nature Reserve, renowned for its geology and Arctic-Alpine plants, such as the rare Snowdon lily. There are eight tenanted upland farms here and nine peaks over 3,000 feet, including the famous Tryfan, where Edmund Hilary trained for his ascent of Everest. The area is home to a variety of wildlife, including otters, feral ponies and rare birds, such as dotterel and peregrine. The 60 miles of footpaths attract 500,000 walkers each year, while the bleak, photogenic landscapes have proved popular with artists. **Note**: mountainous and difficult terrain – please come well equipped and check the weather. Charges apply in the National Park car parks.

Eat, shop, stay: Ogwen has a café and Ranger base, as well as a warden centre run in partnership with Snowdonia National Park and Natural Resources Wales. Two holiday cottages in Dyffryn Mymbyr.

Things to see and do: you can walk to Cwm Idwal and enjoy dramatic mountain views, following in the footsteps of Charles Darwin (who 'discovered' glaciation here). Visit Ogwen Ranger base for more information. **Dogs**: on a lead at all times.

Access: 🦽
Sat Nav: use LL57 3LZ.
Parking: at Ogwen Lake (not National Trust).

Find out more: 01248 605739 or carneddau@nationaltrust.org.uk

With 60 miles of footpaths, peaks of more than 3,000 feet and wildlife galore, the bleak photogenic landscapes of Carneddau and Glyderau, Gwynedd, are irresistible to walkers and artists alike

Cemlyn and the North Anglesey Coast

Cemaes Bay, Anglesey

✚ 🖼 🏠 ♿ 🎒 🛶 🚻 🚽 | 1971 |

Ruggedly beautiful, the north coast of Anglesey has a unique coastline of rocks, small bays and headlands and is a delight for walkers. Cemlyn is recognised for its National Nature Reserve and is a designated Area of Outstanding Natural Beauty and home to the rare spotted rock rose. Renowned for its breeding colonies of Sandwich, common and Arctic terns, Cemlyn Bay is a hive of seabird activity in spring and summer.

Headland paths offer dramatic land and seascapes during autumn and winter. The brackish lagoon is separated from the sea by a remarkable shingle ridge. **Note**: nearest toilets in Cemaes Bay, 3 miles (not National Trust).

Things to see and do: numerous footpaths and downloadable walks to help you explore. Events, including pram walks and walking festival. Summer fair at Swtan, a restored whitewashed cottage nearby (LL65 4EU). **Dogs**: welcome under control near livestock.

Access: ♿
Sat Nav: use LL67 0DY.
Parking: at Bryn Aber car park, Cemlyn.

Find out more: 01248 714795 or cemlyn@nationaltrust.org.uk

Cemlyn and the North Anglesey Coast, Anglesey: outstandingly beautiful National Nature Reserve

Chirk Castle

Chirk, Wrexham LL14 5AF

History comes alive at Chirk Castle, as children learn about the life, and armour, of medieval knights

Completed by Marcher Lord Roger Mortimer in 1310, Chirk is the last Welsh castle from the reign of Edward I still inhabited today. You can explore medieval towers and dungeons, visit the 17th- and 18th-century rooms of the Myddelton family home, including the historic laundry, and discover the story of influential 20th-century tenant and polymath Lord Howard de Walden. The prized gardens contain clipped yews, herbaceous borders and rock gardens. A terrace gives stunning views over the Cheshire and Shropshire plains, while the large estate, divided by King Offa's Dyke, provides habitat for rare invertebrates, wild flowers and veteran trees.

Eat, shop, stay: tea-room serving hot and cold food, drinks and cakes. Seasonal kiosk at Home Farm selling hot and cold drinks and snacks. Gift shops in Home Farm and courtyard, with plant sales and second-hand books. Two holiday cottages on the estate.

Chirk Castle, Wrexham: the hawk-house in the garden

Things to see and do: Indoors Medieval fortress and dungeon, Myddelton family home, Servants' Hall and Victorian laundry to explore. **Outdoors** There are the formal gardens and 194-hectare (480-acre) estate to discover.

Dogs: welcome on leads. Assistance dogs only in formal gardens and Pleasure Ground wood.

Access:
State rooms Adam Tower
Gardens
Parking: at Home Farm by ticket office, then 200 yards (via steep hill) to castle.

Find out more: 01691 777701 or chirkcastle@nationaltrust.org.uk

Chirk Castle		M	T	W	T	F	S	S
Estate								
Open all year*	7–7	M	T	W	T	F	S	S
Garden, shop and tea-room**								
28 Jan–31 Mar	10–4	M	T	W	T	F	S	S
1 Apr–30 Sep	10–5	M	T	W	T	F	S	S
1 Oct–5 Nov	10–4	M	T	W	T	F	S	S
11 Nov–26 Nov	10–4						S	S
2 Dec–23 Dec	10–4	M	T	W	T	F	S	S
State rooms								
28 Jan–26 Feb†	12–4						S	S
1 Mar–31 Mar††	12–4	M	T	W	T	F	S	S
1 Apr–30 Sep††	12–5	M	T	W	T	F	S	S
1 Oct–5 Nov††	12–4	M	T	W	T	F	S	S
11 Nov–26 Nov†	12–4						S	S
2 Dec–23 Dec	11–4	M	T	W	T	F	S	S

*Estate open to 9, June to August.
**Tower and dungeon open as garden.
†Access by guided tour only, timed tickets available on day (places limited). ††Guided tours 11:15 and 11:30 (places limited).

Cilgerran Castle

near Cardigan, Pembrokeshire SA43 2SF

| 1938 |

13th-century castle overlooking the Teifi Gorge – the perfect location to repel attackers. Walk the walls and admire the stunning views. **Note**: in the guardianship of Cadw – Welsh Government's historic environment service. Dogs welcome on leads. Open daily, 2 January to 31 March, 10 to 4; 1 April to 31 October, 10 to 5; 1 November to 31 December, 10 to 4 (closed 24 to 26 December).

Find out more: 01239 621339 or cilgerrancastle@nationaltrust.org.uk

Colby Woodland Garden

near Amroth, Pembrokeshire SA67 8PP

| 1980 |

A short walk from the beach, this hidden wooded valley, with its secret garden and industrial past, is a place for play. There are fallen trees to climb, rope swings and playful surprises everywhere. Spring brings bluebells, camellias, rhododendrons and azaleas, while

Pond-dipping at Colby Woodland Garden, Pembrokeshire: this hidden wooded valley offers so much to discover

the walled garden gives year-round colour, peace and seclusion. There are woodland walks, meandering streams and ponds with stepping stones and log bridges in the wildflower meadow, and the whole valley teems with wildlife. Fun learning activities and exploration packs are available, and there are picnic and campfire spots in the meadow and free games to borrow. **Note**: house not open.

Eat, shop, stay: shop, second-hand books and plant sales. Bothy tea-room (concession). Gallery selling Pembrokeshire arts and crafts. Picnics welcome. Three holiday cottages nearby.

Things to see and do: rope swings, den-building, pond-dipping, camp fires, duck racing, activity sheets, exploration packs and games equipment. Virtual tour and film. Easter trails, wildlife events and holiday activities. **Dogs**: on leads in woodland garden and meadow.

The meandering streams at Colby Woodland Garden provide ample specimens for budding naturalists

Access: 🅿️ 🅿️ 🚻 🔖 📷 🎥 ✏️ 📷
Grounds 🔖 ➡️ ♿
Parking: 50 yards.

Find out more: 01834 811885 or colby@nationaltrust.org.uk

Colby Woodland Garden		M	T	W	T	F	S	S
Woodland and walled gardens*								
3 Jan–17 Feb	10–3	M	T	W	T	F	S	S
18 Feb–29 Oct	10–5	M	T	W	T	F	S	S
30 Oct–22 Dec	10–3	M	T	W	T	F	S	S
Shop								
18 Feb–29 Oct	10–5	M	T	W	T	F	S	S
Gallery and tea-room								
8 Apr–29 Oct	10–4:30	M	T	W	T	F	S	S

*Car park and bothy exhibition open as woodland and walled gardens. Closed 24 to 31 December and 1 January 2018.

Conwy Suspension Bridge

Conwy LL32 8LD

🏠 ⚓ 1965

Designed in the 1820s by Thomas Telford, this graceful bridge with its beautifully restored tiny toll-keeper's house has stunning views over the Conwy Estuary. Kept open by a husband and wife at a time when trade and travel brought Conwy to life, it never closed, whatever the weather. **Note**: sorry no toilet.

Eat, shop, stay: why not bring a picnic to enjoy on the grassed area?

Things to see and do: superb views of the river and castle. **Dogs**: allowed.

Access: Building 🏠 Grounds ♿
Parking: none on site.

Find out more: 01492 573282 or conwybridge@nationaltrust.org.uk

---

Conwy Suspension Bridge
Open 8 March to 5 November. Toll House opening times available at Aberconwy House (01492 592246).

The grace and elegance of Conwy Suspension Bridge, Conwy, belie its immense strength

Craflwyn and Beddgelert

near Beddgelert, Gwynedd

🏛 📷 1994

Craflwyn and Beddgelert, Gwynedd: this beautiful Snowdonian landscape is steeped in history and legend

The 81-hectare (200-acre) Craflwyn Estate is set in the heart of beautiful Snowdonia, within a landscape steeped in history and legend. There's a network of paths and woodland walks to explore and tumbling waterfalls to discover. At Craflwyn you can learn about the Princes of Gwynedd before venturing up to nearby Dinas Emrys, the legendary birthplace of Wales's national emblem, the red dragon. Within a couple of miles of Craflwyn, there are great walks for all abilities, from a village stroll at pretty Beddgelert to the rugged Fisherman's Path down the spectacular Aberglaslyn Pass. **Note**: Craflwyn Hall is run and managed by HF Holidays (surrounding land open to the public).

Eat, shop, stay: picnics welcome at Craflwyn. Local crafts on offer in Tŷ Isaf shop in Beddgelert. The village also has a selection of restaurants, cafés, taverns and hotels (not National Trust). Holiday cottage, chalet and campsite at Hafod y Llan.

A torrent of water sweeps down between rocky wooded banks at Craflwyn and Beddgelert

Things to see and do: you can learn about Prince Llywelyn's legendary faithful hound by visiting Gelert's Grave. Children's adventure packs, maps and guides available from Tŷ Isaf shop in the centre of the village. **Dogs**: welcome under control near livestock.

Access: ♿
Sat Nav: use LL55 4NG. **Parking**: in Craflwyn.

Find out more: 01766 510120 or craflwyn@nationaltrust.org.uk

Cwmdu

Llandeilo, Carmarthenshire

✚ 🍴 🛏 1991

Georgian terrace with pub, post office, chapel and vestry. Representing a rural Welsh village of the past. **Note**: pub and shop run by community. For Sat Nav use SA19 7DY. Pub open 7 to 11, Wednesday to Saturday, 4 January to 30 December. Shop and post office open 9:30 to 1:30, Tuesday to Saturday, 3 January to 30 December (both close 12:30 on Saturdays).

Find out more: 01558 685088 or cwmdu@nationaltrust.org.uk

Dinefwr

Llandeilo, Carmarthenshire SA19 6RT

🏠🏰✚🏛🛋❀🐑🌳🛏🔔🍴 1990

A place of legends and folklore, Dinefwr's long history has featured power, glory, downfall and loss. There is even a direct link with the past through our iconic White Park cattle, which have been kept here for 1,000 years. Walks lead through ancient woods, with gnarled veteran trees, and you can seek the inhabitants of the Bogwood and Mill Pond and walk in the footsteps of medieval princes – viewing 'your kingdom' from the castle on the hill. After exploring the tranquil countryside, you can continue your adventure in atmospheric Newton House, discovering the many changes the years have wrought. **Note**: Dinefwr Castle is owned by the Wildlife Trust and is in the guardianship of Cadw.

Eat, shop, stay: Billiard tea-room (fully licensed). Castle Walk Café serving simple fare to parkland walkers, dogs welcome. Inner courtyard with a gift shop and plant sales. Pre-loved bookshop. China Passage art gallery showcasing local artwork for sale.

Places may occasionally close for events or bad weather

Things to see and do: Indoors Daily 'hidden house' tours. **Outdoors** Seasonal tours of parkland National Nature Reserve. Tractor trailer tours of estate and White Park cattle (summer). School holiday and family activities. Holiday cottages. **Dogs:** welcome in outer park on leads (cattle/sheep grazing). Not permitted in the deer-park.

Access: 🅿♿🚶♿🚻🍽♿🐕⚲
Newton House 🏠♿↕🍽♿
Castle 🏰🍽 Parkland 🚶♿➡
Sat Nav: enter Dinefwr. **Parking:** 50 yards.

Find out more: 01558 824512 or dinefwr@nationaltrust.org.uk

Dinefwr		M	T	W	T	F	S	S
Parkland and tea-room*								
1 Jan–31 Mar	10–4	M	T	W	T	F	S	S
1 Apr–2 Nov	10–6	M	T	W	T	F	S	S
3 Nov–31 Dec	10–4	M	T	W	T	F	S	S
Newton House and shop**								
6 Jan–26 Mar	10–4	·	·	·	·	F	S	S
27 Mar–29 Oct	10–6	M	T	W	T	F	S	S
3 Nov–31 Dec	10–4	·	·	·	·	F	S	S

*Boardwalk and deer-park: close one hour earlier. Newton House: last admission one hour before closing; house and shop open daily during school holidays. **Billiard tea-room: last orders 30 minutes after last house admission. Cadw manages Dinefwr Castle and may alter opening times. Whole property closed 24 and 25 December.

Dinefwr, Carmarthenshire: atmospheric Newton House

Dolaucothi Estate Woodland

near Pumsaint, Llanwrda, Carmarthenshire

🏠♿🏠♿🏕 1944

Hours of woodland walks and a multi-user trail with route information in Dolaucothi Gold Mine visitor reception. **Note:** for Sat Nav use SA19 8US.

Find out more: 01558 650809 or dolaucothi@nationaltrust.org.uk

Dolaucothi Gold Mines

Pumsaint, Llanwrda, Carmarthenshire SA19 8US

🏠♿🏠♿🏕 1941

Not your average National Trust visit, this hidden gem reveals the story of the quest for gold more than 2,000 years ago. You too can try your luck by panning for gold, and anything you find you keep. Or you can venture on an overground tour of the Roman archaeology, go underground to experience the harsh conditions of Victorian times and listen to what 1930s miners had to say in their very own words about their final efforts to search for gold.

Join the hunt for that most elusive of precious metals at Dolaucothi Gold Mines in Carmarthenshire

Would-be 'miners' prepare to go underground at Dolaucothi Gold Mines

Why not join us for the ultimate adventure and discover centuries of stories in just one day? **Note**: steep slopes, stout enclosed footwear essential. Minimum height, no carried children on underground tours. Caravan park on site; pitch charges (including members).

Eat, shop, stay: tea-room (concession) offering light refreshments. Shop specialising in Welsh gold jewellery and gifts. Dolaucothi Arms (tenant-run) offering food and accommodation. Picnic tables in the mine yard.

Things to see and do: **Outdoors** Underground guided tours throughout the day and overground self-guided audio tour of Roman workings. 1930s machinery sheds. Children's trails. Walks around woodland estate. **Dogs**: welcome on leads, although not on guided tours.

Access: 🅿 🅿 ♿ 🏠 🦽 ⬇ 🎧 Tea-rooms ♿ Machinery sheds ♿ Mine yard ♿ ➡
Parking: on site; overflow car park opposite main entrance.

Find out more: 01558 650809 or dolaucothi@nationaltrust.org.uk

Dolaucothi Gold Mines		M	T	W	T	F	S	S
17 Mar–30 Jun	10:30–5	M	T	W	T	F	S	S
1 Jul–31 Aug	10–6	M	T	W	T	F	S	S
1 Sep–5 Nov	10:30–5	M	T	W	T	F	S	S

Shop: opens 11. Caravan Park: open daily, dawn to dusk, 16 March to 5 November.

Dolmelynllyn Estate

near Dolgellau, Gwynedd

🏞 🚶 🛏 1936

Dolmelynllyn Estate covers 696 hectares (1,719 acres) and includes two tenanted farms, with the remaining woodland managed by the Trust. Dolmelynllyn Hall is Grade II listed, with well-preserved formal gardens, an ornamental lake and parkland. The grounds also include a walled kitchen garden and Britain's largest bee-bole wall. Barmouth is a short drive away (12 miles), where you can visit Dinas Oleu, the first parcel of land donated to the Trust by Mrs Fanny Talbot in 1895. From here you can enjoy lovely coastal views over the Mawddach Estuary. **Note**: Dolmelynllyn Hall is a privately run hotel, not a pay-to-enter property.

Eat, shop, stay: four holiday cottages nearby. Two National Trust-owned but tenanted hotels on the estate offering refreshments and light meals. Picnic site.

Things to see and do: estate walks leaflet guides visitors around the more interesting parts of the estate, such as Rhaeadr Ddu waterfall, Cefn Coch gold mines and the wildlife-rich oak woodlands.
Dogs: welcome on leads.

Access: [符]
Sat Nav: use LL40 2TF. **Parking**: on site.

Find out more: 01341 440238 or dolmelynllyn@nationaltrust.org.uk

Once someone's home – a ruined house on the
Dolmelynllyn Estate, Gwynedd, below.
Above, water tumbles and cascades down over rocks

Dyffryn Gardens

St Nicholas, Vale of Glamorgan CF5 6SU

[符][❋][2012]

Colourful displays of flowers light up the borders at Dyffryn Gardens, Vale of Glamorgan

A garden for all seasons, celebrated for its botanical collection, among the best in Wales. Meandering through the gardens, you will discover intimate garden rooms, formal lawns, and an extensive arboretum. The reinstated glasshouse in the kitchen garden houses an impressive collection of rare cacti and orchids. Designed by the eminent landscape architect Thomas Mawson, the gardens are the early 20th-century vision of Reginald Cory. Dyffryn House stands at the heart of the garden. This Grade II* listed house was built as a gallery from which to view the landscape. Partially restored, the house is used as a blank canvas to interpret the gardens and Cory family history.

Eat, shop, stay: tea-room serving kitchen garden produce, including an edible-flower menu in the summer and hearty soups in the autumn. Shop selling plants and gifts.

Things to see and do: network of garden rooms and champion trees in the arboretum to discover. Family events and play area. Tredegar House nearby. **Dogs**: welcome on short leads.

Access: ⓟ⌷⌷⌷⌷ House ⌷⌷
Grounds ⌷⌷⌷⌷⌷⌷
Sat Nav: use CF5 6ST. **Parking**: on site.

Find out more: 02920 593328 or dyffryn@nationaltrust.org.uk

From the formality of the partially restored house and terrace, above, to the informality of splashing in puddles, below, Dyffryn Gardens provides something for everyone

Dyffryn Gardens		M	T	W	T	F	S	S
Gardens, shop and café								
1 Jan–26 Feb	10–4	M	T	W	T	F	S	S
27 Feb–2 Apr	10–5	M	T	W	T	F	S	S
3 Apr–24 Sep	10–6	M	T	W	T	F	S	S
25 Sep–29 Oct	10–5	M	T	W	T	F	S	S
30 Oct–31 Dec*	10–4	M	T	W	T	F	S	S
House								
1 Jan–26 Feb	12–3				T	F	S	S
2 Mar–2 Apr	12–4				T	F	S	S
3 Apr–24 Sep	12–4:30	M	T	W	T	F	S	S
28 Sep–29 Oct	12–4				T	F	S	S
2 Nov–31 Dec*	12–3				T	F	S	S

Last admission one hour before closing. Café: last orders 30 minutes before closing. *Closed 25 and 26 December.

Erddig

Wrexham LL13 0YT

🏠✚🏛♿🐾 1973

Sitting on a dramatic escarpment above the winding Clywedog river, Erddig tells the 250-year story of a gentry family's relationship with its servants. A large collection of servants' portraits and carefully preserved rooms capture their lives in the early 20th century, while upstairs is a treasure trove of fine furniture, textiles and wallpapers. Outdoors lies a fully restored 18th-century garden, with trained fruit trees, exuberant annual herbaceous borders, avenues of pleached limes, formal hedges and a nationally important collection of ivies. The 486-hectare (1,200-acre) landscape pleasure park, designed by William Emes, is a haven of peace and natural beauty, perfect for riverside picnics. Discover the 'cup and saucer' cylindrical cascade or explore the earthworks of a Norman motte-and-bailey castle.

Autumnal fun at Erddig in Wrexham. The extensive gardens and grounds are perfect for letting off steam

Eat, shop, stay: you can enjoy lunch in the Hayloft restaurant, light bites in the café and tea-garden, or fresh coffee in Wolf's Den on busy days. Don't forget to visit our gift shop and second-hand bookshop before leaving.

Things to see and do: **Indoors** Discover how generations of the Yorke family took an almost curatorial attitude to their possessions, bequeathing one of the largest, most diverse and fragile collections in the National Trust.

It is easy to imagine the day-to-day life of a domestic servant in the fully equipped kitchen at Erddig

The perfect spot for tea at Erddig

Outdoors Year-long programme, including spring displays, atmospheric open-air theatre evenings, Christmas and Easter trails, garden tours, orienteering and guided estate walks. Regular sporting activities on the estate include Nordic walking, beginner running groups and buggy walks. Children can let off steam in the Wolf's Den natural play area and fly on the rope swing, climb the obstacles or enjoy building dens. **Dogs**: welcome in country park, but not allowed in the house, garden and play area.

Access: 🅿️📷♿🚾🍴📹🎧🚪♿
Building ♿♿ **Grounds** ♿♿♿
Sat Nav: do not use, follow brown signs.
Parking: on site, 200 yards from ticket office.

Find out more: 01978 355314 or erddig@nationaltrust.org.uk

Erddig		M	T	W	T	F	S	S
House								
18 Feb–24 Mar*	11:30–2:30	M	T	W	T	F	S	S
25 Mar–29 Oct	12:30–3:30	M	T	W	T	F	S	S
30 Oct–31 Dec*	11:30–2:30	M	T	W	T	F	S	S
Garden, restaurant and shop**								
1 Jan–24 Mar	11–4	M	T	W	T	F	S	S
25 Mar–29 Oct†	10–5	M	T	W	T	F	S	S
30 Oct–31 Dec	11–4	M	T	W	T	F	S	S

*Ground floor servants' quarters only. Hourly tours weekdays and self-guided during school holidays and weekends.
**Natural play area open as garden, but closed weekdays, 1 January to 17 February. †Open until 9 every Saturday, 29 July to 26 August. Closed 25 December. Timed tickets operate on Bank Holidays and during busy periods.

Hafod y Llan

near Beddgelert, Gwynedd

♿🍴🛏️⛺ 1998

Hafod y Llan, in the beautiful Nantgwynant Valley, is the largest farm run by the National Trust, part of which is designated a National Nature Reserve and a Site of Special Scientific Interest. It extends from the valley floor to the summit of Snowdon and visitors are free to wander the many paths which cross this unique landscape. **Note**: as this is a working farm, access to the farmyard is by foot only.

Eat, shop, stay: holiday cottage, chalet and campsite on the farm. Refreshments available at nearby Caffi Gwynant (not National Trust).

Things to see and do: a network of paths cross Hafod y Llan, including a low-level adventure trail. At the farm entrance the Watkin Path leads to the summit of Snowdon. **Dogs**: welcome on leads.

Visitors are free to wander the many paths through Hafod y Llan, Gwynedd: the largest farm run by the Trust

Spectacular Henrhyd Falls in Powys: the highest waterfall in South Wales

Access: 🏃
Sat Nav: use SA10 9PH.
Parking: adjoining property.

Find out more: 01874 625515 or henrhydfalls@nationaltrust.org.uk

Hafod y Llan extends from the floor of the Nantgwynant Valley to the summit of Snowdon

Access: 🏃
Sat Nav: use LL55 4NQ. **Parking**: on farm for campsite only. Car park near farm entrance for the Watkin Path (not National Trust).

Find out more: 01766 890473 or hafodyllan@nationaltrust.org.uk

Henrhyd Falls

Coelbren, Powys

🖼 1947

The highest waterfall in South Wales at 90 feet, Henrhyd Falls plunges down into the wooded Graig Llech Gorge – a haven for damp-loving wildlife. An adventurous walk takes you to the falls and down the Nant Llech Valley, passing the site of a disused watermill – the Melin Llech. **Note**: sorry no toilet. Steep descent to waterfall.

Things to see and do: downloadable walk. Additional walk information available locally. Why not visit nearby Brecon Beacons and Aberdulais Tin Works and Waterfall? **Dogs**: welcome on leads.

The Kymin

Monmouth, Monmouthshire NP25 3SF

🖼🖼🔔🍷 1902

Lord Nelson and Lady Hamilton were delighted with this Georgian banqueting house and Naval Temple when they visited in 1802. The Kymin is still a great spot from which to enjoy panoramic views of the Brecon Beacons and Wye Valley. The woods and pleasure grounds are also perfect for picnics. **Note**: road access difficult.

The Kymin, Monmouthshire: this Georgian banqueting house delighted Lord Nelson and Lady Hamilton

Eat, shop, stay: cold drinks and snacks available when the Round House is open. Picnics welcome.

Things to see and do: **Indoors** Our friendly guides offer a taste of a Georgian gentleman's picnic. **Outdoors** Self-guided walks, featuring bluebells in spring. Children's nature quiz and special events throughout the year.
Dogs: welcome in Round House and grounds.

Access: ⓟ ⓓ 🅰 Round House 🦽 🏛
Naval Temple 🏛 Grounds ➡
Parking: limited (narrow lane, single-lane traffic, few passing places).

Find out more: 01600 719241 or kymin@nationaltrust.org.uk

The Kymin			M	T	W	T	F	S	S
Round House									
25 Mar–30 Oct	11–4		M	·	·	·	·	S	S
Grounds									
Open all year	7–9		M	T	W	T	F	S	S

Open Good Friday. Car park open during daylight hours only.

Llanbedrog Beach

Llanbedrog, Gwynedd

🏖 2000

Best known for its colourful beach huts, this wonderful stretch of sand has been enjoyed by generations. Its sheltered waters, fantastic

Small sandy steps at Llanbedrog Beach in Gwynedd

Famed for its warm sheltered waters, craggy landscape and fabulous views, Llanbedrog Beach is a real gem

views over Cardigan Bay and adjacent wooded and craggy landscape make this a real gem of Llŷn. **Note**: toilet (not National Trust).

Eat, shop, stay: shops and cafés at Llanbedrog and at nearby Pwllheli and Abersoch (not National Trust).

Things to see and do: events during summer months. Children's adventure packs, maps and guides available at car park welcome cabin. Beach huts available to hire. **Dogs**: welcome.

Access: 🦽
Sat Nav: use LL53 7TT. **Parking**: on site.

Find out more: 01758 740561 or llanbedrog@nationaltrust.org.uk

Llanerchaeron

Ciliau Aeron, near Aberaeron,
Ceredigion SA48 8DG

🏠🌿♻️🛶🐟🔔🍷 1989

A self-sufficient 18th-century Welsh minor gentry estate. The villa, designed in the 1790s, is the most complete example of the early work of John Nash. It has its own service courtyard with dairy, laundry, brewery and salting house, giving a full 'upstairs, downstairs' experience. The walled kitchen gardens, pleasure grounds, ornamental lake and parkland offer peaceful walks, while the Home Farm complex has an impressive range of traditional, atmospheric outbuildings. A working farm, there are Welsh Black cattle, Llanwenog sheep and rare Welsh pigs as well as chickens, geese and doves. Woodland walks available.

Eat, shop, stay: café serving light meals and cakes (not National Trust). Picnic site. Fresh garden produce and plants, farm meat, local crafts, art, gifts and books for sale. Second-hand bookshop. Two holiday cottages nearby.

Things to see and do: activities during local school holidays, including crafts, gardening, nature activities and self-led trails. Special events days. Cycle hire. **Dogs**: welcome on the woodland walks and in the parkland on leads.

Access: 🅿️♿️🐕🐑🐄📷🚻🚶📖⠿
Visitor building ♿️🚻 Villa 🚶♿️🚻
Grounds ♿️➡️🚻
Parking: 50 yards.

Find out more: 01545 570200 or
llanerchaeron@nationaltrust.org.uk

Llanerchaeron in Ceredigion: the villa, left, is the most complete example of the early work of John Nash. Above, young visitors get into the spirit of the age, with the help of dressing-up clothes

Llanerchaeron		M	T	W	T	F	S	S
Whole property								
18 Feb–26 Feb	11:30–3:30	M	T	W	T	F	S	S
18 Mar–5 Nov*	10:30–5:30	M	T	W	T	F	S	S
Farm and shop**								
1 Jan–12 Feb	11:30–3:30						S	S
27 Feb–17 Mar	11:30–3:30	M	T	W	T	F	S	S
6 Nov–31 Dec†	11:30–3:30	M	T	W	T	F	S	S

Last admission one hour before closing. *Villa opens 11:30. **Garden and woodland walk open as farm. †Closed 24 to 26 December. Geler Jones Rural Life Collection open 12 to 4, Wednesday and Friday, 22 March to 3 November. Parkland and woodland walks open daily.

Marloes Sands and Mere

Marloes, Pembrokeshire

🏛️ 🚶 🐦 1941

Marloes Sands and Mere, Pembrokeshire: perfect for beach games and so much more

A hidden gem, this long sandy stretch is perfect for making a splash, spotting marine life on the shore and gorgeous coastal walks. Just inland you'll find Marloes Mere, a wetland bustling with birdlife. Bring along the binoculars and get closer to nature at our on-site bird hides. **Note**: nearest toilets by Runwayskiln farm, alongside track from the car park to Marloes Mere.

Eat, shop, stay: information point at Martin's Haven. Shop, café and pub in nearby Marloes village (not National Trust).

Things to see and do: for rock-pooling, birdwatching and getting closer to nature why not pick up a nature discovery Tracker Pack (available from the car park)? **Dogs**: welcome under close control.

Access: 🚻 👤 ➡️
Sat Nav: use SA62 3BH. **Parking**: on site.

Find out more: 01348 837860 or marloessands@nationaltrust.org.uk

Martin's Haven

near Marloes, Pembrokeshire

🏛️ 🚶 🐦 🐾 ⛺ 1981

The gateway to Skomer Island and a fabulously wild headland with fine panoramic views of St Bride's Bay. For a really varied and exciting day, why not combine spotting marine wildlife with discovering traces of ancient settlements? **Note**: nearest toilets by the slipway.

Eat, shop, stay: information point at Martin's Haven. Shop, café and pub in nearby Marloes village (not National Trust). Holiday cottages nearby.

Things to see and do: nature discovery Tracker Packs, available from car park, for rock-pooling, birdwatching and getting closer to nature.
Dogs: welcome under close control.

Access: 🅿️ 🚶 ➡️
Sat Nav: use SA62 3BJ. **Parking**: on site.

Find out more: 01348 837860 or martinshaven@nationaltrust.org.uk

The water's edge and rocky outcrops at Martin's Haven in Pembrokeshire, above and below, are ideal for spotting marine wildlife

Mwnt

near Cardigan, Ceredigion

✝️ 🏖️ 🏛️ 1963

Beautiful secluded bay with a sandy beach – perfect for spotting dolphins, seals and other amazing wildlife. Small café and shop. **Note**: steep steps to beach. For Sat Nav use SA43 1QF.

Find out more: 01545 570200 or mwnt@nationaltrust.org.uk

Ogwen Cottage

Nant Ffrancon, Bethesda, Gwynedd LL57 3LZ

🏖️ 2014

Ogwen Cottage is nestled between the dramatic Carneddau and Glyderau mountain ranges, at the starting point for numerous walking routes in the area. It includes a base for our local Ranger team and information point for walkers exploring nearby Cwm Idwal, Tryfan, Y Glyderau and Carneddau. This iconic building has long been associated with mountaineering and adventure, a tradition we're maintaining by providing outdoor learning experiences on site in partnership with The Outward Bound Trust.

Ogwen Cottage, Gwynedd, sits nestled between the dramatic Carneddau and Glyderau mountain ranges

Hikers set off from Ogwen Cottage to spend a day exploring the nearby mountain ranges

Eat, shop, stay: café. Maps and guides available at the Ogwen Ranger base. Two holiday cottages at Dyffryn Mymbyr (7 miles).

Things to see and do: **Indoors** Visit the Ranger base for advice about the area. **Outdoors** Range of rock-climbing and mountain walking routes available in addition to a National Cycle Network, Lon Las Ogwen. **Dogs**: on leads only.

Access: 🚶 Ranger base 🅿️
Sat Nav: use LL57 3LZ.
Parking: at Ogwen Lake (not National Trust).

Find out more: 01248 605739 or ogwen@nationaltrust.org.uk

Ogwen Cottage		M	T	W	T	F	S	S
3 Apr–29 Oct	10–6	**M**	**T**	**W**	**T**	**F**	**S**	**S**

Check website for café opening times.

Paxton's Tower

Llanarthne, near Dryslwyn, Carmarthenshire

🏠🛏 1965

Known as 'Golwg y Byd' (Eye of the World), Paxton's Tower is said to offer Views of seven counties. **Note**: sorry no toilet. Nearest National Trust facilities at Dinefwr in Llandeilo. For Sat Nav use SA32 8HX.

Find out more: 01558 823902 or paxtonstower@nationaltrust.org.uk

Penbryn

near Sarnau, Cardigan, Ceredigion

🛏🚗 1967

One of Ceredigion's best-kept secrets, this beautifully secluded sandy cove lies down leafy lanes, edged with flower-covered banks. **Note**: café (open daily) serving a wide selection of snacks and drinks. For Sat Nav use SA44 6QL. Open daily Easter weekend to end October; weekends only during winter.

Find out more: 01545 570200 or penbryn@nationaltrust.org.uk

Pennard, Pwll Du and Bishopston Valley

near Southgate, Swansea

🏛🛏🚗 1954

Spectacular cliffs, caves where mammoth remains have been found, rare birds, an underground river, bat roosts, silver-lead mining, ancient woodland, smuggling and limestone quarrying are just a few of the wonders of this area. There are also numerous archaeological features and two important

caves – Bacon Hole and Minchin Hole.
Note: due to dangerous rip tides, swimming in Three Cliffs Bay is not advised.

Eat, shop, stay: coffee shop, village stores, tea-rooms and a pub in Pennard (none National Trust). Picnics welcome.

Things to see and do: Pennard provides a great starting point for a variety of walks, on which you can enjoy wild flowers and spot rare birds, such as choughs and Dartford warblers.
Dogs: welcome, but please be aware livestock graze freely across Pennard Burrows.

Access: 🅿♿
Sat Nav: use SA3 2DH.
Parking: at Southgate car park.

Find out more: 01792 390636 or pennard@nationaltrust.org.uk

Pennard, Pwll Du and Bishopston Valley, Swansea: the view from Pennard Cliffs looking down across the golden sands of the beach is worth savouring

Penrhyn Castle

Bangor, Gwynedd LL57 4HT

🏛🏚✝❄⚓🍴 1951

Behind its imposing façade, Penrhyn Castle, Gwynedd, hides neo-Norman stairways and Victorian kitchens

The dominating stone façade of Penrhyn Castle hides more than just its internal red-brick construction. The unique architecture, opulent interiors and fine art collection sit alongside a history of sugar and slate fortunes, of social unrest and the longest-running industrial dispute in British history. Discover Penrhyn's history, its vast rooms, neo-Norman stairways and Victorian kitchens. The extensive grounds are perfect for exploring and enjoying spectacular views of Snowdonia and the North Wales coast. Little explorers can climb trees, make dens and run wild in the adventure playground. There's something for everyone at Penrhyn, just expect the unexpected.

Eat, shop, stay: hot and cold lunches served in the Housekeeper's tea-room. Light bites and cakes available in our Stable coffee shop. Browse through a range of National Trust and local products in the castle and Stables shops. Don't forget our second-hand bookshop.

The Great Hall at Penrhyn Castle is designed to resemble a cathedral, complete with columns and stained glass

Things to see and do: Indoors Take a behind-the-scenes tour or climb aboard an engine in the Railway Museum. **Outdoors** See how we have transformed the Water Garden or find peace in the walled garden. **Dogs**: welcome on leads in grounds. Assistance dogs only in the castle and walled garden.

Access: 🅿️ 🚻 🚪 👖 🐕‍🦺 🏷️ 🖼️ 📷
Castle 👟🪜♿ Stable block 🪜♿ Grounds 👟🪜
Parking: 500 yards.

Find out more: 01248 353084 or
penrhyncastle@nationaltrust.org.uk
Penrhyn Castle, Bangor, Gwynedd LL57 4HT

Penrhyn Castle		M	T	W	T	F	S	S
Castle								
1 Mar–5 Nov†	12–5	M	T	W	T	F	S	S
2 Dec–17 Dec	11–4						S	S
Garden, parkland and Railway Museum								
1 Jan–17 Feb*	11–3	M	T	W	T	F	S	S
18 Feb–28 Feb	11–3	M	T	W	T	F	S	S
1 Mar–5 Nov	10:30–5	M	T	W	T	F	S	S
6 Nov–31 Dec**	11–3	M	T	W	T	F	S	S
Victorian kitchens, café and shop								
18 Feb–28 Feb	11–3	M	T	W	T	F	S	S
1 Mar–5 Nov	11–5	M	T	W	T	F	S	S
11 Nov–31 Dec	11–3						S	S

†Tours: daily, 10:30 to 12. *Excludes Railway Museum.
**Railway Museum open weekends only. Closed 25 December.

Plas Newydd House and Gardens

Llanfairpwll, Anglesey LL61 6DQ

🏠 🏛️ ❄️ 🐕‍🦺 ♿ 1976

The ancestral home of the Marquess of Anglesey sits majestically on the shores of the Menai Strait, a family home enjoying breathtaking views of Snowdonia. The surrounding gardens are great for exploring and include an Australasian arboretum, Italianate terrace garden and extensive woodland walks. There's plenty for little explorers too, including a hand-built tree house, nine-hole Frisbee™ golf course, and adventure playground – you might even meet one of the resident red squirrels!

While children explore the grounds of Plas Newydd House and Gardens, Anglesey, other visitors discover the interior of this lovely family home – including the piano

Sitting majestically on the shores of the Menai Strait, Plas Newydd House and Gardens boasts breathtaking views

The house is home to a Waterloo-inspired military museum, works of art, regular exhibitions and, at its heart, Rex Whistler's famous 58-foot fantasy landscape painting.

Eat, shop, stay: light bites and cakes available from the Old Dairy and local ice-cream from the Sun Room. The Mansion tea-room serves hot and cold lunches. The Old Dairy Shop, Siop Newydd and second-hand bookshop are the perfect place for gifts.

Things to see and do: **Indoors** Learn about family life at Plas Newydd and the secrets behind Rex Whistler's masterpiece. **Outdoors** Enjoy regular walks and talks with the gardeners and a full calendar of events. **Dogs**: welcome on short leads. Assistance dogs only in the mansion and terraced gardens.

Access: 🅿️ 🅳 🚻 ♿ 📶 🎫 📺 👓 📷
Building 🔆 🏛️ 🔆 **Grounds** 🔆 ➡️
Parking: 400 yards from main entrance.

Find out more: 01248 714795 or plasnewydd@nationaltrust.org.uk

Plas Newydd		M	T	W	T	F	S	S
Mansion								
18 Feb–5 Nov	11–4:30	M	T	W	T	F	S	S
2 Dec–17 Dec	11–2:30	·	·	·	·	·	S	S
Gardens, shop and café*								
7 Jan–12 Feb	11–3	·	·	·	·	·	S	S
18 Feb–5 Nov	10:30–5**	M	T	W	T	F	S	S
6 Nov–24 Dec	11–3	M	T	W	T	F	S	S
30 Dec–31 Dec	11–3	·	·	·	·	·	S	S

Rhododendron garden at its best April to June.
*Visitor centre open as shop and café. **Café opens at 11.

Plas yn Rhiw

Rhiw, Pwllheli, Gwynedd LL53 8AB

🏠 ❄️ ♿ 🛏️ 1952

The house was rescued from neglect and lovingly restored by the three Keating sisters, who bought it in 1938. The views from the grounds and gardens across Cardigan Bay are among the most spectacular in Britain. The house is 16th-century with Georgian additions, and the garden contains many beautiful flowering trees and shrubs, with beds framed by box hedges and grass paths. It's stunning whatever the season.

A work of love by three sisters, Plas yn Rhiw, Gwynedd, was rescued from dereliction and restored with care

Eat, shop, stay: tea-room serving a selection of fresh sandwiches, soup, cakes, drinks and ice-cream; picnics also available to take out. Shop selling gifts, plants, books and prints of Honora Keating's landscape watercolours. Three holiday cottages within walking distance.

Things to see and do: **Indoors** Virtual tour available on iPad and guided tours available by arrangement. **Outdoors** Woodland walks and a native-apple orchard. **Dogs**: on woodland walk below shop only (on leads).

Access: 🏠♿🐕♿📺♿♿

Building ♿♿ Grounds ♿♿

Parking: 100 yards (narrow lanes).

Find out more: 01758 780219 or plasynrhiw@nationaltrust.org.uk

Plas yn Rhiw		M	T	W	T	F	S	S
23 Mar–10 Apr	11–5*	M	·	W	T	F	S	S
11 Apr–24 Apr	11–5*	M	T	W	T	F	S	S
26 Apr–22 May	11–5*	M	·	W	T	F	S	S
24 May–5 Jun	11–5*	M	T	W	T	F	S	S
7 Jun–17 Jul	11–5*	M	·	W	T	F	S	S
18 Jul–25 Sep	11–5*	M	T	W	T	F	S	S
27 Sep–5 Nov	11–4*	M	·	W	T	F	S	S

January and February: garden and snowdrop wood open occasional weekends. *House opens at 12.

The garden at Plas yn Rhiw boasts many beautiful flowering trees and shrubs, as well as box hedges and spectacular beds, so there is something to enjoy whatever the season

Porth Meudwy

near Aberdaron, Gwynedd

🏛️🛏️ 1990

Nowhere expresses the essence of the area better than this sheltered cove on the wild and rocky coastline west of Aberdaron. It was from here that the pilgrims set out to Ynys Enlli (Bardsey Island). Today fishermen still bring the daily catch into the cove. **Note**: sorry no toilet.

Porth Meudwy, Gwynedd, above and left: still very much in use by fishermen, this sheltered cove sums up the essence of this wild and rocky area

Eat, shop, stay: shops, pubs and cafés in Aberdaron village (not National Trust). Four holiday apartments in Aberdaron.

Things to see and do: the Wales Coast Path – a birdwatchers' paradise – runs dramatically along the clifftop. **Dogs**: welcome.

Access: 🔾
Sat Nav: use LL53 8DA. **Parking**: ½ mile.

Find out more: 01758 760469 or porthmeudwy@nationaltrust.org.uk

Porth y Swnt

Henfaes, Aberdaron, Pwllheli, Gwynedd LL53 8BE

🔾🔾🔾 2010

This exciting interpretation centre, at the heart of the beautiful fishing village of Aberdaron, shines a light on Llŷn's unique culture, heritage and environment. You can experience the Bardsey Island lighthouse's retired optic up close, follow in the footsteps of pilgrims for a journey across the Sound in the video pod, catch up on what Llŷn's Rangers are up to and form your thoughts in the Sea of Words.

Eat, shop, stay: gift shop in visitor centre. Cafés, pubs and convenience stores in village (not National Trust). Henfaes holiday apartments (Meudwy, Enlli, Daron and Hywyn) are located at the centre of Aberdaron.

Things to see and do: Indoors Audio guide, children's scrapbooks, events during school holidays. **Outdoors** Walks and access to the Wales Coast Path. Adventure packs, beach fun days, seafood festival, guided walks and cycle rides. **Dogs**: beach access restricted during summer.

Access: 🔾🔾🔾🔾 Car park 🔾🔾
Parking: on site.

Find out more: 01758 703810 or porthyswnt@nationaltrust.org.uk

Porth y Swnt		M	T	W	T	F	S	S
2 Jan–31 Mar	10–4	M	T	W	T	F	S	S
1 Apr–30 Jun	10–5	M	T	W	T	F	S	S
1 Jul–31 Aug	10–6	M	T	W	T	F	S	S
1 Sep–30 Sep	10–5	M	T	W	T	F	S	S
1 Oct–31 Dec*	10–4	M	T	W	T	F	S	S

*Closed 24 to 26 December and 1 January 2018.

The impressive retired optic from Bardsey Island's lighthouse at Porth y Swnt, Gwynedd

Porthdinllaen

Morfa Nefyn, Gwynedd

🏚️ 🛏️ 1994

An old fishing village perched on the end of a thin ribbon of land stretching into the Irish Sea, with its clear sheltered waters lapping against stout stone houses, Porthdinllaen really is a jewel.
You can watch fishermen bring in the daily catch, while relaxing with a drink at the Tŷ Coch Inn.
In the summer you can view the ecologically rich seagrasses from a paddle board – and have fun trying to stand up. **Note**: nearest toilet in village. Steps from car park down to beach.

Eat, shop, stay: two holiday cottages available in the heart of the village. Refreshments available at our tenanted pub, Tŷ Coch Inn.

Things to see and do: events during summer for all the family. Wonderful walking on the coastal path – maps and guides available at car park welcome cabin. Find out about village history at 'Caban Gruff'. **Dogs**: welcome.

Access: 🧍 ♿
Sat Nav: use LL53 6DA.
Parking: on site for beach; 1 mile from village.

Find out more: 01758 760469 or porthdinllaen@nationaltrust.org.uk

Porthdinllaen, Gwynedd: the old fishing village, below, sits perched on the end of a thin ribbon of land. The lovely sandy beach, above, is irresistible

Why not share your pictures with us? #nationaltrust

Porthor

Aberdaron, Gwynedd

🏖️🅿️ 1981

This wonderful beach is famous for its 'whistling sands' and glistening waters. If the joys of sandcastles and sunbathing are not enough for you, then why not have a go at surfing? The sea here is perfect. In addition, the Wales Coast Path runs in both directions from the car park. **Note**: nearest toilet in car park.

Famous for its 'whistling sands', Porthor, Gwynedd, also offers excellent surfing

Eat, shop, stay: beachside café and shop offering everything from lunch to sun cream (not National Trust). Four holiday apartments in Aberdaron.

Things to see and do: famous beach and glorious clifftop coast path to explore. Children's adventure pack available from car park. **Dogs**: seasonal restrictions on beach apply from 1 April to 30 September.

Access: ♿ 👣
Sat Nav: use LL53 8LG. **Parking**: on site.

Find out more: 01758 760469 or porthor@nationaltrust.org.uk

Powis Castle and Garden

Welshpool, Powys SY21 8RF

🏛️❄️🅿️🔺🍴 1952

The Herbert family spent more than 400 years transforming a medieval fortress into the comfortable family home you see today. Furnished with sumptuous fabrics and exquisite works of art from around the world, the interior reflects the Elizabethan to Edwardian periods. The UK's largest private collection of Indian treasures is housed in the Clive Museum. From weaponry to a gold bejewelled tiger's head, the collection is unique. The world-renowned gardens are an eclectic mix of Italianate terraces filled with herbaceous borders, a formal garden with clipped yews and a woodland area which boasts a number of champion trees.

Powis Castle and Garden, Powys, sits proudly on a hill, surrounded by terraced Italian gardens and clipped yews

Eat, shop, stay: restaurant (licensed) and garden tea-room. Gift shop and plant sales. Holiday cottage, The Bothy, is located in the heart of the garden.

Things to see and do: **Indoors** Themed tours and daily introductory talks about the castle. Family fun trails. **Outdoors** Talks on the garden every day. Children's activities during school holidays and family trails. **Dogs**: assistance dogs only.

Access: [icons] Building [icon] Grounds [icons] **Sat Nav**: postcode misdirects, enter Powis Castle. **Parking**: on site.

Find out more: 01938 551944 (Infoline). 01938 551929 or powiscastle@nationaltrust.org.uk

Powis Castle and Garden		M	T	W	T	F	S	S
1 Jan–26 Mar*	11–4**	M	T	W	T	F	S	S
27 Mar–1 Oct	11–5**	M	T	W	T	F	S	S
2 Oct–31 Dec*	11–4**	M	T	W	T	F	S	S

*Reduced number of castle state rooms open, 1 January to 17 February and 30 October to 31 December.
**Garden and restaurant: open from 10. Garden: 27 March to 1 October, open to 6. Garden tea-room (opening times vary) and garden shop open. Reduced catering offer in January and February. Closed 25 December.

Visitors admire the spectacular ceiling painting in the Blue Drawing Room at Powis Castle and Garden

Rhossili and South Gower Coast

Coastguard Cottages, Rhossili, Gower, Swansea SA3 1PR

[icons] 1933

There is so much space and the skies seem to stretch on for ever at Rhossili and South Gower Coast, Swansea

Perched on the clifftop overlooking the spectacular Rhossili Bay (Britain's best beach: Trip Advisor Travellers' Choice Awards 2013 and 2014), Rhossili Shop and Visitor Centre offers everything you need to enjoy beautiful Gower, from local information and advice, to tempting treats and gifts to remember your day. **Note**: Worm's Head island access restricted March to August. Very steep steps and slope to beach.

Eat, shop, stay: self-service refreshments and Swansea's famous Joe's ice-cream available all year. Three National Trust holiday cottages nearby.

Things to see and do: visitor information and advice on tides, local beaches, access, facilities and walks available. Free family geocaching trails (booking essential at peak times). **Dogs**: welcome (on leads near livestock please). Beach is dog-friendly all year.

Access: [icons] Visitor Centre [icon] Grounds [icons] **Parking**: large pay and display car park at end of village. Suitable for motorhomes (no overnight stays).

Find out more: 01792 390707 or rhossili@nationaltrust.org.uk

Rhossili and Gower		M	T	W	T	F	S	S
Shop								
3 Jan–15 Feb	10:30–4	·	T	W	T	F	S	S
16 Feb–7 Apr	10:30–4:30	M	T	W	T	F	S	S
8 Apr–4 Sep*	10–5*	M	T	W	T	F	S	S
5 Sep–5 Nov	10:30–4:30	M	T	W	T	F	S	S
6 Nov–23 Dec	10:30–4	M	T	W	T	F	S	S
27 Dec–30 Dec	11–4	·	·	W	T	F	S	·

Car park open 24 hours. *Shop open until 6 August weekends.

St David's Visitor Centre and Shop

Captain's House, High Street, St David's, Pembrokeshire SA62 6SD

 1974

St David's Visitor Centre and Shop, Pembrokeshire: perfect point to start exploring this wild countryside

Overlooking the Celtic Old Cross in the centre of St David's, Wales's smallest historic city, the visitor centre and well-stocked shop is open all year. For a complete guide to the National Trust in Pembrokeshire, visitors can take a tour of our special places, beaches and walks using interactive technology. **Note**: sorry no toilet.

Eat, shop, stay: books, cards, maps, wide range of gifts and local produce. Walks leaflets available. Holiday cottages nearby.

Things to see and do: guided walks, evening talks and events. St David's Head, Porth Clais, Solva and Abereiddi nearby.

Access: Building [🦽]
Parking: none on site.

Find out more: 01437 720385 or stdavidsshop@nationaltrust.org.uk

St David's Visitor Centre		M	T	W	T	F	S	S
2 Jan–18 Mar	9–4	M	T	W	T	F	S	·
20 Mar–31 Dec	9–5*	M	T	W	T	F	S	S

*Closes at 4 on Sundays. Closed 25, 26 December and 1 January 2018.

Segontium

Caernarfon, Gwynedd

 1937

Fort built to defend the Roman Empire against rebellious tribes. **Note**: in the guardianship of Cadw – Welsh Government's historic environment service. Museum not National Trust. For Sat Nav use LL55 2LN. For opening arrangements, please contact Cadw (01443 336105).

Find out more: 01443 336000 or segontium@nationaltrust.org.uk

---

Skenfrith Castle

Skenfrith, near Abergavenny, Monmouthshire NP7 8UH

[▦][▥][♿] 1936

Remains of early 13th-century castle, built beside the River Monnow to command one of the main routes from England. **Note**: in the guardianship of Cadw – Welsh Government's historic environment service. Open every day all year.

Find out more: 01874 625515 or skenfrithcastle@nationaltrust.org.uk

---

Stackpole

near Pembroke, Pembrokeshire

🏠🏛️❄️🚲⛰️🌳🎭🍴 1976

A former grand estate stretching down to some of the most beautiful coastline in the world, including Broadhaven South, Barafundle Bay, Freshwater West and Stackpole Quay. Today it's a National Nature Reserve, recognised for the abundant flora and fauna. Bosherston Lakes are famous for their superb display of lilies and resident otters, and the dramatic cliffs of Stackpole Head are great for wildlife watching. Uncover the history and heritage of this special place too; the former Stackpole Court site and nearby Lodge Park Woods reveal the story behind the magnificent designed landscape.

Eat, shop, stay: The Boathouse tea-room at Stackpole Quay is a popular attraction, offering ready-made picnics for the beach, homemade cakes and scones or local Pembrokeshire ice-cream – perfect after a long walk. Stay at Stackpole's holiday cottages or the Outdoor Learning Centre.

Things to see and do: guided kayak and coasteering sessions. Wildlife walks and talks. Coarse fishing. Family events, from fun runs and beach activity days, to bushcraft with the Rangers. **Dogs:** under close control on the estate.

Stackpole, Pembrokeshire, above and below. This former grand estate is now a National Nature Reserve, so if you get bored by the beach, why not go wildlife watching?

Access: 🅿️📶🚻♿🖼️ Building 🏛️ Grounds 🏛️ ➡️
Sat Nav: for Stackpole Quay use SA71 5LS; Broadhaven South SA71 5DZ; Bosherston Lakes SA71 5DR; Lodge Park Woods SA71 5DE.
Parking: at Stackpole Quay, Broadhaven South, Bosherston Lakes and Lodge Park Woods.

Find out more: 01646 661359 or stackpole@nationaltrust.org.uk

Stackpole		M	T	W	T	F	S	S
Boathouse tea-room								
18 Feb–26 Feb	11–3:30	M	T	W	T	F	S	S
4 Mar–12 Mar	11–3:30						S	S
18 Mar–2 Apr	11–4	M	T	W	T	F	S	S
3 Apr–29 Oct	10–5	M	T	W	T	F	S	S
4 Nov–10 Dec	11–3:30						S	S
16 Dec–29 Dec*	11–3:30	M	T	W	T	F	S	S
Estate								
Open all year	Dawn–dusk	M	T	W	T	F	S	S

*Tea-room closed 24 and 25 December.

Stackpole Outdoor Learning Centre

Old Home Farm Yard, Stackpole,
near Pembroke, Pembrokeshire SA71 5DQ

🏠🏛♿🎨🐕🛏🔔🍴 1976

Located in the heart of the Stackpole Estate, our eco-award-winning centre provides residents with easy access to Bosherston Lakes, Stackpole Quay and award-winning beaches – including Barafundle and Broadhaven South – as well as the historic site of Stackpole Court. The recently refurbished centre can house up to 140 guests and offers flexible accommodation with modern facilities, including a theatre, meeting and classroom space. It is ideal for groups, corporate clients, celebrations, family holidays and couples' getaways. **Note**: contact the centre for activity programmes, prices and availability.

Eat, shop, stay: self-catering or chef-catered options. Meals provided by an experienced in-house National Trust catering team. Full entertainment licence for events with bar. Residents' barbecue area. Shop and information hub. Single and double rooms, bunkhouse accommodation and new campsite at Gupton Farm.

Things to see and do: events, including rock-pool rambles, wild camping, guided walks, open-air theatre and concerts. Hire one of our bikes to explore the area or join our kayaking or coasteering guided tours! **Dogs**: assistance dogs only.

Access: 🅿♿🚻🔆🖼
Parking: free for guests.

Find out more: 01646 661425 (reception). 01646 661359 (estate office) or stackpoleoutdoorlearning@nationaltrust.org.uk

Stackpole Outdoor Centre
Open every day all year

Please contact the centre for more information on residential group bookings, courses and activities.

Stackpole Outdoor Learning Centre, Pembrokeshire. Set within the very heart of the Stackpole Estate, the centre offers an extensive choice of activities

Tredegar House

Newport NP10 8YW

[icons] [2012]

For centuries, the flamboyant Morgan family called this Grade I listed 17th-century Restoration mansion their home. With tales of giant birds' nests, riotous parties, dark arts, war heroism and animal menageries – the Morgan's was certainly no ordinary household. You can hear about the lives of their servants and connect with the hands-on spaces that served the family. Enjoy lakeside walks and an avenue of ancient oak trees within the 36-hectare (90-acre) parkland, then meander through the formal walled gardens and explore the impressive Grade I listed stables. An oasis hidden a stone's throw from the industrial setting of Newport. **Note**: roofing works and roadworks will cause disruption (check before visit).

If walls could talk, then Tredegar House, Newport, would have many stories to tell. The Restoration mansion, left, with its fabulous interiors, above, saw some wild goings on

Tredegar House		M	T	W	T	F	S	S
House and garden†								
18 Feb–31 Mar	11–4	M	T	W	T	F	S	S
1 Apr–5 Nov	11–5	M	T	W	T	F	S	S
25 Nov–17 Dec	10:30–5						S	S
Tea-room and shop								
7 Jan–12 Feb	11–3						S	S
18 Feb–31 Mar	10–4	M	T	W	T	F	S	S
1 Apr–5 Nov	10–5	M	T	W	T	F	S	S
8 Nov–17 Dec*	11–3			W	T	F	S	S
Park								
Open all year	Dawn–dusk	M	T	W	T	F	S	S

†Garden: opens 10:30. House: last entry one hour before closing.
*Christmas event weekends: tea-room and shop open 10 to 5.

Eat, shop, stay: tea-room serving light lunches, homemade cakes and hot drinks. Cosy gift shop selling souvenirs, books, gifts and plants.

Things to see and do: **Indoors** Introductory talks. Family trails and hands-on activities. Yearly programme of things to do. Traditional Christmas experience. **Outdoors** Lakeside walks, formal gardens and seasonal garden talks. Dyffryn Gardens nearby. **Dogs**: welcome in the parkland, formal gardens and tea-room.

Access: [icons]
House [icon] Reception [icon] Grounds [icons]
Parking: on site.

Find out more: 01633 815880 or tredegar@nationaltrust.org.uk

Tudor Merchant's House

Quay Hill, Tenby, Pembrokeshire SA70 7BX

[icon] [1937]

Over 500 years ago when Tenby was a busy trading port, a merchant built this three-storey house to live in and trade from. Today, this unaltered house and shop have been furnished with exquisitely carved replicas and brightly coloured wall-hangings which re-create the atmosphere of life in Tudor Tenby. **Note**: sorry no toilet.

Eat, shop, stay: shop range includes specially made Tudor-style pottery (design based on finds at the house), pewterware, horn cups, glass, beeswax candles and books about the Tudors.

Things to see and do: Tudor Family Fortunes game, superstitions scrolls, lay the high table, costumes to try on and replica toys. Easter, Hallowe'en and Tudor-themed family events. Colby Woodland Garden and Stackpole nearby. **Dogs**: assistance dogs only.

Access: [icons] Building [icon]
Parking: very limited on-street parking. Several pay-and-display car parks, not National Trust (charge including members).

A young visitor gets a feel for the past as he turns the spit at Tudor Merchant's House, Pembrokeshire

Find out more: 01834 842279 or tudormerchantshouse@nationaltrust.org.uk

Tudor Merchant's House		M	T	W	T	F	S	S
18 Feb–26 Feb	11–3	M	T	W	T	F	S	S
4 Mar–2 Apr	11–3	·	·	·	·	·	S	S
8 Apr–21 Jul	11–5	M	·	W	T	F	S	S
22 Jul–3 Sep	11–5*	M	T	W	T	F	S	S
4 Sep–3 Nov	11–5**	M	·	W	T	F	S	S
4 Nov–24 Dec	11–3	·	·	·	·	·	S	S

Open Tuesday in Bank Holiday weeks, 11 to 5. *Tuesday and Wednesday: open until 6:15 for costumed guided tours (booking essential). **Closed Tuesday, except for 31 October.

Tŷ Mawr Wybrnant

Penmachno, Betws-y-Coed, Conwy LL25 0HJ

[icons] 1951

Hidden in the beautiful Conwy Valley, this traditional upland farmhouse was the birthplace of Bishop William Morgan, who first translated the Bible into Welsh. This is one of the most important houses in the history of the Welsh language. Two copies of William Morgan's original Bible are on display. **Note**: access via narrow track.

Eat, shop, stay: picnics welcome. Four holiday cottages available near Betws-y-Coed and Hendre Isaf bunkhouse at Pentrefoelas (9 miles).

Things to see and do: **Indoors** Enjoy an introductory talk, visit the exhibition room and browse the extensive Bible collection. Virtual tour also available. **Outdoors** Tudor kitchen garden, woodland walks and two animal puzzle trails. **Dogs**: under close control.

Access: [icons] Building [icon] Grounds [icon]
Sat Nav: no access from A470.
Parking: 500 yards.

Find out more: 01690 760213 or tymawrwybrnant@nationaltrust.org.uk

Tŷ Mawr Wybrnant		M	T	W	T	F	S	S
6 Apr–5 Nov	12–5	·	·	·	·	T	F	S	S

Open Bank Holiday Mondays.

Tŷ Mawr Wybrnant, Conwy: traditional stone farmhouse

Additional coastal and countryside car parks in Wales

Ceredigion
Mwnt	SA43 1PS
Penbryn	SA44 6QL

Llŷn Peninsula
Uwchmynydd	LL53 8DD

Pembrokeshire
Broadhaven	SA71 5DR
Bosherston	SA71 5DW
Porthclais	SA62 6RR

Snowdonia
Cregennan	LL39 1LX
Nantmor	LL55 4YG

Swansea (Gower)
Rhossili	SA3 1PR

Northern Ireland

Giant's Causeway, County Antrim
Competition entry from Steve Haydon

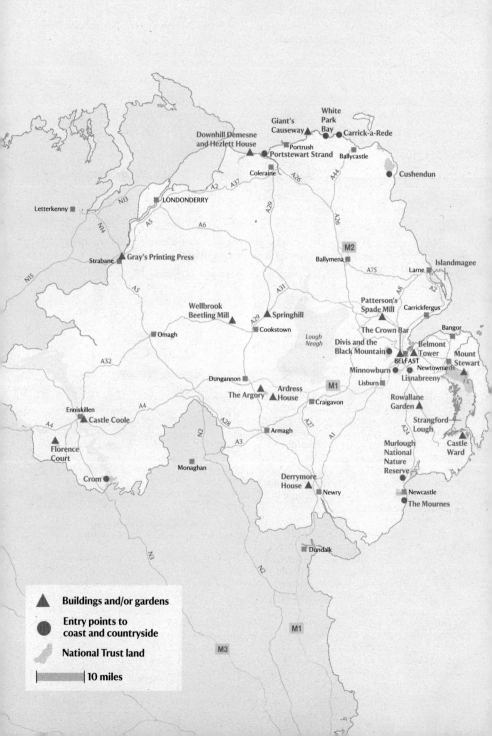

Buildings and/or gardens

Entry points to coast and countryside

National Trust land

10 miles

Giant's Causeway
White Park Bay
Downhill Demesne and Hezlett House
Carrick-a-Rede
Portrush
Portstewart Strand
Ballycastle
Coleraine
Cushendun
Letterkenny
LONDONDERRY
Gray's Printing Press
Strabane
Islandmagee
Ballymena
Larne
Patterson's Spade Mill
Carrickfergus
Wellbrook Beetling Mill
Springhill
Bangor
Omagh
Cookstown
The Crown Bar
Belmont Tower
Divis and the Black Mountain
BELFAST
Mount Stewart
Minnowburn
Newtownards
Lisnabreeny
Dungannon
Lisburn
Ardress House
The Argory
Craigavon
Rowallane Garden
Enniskillen
Castle Coole
Armagh
Strangford Lough
Florence Court
Monaghan
Castle Ward
Crom
Murlough National Nature Reserve
Derrymore House
Newry
Newcastle
The Mournes
Dundalk

Ardress House

64 Ardress Road, Annaghmore, Portadown,
County Armagh BT62 1SQ

🏠 🐾 ❄ ♿ 1959

Although built in the 17th century, Ardress House, County Armagh, contains fine Georgian interiors

Nestling in 40 hectares (100 acres) of rolling countryside, this 17th-century farmhouse is an elegant example of 18th-century remodelling, with detailed plasterwork and fine Georgian interiors. The cobbled farmyard is the perfect spot for children to feed the resident chickens, and the nearby apple orchards are great for exploring.

Eat, shop, stay: takeaway hot and cold drinks and ice-cream available. Picnics welcome in the garden or woodlands.

Things to see and do: original cobbled farmyard, including dairy, smithy and threshing barn, miniature Shetland ponies, donkeys, Soay sheep, geese and chickens. Children's outdoor and indoor play, including ride-on tractors and dressing-up. **Dogs**: on leads in garden only.

Access: 🏠 Building 📶 ♿ Grounds 🅿 ➡
Parking: 10 yards.

Find out more: 028 8778 4753 or
ardress@nationaltrust.org.uk

Ardress House		M	T	W	T	F	S	S
House and farmyard								
16 Feb–19 Feb	1–6				T	F	S	S
11 Mar–9 Apr	1–6						S	S
14 Apr–23 Apr	1–6	M	T	W	T	F	S	S
29 Apr–25 Jun	1–6						S	S
1 Jul–28 Aug	1–6	M			T	F	S	S
2 Sep–30 Sep	1–6						S	S
1 Oct–29 Oct	12–5							S
Lady's Mile Walk								
Open all year	Dawn–dusk	M	T	W	T	F	S	S

House: admission by guided tour, last tour one hour before closing. Open Bank Holiday Mondays and all other public holidays in Northern Ireland. Closed 25, 26 December and 1 January 2018.

The Argory

144 Derrycaw Road, Moy, Dungannon,
County Armagh BT71 6NA

🏠 ❄ ♿ 🔔 🍴 1979

The spectacular West Hall of The Argory, County Armagh, shimmers with a golden hue

This Irish gentry house can trace more than 190 years of history. Built in the 1820s for the MacGeough Bond family, the house and surrounding riverside estate came into existence due to a quirky stipulation in a will. The interior of this understated and intimate house still evokes the eclectic tastes and interests of the family. The rose garden, with its unusual sundial, pleasure gardens and wooded walks along the River Blackwater are ideal for exploring.

Eat, shop, stay: Courtyard Coffee Shop serving home-baked scones, sandwiches, paninis and cakes. Gift shop offering a wide range of products: jewellery, books and items for the home and garden. Bookshop with second-hand books for all tastes and interests. Picnics welcome.

Things to see and do: **Indoors** Guided house tours and children's indoor bug trail. Farmyard fun in the stables and laundry yard. **Outdoors** Variety of walks and trails. Children's play area with zip line. **Dogs**: on leads in grounds and garden.

Access: 🅿️♿🏷️👁️ Grounds ♿ ➡️
Parking: 100 yards.

Find out more: 028 8778 4753 or argory@nationaltrust.org.uk

The Argory		M	T	W	T	F	S	S
Courtyard café and shop								
4 Feb–5 Mar*	12–5	·	·	·	·	·	S	S
House, courtyard café and shop								
11 Mar–9 Apr	12–5	·	·	·	T	F	S	S
10 Apr–23 Apr	12–5	M	T	W	T	F	S	S
27 Apr–28 May	12–5	·	·	·	T	F	S	S
1 Jun–30 Jun	12–5	·	·	W	T	F	S	S
1 Jul–31 Aug	12–5	M	T	W	T	F	S	S
1 Sep–30 Sep	12–5	·	·	·	T	F	S	S
1 Oct–22 Oct	12–4	·	·	·	·	·	S	S
26 Oct–1 Nov	12–4	M	T	W	T	F	S	S
Grounds								
Open all year	10–5	M	T	W	T	F	S	S

House: admission by guided tour, last tour one hour before closing. Open Bank Holiday Mondays and all other public holidays in Northern Ireland. *Courtyard café and shop open 12 to 5, half-term (16 and 17 February). Closed 25, 26 December and 1 January 2018.

The grounds of The Argory are perfect for exploring and letting off steam

Belmont Tower

82 Belmont Church Road, Belfast, County Down BT4 3FG

🏠 Ⓣ 2013

Once a primary school, Belmont Tower in County Down is now an inspirational, multi-functional space

For more than 100 years this prominent Gothic-style late-Victorian building buzzed to the sound of children playing and learning in its former life as Belmont Primary School. Today this inspirational space has been restored and adapted to offer classes, conference facilities, coffee shop and gift shop.

Eat, shop, stay: freshly prepared food and delicious scones at Belmont Tower Café.

Things to see and do: community groups, such as Belfast Historical Society and baby sensory. **Dogs**: assistance dogs only.

Access: 🏷️🔊♿♿🔢
Parking: on site and on street at Belmont Road and Belmont Church Road.

Find out more: 028 9065 3338 or belmonttower@nationaltrust.org.uk

Belmont Tower		M	T	W	T	F	S	S
2 Jan–30 Dec	9–4*	M	T	W	T	F	S	·

*Saturdays and July: closes at 3. Open evenings and other times for booked classes and events. Closed 14 to 18 April, 12 and 13 July, 25 and 26 December.

Carrick-a-Rede

Ballintoy, County Antrim BT54 6LS

 1967

Connected to the cliffs by a rope bridge across the Atlantic Ocean, this rocky island is the ultimate clifftop experience. Jutting out from the rugged North Antrim Coast Road, the 30-metre-deep and 20-metre-wide chasm separating Carrick-a-Rede from the mainland is traversed by an amazing rope bridge that was traditionally erected by salmon fishermen. If you are bold enough to make the crossing, you will be rewarded by unique geology and wildlife, and enjoy uninterrupted vistas across the seas of Moyle to Rathlin Island and far beyond to the Scottish islands. Carrick-a-Rede offers clifftop birdwatching and windswept coastal scenery. **Note**: number crossing bridge at any one time restricted. Open weather permitting. Entrance 119a Whitepark Road.

All that connects Carrick-a-Rede, County Antrim, to the mainland is a rope bridge originally erected by fishermen. Crossing it is an unforgettable experience

Eat, shop, stay: Weighbridge tea-room offering great coffee, delicious home-baked scones and sweet treats, hot snacks and light lunches. Gift shop area showcasing local crafts and unique range of Carrick-a-Rede souvenirs.

Things to see and do: coastal path – part of the Causeway Coast Way from Portstewart to Ballycastle and the Ulster Way. Birdwatching and coastal scenery. Unique flora and fauna. Guided tours (by prior arrangement).
Dogs: on leads (not permitted to cross bridge).

Access: 🅿♿🚻♿📷 Grounds 🦽🦽▶
Parking: on site.

Find out more: 028 2076 9839 or carrickarede@nationaltrust.org.uk

Carrick-a-Rede		M	T	W	T	F	S	S
Bridge								
1 Jan–31 Jan	9:30–3:30	M	T	W	T	F	S	S
1 Feb–26 Feb	9:30–5	M	T	W	T	F	S	S
27 Feb–25 Jun	9:30–6	M	T	W	T	F	S	S
26 Jun–3 Sep	9:30–7	M	T	W	T	F	S	S
4 Sep–29 Oct	9:30–6	M	T	W	T	F	S	S
30 Oct–31 Dec	9:30–3:30	M	T	W	T	F	S	S

Last entry to bridge 45 minutes before closing. Car park and North Antrim coastal path open all year. Bridge open weather permitting. Closed 24 to 26 December.

Castle Coole

Enniskillen, County Fermanagh BT74 6HN

🏠♿🔔⚓☂ 1951

Castle Coole stands out as one of the finest examples of Neo-classical architecture in Ireland. With an elegant and restrained exterior, the interior is brimming with opulence, luxury and colour. The surrounding soft, rolling parkland, interspersed with mature oaks, woodlands and paths, is perfect for refreshing walks. You can also explore the historic outbuildings on the estate, such as the 18th-century ice house. Families can relax and have fun in the outdoor play area.

Eat, shop, stay: Tallow House tea-room, serving snacks, lunches and afternoon teas. Gift shop selling souvenirs and second-hand bookshop (volunteer-run).

Things to see and do: Indoors Events throughout the year. 'Upstairs downstairs' guided tours of the mansion. Enjoy the cosy Tallow House tea-room. **Outdoors** Events, including Easter Sunday egg hunts. Trails and walks. **Dogs**: under control.

Access: 🅿♿♿♿📷🖼📱
Building 🏠🏠🖼 Grounds 🏠➡
Parking: 150 yards.

Find out more: 028 6632 2690 or castlecoole@nationaltrust.org.uk

Castle Coole		M	T	W	T	F	S	S
Grounds								
1 Jan–28 Feb	10–4	M	T	W	T	F	S	S
1 Mar–31 Oct	10–7	M	T	W	T	F	S	S
1 Nov–31 Dec	10–4	M	T	W	T	F	S	S
House, tea-room and shop								
11 Mar–19 Mar	11–5	·	·	·	·	F	S	S
25 Mar–9 Apr	11–5	·	·	·	·	·	S	S
14 Apr–23 Apr	11–5	M	T	W	T	F	S	S
29 Apr–31 May	11–5	M	·	W	T	F	S	S
1 Jun–31 Aug	11–5	M	T	W	T	F	S	S
1 Sep–30 Sep	11–5	M	·	W	T	F	S	S

House: admission by guided tour (last tour one hour before closing). Open Bank Holiday Mondays and all other public holidays in Northern Ireland.

The restrained exterior of elegant Castle Coole in County Fermanagh, below, contrasts with the opulence and colour of its interiors, above

Castle Ward

Strangford, Downpatrick,
County Down BT30 7BA

🏠🏛🏚♿✦🧺🖼🚪🛏🔺🔔🍷 1953

High on a hillside, with views across the tranquil waters of Strangford Lough, the distinctly different styles of Gothic and classical collide at Castle Ward. This eccentric 18th-century mansion within a 332-hectare (820-acre) walled demesne is one of the most peculiar architectural compromises between two people. The former home of the Viscounts Bangor, guided tours reveal the history of the different façades. In the farmyard, you can visit the water-powered corn mill, or stroll among flowers and subtropical plants in the Sunken Garden, while the extensive grounds are criss-crossed by a 21-mile network of family-friendly multi-use trails. The impressive

laundry, tack room, children's Victorian play centre and adventure playground provide further opportunities to explore the demesne. **Note**: 1 March to 30 November visitor access to livestock grazing areas may be restricted.

Eat, shop, stay: Stableyard tea-room. Gift shop selling local produce and souvenirs. Second-hand bookshop. Holiday cottage, bunkhouse, caravan and campsite with glamping pods.

Set within extensive grounds, family friendly Castle Ward in County Down, below, presents two distinctly different faces to the world – Gothic and, as here, classical

Things to see and do: **Indoors** Guided house tours. **Outdoors** Network of multi-use trails. Bicycles for hire. Farmyard with animals. Victorian play centre, adventure playground. Tracker Packs and children's activities. Events, including Easter Fair, Pumpkinfest, Jazz in the Grounds and Christmas. Iconic filming locations – Winterfell in HBO's *Game of Thrones*.

Dogs: on leads in grounds only (livestock grazing areas out of bounds).

Access: 🅿️ 🅳 🐕 ♿ ⬆️ 🖥️ ⬇️ ••
Building ♿♿♿ Grounds ♿♿➡️
Parking: on site.

Find out more: 028 4488 1204 or castleward@nationaltrust.org.uk

Castle Ward		M	T	W	T	F	S	S
Parkland, trails and garden								
1 Jan–16 Mar	10–4	M	T	W	T	F	S	S
17 Mar–29 Oct	10–6	M	T	W	T	F	S	S
30 Oct–31 Dec	10–4	M	T	W	T	F		S	S
House, stableyard and farmyard								
17 Mar–29 Oct	12–5*	M	T	W	T	F	S	S
Tea-room, gift shop and second-hand bookshop								
4 Jan–16 Mar	11–4	·	·	W	T	F	S	S
17 Mar–29 Oct	10–5	M	T	W	T	F	S	S
1 Nov–31 Dec	11–4	·	·	W	T	F	S	S

*Stableyard and farmyard open at 10. House: last admission one hour before closing. Timed tickets apply to guided house tours. Corn mill demonstration on Sundays, 2 to 5, 16 April to 24 September. Gates open when grounds open. Closed 25 and 26 December.

The clock tower and corn mill, left, and the Saloon, below, show the Gothic side of eccentric Castle Ward

Crom

Upper Lough Erne, Newtownbutler,
County Fermanagh BT92 8AJ

🏠🚻🐾🛏️⛺🎣🍽️ 1987

**Tranquil Crom, County Fermanagh, sits on the
peaceful southern shores of Upper Lough Erne**

Home to islands, ancient woodland and
historical ruins, this 810-hectare (2,000-acre)
demesne sits in a tranquil landscape on the
peaceful southern shores of Upper Lough Erne.
One of Ireland's most important conservation
areas, it has many rare species and is great
for relaxing walks, cycling and boat trips.
Note: 19th-century castle not open to public.

Eat, shop, stay: lunch, snacks and afternoon
tea, gifts and souvenirs available in visitor
centre. Convenience goods and outdoor
clothing also for sale. Holiday cottages,
campsite and glamping pods.

Things to see and do: historic castle ruins.
Cot trips (Bank Holiday Mondays).
Boat and canoe hire. **Dogs**: under control.

Access: 🅿️🚐♿🚻🅿️👁️
Building ♿🅿️ **Grounds** ♿➡️🦽
Parking: 100 yards.

Find out more: 028 6773 8118 or
crom@nationaltrust.org.uk

The Crown Bar

46 Great Victoria Street, Belfast,
County Antrim BT2 7BA

🏠🍽️ 1978

Belfast's most famous pub remains one of the
finest examples of a high-Victorian gin palace
complete with period features. **Note**: run by
Mitchells & Butlers. Open Monday to Saturday,
11:30 to 11; Sunday, 12:30 to 10 (telephone to
check public and Bank Holiday openings).

Find out more: 028 9024 3187 or
info@crownbar.com

Cushendun

County Antrim

🚻🏞️ 1954

Nestled at the mouth of the River Dun
(Brown River) at the foot of Glendun,
Cushendun is a very charming historic
village steeped in character and folklore.
The surrounding hills are a patchwork of
farms, small fields, hedgerows and traditional
stone walls. Sheltered harbour and beautiful
beach. Views of Scotland.

Eat, shop, stay: Corner House tea-room in the
village offers great coffee, delicious home-baked
scones, sweet treats and a tasty hot food menu
using fresh local produce. Pub and restaurant
facilities also available in the village.

Steeped in folklore and charm, historic Cushendun, County Antrim, nestles at the mouth of the River Dun

Things to see and do: attractive white Cornish-style houses designed by Clough Williams-Ellis. Explore the grounds of historic Glenmona House. Fine circular walking trail. River fishing, sea angling, boating, horse-riding and golf course nearby.

Access: 🔣🔣
Sat Nav: use BT44 0PH. **Parking**: car park adjacent to Corner House tea-room and at Glenmona House.

Find out more: 028 2176 1560 (Corner House tea-rooom). 028 2073 3320 (North Coast Office) or cushendun@nationaltrust.org.uk

Derrymore House

Bessbrook, Newry, County Armagh BT35 7EF

🔣🔣 1953

Resting peacefully in a landscape demesne, this 18th-century thatched cottage is rich in history and a great place for walks. **Note**: sorry no toilet. Grounds open all year, dawn to dusk. Treaty Room open 2 to 5:30, 1 and 29 May, 12 July, 28 August and 9 September.

Find out more: 028 8778 4753 or derrymore@nationaltrust.org.uk

Divis and the Black Mountain

Hannahstown, near Belfast, County Antrim

🔣🔣🔣 2004

Sitting in the heart of the Belfast Hills, this 809-hectare (2,000-acre) mosaic of upland heath and blanket bog is a great place for a wild countryside experience. There are four walking trails to explore, affording panoramic views across Belfast and a wealth of flora, fauna and archaeological remains to discover. **Note**: cattle roam freely during summer months. Mountain environment and weather conditions can change rapidly.

Eat, shop, stay: tea, coffee and light refreshments available in The Barn (seasonal opening).

For a wild countryside experience, head to Divis and the Black Mountain in County Antrim

Things to see and do: guided walks on biodiversity and archaeology. **Dogs**: welcome, but please note cattle roam freely during summer.

Access: 🔣🔣🔣🔣 Visitor centre 🔣 Mountain 🔣
Sat Nav: use BT17 0NG. **Parking**: on Divis Road, opposite Divis Mountain gates.

Find out more: 028 9082 5434 or divis@nationaltrust.org.uk

Downhill Demesne and Hezlett House

Mussenden Road, Castlerock,
County Londonderry BT51 4RP

🏠 🏛 ⛽ ✤ 🥾 ⛺ 🔔 🍽 1949

The sheltered gardens, cliff-edge landmark and striking ruins of a grand headland mansion bear testament to the eccentricity of the Earl Bishop who once made this 18th-century demesne his home. Mussenden Temple, perched atop sheer cliffs, offers panoramic views of the famous north coast and is a great place for walking and kite-flying. Nearby at Hezlett House, life in a rural 17th-century cottage is told through the people who once lived there. One of the oldest thatched cottages left standing in Northern Ireland, it boasts a rare cruck frame and houses the Downhill Marble Collection.

Eat, shop, stay: tea and coffee facilities at Hezlett House and Bishop's Gate. Picnics welcome in gardens.

Things to see and do: **Indoors** Hezlett House guided tours on request (booking essential). **Outdoors** Numerous events throughout year, including Easter Egg hunts and Kite Festival. Brand new outdoor Bishop's Play Trail. **Dogs**: on leads only.

Access: 🅿🚻 **Building** ♿ **Grounds** ♿
Parking: at Lion's Gate.

Find out more: 028 7084 8728 or downhilldemesne@nationaltrust.org.uk
Hezlett House, 107 Sea Road, Castlerock, County Londonderry BT51 4TW

Downhill and Hezlett		M	T	W	T	F	S	S
Downhill Demesne grounds								
Open all year	Dawn–dusk	M	T	W	T	F	S	S
Downhill Demesne facilities								
17 Mar–10 Sep	10–5	M	T	W	T	F	S	S
16 Sep–29 Oct	10–5						S	S
Hezlett House								
18 Mar–9 Apr*	11–5						S	S
10 Apr–23 Apr	11–5	M	T	W	T	F	S	S
29 Apr–18 Jun	11–5						S	S
19 Jun–3 Sep	11–5	M	T	W	T	F	S	S

Open Bank Holiday Mondays and all other public holidays in Northern Ireland. *Hezlett House also open 17 March. Hezlett House and facilities closed 24 to 26 December.

Mussenden Temple at Downhill, County Londonderry

Florence Court

Enniskillen, County Fermanagh BT92 1DB

🏠 🏛 ❀ ⚇ ⚐ 🔔 🍷 1954

Surrounded by lush parkland and thick woodland with Benaughlin mountain rising in the background, Florence Court enjoys a majestic countryside setting in west Fermanagh. There is something for everyone to enjoy at this extensive and welcoming place. On a guided tour of the Georgian mansion you can hear stories about the Cole family and their staff, who lived here for over 250 years. Outdoors take a gentle walk or long cycle along 10 miles of trails in the adjoining forest park and see fascinating industrial heritage features, including the water-powered sawmill and blacksmith's forge. The gardens are home to the mother of all Irish yew trees, as well as the kitchen garden which is being restored to its 1930s character.

Set in majestic countryside, welcoming Florence Court in County Fermanagh, this page and opposite, offers something for everyone, whether their interests lie in the great outdoors or family stories, Georgian architecture and interior design

Access: 🅿️ 🄳 ♿ 🐕 ♿ 🄻 ♿ 🖼️ 🎧 ⓥ 🎵 🅰️
Building 🄻 ♿ ♿ **Grounds** ♿ ➡️ 🦽
Parking: 100 yards to Visitor Centre.

Find out more: 028 6634 8249 or florencecourt@nationaltrust.org.uk

Eat, shop, stay: Stables tea-room serving snacks, lunches and afternoon tea. Coach House gift shop. Second-hand bookshop (volunteer-run). New Visitor Centre providing information, house tour tickets, retail and drinks to go. Why not stay for longer in the Butler's Apartment?

Things to see and do: Indoors Guided house tours. Laundry yard with washroom, dairy, ironing and drying room. Explore our forge, sawmill and carpenter shop. **Outdoors:** Events and Ranger walks throughout year. Children's Tracker Packs. Network of 10 miles of multi-use trails. Bike hire available from the Visitor Centre. Kitchen Garden restoration project. **Dogs**: under control, on leads in Walled Garden.

Florence Court		M	T	W	T	F	S	S
Gardens and park								
1 Jan–28 Feb	10–4	M	T	W	T	F	S	S
1 Mar–31 Oct	10–7	M	T	W	T	F	S	S
1 Nov–31 Dec	10–4	M	T	W	T	F	S	S
House, tea-room, visitor centre and shop								
11 Mar–19 Mar	11–5					F	S	S
25 Mar–9 Apr	11–5						S	S
14 Apr–23 Apr	11–5	M	T	W	T	F	S	S
29 Apr–31 May	11–5	M	T	W	T		S	S
1 Jun–31 Aug	11–5	M	T	W	T	F	S	S
2 Sep–30 Sep	11–5	M	T	W	T		S	S
1 Oct–29 Oct	11–5						S	S

House: admission by guided tour (last tour one hour before closing). Open Bank Holiday Mondays and all other public holidays in Northern Ireland. Open Republic of Ireland Bank Holiday 30 October. Grounds closed 25 December. Visitor Centre open weekends November and December.

Giant's Causeway

44 Causeway Road, Bushmills,
County Antrim BT57 8SU

⬆️🏛️👥〰️ 1962

Follow in the legendary footsteps of giants at Northern Ireland's iconic World Heritage Site. The famous basalt columns of the Causeway landscape, left by volcanic eruptions 60 million years ago, are home to more than Finn McCool. Its nooks and crannies are dotted with dainty sea campion, and defensive fulmars protect their cliff nests. Windswept walking trails wind through this Area of Outstanding Natural Beauty, with an all-accessible walk at Runkerry Head and more challenging terrain along the Causeway Coast Way. The interactive exhibition and innovative audio-guides unlock the secrets of the landscape and regale visitors with legends of giants.

Eat, shop, stay: light lunches and tasty snacks available in Visitor Centre café. Causeway Hotel bar and restaurant offer delicious lunch and evening meal menus based around fresh local produce. The award-winning gift shop showcases locally handcrafted gifts and exclusive Giant's Causeway souvenirs.

Things to see and do: **Indoors** Interactive exhibition brings the stories of the Causeway to life. **Outdoors** Audio-guides (11 languages) reveal the landscape's secrets. Walking trails for all abilities. Entertaining guided tours. Family fun events. **Dogs**: on leads only.

Access: 🅿️🅳♿🏛️🚻♿🔄🔗⬆️∴🔍
Visitor Centre ♿♿ **Causeway Hotel** ♿🚻
Grounds ♿♿➡️
Parking: on site and park and ride in Bushmills village.

Find out more: 028 2073 1855 or giantscauseway@nationaltrust.org.uk

Giant's Causeway		M	T	W	T	F	S	S
Stones and coastal path								
Open all year	Dawn–dusk	M	T	W	T	F	S	S
Visitor Centre								
1 Jan–28 Feb	9–5	M	T	W	T	F	S	S
1 Mar–30 Jun	9–6	M	T	W	T	F	S	S
1 Jul–31 Aug	9–7	M	T	W	T	F	S	S
1 Sep–31 Oct	9–6	M	T	W	T	F	S	S
1 Nov–31 Dec	9–5	M	T	W	T	F	S	S

Last admission to Visitor Centre one hour before closing. Closed 24 to 26 December.

Legends of giants abound at Giant's Causeway in County Antrim, above and below. This geological wonder, with its fabulous flora and fauna, is accessible to all

Gray's Printing Press

49 Main Street, Strabane,
County Tyrone BT82 8AU

🏠 1966

The indelible story of printing is told behind
this Georgian shop front in Strabane, once
reputed as Ireland's printing capital.
Note: open 12 to 3 (times subject to change)
on 15 April, 10 June, 1 July, 9 September
and 28 October.

Find out more: 028 7084 8728 or
grays@nationaltrust.org.uk

Islandmagee

near Larne, County Antrim

▦ ▦ ▦ ▦ ▦ ▦ 1996

Islandmagee in County Antrim is steeped in history

Once the site of smuggling and home to an
ancient monastery, the Islandmagee peninsula's
coastline is steeped in history. An Area of Special
Scientific Interest, it has some of Northern
Ireland's largest colonies of cliff-nesting
seabirds and offers views of the famous Antrim
coast. **Note**: paths uneven and steep in places.

Eat, shop, stay: Earl's café in Mullaghboy
village serving food, tea and coffee and
The Rinkha in Ballystrudder village offering
famous ice-cream (neither National Trust).
Picnics welcome.

Things to see and do: coastal walks.
Dogs: on leads only.

Access: Portmuck and Skernaghan ♿
Sat Nav: use BT40 3TP. **Parking**: at Portmuck
and Brown's Bay for Skernaghan Point
(not National Trust).

Find out more: 028 9064 7787 or
islandmagee@nationaltrust.org.uk

Lisnabreeny

near Belfast, County Down

🏠 ▦ ▦ ▦ ▦ 1938

The path through this easily overlooked haven
on the edge of Belfast climbs along a tumbling
stream through a wooded glen and across
rolling farmland to emerge at a hilltop rath
at the summit of the Castlereagh Hills. This
picturesque setting affords sweeping views
across the city and beyond. **Note**: sorry no
toilet. Uneven paths and steep steps.

Things to see and do: viewpoint
and Second World War memorial
commemorating US servicemen who died
in Northern Ireland. Walks through glen,
woodlands and ancient rath. Yearly guided
walk. **Dogs**: welcome on leads.

Access: Glen ♿
Sat Nav: use BT8 6SA. **Parking**: on
Lisnabreeny Road (no parking on Manse Road).

Find out more: 028 9064 7787 or
lisnabreeny@nationaltrust.org.uk

Lisnabreeny, County Down: haven on the edge of Belfast

Minnowburn

near Belfast, County Down

🏛 🌿 ❄ 🎿 🔔 1952

Kayaking on the River Lagan at Minnowburn, County Down

Just a few miles from Belfast city centre yet in the heart of the country, this 52 hectares (128 acres) of naturally mixed countryside is a paradox all of its own. Sitting within the Lagan Valley Regional Park, it has riverside, meadow and woodland walks and is rich in wildlife. **Note**: sorry no toilet. Trails are uneven and steep in places.

Eat, shop, stay: Piccolo Mondo van (not National Trust) serves food, tea and coffee in car park six days a week. Lock Keeper's Inn (not National Trust) serving food, tea and coffee, ¾ mile along riverside path. Picnic tables in Terrace Hill garden.

Things to see and do: guided walks, including heritage, history and woodlands. Waymarked walks, including the Giant's Ring and Terrace Hill trails. Riverside and pond walks. **Dogs**: on leads only.

Access: 👤
Sat Nav: use BT8 8LD. **Parking**: on site.

Find out more: 028 9064 7787 or minnowburn@nationaltrust.org.uk

Mount Stewart

Portaferry Road, Newtownards,
County Down BT22 2AD

🏛 ❄ 🌿 🔔 🍴 1976

Voted one of the world's top ten gardens, Mount Stewart reflects a rich tapestry of design and planting artistry bearing the hallmark of its creator. Edith, Lady Londonderry's passion for bold planting schemes, coupled with the mild climate of Strangford Lough, means rare and tender plants from across the globe thrive in this celebrated garden, with the formal gardens exuding a distinct character and appeal. Explore the exquisite house, recently restored to glory. Experience a changing offer that is filled with fascinating stories about the Londonderry family, a world-class collection of paintings and many other internationally significant items. For a different view of Mount Stewart, stroll around miles of new walking trails and discover a landscape lost in time.

Eat, shop, stay: locally sourced gifts in our shop. Garden shop selling a range of gardening items and plants specially propagated from our world-class garden. Tea-room with a range of homemade food and many products made from local produce.

Elegant corner of exquisite Mount Stewart, County Down

Access: [icons]
Building [icons]
Grounds [icons]
Parking: 200 yards.

Find out more: 028 4278 8387 or
mountstewart@nationaltrust.org.uk

Mount Stewart		M	T	W	T	F	S	S
Formal and lakeside gardens, trails, tea-room and shop								
1 Jan–3 Mar	10–4*	M	T	W	T	F	S	S
4 Mar–29 Oct	10–5	M	T	W	T	F	S	S
30 Oct–31 Dec	10–4*	M	T	W	T	F	S	S
House								
1 Jan–26 Feb	11–3						S	S
4 Mar–29 Oct	11–5	M	T	W	T	F	S	S
4 Nov–31 Dec	11–3						S	S
Temple of the Winds								
5 Mar–29 Oct	2–5							S

*Tea-room and shop: close at 5 weekends, Bank Holidays
and public holidays. House: admission by free-flow
(guided tours on selected days); October open times
for house may change (check website for details).
Open Bank Holiday Mondays and all other public holidays
in Northern Ireland. Closed 25 and 26 December.

Things to see and do: **Indoors** You can
explore the recently restored family home and
discover a wealth of new treasures. Seasonal
events and continuing conservation in action.
Outdoors Why not stroll around the walled
garden, discover interesting new walks and join
a garden tour? Don't miss the lakeside walk,
where the colours and smells vary from season
to season. In the formal gardens, look out for
our topiary and collection of statues. The
natural play area and walking trails will take you
through a truly magical landscape of woodland
and farmland, set within an iconic rolling
drumlin landscape beside Strangford Lough.
Dogs: welcome on short leads in all areas.

As well as the celebrated formal garden, seen here with
the south front of the house, below, visitors can
enjoy a wilder experience and discover a landscape lost
in time on Mount Stewart's walking trails, above

The Mournes

near Newcastle, County Down

🏛️♿🚶 1992

The Mournes in County Down offer fabulous walking

These famous wildlife-rich mountains are criss-crossed by well-marked coastal and mountain paths. Great for exploring, the National Trust-maintained paths stretch from the shore into the heart of the Mournes, offering views over Dundrum Bay to the Isle of Man on a clear day.

Eat, shop, stay: picnics welcome. Nearest shops, restaurants and cafés in Newcastle (none National Trust).

Things to see and do: outstanding views from Bloody Bridge. Coastal path to St Mary's Chapel ruins. Birdwatching. **Dogs**: welcome under control.

Access: ♿
Sat Nav: use BT33 0EU for Slieve Donard and BT33 0LA for Bloody Bridge.
Parking: for Slieve Donard, park in Newcastle; for Bloody Bridge, park on A2.

Find out more: 028 4375 1467 or mournes@nationaltrust.org.uk

Murlough National Nature Reserve

near Dundrum, County Down

🏛️♿🚶🐾 1967

Home to seals, Neolithic sites and Ireland's first nature reserve, Murlough is one of the most extensive examples of dune landscape in Ireland. A network of paths and boardwalks through these ancient dunes, woodland and heath makes it ideal for relaxed walks and spotting a wonderland of wildlife. **Note**: limited toilet facilities.

Eat, shop, stay: beach café (seasonal opening, not National Trust). Picnics welcome on beach or in car park.

Murlough National Nature Reserve in County Down

Things to see and do: self-guided nature walk and series of guided walks. Volunteer events and family activities throughout year. **Dogs**: welcome on leads, restrictions apply when ground-nesting birds breeding or cattle grazing.

Access: **Grounds**
Sat Nav: use BT33 0NQ. **Parking**: on site.

Find out more: 028 4375 1467 or murlough@nationaltrust.org.uk

Murlough		M	T	W	T	F	S	S
Nature reserve								
Open all year	Dawn-dusk	**M**	**T**	**W**	**T**	**F**	**S**	**S**
Facilities								
11 Mar-9 Apr	10-6	·	·	·	·	·	**S**	**S**
14 Apr-23 Apr	10-6	**M**	**T**	**W**	**T**	**F**	**S**	**S**
29 Apr-28 May	10-6	·	·	·	·	·	**S**	**S**
29 May-3 Sep	10-6	**M**	**T**	**W**	**T**	**F**	**S**	**S**
9 Sep-1 Oct	10-6	·	·	·	·	·	**S**	**S**

Open Bank Holiday Mondays and all other public holidays in Northern Ireland.

Patterson's Spade Mill

751 Antrim Road, Templepatrick, County Antrim BT39 0AP

1991

Travel back in time and witness history literally forged in steel at the last working water-driven spade mill in daily use in the British Isles. Dig up the history and culture of the humble spade and visit bygone life fashioning steel into spades during the industrial era.

Eat, shop, stay: handcrafted spades on sale and made to specification. Tea and coffee available from drinks machine.

Things to see and do: guided tours and demonstrations for all the family. **Dogs**: on leads only.

Sparks fly at Patterson's Spade Mill, County Antrim

Access: **Building** **Grounds**
Parking: 50 yards.

Find out more: 028 9443 3619 or pattersons@nationaltrust.org.uk

Patterson's Spade Mill		M	T	W	T	F	S	S
14 Apr-23 Apr	12-4	**M**	**T**	**W**	**T**	**F**	**S**	**S**
29 Apr-28 May	12-4	·	·	·	·	·	**S**	**S**
29 May-27 Aug	12-4	**M**	**T**	**W**	·	·	**S**	**S**
2 Sep-24 Sep	12-4	·	·	·	·	·	**S**	**S**

Admission by guided tour, last admission one hour before closing. Open Bank Holiday Mondays and all other public holidays in Northern Ireland from 14 April to 24 September.

Portstewart Strand

Portstewart, County Londonderry

🏠 ♿ ♨ 👕 🍽 1981

Surfs up at Portstewart Strand in County Londonderry: one of the finest beaches in Northern Ireland

Sweeping along the edge of the north coast, this 2-mile stretch of golden sand is one of Northern Ireland's finest beaches and affords uninterrupted views of the coastline. It's an ideal place for lazy picnics, surfing and long walks into the wildlife-rich sand dunes.

Eat, shop, stay: award-winning Harry's Shack with great new catering offer. Mobile beach retail and information service.

Things to see and do: waymarked nature trail. Barmouth Estuary bird hide. Events during peak season. **Dogs**: on leads only.

Access: 🅿 ♿ 👁 🚻 Café 👶 Beach 👶 ➡
Sat Nav: use BT55 7PG. **Parking**: on beach.

Find out more: 028 7083 6396 or portstewart@nationaltrust.org.uk

Portstewart Strand		M	T	W	T	F	S	S
Beach								
Open all year*	Dawn–dusk	M	T	W	T	F	S	S
Facilities								
13 Mar–2 Apr	10–5	M	T	W	T	F	S	S
3 Apr–30 Apr	10–6	M	T	W	T	F	S	S
1 May–3 Sep	10–7	M	T	W	T	F	S	S
4 Sep–1 Oct	10–5	M	T	W	T	F	S	S

*Open to pedestrians. Beach closed to vehicles one hour after last admission. Opening times may vary depending on weather and tides.

Rowallane Garden

Saintfield, County Down BT24 7LH

❄ 🔔 👕 1956

Carved into the County Down drumlin landscape since the mid-1860s, this inspirational 21-hectare (52-acre) garden is 'a world apart'. The passion and shared vision of the Reverend John Moore, and later his nephew Hugh Armytage Moore, created a garden where you can leave the outside world behind and immerse yourself in nature's beauty. The formal and informal garden spaces are home to magical features mingled with native and exotic plants, such as drifts of rare rhododendrons. It is a great place for a leisurely walk or just to relax on a seat and soak up the atmosphere.

Eat, shop, stay: garden café with views across the gardens. Café shop selling Rowallane Garden soap, honey and pottery, alongside other gift items. Second-hand bookshop. Pottery providing unique Rowallane Garden items and garden pots.

Inspirational Rowallane Garden, County Down: formal and informal spaces are home to native and exotic plants

Pumpkins galore at Rowallane Garden: you can leave the outside world behind in this magical place

Things to see and do: events throughout the year for all ages. **Dogs**: on leads in garden.

Access: [icons] Grounds [icons]
Parking: on site.

Find out more: 028 9751 0131 or rowallane@nationaltrust.org.uk

Rowallane Garden		M	T	W	T	F	S	S
Garden								
1 Jan–28 Feb	10–4	M	T	W	T	F	S	S
1 Mar–30 Apr	10–6	M	T	W	T	F	S	S
1 May–31 Aug	10–8	M	T	W	T	F	S	S
1 Sep–31 Oct	10–6	M	T	W	T	F	S	S
1 Nov–31 Dec	10–4	M	T	W	T	F	S	S
Café								
6 Jan–26 Feb	11–3					F	S	S
1 Mar–30 Apr	11–4	M	T	W	T	F	S	S
1 May–31 Aug	11–5	M	T	W	T	F	S	S
1 Sep–31 Oct	11–4	M	T	W	T	F	S	S
2 Nov–31 Dec	11–3				T	F	S	S

Open Bank Holiday Mondays and all other public holidays in Northern Ireland. Closed 25 and 26 December.

Springhill

20 Springhill Road, Moneymore, Magherafelt, County Londonderry BT45 7NQ

[icons] 1957

Hundreds of years ago the Lenox-Conyngham family chose this bucolic spot to build their home and, after ten generations, this 17th-century plantation house is still regarded as 'one of the prettiest houses in Ulster'. The welcoming family home they created is brought to life on enlightening guided tours of its portraits, furniture and decorative arts. The old laundry houses Springhill's celebrated costume collection of 18th- to 20th-century pieces that capture its enthralling past. There is a visitor centre, a natural play trail and short walks around the estate that are perfect for a leisurely stroll.

Eat, shop, stay: soup, scones, hot and cold drinks, snacks and ice-cream available from the visitor centre. Retail area with a range of items for the home and garden. Bookshop with second-hand books for all tastes and interests.

Springhill, County Londonderry: pretty 'Plantation' home

Things to see and do: **Indoors** Guided house tours and children's indoor bug trail. Costume exhibition and children's dress-up area. **Outdoors** Woodland walks, children's natural play trail and Springhill nursery selling plants and shrubs. **Dogs**: on leads in grounds only.

Access: [icons] Building [icons]
Parking: 50 yards.

Find out more: 028 8674 8210 or
springhill@nationaltrust.org.uk

Springhill		M	T	W	T	F	S	S
Visitor centre and café								
4 Feb–5 Mar*	12–5	.	.	.	.	.	S	S
House, visitor centre, café and costume museum								
11 Mar–9 Apr	12–5	.	.	.	.	.	S	S
10 Apr–23 Apr	12–5	M	T	W	T	F	S	S
28 Apr–28 May	12–5	.	.	.	.	F	S	S
1 Jun–30 Jun	12–5	.	.	.	T	F	S	S
1 Jul–31 Aug	12–5	M	T	W	T	F	S	S
2 Sep–30 Sep	12–5	.	.	.	.	.	S	S
1 Oct–22 Oct	12–4	.	.	.	.	.	.	S
26 Oct–1 Nov	12–4	M	T	W	T	F	S	S
Grounds								
Open all year	10–5	M	T	W	T	F	S	S

House: admission by guided tour, last tour one hour
before closing. Open Bank Holiday Mondays and all other
public holidays in Northern Ireland. *Visitor centre and
café open 12 to 5, half-term (16 and 17 February).
Closed 25, 26 December and 1 January 2018.

**The walled garden and parkland at Springhill offer
plenty of opportunities for discovery and fun**

Strangford Lough

County Down

[icons] 1969

**As Britain's largest sea lough, Strangford Lough,
County Down, is one of Europe's key wildlife habitats**

The tidal treasures of Britain's largest sea lough
and one of Europe's key wildlife habitats await
discovery. This delicately balanced landscape
is rich in natural and built heritage. Northern
Ireland's first Marine Conservation Zone and
the winter home for up to 90 per cent of the
world's light-bellied brent geese.

Eat, shop, stay: nearest tea-room and shop at
Mount Stewart and Castle Ward. Also numerous
restaurants serving dishes made from local
produce, including meat produced on the
surrounding land and seafood from the lough,
and arts and crafts shops (none National Trust).

Things to see and do: birdwatching
(some of the best in UK), rock-pooling and
geocaching. Red squirrels and seals to spot.
Canoe and cycle trails. **Dogs**: under control.
Temporary exclusion where livestock are
grazing (look out for notices).

Access: [icon]
Sat Nav: use BT22 1RG.
Parking: small car park at Ballyquintin or
parking around Lough (not all National Trust).

Find out more: 028 4278 7769 or
strangford@nationaltrust.org.uk

Wellbrook Beetling Mill

20 Wellbrook Road, Corkhill,
Cookstown, County Tyrone BT80 9RY

 1968

You can step back in time and discover how yarn was spun at Northern Ireland's last working water-powered linen beetling mill. Hands-on demonstrations reveal the importance of the linen industry in 19th-century Ireland. The glen is ideal for relaxing walks and perfect for a picnic by the Ballinderry River.

Eat, shop, stay: small cottage shop. Picnic tables near river.

Things to see and do: **Indoors** Tours of the mill, covering history and linen-making processes. **Outdoors** Walks up to the head-race. **Dogs**: on leads in grounds only.

Time stands still at Wellbrook Beetling Mill, County Tyrone

Access: 🅿️🏛️👶♿🎧 Building 🦽🔖 Grounds 🦽🔖
Parking: 10 yards.

Find out more: 028 8674 8210 or
wellbrook@nationaltrust.org.uk

Wellbrook Beetling Mill	M	T	W	T	F	S	S
11 Mar–30 Sep	2–5					**S**	**S**

Admission by guided tour. Last tour one hour before closing. Open Bank Holiday Mondays and all other public holidays in Northern Ireland. Closed 25, 26 December and 1 January 2018.

White Park Bay

near Ballintoy, County Antrim

🏛️🖼️🚶 1939

White Park Bay, County Antrim: rich in wildlife and history

Embraced by ancient dunes, Neolithic settlements and passage tombs, this arc of white sand nestles between two headlands on the North Antrim coast. Home to a range of rich habitats for a myriad of wildlife, its secluded location makes it ideal for quiet relaxation and peaceful walks.

Eat, shop, stay: shops, restaurants and cafés in nearby towns (none National Trust). Picnics welcome.

Things to see and do: you can discover one of the first Neolithic settlements in Ireland with three passage tombs, including Druid's Altar. Part of the Causeway Coast Way and the Ulster Way.

Access: 🅿️
Sat Nav: use BT54 6NH. **Parking**: on site.

Find out more: 028 2073 3320 or
whiteparkbay@nationaltrust.org.uk

Ever dreamed of waking up in a National Trust house, which has a family history stretching back centuries?

Such historic houses make great places to stay, to hold family gatherings, a party or wedding – making it an experience to remember. You can stay at one of the three Historic House Hotels of the National Trust located in the Vale of Aylesbury, North Wales and the City of York.

Hartwell House Hotel, Restaurant and Spa

The most famous resident of this elegant stately home was Louis XVIII, the exiled King of France, who lived here with his Queen and members of his court for five years from 1809. Only one hour from central London, the magnificent grounds include a romantic ruined church, lake and bridge.

www.hartwell-house.com   01296 747444

Bodysgallen Hall Hotel, Restaurant and Spa

This Grade I listed 17th-century house has the most spectacular views towards Conwy Castle and Snowdonia. The romantic gardens, which have won awards for their restoration, include a rare parterre – filled with sweet-smelling herbs – as well as several follies, a cascade, walled garden and formal rose gardens. Beyond, the hotel's parkland offers miles of stunning walks.

www.bodysgallen.com   01492 584466

Middlethorpe Hall Hotel, Restaurant and Spa

Built in 1699, this quintessentially William and Mary house was once the home of the 18th-century diarist Lady Mary Wortley Montagu. Furnished with antiques and fine paintings and set in manicured gardens with parkland beyond, Middlethorpe Hall's country-house character remains unspoilt.

www.middlethorpe.com   01904 641241

Start planning your visit to a Historic House Hotel today

Themed index

General interest

Lanhydrock, Cornwall

Devon and Dorset

Finch Foundry, Devon

Lydford Gorge, Devon

Somerset and Wiltshire

Dunster Castle, Somerset

The Cotswolds, Buckinghamshire and Oxfordshire

Nuffield Place, Oxfordshire

Berkshire, Hampshire and the Isle of Wight

Bembridge Windmill, Isle of Wight

Kent, Surrey and Sussex

Claremont Landscape Garden, Surrey

London

East of England

Oxburgh Hall, Norfolk

Clumber Park, Nottinghamshire

West Midlands

North West

Rufford Old Hall, Lancashire

The Lakes

Low Wray Campsite, near Wray Castle, Cumbria

Yorkshire

Fountains Abbey, North Yorkshire

General interest continued

North East

Cherryburn, Northumberland

Cymru Wales

Bodnant Garden, Conwy

Penrhyn Castle, Gwynedd

Northern Ireland

Crom, County Fermanagh

Additional coastal and countryside car parks

Quick stops

Dyrham Park, Gloucestershire

Collections

Saltram, Devon

Chastleton House, Oxfordshire

Smallhythe Place, Kent

Felbrigg Hall, Norfolk

Collections continued

1 Armour
2 Carriages
3 Ceramics
4 Costume and fashion
5 Dolls, doll's-houses and
   miniature rooms
6 Furniture
7 Glass and silverware
8 Musical instruments
9 Paintings
10 Wall hangings, embroideries
   and needlework

East Midlands

Hardwick, Derbyshire

West Midlands

Attingham Park, Shropshire

Wightwick Manor, West Midlands

North West

The Lakes

Hill Top, Cumbria

Yorkshire

North East

Wallington, Northumberland

Cymru Wales

Northern Ireland

Mount Stewart, County Down

Famous people

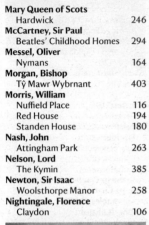

Film and television

This is a small selection of the largest and most popular films and TV dramas filmed at National Trust places.

Knole, Kent

Basildon Park, Berkshire

Murlough National Nature Reserve, County Down

Ashridge Estate, Hertfordshire

Enjoy spectacular views at a cottage in the Lake District

Take part in a Working Holiday in Cornwall

Sleep under the stars at a campsite in Cambridgeshire

National Trust Holidays

Choose from over 400 quirky cottages and a selection of campsites and bunkhouses, or join one of our unique Working Holidays. All perfectly placed for discovering the best of every season.

By booking a holiday with us you're helping to look after special places, for ever, for everyone.

Find out more at:
nationaltrustholidays.org.uk

Alphabetical index

The big list of wild adventures

With help from kids all over the country, we've put together the ultimate 50 things to do before you're 11¾. From making mud pies and catching a crab, to planting seeds and exploring caves, there's loads to discover, wherever you go.

To join in for free, download the app or visit nationaltrust.org.uk/50things

Make more of your membership

Your membership card gives you free, unlimited access to most of the places we look after during normal opening hours. Just bring it along with you every time you visit.

To make it easier to discover special places, your membership includes free parking at most of our places. Please display the car-park sticker (to be found at the front of the *Handbook*) on your windscreen.

Some of our car parks are now pay and display for non-members. At these, you'll be able to scan your membership card to get a free parking ticket to display alongside your sticker. And your scan will help us to direct financial support to the places you visit, for the upkeep of facilities and for conservation projects.

You may also be asked to show your card at staffed car parks. So remember: always bring your membership card.

And that's not all you get from being a member...

Visit special places abroad

We are part of the International National Trusts Organisation (INTO), a global network of charities and foundations which look after heritage sites of natural and historical importance. This means your current membership card may entitle you to free or discounted entry to other places looked after by INTO members.

For a full list of participating nations, visit **nationaltrust.org.uk/overseas-visitors/ overseas-organisations**

Entry to places owned by us but maintained by English Heritage or Cadw is also free to our members. If this is the case, it will be stated in the entry's Important Note.

Carers go free

Carers and essential companions of disabled visitors also enjoy free entry to all places on request.

To make things easier, you can order an annual Admit One Card by calling 0344 800 1895 or emailing **enquiries@nationaltrust.org.uk**

Four-legged friends

We love to welcome dogs wherever we can, but it isn't possible at all of our special places. To avoid disappointment, check the 'Dogs' message at the end of 'Things to see and do' before setting out. At our dog-friendly places you'll find water bowls, exercise areas and shady spaces.

Access

The symbols on page 2 indicate the access and facilities at each place.

Please ring before your visit in case a particular provision needs to be booked.

Photography

You are welcome to take pictures during your visits for personal use. However, to avoid disturbing fellow visitors, please don't use a flash or tripod when indoors. Also pictures taken indoors are at the discretion of the Property/General Manager, as they may need to get permission from the owner of loan items. Mobile phones can also be used – without flash please.

All requests for commercial filming and photography need to go through our Head of Filming and Locations (020 7824 7128).

Other ways to support the National Trust

As a charity, we rely on membership fees to look after special places for ever, for everyone. So from everyone who loves these places, and everyone who ever will, thank you. If you'd like to do more, here are some other ways you can support the places that matter to you.

Events
From live music and open-air theatre to organised sports and conservation walks, we have a busy programme of events. Find out what's happening near you at **nationaltrust.org.uk/visit/whats-on/events**

Donations
Every penny helps us look after places of natural beauty and historic importance. From supporting an appeal to leaving a gift in your Will, see how you can help at **nationaltrust.org.uk/get-involved/donate**

Volunteering
We wouldn't exist without the passion and hard work of thousands of volunteers. If you'd like to learn some new skills, share your experience and find rewarding work, please visit **nationaltrust.org.uk/get-involved/volunteer**

Supporter groups
Our supporter groups find enjoyable ways to raise funds. From group talks to group walks, enjoying days out to organising social events, find out more at **nationaltrust.org.uk/get-involved/volunteer/ways-to-volunteer/supporter-groups**

Heritage Lottery Fund
Using money raised through the National Lottery, the Heritage Lottery Fund (HLF) has awarded grants totalling well over £100 million to the National Trust in the last 20 years. Through these grants it has supported many of our most important projects including the Giant's Causeway, Knole, Castle Drogo and Quarry Bank Mill.

If you would like to know more please visit **hlf.org.uk**

The Royal Oak Foundation
Through the generous support of its members and donors across the USA, Royal Oak makes grants to the National Trust. Royal Oak members enjoy free access to National Trust places as well as lectures and tours in the USA.

For more information please visit **royal-oak.org**

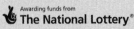

Have your say

Annual General Meeting
Our Annual General Meeting (AGM) each autumn is an opportunity for you to meet our Trustees and staff, ask questions and contribute to debates. Most importantly, you can exercise your right to vote on both resolutions and elections to our Council.

You can also vote online and watch the live AGM webcast. There will be more details in the autumn magazine and on our website **nationaltrust.org.uk/agm**

Governance
A guide to the Trust's governance arrangements is available on our website **nationaltrust.org.uk/about-us** and on request from The Secretary.

Our Annual Report and Financial Statements are available online at **nationaltrust.org.uk/annualreport** and on request from **annualreport@nationaltrust.org.uk**

Privacy policy

The National Trust makes every effort to comply with the principles of the Data Protection Act 1998. The National Trust's Privacy Policy sets out the ways in which we process personal data. The full Privacy Policy is available on our website **nationaltrust.org.uk**

Use of personal information
Personal information provided to the National Trust via our website, membership forms, fundraising responses, emails and telephone calls will be used for the purposes outlined at the time of collection or registration in accordance with the preferences you express.

By providing personal data to the National Trust you consent to the processing of such data by the National Trust as described in the full Privacy Policy. You can alter your preferences as explained in the following paragraph.

Verifying, updating and amending your personal information
If, at any time, you want to verify, update or amend your personal data or preferences please write to:

National Trust, Supporter Services Centre, PO Box 574, Manvers, Rotherham, S63 3FH

Verification, updating or amendment of your personal data will take place within 28 days of receipt of your request.

If subsequently you make a data protection instruction to the National Trust which contradicts a previous instruction (or instructions), then the Trust will follow your most recent instructions.

Subject access requests
You have the right to ask us, in writing, for a copy of all the personal data held about you (a 'subject access request').

There's a payment fee of £10.

To access your personal data held by the National Trust, please apply in writing to:

The Data Protection Officer, National Trust, Heelis, Kemble Drive, Swindon, Wiltshire, SN2 2NA.

Getting in touch

To discuss a visit
We support the National Code of Practice for Visitor Attractions. This means we are always happy to receive your comments and answer your questions.

If you want to know something before you visit, such as what facilities are available on site, please contact the place directly.

If possible, please speak to a member of staff on site. Alternatively, many places provide comment cards and boxes. You can email and telephone our places too. All your comments will be read, considered and action taken where necessary, but please be aware, it isn't possible for us to reply to every comment individually.

Telephone numbers and email addresses are included in the entry for each place in this *Handbook*.

You can find regularly updated information about the places we look after on **nationaltrust.org.uk**

Or to find an event happening near you, visit **nationaltrust.org.uk/visit/whats-on/find-an-event**

If you'd like this information in an alternative format please telephone 0344 800 1895 or email enquiries@nationaltrust.org.uk

Online Help Centre
Visit **nationaltrust.org.uk/help-centre** for an easy and quick way to find the answers to any questions, from membership queries to property feedback and more. Information on the best way to contact us is there as well.

Help with your membership
Manage your membership online at **nationaltrust.org.uk/mynationaltrust**, where you can register for an account and make updates to your address, contact information, contact preferences and Direct Debit payments. You can also view your membership details and request replacement items. For all other queries, please try the online Help Centre (see above) or contact the Supporter Services Centre (see below).

Supporter Services Centre
enquiries@nationaltrust.org.uk
PO Box 574,
Manvers,
Rotherham, S63 3FH
0344 800 1895 (phone)
0344 800 4410 (minicom)
Lines open seven days a week (9 to 5:30 weekdays, 9 to 4 weekends and Bank Holidays)

National Trust Holidays
0344 335 1287 (enquiries)
cottages@nationaltrust.org.uk

Our online shop
If you have a question about an order or purchase made from our website, please contact our online shop order fulfilment team.
online.shop@nationaltrust.org.uk
0300 123 2025
Lines open Monday to Friday, from 9 to 5.

Sponsor **Louise McRae**	Art direction **Craig Robson**	Editor **Lucy Peel**	Content management **Roger Shapland** **Dave Buchanan**	Printed **Wyndeham Group**
Publisher **Katie Bond**	Image selection **Chris Lacey**	Editorial assistance **Anthony Lambert** **Dee Maple** **Wendy Smith**	Design **Steers McGillan Eves**	NT LDS stock no: 50000658
Production **Graham Prichard**	Maps in Minutes™/Collins Bartholomew 2015		Origination **Zebra**	ISBN: 978-0-7078-0440-8